Outside the Bubble

Oxford Studies in Digital Politics

Series Editor: Andrew Chadwick, Professor of Political Communication
in the Centre for Research in Communication and Culture and
the Department of Social Sciences, Loughborough University

Outside the Bubble

SOCIAL MEDIA AND POLITICAL PARTICIPATION
IN WESTERN DEMOCRACIES

CRISTIAN VACCARI AND AUGUSTO VALERIANI

Oxford University Press is a department of the University of Oxford. It furthers
the University's objective of excellence in research, scholarship, and education
by publishing worldwide. Oxford is a registered trade mark of Oxford University
Press in the UK and certain other countries.

Published in the United States of America by Oxford University Press
198 Madison Avenue, New York, NY 10016, United States of America.

Library of Congress Cataloging-in-Publication Data
Names: Vaccari, Cristian, author. | Valeriani, Augusto, author.
Title: Outside the bubble : social media and political participation in
western democracies / Cristian Vaccari and Augusto Valeriani.
Description: New York, NY : Oxford University Press, 2021. |
Series: Oxford studies digital politics series |
Includes bibliographical references and index.
Identifiers: LCCN 2021013391 (print) | LCCN 2021013392 (ebook) |
ISBN 9780190858476 (hardback) | ISBN 9780190858483 (paperback) |
ISBN 9780190858506 (epub)
Subjects: LCSH: Political participation—Technological innovations—Europe. |
Political participation—Technological innovations—United States. |
Social media—Political aspects—Europe. | Social media—Political
aspects—United States. | Communication in politics—Europe. |
Communication in politics—United States.
Classification: LCC JN40 .V34 2021 (print) |
LCC JN40 (ebook) | DDC 323/.042094—dc23
LC record available at https://lccn.loc.gov/2021013391
LC ebook record available at https://lccn.loc.gov/2021013392

DOI: 10.1093/oso/9780190858476.001.0001

9 8 7 6 5 4 3 2 1

Paperback printed by LSC Communications, United States of America
Hardback printed by Bridgeport National Bindery, Inc., United States of America

Contents

Acknowledgments

This book concludes a journey that began in early 2012, when we got together to draft a funding application whose success enabled us to develop the kind of in-depth comparative research on social media and political participation that we had always dreamed of. We came to this topic from different but converging trajectories. Cristian had been mostly interested in the relationship between the Internet and politics during and around election campaigns, while Augusto had mostly focused on the impact of digital media on public diplomacy and foreign politics. We had traveled the world (Cristian mostly to the United States and the United Kingdom, Augusto mostly to the Middle East and North Africa), interviewed media and political elites, and analyzed various kinds of data, mostly collected by other institutions that made them available to us, to shed light on the issues we were interested in. This project provided us with the unique opportunity to devise our own research and collect our own data, and to do so across a wide variety of countries. As our dream turned into reality, we asked many questions, took many detours, made many mistakes, and learned many lessons. Perhaps the most important lesson we learned is that our journey will never end and that we will need to continue learning if we are to keep walking.

Our individual and joint academic enterprises would not even be imaginable without Roberto Grandi. From our times as undergraduate students at the University of Bologna and throughout our scholarly careers, Professor Grandi has been a generous, insightful, and sensible mentor, critic, and friend to both of us. When French writer Daniel Pennac received an honorary degree from the University of Bologna, he argued in his *lectio magistralis* that professors can act either as *gardiens du temple*, policing particular disciplinary, methodological, and stylistic boundaries, or as *passeurs*, striving to awaken consciousness and instill a sense of wonder for what is beautiful, novel, and important—regardless of where it comes from and irrespective of what canons it espouses or violates. Professor Grandi is the best embodiment of a *passeur* we could have met, and we hope that we are passing on at least some of the brilliance, wisdom, and humanity he has generously showered on us to the other scholars we are fortunate to be working with.

We are also enormously grateful to Andrew Chadwick for his intellectual leadership and support. Andy's work greatly inspired our early steps as researchers and our understanding of the complex relationships between media and power. As a colleague, mentor, and collaborator, he has been a model of collegiality, vision, and intellectual acumen. Cristian is grateful to have worked closely with Andy as a coauthor for the past eight years, and we are both thankful for his leadership, support, and friendship.

As we embarked on the intellectual journey that finally resulted in this book, we were fortunate to encounter many enlightened travel mates who were asking similar questions to ours and shared their experiences and wisdom with us. Lorenzo Mosca and Giovanna Mascheroni, the co-investigators on our grant, were a constant source of feedback and support during our project meetings. They were also generous in removing any obstacles for us to freely use the data collected as part of the project for various publications, including this book. We are grateful to Josh Tucker for building strong bridges between our project and the Social Media and Political Participation (SMaPP) lab at New York University, which later developed into the Center for Social Media and Politics. Cristian was also fortunate to be part of SMaPP Global, an international network that enabled us to receive invaluable feedback on this project from an outstanding group of scholars. Rasmus Kleis Nielsen has been a constant source of encouragement, advice, and inspiration, and under his leadership the Reuters Institute for the Study of Journalism at the University of Oxford has become a beacon for global research on media and politics, providing valuable insights that we and many others have been fortunate to build upon. Cristian is also grateful to Rasmus for his mentorship and support during and after his transition into the new role of editor-in-chief of *The International Journal of Press/Politics*, and for the extraordinary legacy that Rasmus and the journal's other past editors have entrusted him with.

Our intellectual adventures have been made possible by the many scholarly giants on whose shoulders we stand and whose hands we were very fortunate to hold at crucial points in our careers. We are particularly grateful to Bruce Bimber, Marcella Emiliani, Marino Livolsi, Gianpietro Mazzoleni, Gianfranco Pasquino, Sam Popkin, Monroe Price, Michael Schudson, Carlo Sorrentino, and James Thurber for generously supporting us with wisdom, encouragement, and opportunities at many different points in time and for being intellectual compasses we can always rely on.

Our work has greatly benefited from the constructive and insightful feedback that many colleagues have provided along the way as we presented our ideas at conferences, seminars, and workshops, as well as during informal exchanges over email, coffee, social media, or online videoconferencing. To adequately represent so many contributions over nearly a decade is a daunting task, and we know that this list cannot ever be complete, but we feel it is worth recognizing all those who inspired or supported us one way or another, with apologies to those we may have accidentally forgotten: Chris W. Anderson, Nick Anstead, Jesse Baldwin-Philippi, Pablo Barberá, Frédérick Bastien, Marco Bastos, Nick Beauchamp, Sara Bentivegna, Giuliano Bobba, Giovanni Boccia Artieri, Leticia Bode, Rich Bonneau, Rosa Borge Bravo, Michael Bossetta, Shelley Boulianne, Jonathan Bright, Erik Bucy, Donatella Campus, Marta Cantijoch, Ana Sofia Cardenal, Andreu Casero-Ripollés, Luigi Ceccarini, Diego Ceccobelli, Michael Chan, Jean-Gabriel Contamin, Lauren Copeland, Michael Delli Carpini, Lorenzo De Sio, Kate Dommett, Elizabeth Dubois, Johanna Dunaway, Anamaria Dutceac Segesten, Shira Dvir Gvirsman, Dean Eckles, Suzanne Elayan, Gunn Enli, Frank Esser, Richard Fletcher, Deen Freelon, Jason Gainous, R. Kelly Garrett, Thierry Giasson, Rachel Gibson, Fabio Giglietto, Homero Gil de Zúñiga, Sandra González-Bailón, Fabienne Greffet, Tim Groeling, Andy Guess, Philip Habel, Dan Hallin, Oliver Heath, Matt Hindman, Phil Howard, Stefano Iacus, Laura Iannelli, Dan Jackson, Mike Jensen, Abby Jones, Andreas Jungherr, Johannes Kaiser, Rune Karlsen, Dave Karpf, Norbert Kersting, Young Mie Kim, Karolina Koc-Michalska, Dan Kreiss, Michal Krzyzanowski, Ana Langer, Regina Lawrence, Sophie Lecheler, Guido Legnante, Darren Lilleker, Guillermo López-García, Paolo Mancini, Alice Mattoni, Shannon McGregor, Solomon Messing, Asimina Michailidou, Sabina Mihelj, Mike Miller, Judith Moeller, Patricia Moy, Kevin Munger, Maria Francesca Murru, Jonathan Nagler, Sarah Oates, Jennifer Oser, Jennifer Pan, Zizi Papacharissi, Josh Pasek, Elena Pavan, Barbara Pfetsch, Matt Powers, Cornelius Puschmann, Mario Quaranta, Jason Reifler, Molly Roberts, Franca Roncarolo, Luca Rossi, Patricia Rossini, Naomi Sakr, Holli Semetko, Kaat Smets, David Smith, Stuart Soroka, Sergio Splendore, James Stanyer, Kari Steen-Johnsen, Václav Štětka, Sebastian Stier, Talia Stroud, Jenny Stromer-Galley, Martin Sykora, Yannis Theocharis, Kjerstin Thorson, Ben Toff, Mariano Torcal, Terri Towner, Emiliano Treré, Filippo Trevisan, Filippo Tronconi, Damian Trilling, Rebekah Tromble, Nikki Usher, Lidia Valera-Ordaz, Peter Van Aelst, Thierry Vedel, Emily Vraga, Claes de Vreese, Claudius Wagemann, Silvio Waisbord, Brian Weeks, Chris Wells, Christine Williams, Magdalena Wojcieszak, Scott Wright, Dominic Wring, Danna Young, and Barbie Zelizer. We are also thankful to the editors, associate editors, and anonymous reviewers of the journals that published work we conducted as part of this project, as well as the journals that rejected our work but provided constructive feedback that helped us improve it.

As we completed this book, we were greatly saddened by the passing of three maestros whose work greatly influenced ours. Jay Blumler inspired generations of researchers to understand the implications of political communication for democracy in a comparative perspective. Martin Johnson was one of the friendliest and sharpest scholars whose company we have ever enjoyed, having the good fortune of sharing with him a passion not only for the study of political communication but also for the city of Bologna. Giovanni Sartori taught us, and countless other scholars around the world, what democracy is, what it can be, and what it cannot be, and his contribution has been invaluable in shaping how we think about the normative implications of our research.

The data on which this book is based were collected as part of a project generously funded by the Italian Ministry for Education and Research (MIUR) between 2013 and 2016. The project was titled "Building Inclusive Societies and a Global Europe Online: Political Information and Participation on Social Media in Comparative Perspective" (project code RBFR12BKZH). Cristian was the principal investigator and Augusto a key research fellow. The grant scheme under which our project was funded—named "Future in Research"—aimed to support and empower early career scholars. We are grateful we had the opportunity to collaborate and conduct our own large-scale study as part of this grant, which also funded a variety of events that enabled us to discuss and disseminate our research before it coalesced into this book. Being in charge of a generous budget for long-term investment at a relatively early stage in our careers provided an invaluable boost to our development as researchers. We hope young Italian scholars continue to enjoy these and other kinds of opportunities so they can spread their wings and fly as high and as far as they possibly can.

Collecting high-quality representative survey data across nine different countries over four years has been no small challenge. In this endeavor, we were fortunate to count on the support of Ipsos, a global company with an impressive track record and a very strong research culture. We are grateful to Simone Telloni and Barbara Toci for constantly ensuring that the needs of our project were met, often adapting to our sudden changes of direction, so that the quality of the data presented in this book is as high as possible.

The Department of Social and Political Sciences at the University of Bologna served very effectively as the administrative home of our project. We are indebted to all its administrative personnel, particularly Simona Nardini, for constantly assisting us, understanding the needs of our research, and helping us steer clear of the most perilous bureaucratic traps. We also thank Fabio Giusberti and Filippo Andreatta, who served as heads of department during our project and throughout the writing of this book, for their steady support and encouragement. Shortly after securing the grant for this project, Cristian was offered a life-changing opportunity to work at the Department of Politics and International

Relations at Royal Holloway, University of London, on a double appointment with the University of Bologna. Nathan Widder and Alister Miskimmon, who served as heads of department during the project, were invaluable in helping Cristian manage an exciting but challenging personal and professional transition, as were Ben O'Loughlin's friendship, humor, and intellectual companionship. We met twice at Royal Holloway for very fruitful planning sessions in 2014 and 2016, which were crucial to the development of this book and the strengthening of our personal bond—in spite of also coinciding with the disappointments of Italy's defeat to Costa Rica in the 2014 football World Cup and the outcome of the Brexit referendum in 2016! Cristian is also grateful to Royal Holloway and Loughborough University, where he moved in 2018, for providing one semester each of sabbatical leave, during which a substantial part of this book was drafted. At Loughborough University, Cristian also enjoyed invaluable support from James Stanyer and John Downey in their roles as heads of subject for communication and media.

We are both thrilled and honored that this book is published by Oxford University Press and in the Oxford Studies in Digital Politics series, which has immensely contributed to the advancement of the international scholarship to which we hope to contribute. We are particularly grateful to the series editor Andy Chadwick for his constant encouragement, advice, and support throughout the planning, preparation, and completion of the book, and to Angela Chnapko for how she carefully and insightfully shepherded us through the various stages of the publication process. We also greatly appreciate the very helpful and constructive comments from the anonymous colleagues who reviewed our book project and full manuscript. We have followed their feedback to the best of our ability, and we believe the process has greatly strengthened our work. Needless to say, any shortcomings in our execution of the advice we gratefully received are solely our responsibility.

Finally, this book, like all our other professional achievements, would not have been possible, nor meaningful to us, without the love and support of our families. Cristian is forever grateful to his parents for teaching him to believe in himself, to care for others and the world, and to always strive to grow and improve; to Margherita for being a loving partner and a wise companion through thick and thin; and to Carola and Edoardo for reminding him, every moment of every day, of what it all means and why it all matters. Augusto is grateful to his parents and grandparents for showing so clearly that, while there are many possible ways to walk through life, dedication, integrity, and love should always guide each of our steps; to Silvia for constantly pushing him toward new adventures together; and to Ilde and Tina for being a "blessed island" of joy and love.

Loughborough (United Kingdom) and Reggio Emilia (Italy), February 2021

Introduction

June 23, 2017. It is 10 p.m. in Pilton, Somerset, United Kingdom, on Day One of Glastonbury Music Festival. Held for the first time in June 1970, Glastonbury has become the signature British summer music event, following in the footsteps of the legendary hippie mass gatherings organized during the Seventies. The star British band Radiohead are on the main stage—aka "the Pyramid"—to headline the opening night. Suddenly, thousands in the public start a chant that you would not expect during a music event: to the tune of the White Stripes' "Seven Nation Army," the crowd sings with one voice: "Oh, Jeremy Corbyn!" At some point, even Thom Yorke, Radiohead's frontman, joins in. The BBC is broadcasting the festival live, and hundreds of Twitter users who are either attending the concert or dual-screening the TV show from their homes start commenting on this impromptu political media event using hashtags such as #glastonbury2017, #radiohead, and #bbcglasto. Radiohead's show has unexpectedly turned into a celebration of the then Labour Party leader, joined by an audience largely made up of younger voters, often described as disengaged from mainstream politics.

This was actually not the first time that the crowd of Glastonbury 2017 raised its voice to show sympathy for the Labour leader. Similar "Oh, Jeremy Corbyn!" choruses had started erupting from the very beginning of the festival, when people were queuing at the gates, and continued throughout the happening. After the Radiohead performance, the crowd's Corbyn chant was particularly loud when the British rap star Stormzy danced and free-styled over it on stage, and most importantly, when Corbyn himself walked into the Pyramid invited by Michael Eavis, the festival funder and long-standing left-wing activist, to give a highly acclaimed speech before introducing the U.S. hip-hop duo Run the Jewels.

Glastonbury 2017 was a topical moment in the so-called "Corbynmania." With this term, as well as the variation "Jez-mania," British media referred to the strong popularity Jeremy Corbyn enjoyed among young voters after he was unexpectedly elected Labour leader in 2015. Corbyn, a seasoned Westminster backbencher who had started his leadership campaign with few hopes of even

Outside the Bubble. Cristian Vaccari and Augusto Valeriani, Oxford University Press. © Oxford University Press 2021.
DOI: 10.1093/oso/9780190858476.003.0001

getting on the ballot, eventually secured a sound victory in 2015, confirmed it in 2016, and, just a couple of weeks before the 2017 Glastonbury acclamation, led Labour to a surprising 40% of the popular vote in the general election, gaining thirty parliamentary seats and coming surprisingly close to beating the Conservative Party, which lost its majority instead. Even two years later, when Labour was resoundingly defeated in the 2019 general election, the party still commanded a large majority among younger voters (Lord Ashcroft, 2019).

Moreover, and maybe most importantly, between 2015 and 2017 the number of Labour members almost doubled, passing the half-million mark (Audickas et al., 2019).[1] The number of Labour registered supporters—a lighter form of affiliation via online subscription—also increased substantially (BBC News Online, 2015). Although those who joined—or rejoined—the party during the Corbyn era were not all cut from the same cloth, most did not look like conventional party activists (as described, for instance, by Dalton, 2018). Compared with existing members, those who joined Labour for the first time after the 2015 general election were more likely to be younger and female, and to not have a university degree (Whiteley et al., 2019).

Corbyn's strategy to bring not only votes but also fresh energy to the Labour Party has been described as a successful mix of traditional volunteering, grassroots mobilization, and a robust social media effort both at horizontal (citizen to citizen) and vertical (organization to citizens) levels (Chadwick, 2017a; Pickard, 2018). Momentum, an organization independent from Labour created in 2015 to support Corbyn's leadership and his commitment to bring the party back to its original socialist vocation, was crucial. Momentum functions as a grassroots campaigning network that coordinates activists' efforts by offering them organizational tools (both digital and traditional), by producing original material or recirculating user-generated content (such as memes) that users can share online, and more broadly, by helping activists engage with each other and with voters (Dennis, 2020). At the same time, the organization constantly launches issue-based campaigns, organizes events and rallies, and even runs its own festival. Momentum exemplifies what Andrew Chadwick and Jennifer Stromer-Galley (2016) defined a "party-as-movement mentality," i.e., a party that connects with its base and with citizens in a more decentralized fashion than traditional organizations and that enables supporters to participate on their own terms (Gibson, 2015). By incorporating some of the organizational features typical of social movements and by leveraging digital and social media, this approach to political action partially disrupts hierarchical and exclusively top-down models and as a result can cement new political loyalties, unleash new political energies, and amplify new citizen voices (Chadwick & Stromer-Galley, 2016).

Granted, the forms of membership and identification encouraged by these new assemblages are less stable than in the past, as Bruce Bimber (2003) noted when he theorized that digital media would enhance new ephemeral forms of event-based membership. As public moods change, so do these manifestations of activism. Before his 2017 coronation, Corbyn had canceled his scheduled Glastonbury appearance in 2016, just after the Brexit referendum where he had been criticized for his half-hearted campaign for Remain. He canceled again in 2019, amid criticism that Labour was not doing enough to stop Brexit. The young, largely pro-Remain festival crowd was apparently not willing to give carte blanche to the same leader they loudly cheered on two years before. And even if, as mentioned earlier, a majority of young Britons voted for Labour in the catastrophic (for Corbyn) 2019 general election, as the decade was closing, the Corbyn-mania has already become a relic of the past, as the party seeks to move on and recover from a historic loss.

Still, this story highlights one of the implications of the contemporary media environment, and the forms of political action that various types of organizations have devised to take advantage of it. Citizens previously unaware of, or uninterested in, opportunities to get involved in politics might find information and motivation to become engaged in causes, around events, and in support of leaders and organizations that revolve around politics. In turn, these new recruits may then activate information and participation cascades within their online and offline social networks. In this book, we argue that social media are part of the reason why Western democracies are witnessing an increase in different forms of political participation, some of which involve citizens who were previously not deeply engaged in public affairs.

At the turn of the millennium, several authors (e.g., Dalton & Wattenberg, 2000; Putnam, 2000; Alex-Assensoh, 2005) warned that citizens' political participation was dramatically declining in Western democracies. Other scholars (e.g., Bennett, 2008; Stolle et al., 2005) argued that these pessimistic assessments missed the point because understanding citizens' political engagement in contemporary democracies required a new citizen-focused framework. This approach led to more inclusive definitions of participation and a renewed attention to extra-institutional forms of engagement, focusing in particular on protest, which characterized the first wave of research on social media and political participation (e.g., Bennett & Segerberg, 2013; Castells, 2015; Papacharissi, 2015). However, as we argue in this book, citizens' engagement in activities aimed at influencing processes and outcomes characterizing representative institutions is also not doomed to the irreversible decline that seemed to be unfolding one or two decades ago. We argue that social media are one of the reasons for this reversal.

As with every widely popular medium, scholarly assessments of the normative implications of digital media have swung like a pendulum between optimism and pessimism (Miller & Vaccari, 2020). The project that made this book possible was conceived at a time of widespread enthusiasm following the successful Internet-driven campaigns of Barack Obama in the United States (e.g., Cogburn & Espinoza-Vasquez 2011; Kreiss, 2012; Parmelee & Bichard, 2012; Gainous & Wagner, 2013) and, to some degree, the upheavals in some Middle Eastern and North African countries that were (prematurely) labeled as the "Arab Spring" and seen as driven by digitally enabled activism (Howard, 2010; Tufekci & Wilson, 2012; Howard & Hussain, 2013). As we complete this manuscript, the climate of opinion around digital media is much darker amid concerns for disinformation, hyper-partisanship, and hateful and intolerant speech (e.g., Persily, 2017; Bennett & Livingston, 2018; Gillespie, 2018; Rossini, 2019; Bail, 2021), where social media seem to be part of the problem rather than the solution (Vaidhyanathan, 2018). These are important political and societal problems, and we will address some of them in outlining our theoretical framework (Chapter 1) and in presenting our empirical analyses (Chapter 5), as well as reflecting on them in the Conclusion of this book. However, as we argue in Chapters 1 and 2, the relationship between social media and political participation in Western democracies still merits systematic empirical investigation. Our approach to this question is distinctive because it considers national contexts other than the United States and addresses differences between specific groups of citizens. Although some of the moderately optimistic normative conclusions that we draw from our findings may not fit well with the current climate of opinion around social media and democracy, they are informed by what we argue is one of the most comprehensive empirical analyses of the relationship between social media and participation to date.

Social Media and the Value of Democratic Participation

The present book investigates the implications of different types of political experiences on social media for patterns of citizens' institutional participation in Western democracies. Most theories of democracy, including the competitive approach proposed by Schumpeter (1942), identify a crucial connection between citizen participation and democratic governance, as voting enables citizens to select teams of representatives who govern them. In their seminal essay on how to assess the quality of democracy, Larry Diamond and Leonardo Morlino list participation as their second of eight criteria and argue that "democratic quality is high when citizens participate in the political process not only by voting, but by joining political parties and civil society organizations, partaking in the discussion of public policy issues, communicating with and demanding accountability from elected representatives, monitoring the conduct of public office-holders, and engaging in public issues at the local community level" (Diamond & Morlino, 2005: xvi). Similarly, Pippa Norris (2000: 22) argues that one of the key functions that news media must fulfill in a representative democracy is to serve as "mobilizing agents" to promote citizen participation. In this book, we assess the extent to which social media fulfill this role.

We do not assume that citizens' participation inevitably enriches the quality of the democratic environment they live in. Indeed, some scholars (e.g., Huntington, 1975) identify risks that might result from massive participation, such as overloading institutions with excessive demands and paving the way for authoritarian drifts. However, a democracy lacking a minimally engaged and active citizenry could be even more dysfunctional, as the inputs and incentives the elites receive from voters reflect the views and interests of small and unrepresentative minorities and thus lead public officials and parties to pursue policies that do not benefit most of the people, ultimately weakening the legitimacy of the democratic project. Verba and Nie (1972: 5) contend that citizens' democratic participation not only is instrumental to a functioning democracy but also should be seen as a democratic end in itself. Citizens' active engagement is instrumental to a working democracy since it is the most effective way for citizens to communicate their demands to those aiming to represent them, thus spurring responsiveness and accountability within democratic institutions. Conversely, the lack of active involvement into democratic life generates a spiral of disengagement and the decline of citizens' trust in their ability to have a say in crucial matters affecting their lives (Verba & Nie, 1972: 5). In turn, this could result in generalized lack of trust in the value and merits of democracy, potentially threatening the legitimacy and stability of its institutions. Relatedly, even critical appraisals of citizens' competence and ability to vote in a way that appropriately reflects their issue preferences still maintain that citizen participation can lead to the development of desirable democratic virtues (Achen & Bartels, 2017).

There is extensive evidence that participation connected to institutional politics, from electoral turnout (Gray & Caul, 2000; Texiera, 1987) to engagement in party-related activities (Rosenstone & Hansen, 1993; Whiteley, 2011a) declined from the end of the 1960s through to the end of the century. This period, termed the "second age of political communication" by Blumler and Kavanagh (1999), was dominated by televised politics and electorally focused parties. As Robert Entman (1990) argued, mass participation was replaced by mass spectatorship, leading to a "democracy without citizens," where strategic elites communicate carefully crafted appeals to a largely passive televised audience. Whether, as argued by Robinson (1976) and Putnam (2000), television had a direct responsibility in the decline of citizen participation or, as Norris (2000) and Bennet

(1998) contended, television was actually helping citizens remain engaged amid a host of other societal and political factors that were depressing participation, few dispute that political participation declined across most Western democracies for most of the second half of the twentieth century.

The digital era of political communication has often been seen as a more fertile terrain for participation. As documented by Shelley Boulianne (2015, 2019, 2020), a large and robust corpus of empirical studies has found positive associations between different uses of social media and political participation. Thus, social networking platforms might have helped turn the tide of widespread political disengagement that had worried scholars of democracy in the previous three decades. Nevertheless, as Boulianne observed (2015), studies of social media and participation focus, with very few exceptions, on single countries, employ relatively small data sets, and are based on highly heterogeneous—and, we add, not always ideal—measures both on the right-hand side (social media uses) and left-hand side (political participation) of the equation. Moreover, studies considering differential effects of social media use on participation among specific types of citizens are still rare. By overcoming some of these limitations, the research presented in this book aims to enhance our understanding of the relationship between digital media and political participation both conceptually and empirically.

Different Platforms, Different Users, Different Outcomes

To understand the relationship between social media and political participation, we focus on *politically relevant outcomes* of citizens' use of social media rather than on the technical affordances of those platforms or the sheer frequency with which people use them. The affordances of social media matter, as they make certain political outcomes relatively more or less likely (Chadwick, 2019), but it is those outcomes that in the end may result in higher or lower levels of participation. In the present book we consider three politically relevant outcomes of social media usage that we theorize could affect political participation: (a) levels of *political agreement* encountered on social media, (b) *accidental exposure to political news*, and (c) being targeted by *electoral mobilization*.

We start our investigation by assessing how common, or uncommon, these outcomes are among representative samples of Internet users in nine Western democracies. This enables us to advance the debate on social media's role in enabling dissemination of different types of political content and, in particular, in fostering or hindering exposure to disagreeable or unsearched-for political information. Our analyses show that technologically deterministic accounts of digital and social media as "echo chambers" (Sunstein, 2009) or "filter bubbles" (Pariser, 2011) isolating all individuals from political information they disagree with, or are not interested in (Prior, 2007), are at best exaggerated and at worst unfounded (as also recently argued, among others, by Bruns, 2019). Across the Western democracies we study, most social media users encounter similar amounts of agreeable and disagreeable political content, and it is much more common for users to predominantly see political messages they disagree than agree with. These patterns contrast remarkably with face-to-face conversations, where the opposite occurs. Moreover, social media often expose individuals to political information accidentally—i.e., while they are using these platforms for other purposes—and enable both organized political actors and activist citizens to reach substantial numbers of users with electoral mobilization messages designed to persuade them to vote for a party or candidate. Therefore, while ideological self-segregation and avoidance of politics are theoretically possible outcomes of the choice affordances of social media, our findings indicate that substantial numbers of their users encounter and engage with political content that they do not necessarily seek or agree with. In a nutshell, as the title of this book suggests, politics on social media can break *outside the* (ideological and topical) *bubbles* that might indeed characterize the online experiences of political junkies but hardly shape those of most ordinary users.

We also identify the sociodemographic, attitudinal, behavioral, and systemic factors that lead individuals to experience the outcomes we study. More than demographic characteristics or general attitudes toward politics, patterns of social media use predict the political experiences citizens do or do not engage in. Conversely, variables related to political involvement, such as interest in politics, are not always crucial in explaining political experiences on social media. Social media can create favorable opportunities for participation that reach beyond the usual suspects—the politically informed and engaged—that earlier research on the pre-social-media Internet suggested were the only targets and beneficiaries of online political communication (Bimber & Davis, 2003; Norris, 2003).

Mobilizing the Political Junkie, the Inattentive, or the Disaffected?

The second distinctive feature of our approach is that we theorize and empirically evaluate the role of social media in promoting citizens' political participation as *varying in strength among different sectors of the population.* Instead of assuming that political experiences on social media have the same participatory implications for everyone—as most research has done so far, at least implicitly, by focusing on generalized statistical relationships—we argue and demonstrate that such associations are differential—i.e., their strength varies between different groups. Thus, we first show that exposure to political viewpoints that are predominantly congruent with one's own, accidentally encountering political news, and being targeted by electoral mobilization via social media all exhibit positive and significant correlations with political participation. Then, we differentiate between citizens based on their levels of political involvement, which previous research (Verba et al., 1995) has shown time and again to predict political participation. We employ measures of both long-term (*interest in politics*) and short-term (*attention to election campaigns*) political involvement. We theorize that citizens with higher levels of political involvement should enjoy lower marginal participatory gains from political experiences on social media than citizens with lower levels of involvement. For the highly involved, any additional piece of information and any call to action that social media may convey fall against the backdrop of a high volume of existing knowledge, strong political convictions, and robust networks of recruitment, so it may not make a massive difference. By contrast, for the less involved, even a small amount of political content may be consequential, as it constitutes a comparatively larger addition to a smaller existing informational inventory and a weaker structure of opportunities for political action. Thus, for the less involved, political experiences on social media are more likely to provide genuinely new avenues for participation.

Consistent with this theory, our analyses reveal that, if citizens engage in political experiences on social media, it is those who are *less* interested in politics and *less* attentive to a general election campaign who see their levels of participation increase the most, while the corresponding participatory increases are much smaller among users who report higher levels of interest and attention. This suggests that social media may foster political equality rather than augment existing participatory gaps. These insights highlight the benefits of studying the differential participatory effects of social media, as opposed to the one-size-fits-all approaches that have so far been dominant in the literature. We draw from these findings a moderately optimistic assessment of the role of social media in Western democracies. Not only do they enhance overall levels of participation, but they also seem to particularly benefit those less engaged citizens who need this encouragement the most, at least if we value equality of political voice in a democracy.

As well as participation, another crucial component of democracy is pluralistic electoral competition, which guarantees, if not responsiveness (Schumpeter, 1942; Dahl, 1989; Diamond & Morlino, 2005), at least the possibility of alternation in government (Achen & Bartels, 2017). Competing political elites need support from citizens, in terms of both votes and resources that can be directed to mobilize support in the electorate. If one group manages to build and organize this support more extensively and effectively, it will be more likely to attract votes and, thus, power. Hence, political participation, and the promotion thereof, can have important effects on electoral competition. To illuminate the impact of social media on political competition, we investigate whether political experiences on social media have similar or different implications on voters of different ideological persuasions.

Our results show that, for the most part, the relationship between the political experiences on social media that we study (encountering agreeing messages, accidentally seeing political content, and being exposed to electoral mobilization) and political participation does not vary according to citizens' ideology. In particular, we find no evidence that voters who locate themselves to the extremes (right or left) of the political spectrum are disproportionately activated by these political experiences online. There is, however, some evidence that supporters of the moderate right yield slightly greater participatory benefits than those who identify with the moderate left. These findings suggest that the advantage progressives enjoyed online in the past decade (Vaccari, 2013; Kreiss, 2012) may have vanished. Still, to the extent that conservatives are currently reaping greater participatory benefits from social media, as argued, among others, by Schradie (2019), it is mostly citizens who locate themselves around relatively moderate center-right positions, rather than those who gravitate toward the extreme right, who are becoming more active compared with others, and the differences between moderate right and moderate left voters are small in magnitude. Overall, the political experiences on social media that we study in this book seem to constitute rising tides that lift most ideological boats.

In this context, we also address the ongoing debate on the relationship between digital media and populism. The success of political actors espousing populism, defined by Cass Mudde (2004: 543) as "an ideology that considers society to be ultimately separated into two homogeneous and antagonistic groups, 'the pure people' versus 'the corrupt elite,' and which argues that politics should be an expression of the *volonté generale* (general will) of the people," has transformed political competition in most Western democracies in the past few years (Norris & Inglehart, 2019). Various scholars have highlighted that contemporary media ecologies, and social media in particular, can provide a fertile breeding ground for authoritarian populists (Engesser et al., 2017; Bennett & Livingston, 2018; Hallin, 2019; Gil de Zúñiga et al., 2020). To shed light on this issue, we assess the differential effects of the three political experiences we study on participation among voters who did and did not vote for populist parties and presidential candidates in the previous elections. Similar to Boulianne and colleagues (2020), we find no evidence that citizens who voted for populist political actors were disproportionately sprung into political action by exposure to agreeing viewpoints, accidentally encountering political news, or electoral mobilization on social media. Although our data cannot illuminate the ways in which populist political actors use social media to persuade prospective voters (on which point see, e.g., Bucy et al., 2020; Hameleers et al., 2018; Roemmele & Gibson, 2020; Zhang et al., 2018), our findings suggest that political experiences on social media are not activating populist voters to participate in politics to a greater extent than supporters of other, non-populist parties.

Context Matters, but How?

Although there are now hundreds of published studies on social media and participation, most of them focus on just one country and the few comparative studies that are available—including some of our own (Valeriani & Vaccari, 2016; Vaccari & Valeriani, 2016; Vaccari, 2017)—only consider as few as two or three countries. As a result, we do not know whether the patterns found in highly researched political systems such as the United States apply to other, important but less frequently studied, Western democracies. We also have no reliable knowledge on whether and how the relationship between social media and political participation varies in strength or form across different political contexts. Finally, we can only speculate on how different political and media institutions may or may not make any difference to these patterns.

To address this gap, our research compares *nine diverse Western democracies*— Denmark, France, Germany, Greece, Italy, Poland, Spain, the United Kingdom, and the United States—that share relevant features as stable democratic regimes but also differ under theoretically fertile respects. These differences enable us to more confidently establish the robustness of our findings across a wide variety of contexts and to assess how specific systemic characteristics shape the relationship between political experiences on social media and political participation.

We root our analysis in an original theoretical framework that focuses on three systemic factors: (a) whether electoral competition is organized around *majoritarian* or *proportional* rules and patterns, (b) how *mass media systems* function, and (c) whether political systems are *party-centric* or *candidate-centric*. Based on theoretically grounded considerations, we assess how each of these factors moderates the relationship between political participation and one of the social media experiences we focus on.

Our results show that the correlation between predominant exposure to political agreement on social media and participation is stronger in majoritarian than proportional systems. Where electoral rules incentivize catch-all parties, characterized by looser ideological connections with their voters, the experience of supportive political views on social media plays a stronger mobilizing role for citizens. We also find evidence—albeit less conclusive than in the previous case—that the association between exposure to electoral mobilization on social media and participation is stronger in countries characterized by party-centric systems, where parties are better organized and more capable of providing participatory opportunities for citizens both during and outside election campaigns. Contrary to our expectations, we find that the characteristics of media systems do not moderate the relationship between accidental exposure to news on social media and participation.

To sum up, systemic differences have a limited, but still observable, impact on the relationship between political experiences on social media and participation. This confirms the importance of comparative research to develop a more granular and context-sensitive understanding of the implications of social media on democratic life. Neither the United States, which has dominated the literature on digital media and politics so far, nor any other political system should be taken as the gold standard on which to develop, or inductively derive, universal theories.

Outline of the Book

This book is organized around six chapters.

In Chapter 1, we introduce the conceptual building blocks on which we base our analysis and set out our position in the debate on the implications of social media for citizens' political participation. We argue that social networking platforms may contribute to strengthening participation due to several features characterizing them as spaces where political content is easily accessible in often unplanned circumstances. We engage with a broad theoretical and empirical literature to substantiate three main hypotheses that suggest a positive direct relationship between political participation and, respectively, predominant exposure to political agreement, incidental exposure to political news, and exposure to electoral mobilization messages. We then discuss our expectations on how different sets of individual and systemic variables may moderate such relations. As concerns individual factors, we focus on two indicators of political involvement (as specified earlier, interest in politics and attention to the latest election campaign) and ideology (which we supplement with voting for populist political actors to better understand the relationship between social media and populism). As regards political involvement, we theorize that the effects of political experiences on social media should be stronger for citizens who are less involved than for those who are more involved. With respect to ideology, we outline alternative scenarios for electoral competition that may result from different patterns of differential effects across different ideological groups. With respect to systemic factors, we theorize that three variables may play a role: electoral competition (majoritarian vs. proportional), media systems (liberal vs. other types), and political organizations (party- vs. candidate-centric). Specifically, we hypothesize that each of these variables may moderate the relationship between participation and exposure to political agreement, accidentally encountering political news, and being targeted by electoral mobilization on social media. Chapter 1 also discusses our rationale for country selection and outlines the main characteristics of the nine Western democracies we study.

In Chapter 2, we define political participation as a fluid set of repertoires of political action spanning across face-to-face and digitally enabled activities. We consider an activity as constituting political participation if it aims to exercise *influence on politically relevant outcomes*. In this sense we focus on, and measure, citizens' attempts to affect three types of outcomes: *policy decisions* (primary influence), the *selection of public officials* who make those decisions (secondary influence), and *other citizens' political preferences and actions* (tertiary influence). Chapter 2 also introduces the main characteristics of the custom-built, comparative survey data sets we employ for this research, on which we provide extensive additional information in our Online Appendix, available at https://bit.ly/outside-the-bubble.

In Chapter 3, we assess how common, or uncommon, the three political experiences on social media we consider are among representative samples of Internet users in the nine countries we study. We also identify the sociodemographic, attitudinal, behavioral, and systemic factors that predict whether individuals have these experiences. Uncovering these patterns allows us to assess whether political content on social media disproportionately caters to certain groups in the population, and, if so, to identify which groups these are, thus beginning to unveil the extent to which social media reinforce or disrupt existing political inequalities.

Chapter 4 opens a triplet of chapters where we present our analyses on the relationship between political experiences on social media and participation. Here, we focus on the *direct effects* of being exposed to agreeing views, encountering unsearched political news, and being targeted by electoral mobilization messages. We illustrate the results of multivariate analyses that reveal the statistical associations between these experiences and levels of political participation. Our models show that, although social media are fertile grounds for exposure to contrarian opinions (as shown in Chapter 3), encountering disagreement is less fruitful, in terms of spurring political participation, than the—less common— condition of predominantly interacting with opinions one agrees with. We also find a positive but weaker relationship between incidental exposure to news and participation. Conversely, being targeted by electoral mobilization shows the strongest association, among the three experiences we consider, with participation.

In Chapter 5, we assess whether political experiences on social media can reduce participation gaps between types of citizens with high and low levels of political involvement, as well as assess differential effects among citizens of different ideologies. By adding interaction terms to our models, we estimate whether the relationship between participation and each of the three political experiences on social media we study differs among citizens with different levels of interest in politics and attention to election campaigns. The results broadly confirm our general expectation of social media as participation equalizers, as our relationships of interest tend to become weaker as levels of political involvement increase, and vice versa. We also find that the political experiences on social media that we study have similar relationships with participation across respondents who locate themselves at different points in the left–right ideological spectrum, albeit with slightly stronger relationships among moderate center-right voters. Finally, we show that respondents who voted for populist political actors did not experience disproportionately larger participatory gains from political experiences on social media than those who voted for non-populist parties and candidates. These results suggest that social media may not be substantially tilting the scales of electoral competition, at least with regard to their ability to help different political actors activate their voters.

Finally, Chapter 6 presents the results of our comparative analysis. Here, we assess whether the participatory gains resulting from political experiences on social media vary as a function of the characteristics of electoral competition, mass media, and political parties. We open the chapter by questioning the standardization hypothesis of social media and politics—i.e., the idea that the effects of social media on political outcomes should be broadly similar across different Western democracies—which often implicitly or explicitly translates into the notion of an Americanization of social media and politics. We conversely explain why we expect to see cross-country differentiation based on systemic variables, as hypothesized in Chapter 1. We test our expectations by enriching our models with interaction terms between political experiences on social media and variables clustering together majoritarian versus proportional electoral systems, liberal versus polarized pluralist and democratic corporatist media systems, and party-centric versus candidate-centric political systems. The results suggest that system-level political characteristics such as electoral competition and party-centeredness matter, but less than the individual-level political attitudes investigated in Chapter 5. Comparing different political systems enables us to add nuances to our understanding of the role of social media in contemporary democracies.

Finally, in the Conclusion we summarize our findings and discuss their implications for the study of social media and democracy. First, social media can be fertile terrains for the propagation of political opinions, efficient vehicles for serendipitous encounters with political news, and viable channels of electoral mobilization—all of which have positive, albeit limited, implications for political participation. Second, social media are not necessarily and not only "weapons of the strong" (Schlozman et al., 2010) that disproportionally empower citizens who are already more likely to participate in politics. Under certain conditions, political experiences online benefit the less involved more than the highly involved, thus gradually broadening the pool of participants. Third, any effects that social media may have on political participation do not occur in a vacuum but are to some degree shaped by political institutions.

A final note concerns the style with which we will present our analyses. This book reports original research based on custom-built survey data, which we analyzed with sometimes complex statistical techniques that are commonly employed for these purposes in the literature in political science and political communication. Throughout the chapters, we have aimed to provide as much information as possible on the ways we processed and analyzed the data, while trying not to overburden readers with too many technical details. We have, however, prepared a detailed Online Appendix, which provides extensive information on our sample and data collection, the wording of all the questions we used in the analyses, additional statistical models, and discussion of the techniques we used to preprocess the data to better approximate the conditions that enable social scientists to make causal inferences based on observational data such as those employed in this study. We encourage readers who are particularly interested in these aspects to consult this Online Appendix, which we will reference whenever appropriate throughout the book.

1

Why Social Media Matter

Knock Down the House is a documentary on the primary campaigns of four out-sider Democratic women candidates running for the 2018 U.S. midterm con-gressional elections (Lears, 2019). The four underdogs were supported in their campaigns by Justice Democrats and Brand New Congress, two organizations aiming to help progressive Democrats get elected. Among the candidates fea-tured in the documentary, only Alexandria Ocasio-Cortez (who later came to be known simply by her initials AOC) won the primary and was eventually elected as the representative for New York's 14th District. AOC's popularity grew expo-nentially during and after the election, partly due to her sharp argumentative style in Congress, but also thanks to her sophisticated communication on social media. In one of the most emotional scenes of the documentary, the cameras follow AOC into the polling station. As Ocasio-Cortez has just cast her vote, she stumbles into a man who wants to shake her hand and express support. The man, who does not seem to be completely at ease in the situation, says to her: "I saw the video clip, but I saw, I didn't see it all through, but the first two minutes convinced me to come here." The clip is very likely to be *The Courage of Change*, a highly emotional video produced by AOC's campaign to be circulated on social media, in which the candidate tells her personal story and the motivations behind her choice to run for office. The clip, which had more than one million views on YouTube by June 2019, is actually two minutes long, but AOC's sup-porter admits that he "didn't see it all through." It is hard to imagine that some-one who does not even get through to the end of a captivating two-minute online video would be willing to watch a ninety-minute political debate on TV, read a political column in a newspaper, or read a candidate's policy proposals on her website. We can reasonably suppose that AOC's polling station supporter is not a political junkie and that he possibly stumbled upon the video on social media by chance, just as he stumbled into his favored candidate at the polling station. However, at least according to the story this voter tells Ocasio-Cortez, the effect of such a minimal digital political experience was strong enough to push him to get out and vote: the fragment of the video was what made the difference for him

Outside the Bubble. Cristian Vaccari and Augusto Valeriani, Oxford University Press. © Oxford University Press 2021.
DOI: 10.1093/oso/9780190858476.003.0002

between participation and abstention. In a nutshell, this vignette illustrates two important propositions this book aims to assess: (1) that on social media political experiences can happen to a highly diverse plethora of citizens, and (2) that these experiences can sometimes make a difference when it comes to political participation—including for less engaged citizens.

This chapter sets out our main argument on how and why social media matter for citizens' political participation. We contend that social networking platforms may contribute to strengthening participation and that research has so far failed to fully grasp these realities as a consequence of three theoretical and empirical fallacies. We call them the *affordances-as-destiny fallacy*, the *one-effect-fits-all fallacy*, and the *contextual vacuum fallacy*. We propose a framework that overcomes these fallacies by refocusing our attention on the different uses individuals make of social media; on the extent to which their effects differ among subjects with different levels of political involvement and ideology; and on the role of systemic factors that vary across countries, such as characteristics of media systems, patterns of electoral competition, and the strength of party organizations.

Social Media and Everyday Politics

danah boyd and Nicole Ellison (2007) define social media as online services that allow individuals to construct public or semi-public profiles, build connections with other users, and explore such connections as well as those made by other users. These networks also enable users to post different types of content (textual, visual, and audiovisual); share links to such content; and comment on, share, and edit content posted by others. Nowadays, most users access social media from both mobile and fixed devices. In our surveys, when we asked respondents how frequently they access the Internet and social media from different devices, 57.6% told us they do that "several times a day" using a smartphone, 39.7% using a laptop computer, 35.6% using a desktop computer, and 18.8% using a tablet (see Chapter 2 for a discussion of our data). The broad social adoption of these platforms and their widespread use in mobility contribute to deeply embedding these technologies in the everyday lives of many, possibly most, citizens in contemporary Western democracies (Highfield, 2016).

When they access social media, citizens have multiple opportunities to engage with political and media actors that compete for their attention, resources, and loyalty. Most people, however, choose not to purposefully follow such elites online (Nielsen & Vaccari, 2013). Most social media users most of the time employ these platforms to engage with other citizens—be they members of their families, friends, colleagues, distant acquaintances, or at times perfect strangers. Just as most citizens are not particularly interested in or attentive to politics (Dalton & Wattenberg, 2002; Hibbing & Thesis-Morse, 2002), *most of the relationships users entertain on social media are nonpolitical.* Thus, most of the interactions that occur on social media are also nonpolitical, or at least not *primarily* and *intentionally* political.

Nonpolitical exchanges among social media users, however, can result in references to, and possibly discussions of, political topics. On occasion, such political interactions are sparked by political content produced by elite actors such as politicians, governments, and journalists, which other users can easily find and circulate on social media. This is because social media offer a variety of low-cost and low-threshold opportunities for individuals to share political content or express political views (Chadwick, 2009), even if only by "liking" or "sharing" someone else's contributions. These individual actions may seem inconsequential and irrelevant in themselves, and they often are, but they may scale up quickly if enough other users join in, potentially adding up to a non-negligible amount of political stimulation for those on the receiving end. Importantly, exposure to and discussion of political content on social media do not need to happen because of deliberate and premeditated users' choices. They often happen informally, occasionally, and accidentally, because on social media there is generally not a rigid distinction between spaces where people can and should talk about politics and spaces where people cannot or should not do so (Wojcieszak & Mutz, 2009).

One important way in which social media have contributed to changing the context of contemporary political communication is by providing what Scott Wright (2012) calls "third spaces"—public environments where informal interactions and everyday political talk occur continuously but not purposefully. *It is because social media are not seen, employed, and experienced as eminently political arenas by most users that they can play a role in exposing citizens to relevant political content that they may not have otherwise encountered and that may, in turn, enhance their participation.* This chapter outlines this argument in full. Before we do that, however, we will ground this premise—that most of what social media users do on these platforms most of the time has little to do with politics—on firmer empirical foundations.

Many readers of this book may be passionate about politics, and they may in fact disagree with our contention that social media are mostly nonpolitical spaces that only occasionally become political. For many of our readers, the opposite may be true, especially during topical events such as elections, crises, and political scandals. This idea may particularly resonate among those who, like us, are avid Twitter users. If our readers feel this way, it is because they, and we, are interested in politics, and as a result politics plays a larger role in our social media lives than other topics. However, this is not the case for most of our fellow citizens, who generally do not pay much attention to politics, do not invest many cognitive or affective energies in it, and as a result do not spend a lot of their time and efforts on social media reading, writing, or commenting about politics.

Let us consider some empirical data from our surveys. We asked our respondents who are social media users to estimate, on a scale from 0 to 10, the proportion of the messages they posted and read on social media in the previous two months that had to do with politics, the general elections in their countries, or public affairs more generally. Figure 1.1 shows that 38.8% of our respondents claimed that *none of the messages they posted were about politics*, and 24.4% claimed that *none of the posts they read were about politics*. The remainder of the sample, however, answered with a number higher than 0; i.e., they claimed they posted (61.2%) and read (75.6%) at least a few political messages. Importantly, our respondents claimed that the proportion of messages they read was higher than the proportion of messages they posted, and more people placed themselves on the lower end of the spectrum (i.e., answers 1–5) than on the higher end (6–10). The average among the whole sample is 3 for posting and 3.99 for reading political messages. Hence, most social media users publish and, especially, come across political messages at least some of the time, but political content is by no means the sole, nor the primary, component of most users' everyday experience of these platforms.

Moreover, the specific social media platforms people use matter for the quantity of political messages they post and read. Among those who claimed to log into different platforms more than once per day, the average responses for reading political messages differed widely between Twitter users (5.80 on a 0–10

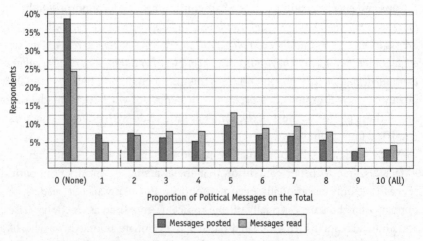

Figure 1.1. Proportion of Published and Read Posts on Social Media That Were About Politics in the Past Two Months

Note: N = 15,352.

scale) and Facebook users (4.74), and the same was true for posting political messages, where regular Twitter users averaged 5.29 compared with 3.55 for regular Facebook users. Among the platforms we measured (which also include Instagram, YouTube, the now-defunct Google Plus, and other sites respondents could identify in open-ended form), Facebook was the one whose regular users claimed to read and post the least about politics, and Twitter was the one whose regular users claimed to read and post the most about politics. Considering that Facebook is by far the most popular social media platform around the world and in Western democracies (We Are Social, 2019), if there is such a thing as an average social media user, that person is much more likely to be on Facebook than on Twitter, and their experience of politics can be expected to be substantially more rarefied than for the average Twitter user. Still, most politicians, journalists, and commentators tend to be heavier users of Twitter than Facebook, and most academic research on social media—especially that based on digital trace data— has hitherto focused on Twitter rather than Facebook (Bode & Vraga, 2018). This is one of the reasons why both public and scholarly debates about social media and politics have, in our view, failed to capture some relevant dynamics that this book aims to explore.

Social Media and the Flow of Political Information Across Personal and Public Spaces

So far, we have pointed out that social media enable low-cost diffusion of political messages by elites and individuals, and we have highlighted that relatively small but not insubstantial quantities of these messages reach vast amounts of users, many of whom may not be particularly interested in politics in the first place. This is not conceptually different to what general-purpose mediums such as television have arguably done for decades, i.e., exposing individuals to public affairs content even though they are not particularly interested in it, let alone actively seeking it (Neuman et al., 1992; Graber, 2001). As we saw earlier, social media seem to have the potential to achieve similar goals, even though different platforms are differently suited to fulfill them. What is peculiar about social media, however, is that they bring together political and nonpolitical interactions, as well as exchanges with both elites and non-elites. As such, social media facilitate the fusion of two different domains that political communication research has generally treated separately: *public* political communication (accessible to and observable by everyone) and *private* political communication (occurring among private actors and, thus, normally confined to them; see Henn et al., 2016). Manuel Castells's (2007) concept of "mass-self communication"

aptly describes this fusion of public and private modes in the production, distribution, and fruition of political messages (see also Flanagin, 2017). This point is
particularly important for political participation, which in itself is an act where
individuals bring (some facets of) their private personas into (a subset of) the
public domain to make their voices heard with respect to some authoritative
allocation of value (Easton, 1965).

The public–private, or mass–self, communicative fusion enabled by social
media has important implications not just for the circulation of political content,
but also for the conditions in which such content is communicated. When individuals generate, share, or endorse content on social media, they make it more
likely that such messages will be seen by other users in their networks.[1]

If and when those messages are seen, they carry two important additional
features superimposed to their content: *social cues* related to the characteristics
of the sender and *social endorsements* tied to the popularity of the message within
the network.

SOCIAL CUES

Most people rarely have the time, attention, cognitive resources, and motivation
to process the deluge of content that competes for their eyes, hearts, and minds
on social media—or, for that matter, outside of it. Faced with what is known
as "information overload" (Eppler & Mengis, 2004), individuals rationally
resort to heuristics—rules aiming at solving problems or achieving cognitive
goals without collecting or processing all the information that is theoretically
available. Politics is one of the domains where such heuristics are most helpful
(Popkin, 1994) because most individuals are not particularly interested in it and
even those who are cannot rationally expect to be able to generate meaningful
political change by being better informed and acting upon such information on
their own (Downs, 1957; Lupia & McCubbins, 1998). Evaluating the content
and implications of a message based on its source is one very important heuristic
that citizens often employ when processing political messages (Mondak, 1993).
Voters quickly assess whether they agree on a policy based on whether they generally favor the politician, party, or group proposing it. They also decide whether
to trust some information based on how credible they consider the individual or
organization that provides it.

On social media, however, sources are often *layered*, i.e., more than one
source is involved in bringing content to our attention. A political message can
reach users directly because someone—ordinary citizen, activist, journalist, or
politician—writes something, shares a picture or video, or posts a link to some
content they or their organizations have published online. Such a message,

however, can also reach users *indirectly*, because someone else has shared some content that another user originally produced.

When assessing the content, political or otherwise, of a post on social media, users can be expected to rely, among other things, on the characteristics of both its direct and indirect sources that are known and relevant to them. Source cues help social media users make quick and relatively undemanding decisions as to whether a message deserves their limited attention. If this first threshold is passed, source cues can also influence how users interpret the meaning of such content—based on who shared it and, possibly, how they commented on it. As social media are used to maintain relationships of different intensity with one's family, close and distant friends, acquaintances, groups, organizations, brands, and public figures, users process these different source cues according to the types of relationships they entertain with them.

The power of source cues has been widely demonstrated by research on social media and political behavior. For instance, an experiment found that Facebook users became more likely to vote when they saw posts showing that their close ties—i.e., users with whom they interact most often—had voted (Bond et al., 2012). Similarly, Kaiser and colleagues (2021) found that people who accidentally come into contact with news in an experimental setting mocking up the Facebook news feed are more likely to actually read such news if it has been shared by someone with whom they have a strong social connection. Anspach (2017) showed that individuals who are not interested in the news are more likely to read it on social media when some of their close friends and family members share it. The same study found that even partisan voters are willing to engage with news from the other end of the political spectrum if people who are socially close to them recommend it.

To summarize, social media help disseminate political information with a personal touch, and whether the source is a close friend or family member or a distant acquaintance, the fact that there is a source to which recipients can assign value (whether in terms of rational utility, social proximity, or ideological affinity) adds meaning to the message. If shared by trusted and valued sources, political content can appear as more relevant and appealing even among users who are not highly engaged with politics.

SOCIAL ENDORSEMENTS

Social endorsements provide social media users with cues they can employ to activate another type of information shortcut—the bandwagon heuristic, based on which individuals attribute value to the opinions of others and orient their behaviors accordingly (Messing & Westwood, 2014: 1047).

When users "like" or share content on social media, they make such content more likely to be seen by others they are in contact with. Moreover, most social media platforms provide numeric tallies summarizing the number of users who endorsed any content, and some platforms also highlight who among the user's contacts has done that. As a result, when users see a message on social media, they can also see ostensibly objective data on its popularity. Messing and Westwood (2014) demonstrate that these visible and quantified social endorsements play a strong role in helping users decide which content to access and engage with in digital environments. Even users with strong political views are willing to read content from a source they normally disagree with, as long as it has been endorsed by many other users. This is a very important finding because decades of research in political communication suggest that one of the most powerful mechanisms driving citizens' contact with information is selective exposure—that is, individuals choose what they see based on their (real or perceived) ideological congruence with the source, the content, or both (Bennett & Iyengar, 2008; Stroud, 2011; Arcenaux & Johnson, 2013). If social endorsements can thwart selective exposure, they may also counterbalance another factor that normally limits individuals' engagement with political information—their lack of interest in and desire for political content (Prior, 2007). Just as users who have partisan allegiances are willing to temporarily set them aside to read or watch content that, albeit incongruent with their views, has been endorsed by many others, users who are not interested in politics may still be encouraged to read political content that has been widely endorsed by others.

Although we have presented social cues and social endorsements as general mechanisms, the extent to which they influence the ways in which individuals process a given message may vary substantially across different types of individuals. For instance, Bond and colleagues (2017) found that social cues affect users' behaviors in different ways depending on individuals' demographic characteristics, their attitudes toward political expression on social media, and the structure of their digital networks. These results highlight that one-size-fits-all theories and explanations are not well positioned to capture the nexus between political experiences on social media and political participation, as we discuss later in this chapter.

Social Media and Political Participation: The Story So Far

In this book, we define political participation as a constellation of political actions—performed across the online and offline realms—that are aimed at influencing specific policies, the selection of public officials who determine such policies, and other citizens' political preferences and behaviors (see Chapter 2 for a broader discussion). Since social media help channel meaningful political information, which might include calls for action, and facilitate political expression through low-cost and low-threshold endeavors, do they also enhance political participation? Most research on this topic suggests they do, even though many aspects of this phenomenon are still obscure. Shelley Boulianne has conducted three important meta-analyses of survey-based research on this topic: one includes 36 studies, mostly from the United States (Boulianne, 2015); the second covers 133 studies from 27 countries (Boulianne, 2019); and the third is based on 243 studies from 50 countries (Boulianne, 2020). All three reviews conclude that research has generally found positive and significant correlations between social media use and political participation across different political systems and contexts. The strength and significance of such correlations, however, vary depending on which type of social media use was investigated. Generic social media use had the weakest association with participation, and political self-expression had the strongest association (Boulianne, 2019: 47). There is, indeed, little reason to expect that just using social media may lead to higher levels of participation—some research even suggests that in and of itself it may lead to lower participation because it displaces other activities (Theocharis & Lowe, 2016). Thus, to understand how and why social media may contribute to political participation, we need to focus on *specific political experiences* resulting from social media use, as we discuss later in this chapter.

While most, though not all, survey-based research has focused generically on social media use as a possible predictor of participation, experimental research has measured the impact of very specific messages, and their sources, on participation (Bond et al., 2012; Coppock et al., 2016; Jones et al., 2017). Other studies have addressed the role of more specific, but still relatively broad, types of politically relevant behaviors on social media. For instance, survey-based research by Cantijoch and colleagues (2015) found that lower-intensity online political activities, such as seeking information on the Internet, spill over to subsequent levels of engagement in political discussion online, and Gil de Zúñiga and colleagues (2014) found positive relationships between political self-expression on social media and political participation. Other studies (e.g., Gil de Zúñiga et al., 2015; Vaccari et al., 2015) have focused on very specific expressive practices, such as political dual screening, finding positive correlations with political participation online and offline. Finally, a large body of research has addressed the nexus between uses of social media and extra-institutional participation or protest. Here, too, most studies reveal positive correlations between social media use and participation. For instance, Tufekci and Wilson (2012) found that social media users were more likely than nonusers to join the Egyptian uprisings in January 2011. More specifically, Valenzuela (2013) found

that political discussion and activism on social media mediated the positive relationship between frequency of social media use and involvement in contentious
political action offline in Chile. Social media also played an important role in
the emergence and identity construction of the #BlackLivesMatter movement
for racial equality in the United States (Yang, 2016). These findings refute pessimistic views—frequently lacking solid empirical ground—of digital activism
as a distraction from offline activities (Dennis, 2018).

Three Fallacies of Existing Scholarship on Social Media and Participation

While the studies cited so far provide some useful starting points, in our view
their main limits are not methodological—the research design they employed,
the data they collected, the analyses they conducted—but conceptual and theoretical. Just as the rest of the public, most scholars—us included—witnessed the
ascendancy of social media in democratic life and rushed to answer the many
pressing and fascinating questions raised by these new phenomena. As a result,
most studies were conducted based on established theories and concepts that,
while definitely helpful as starting points, could not fully capture what is important and distinctive about social media and why. In particular, the vast majority of existing research has been limited by three types of fallacies, which we
identify as the affordance-as-destiny fallacy, the one-effect-fits-all fallacy, and the
contextual vacuum fallacy.

In a nutshell, the affordances-as-destiny fallacy has to do with "what" aspects of
social media use are studied, the one-effect-fits-all fallacy entails "who" is affected
by social media and "how," and the contextual vacuum fallacy involves "where"
and "when" these patterns emerge with different strengths. These theoretical
blind spots have important implications for the types of phenomena and relationships researchers focused on and the studies they devised to investigate them. We
now review each of these fallacies in detail and suggest how to overcome them to
expand our knowledge. To be clear: we are not arguing that any and all research
on social media and participation has equally and wholly been affected by all
three fallacies, but we contend that, overall, the cumulative knowledge deriving
from existing research on these topics suffers from these limitations.

THE AFFORDANCES-AS-DESTINY FALLACY

The *affordances-as-destiny* fallacy is the assumption that certain technical possibilities enabled by social media tend to more or less automatically produce

specific political outcomes. The most obvious example is the idea that because social media users can choose whom they connect with (whether it be individuals, groups, or organizations), two linear and uniform patterns must by necessity arise. First, people who are not interested in politics are expected to tightly isolate themselves from political content (Prior, 2007; Pariser, 2011). Second, individuals who care about politics and have clearly defined views are predicted to envelop themselves in cocoons of opinion-reinforcing interactions with others they agree with, while isolating themselves from disagreeing viewpoints (Sunstein, 2009). These assumptions are doubtful on two grounds.

First, the affordances of digital and social media are multiple and evolving. If we conceptualize them as facilitating one single set of outcomes, we lose sight of much of their complexity. Sure, social media users can choose whom to "friend" and "follow," but as we argued earlier, those same users can also be exposed to unchosen and, at times, unwanted content via their contacts' low-cost and low-threshold decisions to share, like, or comment on politically relevant content, thus in part counterbalancing the effects of selectivity by choice. A particular type of affordance that is often seen as destiny involves the curation algorithms that most social media platforms use to present users with a selection of the content their contacts have posted or interacted with (Bucher, 2018). Most social media algorithms tend to curate users' experience by increasing their likelihood of being exposed to messages coherent with their previously revealed preferences for some types of content, or messages posted by other users with whom they are more closely connected. To the extent that individuals are more likely to engage with content they agree with ideologically and to cluster with politically like-minded users, algorithmic curation may reduce the diversity of political content individuals are exposed to. However, research on the effects of algorithmic filtering has shown them to be relatively modest compared to users' choices (Bakshy et al., 2015; Möller et al., 2018). Algorithms are shaped by human and corporate decisions, and they do not even necessarily achieve the goals their creators aspire to, often because users adapt their behavior or start behaving in ways the algorithm's creators had not anticipated (Gillespie, 2016). Moreover, digital platforms need to reconcile often mutually contradictory goals, and the balance between different objectives can often change, leading to incremental and sometimes inconsistent updates to algorithmic policies and code.

The second reason why the affordances of social media should not be treated as destiny is that social media users differ widely in their preferences and behaviors toward political content, and thus they are likely to make different uses of politically relevant digital affordances.

For starters, some affordances are used asymmetrically by individuals, so the pursuit of one goal does not necessarily imply the denial of its contrary. As an example, people are more likely to actively look for content that reinforces their views online than they are to avoid or censor content that challenges their views. Seeking congruence does not mean escaping dissonance (Holbert et al., 2010).

Moreover, individuals choose with whom they interact on social media based on multiple criteria and considerations. Political homogeneity may surely be one of them—especially for the minority of the population that are highly interested in politics—but it sits alongside others, such as commonalities in lifestyles, interests, and family, to name just a few. As noted in Huckfeldt and colleagues' (2004) research on face-to-face conversations, people do not necessarily forgo relationships with others with whom they share common interests and personal ties solely because they disagree with them about politics. Even though social media users can "prune" their news feeds from contacts who share content they are not interested in or dislike, Bode (2016a) showed that only a minority of social media users do that, and this is more common among people who talk about politics more frequently and who have more extreme ideological views. Boutyline and Willer (2017) found that Twitter users with conservative and more extreme political orientations are more likely to follow like-minded users than other users are.

Third, some individuals actually enjoy learning about new topics and engaging with political viewpoints that differ from their own, and those types of people are likely to employ the choice affordances of social media to find contrarian opinions (Vaccari et al., 2016). Dutton and colleagues (2019) surveyed Internet users in seven countries and found that large percentages of respondents reported engaging in behaviors that reduce the likelihood of being self-segregated into echo chambers, augmenting the number of information sources one is exposed to. Most Internet users learn new and unexpected political information through their digital searches by combining different platforms and enrich the diversity of their sources by checking some of the news they encounter online. The authors conclude: "Even if filter bubbles did exist for some users within some specific platforms, people's choices help them encounter countervailing information" (Dutton et al., 2019: 241).

Finally, the affordances of social media are more complex than conventionally assumed, and because users can employ them in different ways depending on their specific goals, they rarely lead to the same outcomes in different contexts. Colleoni and colleagues (2014) show that some features of Twitter enable users to disseminate messages through networks that reflect their preferences, but other affordances of the same platform facilitate the diffusion of content to a much broader realm that goes beyond individually customized networks. Along the same lines, Barberá and colleagues (2015) showed that ideological clustering among Twitter users varies depending on the type of event users are discussing and can even change as an event unfolds.

The way out of the affordance-as-destiny fallacy is to treat the concrete outcomes of theoretically relevant affordances of social media as empirical questions rather than as fixed assumptions, and to measure those outcomes as variables rather than as constants. In this book, we focus on three such relevant outcomes, which we call *political experiences*; we operationalize them with precise survey questions; and we employ them as independent variables in our models. The experiences we consider are the extent to which respondents engage with political messages they agree or disagree with, the frequency with which they accidentally encounter political information while on social media for other purposes, and whether they received electoral mobilization messages encouraging them to vote for a party or candidate. Instead of assuming that such outcomes stem directly and uniformly from some platforms' affordances, we ask how widespread they are among social media users, we investigate among what types of users they are more and less common, and we estimate the relationship between these experiences and political participation. The fact that we measure (survey respondents' recollections of) political experiences that actually occurred on social media means that our analysis already incorporates the filtering function of users' deliberate choices as well as of platform algorithms, including the direction in which they may skew such experiences. In other words, while we cannot know how frequently each of these experiences might have occurred for our respondents in a choice-free and algorithm-free setting, we know what users experienced once those choices and algorithms kicked in. Thus, although we cannot address the important debate on the political and social implications of platforms' algorithmic curation and filtering, we can at least trust that our measurements incorporate the key impact of these mechanisms.

THE ONE-EFFECT-FITS-ALL FALLACY

The *one-effect-fits-all* fallacy is the assumption that the relationship between political interactions on social media and political participation can be expected to be roughly similar, if not the same, across different subgroups within the population. This assumption is central to the question of whether social media can widen or reduce existing democratic inequalities in political participation. Most research to date has investigated the *direct*, generalized effects of social media use on political participation, while largely overlooking *differential effects*, whose strength varies between different subgroups and whose direction may even differ across them (i.e., a relationship may be positive for one group and negative for another). Research addressing these questions has almost exclusively looked at sociodemographic divides between younger and older people (Xenos et al., 2014; Boulianne & Theocharis, 2020) and between citizens with higher and lower socioeconomic status (Schlozman et al., 2010). Studies have mostly focused on how these factors influence online participation, rather than the relationship between specific political experiences on social media and political participation. For instance, research assessing differences across age cohorts mostly emphasizes that younger citizens are more avid users of digital technology and social media than older ones (Holt et al., 2013; Andersen et al., 2020). This divide between younger and older cohorts has important political implications, but it may not stand the test of time, as generational gaps are closed by market forces and the societal domestication of technology. Much more persistent, at least at the individual level, are the divides between citizens who are involved in politics and those who are not. Political involvement has been shown to be very difficult to change throughout individuals' life cycles (Prior, 2010) while also being a crucial driver of political participation (Verba et al., 1995). Therefore, whether political experiences on social media can close the participatory gap between citizens with high and low levels of political involvement is a crucial question for democratic equality, but one that has not been thoroughly addressed so far.[2]

One antidote to what we call the one-effect-fits-all fallacy is to focus on the attitude-based differential effects of social media use on political participation. Thus, in this book we assess whether relevant political experiences on social media are more strongly related to political participation among users who are more involved or among those who are less involved in politics. We also shed light on differential effects based on ideology.

In the pre-social-media age, Mike Xenos and Patricia Moy (2007) found that political information acquired online had greater effects on participation among citizens highly interested in politics, thus suggesting that digital media at that time may have exacerbated rather than reduced attitude-based gaps in participation. However, their important study predates the diffusion of social media, and there is an important difference between contemporary digital political experiences and the early years of Internet politics, when a minority of citizens had Internet access and most of those who did were at least moderately interested in politics (Norris, 2001). Back then, the Web predominantly functioned as a vast information repository where users constantly had to choose where to go and what to look for (Bimber & Davis, 2003). Moreover, the idea that the use of digital media could almost exclusively help those who were already interested in politics find out ways to become more active proved to be simplistic even in the pre-social-media era. Bruce Bimber and colleagues (2015) analyzed data from three different waves of the British Election Study (2001, 2005, 2010) and found that the relationship between Internet use and political participation was in some cases stronger among the less than among the most interested, depending on the specific type of action to be predicted. Based on these findings, the authors concluded that "the question of whether digital media reinforces or remedies inequality in traditional political behavior is wrongly put. It likely does both, and the relationship varies across time" (Bimber et al., 2015: 37–38).

The pool of social media users is currently much more diverse than the early adopters of the first Internet age, and, as we have argued, social media have the potential to expose even relatively uninterested citizens to politically relevant messages, coupled with social cues and social endorsements that can augment their salience. These transformations require a fresh approach to the differential effects of social media use on political participation. We should abandon the assumption that *only* the politically interested access politically relevant content on digital platforms in favor of a more nuanced view of the different political opportunities that different groups may encounter online. On the one hand, the more politically active groups in the population can leverage social media to find relevant political information and avenues to participation. On the other hand, less politically involved users of social media may also benefit from political experiences on those platforms. Hence, social media may have positive participatory implications for citizens with both high and low levels of political engagement.

Crucially, however, a *law of diminishing returns* may cap the participatory benefits of social media among the most engaged but not among the least engaged. The more politically involved a user is, the larger the amount of political information that should be stored in her memory, and, therefore, the smaller the contribution that any extra piece of information channeled by social media should make. Conversely, the *marginal utility*—in terms of potential for political activation—resulting from political experiences on social media should be greater among citizens who are less politically involved, as any bit of additional information may add greater value to their existing repositories of political knowledge. By shedding light on these differential effects, we can evaluate whether political experiences on social media reduce or augment existing societal gaps in political participation.

Another important aspect in which social media may not affect political participation evenly among users is their ideology. In the pre-social-media age, progressive voters and political actors were earlier adopters of campaign websites and online political news (Vaccari, 2013; Kreiss, 2012), and this may have helped boost the left's competitive chances. However, since at least 2016 it has become clear that conservative and, in some cases, authoritarian political actors can also effectively marshal social media and other digital campaigning tools to spread their messages (Freelon et al., 2020). While analyses of specific campaigns and their effects (e.g., Wells et al., 2016) can be useful for illuminating the ways in which different technologies may have helped some political actors and causes and damaged others, only a systematic assessment of the relationship between political experiences on social media among voters with different ideological preferences can help us understand whether they are tilting the scales of political competition.

THE CONTEXTUAL VACUUM FALLACY

Finally, the *contextual vacuum* fallacy stems from the neglect for the role that systemic features play in shaping the relationship between political experiences on social media and political participation. On its surface, this is mostly the result of research design limitations, as the literature on social media and participation mainly comprises single-country case studies, mostly based in the United States. The roots of this problem, however, lie in underdeveloped theorizing about the role of systemic characteristics in shaping the relationship between social media and participation. Comparative research in political communication is still developing its foundations (Esser & Pfetsch, 2004; Rojas & Valenzuela, 2019). Most comparative research has focused on journalism and the mass media (Hallin & Mancini, 2004, 2011; Albaek et al., 2014; Hanitzsch et al., 2019), and, as a result, our understanding of the role of systemic factors is still very limited when it comes to online political communication (Anstead & Chadwick, 2009; Vaccari, 2013). Different mass media—the printing press, radio, and television—relied on relatively standardized (though by no means universal) technologies, but their institutional adaptation involved the creation of media organizations that generally operated at the national and subnational level and offered media content that was sensitive to local demand and reflexive of local language, political culture, norms, and incentives. By contrast, even though it would be naïve to speak of the Internet as one and the same around the world, at least across Western democracies the most important social media platforms are operated by the same (American and, increasingly, Chinese) global companies and present their users with the same interface, the same mobile applications, and the same affordances.[3] While these global platforms still need to uphold the laws of the countries where they operate, regulation of social media in Western democracies has hitherto been very light.

It is thus understandable that most scholars have identified the globally undifferentiated affordances of social media as the main potential source of their political impact, and that this impact has been understood as being largely similar across different democracies. This approach, however, overlooks the role played by political context and institutions. How individuals behave on social media, what they experience there, and how those behaviors and experiences impact broader participatory practices is shaped in part by context. Political and media institutions are important components of such context.

On the one hand, political institutions matter because they constitute the "rules of the game" (North, 1990) of most relevant interactions in the political system, including citizens' participation. Institutions comprise laws, rules, and norms. For instance, electoral laws that stipulate the formulas to convert votes into public offices drastically shape the incentives that different types of parties have to compete in elections, as well as the reasons why citizens vote for them (Norris, 2004). Institutions also include political organizations, such as governments, parliaments, parties, and interest groups, all of which shape the structure of opportunity that citizens face when they assess their prospects for taking action on issues they care about. The characteristics of political organizations are of great importance. Their strategies and approaches in engaging with citizens, both in physical and digital spaces, the societal cleavages they articulate, and the levels of legitimacy they enjoy all shape the extent to which citizens may feel they have, or lack, viable channels through which to provide input into the political system.

Mass media systems are also an important part of the context in which political experiences on social media take place and may impact patterns of participation. As Chadwick (2017b) showed, contemporary media systems are "hybrid," as they are characterized by the integration between the logics of older and newer media. Thus, any study of contemporary political communication should take into account how different media, both older and newer, interact and contribute to the phenomena of interest. If newer and older media are intertwined, then what citizens expect, experience, and gain from their encounters with politics on social media is highly dependent on the features characterizing national mass media institutions and their relationship with the political system.

Moreover, it is precisely because social media platforms technically operate in (nearly) identical ways across different Western democracies that they constitute a very promising site for comparative research. This is a unique feature of the social media environment. Mass media systems may show similarities across different countries, such as the presence of a vibrant opinion press, or a high fragmentation of the market, or strong public service media. However, comparing mass media in different countries always requires drawing equivalences, or analogies, between different media organizations, each operating in a different language, culture, business environment, legal system, and so on.[4] By contrast, when it comes to social media, the uncontested dominance of the very same few platforms—at least in Western Europe and North America— allows comparative researchers to assume that the social media affordances with which most users interact are very similar, if not the same, across all countries. Technically, Facebook in Italy functions in the same way as Facebook in Germany or in the United Kingdom.[5] While we still need to take into account the differences between the main platforms, as Facebook functions differently from Twitter, comparing how social media platforms function in different countries is less methodologically problematic than comparing different mass media organizations across different countries. This, in turn, creates ideal conditions in which to focus on the role of individual and systemic variables, which we can safely assume will not be confounded by large unaccounted-for cross-country differences in the technical functioning of the platforms.[6]

Addressing the contextual vacuum fallacy requires, first, theorizing how systemic characteristics related to both political and mass media institutions may shape the relationship between social media use and political participation and, second, designing comparative research that leverages differences between systemic features (identified as relevant by theory) across otherwise relatively similar countries. This combination of theory and research design enables us to identify and disentangle how some relevant systemic differences shape the relationship between political experiences on social media and political participation.

Political Experiences on Social Media and Participation: Direct Effects

In this book, we argue that specific political experiences on social media have the potential to make politics relevant to users in ways that are distinctive from the types of political messages they receive when discussing politics face to face, getting news via the mass media, or purposefully accessing political information on the Web—for instance, by querying search engines or visiting the websites of news organizations or political parties.

We focus on three different types of political "experiences" (a term that we use to differentiate them from more purposeful types of activities, as we explain in Chapter 2) on social media: *engaging with agreeing viewpoints, accidentally encountering political news*, and *being targeted by electoral mobilization messages*. Although conceptually and empirically distinct, these experiences share two important properties. First, they do not require high levels of intentionality and could conceivably occur, at least occasionally, to both the highly politically engaged and those who are less involved. Second, the experiences we study entail exposure to politically relevant content, whether it be viewpoints one identifies as similar to one's own, political news accessed by accident, or messages by other users encouraging one to vote in a certain way. The fact that politics is not a central component of a typical user's everyday experience on social media, as discussed earlier, suggests that these experiences typically stand out against a backdrop of nonpolitical communication ordinarily occurring on these platforms. Based on existing research and our own theorizing, in the next pages we develop expectations of how these three political experiences on social media may contribute to citizens' repertoires of participation. By focusing on the direct effects of these experiences on participation, we hope to address what we identified as the affordances-as-destiny fallacy.

ENGAGING WITH AGREEING VIEWPOINTS

Let us start from the extent to which social media users *engage with agreeing viewpoints*, shared by other users and sources. The effects on political participation of exposure to, and engagement with, consonant versus crosscutting political views in face-to-face conversations have been widely researched (e.g., Mutz, 2002; McClurg, 2006; Nir, 2011; Matthes et al., 2019). In one of the most influential studies, Diana Mutz (2006) has shown that "hearing the other side"— i.e., interacting predominantly with people with political views different from one's own—educates citizens to be tolerant and facilitates deliberation, but it depresses participation. People who discuss politics with others they mostly agree with tend to participate in politics more than those who encounter disagreement. The main argument behind Mutz's research is that individuals are hardwired to seek validation from others, and exposure to contrarian views reduces their confidence in their own political beliefs and, thus, undermines their motivations toward political action. By the same token, engaging with a prevalence of agreeing viewpoints reassures individuals that their views are cogent and popular within their social networks, thus reinforcing self-confidence and, in turn, fostering participation.

Other scholars, while generally confirming that political homophily has a positive effect on participation, have added important nuances to this picture. According to Scott McClurg (2006), the levels of political sophistication that can be found in a given network have a stronger influence on citizens' participation than the political viewpoints expressed therein. Thus, political discussion with disagreeable others can still enhance participation if such disagreeing discussants have high levels of sophistication. Similarly, Min and Wohn (2018) found that exposure to counter-attitudinal information on social media is positively associated with online and offline participation if it originates from weak (but not strong) ties, and that the relationship is stronger among respondents who claim to closely engage with this disagreeing content. Moreover, Lilach Nir (2011) argued that what actually depresses political participation is not encountering disagreeing viewpoints per se, but the sense of isolation resulting from the lack of supportive political discussion to balance the costs of engaging with counter-attitudinal viewpoints. Nir's research highlights that agreement and disagreement can coexist in networks of political conversations, and that it is therefore more appropriate to conceptualize these networks based on at least three different ideal-typical categories: predominantly supportive, predominantly adversarial, or evenly balanced. We adopt this distinction in our own measurement of exposure of agreement and disagreement on social media.

Following Mutz's and others' research, we expect that users who engage with predominantly supportive viewpoints on social media should participate more than those who engage with predominantly adversarial or evenly balanced political messages. Importantly, however, we do not expect exposure to agreeing viewpoints to be the most common political experience, when compared with exposure to oppositional or balanced messages. As discussed earlier, social media combine high selectivity with high potential for accidental exposure to content shared by users' contacts. While earlier research (e.g., Gaines & Mondak, 2009) suggested that the affordances of social media facilitated the creation of silos of like-minded individuals, more recent studies (e.g., Barberá et al., 2015; Flaxman et al., 2016; Dubois & Blank, 2018) have shown that the experience of political disagreement on social media is far from being residual, and that these platforms could even provide an injection of diversity for citizens who are part of highly consonant networks offline (Vaccari et al., 2016). Accordingly, various studies confirm that citizens report encountering higher levels of disagreement on social media than in other communicative settings, including face-to-face conversation (Anspach, 2017; Barnidge, 2017; Diehl et al., 2016).

ACCIDENTALLY ENCOUNTERING POLITICAL NEWS

The second politically relevant experience we consider is inadvertent exposure to political news on social media. According to democratic theory (Dahl, 1956) an informed citizenry is essential for the health and functioning of democracy. However, obtaining political information is a costly endeavor for citizens (Downs, 1957), who often lack time to search, cognitive resources to process, and sometimes even money to pay for such information. One partial remedy to this democratic conundrum is that, for some citizens, acquiring political news is a valuable and enjoyable activity in itself. These voters are therefore willing to pay the necessary costs to be well-informed citizens, up to a point. For most of their fellow citizens, however, politics is neither interesting nor entertaining in itself, and these voters can only be expected to acquire information when it is presented to them in a way that is convenient, easy to process, and helpful for making decisions (Lupia & McCubbins, 1998). The news media can play a role in this process, by alerting otherwise inattentive audiences to major crises, scandals, and problems that deserve their attention (Zaller, 2003). Similarly, social media can reduce the costs of political information by exposing individuals to political content incidentally, while they are using these platforms for reasons other than news or politics. As discussed earlier, encountering political content is not the main motivation for most people in using social media, but at the same time most social media users encounter at least some political messages there. When that happens, users can acquire relevant information at a low cost.

However, it could be argued that exposure to information, especially if accidental, does not necessarily mean engagement with it, and, indeed, Karnowski and colleagues (2017) found that previous knowledge of and interest in a specific topic are important determinants of users' actual interaction with incidentally encountered news on social media. The convenience with which social media users can stumble upon public affairs information can even instill a false sense of security that news that is important enough will find its way to them (Toff & Nielsen, 2018). Gil de Zúñiga and colleagues (2017) characterize this attitude as "News Find Me" (NFM) to describe the belief that one can stay informed by simply using the Internet, connecting with others on social media, and talking with peers with no need to actively search for news. The implications of NFM attitudes for democratic engagement are far from unambiguously positive, however. In a survey-based study of ten countries, Gil de Zúñiga and colleagues (2020) found that NFM is negatively associated with political interest, knowledge, and voting. However, there is a difference between believing that "news will find me," as an attitude, and accidentally encountering news on social media, as an experience. In other words, NFM is an intriguing concept, but it focuses on citizens' perceptions of news within high-choice media environments rather than their actual exposure to it.

That being said, there is no question that accidental exposure to news on social media is a complex and multifaceted experience, whose effects are dependent on users' broader attitudes toward politics and news. In this sense, Kümpel (2020) makes a compelling theoretical case that incidental exposure to news online may generate a "Matthew Effect" that exacerbates existing disparities in access to information. Similarly, Matthes and colleagues (2020) contend that the implications of unsearched exposure to political news may be conditional on users' specific intentions—particularly whether they are on social media for political reasons—and how closely they engage with the content they incidentally encountered. On this basis, the authors propose a distinction between simple scanning (which they define as "first level incidental exposure") and substantial processing ("second level incidental exposure") of unsearched news, which they argue might be more likely among more interested users. However, as Matthes and colleagues themselves suggest (2020: 1043–1044), these nuances can be better captured by research designs other than surveys that can more precisely measure and manipulate what content users engage with and how intensely. One such study employed eye-tracking technology to show that users' visual engagement with political posts and news on social media is not dependent on general interest in these types of content, which suggests that incidental exposure to political news might have at least some potential for informing uninterested users (Vraga et al., 2019).

In sum, the theoretical and empirical debate around the implications of accidental exposure to news for political participation is rich and nuanced, and the findings have varied, partly as a result of differences in scholars' approach. Overall, however, we expect that accidental exposure to political news on social media may have a positive relationship with participation (Valeriani & Vaccari, 2016).

BEING TARGETED BY ELECTORAL MOBILIZATION MESSAGES

Electoral mobilization by political actors (usually studied as face-to-face personalized communications such as door-to-door canvassing) has been found to increase voter turnout (Green & Gerber, 2015) and other types of political activities (Huckfeldt & Sprague, 1992; Rosenstone & Hansen, 1993). Mobilization by parties and candidates is often aimed specifically at gaining citizens' votes. However, these messages can spill over into stimulating non-electoral activity by their recipients. As contended by Verba and colleagues (1995), many citizens abstain from political activities because nobody has ever asked them to do so. Thus, mobilization efforts can enable citizens to become part of networks of political action that may have long-term implications for their ability to participate. Once people are included in the distribution list of a political organization, they are more likely to be contacted for future initiatives, and they may accept some of those invitations. Moreover, after being reached by these messages, citizens may also become more aware of such organizations and may decide to call on them in the future if they want to get involved.

Electoral mobilization is not an exclusive domain of strategic political actors but can also be pursued by citizens in a spontaneous manner (Rosenstone & Hansen, 1993). Such unorganized or informal mobilization has always represented an important complement to the activities directly run by political actors who, due to resource constraints and capacity shortages, frequently limit their efforts to targets they consider more receptive. This means that the citizens who are more likely to be mobilized are often those who are keener to participate in the first place. This is a rational organizational behavior, as research shows that messages aiming to get out the vote are more effective on citizens with a higher propensity to vote (Enos et al., 2014), so it is not surprising that political actors direct scarce resources toward those groups that they believe will yield more bang for their buck. Relatedly, Hassell and Monson (2014) found that campaigns are more likely to send fundraising mail to previous donors than to potentially new ones.

However, digital media have changed the process of electoral mobilization in important ways. First, by lowering the costs of message distribution, the Web has created incentives for political actors to target broader constituencies in their mobilization efforts (Krueger, 2006). At the same time, the abundance of digital trace data on users' attitudes and behaviors has enabled more effective targeting (Issenberg, 2012), potentially increasing the effectiveness of mobilization. That being said, the extent to which extremely sophisticated data are really of use to campaigns is still unclear (Hersh, 2015), and these operations require substantial and sustained investments in infrastructure, which are often neglected by political organizations (Kreiss, 2016). And while the U.S. regulatory environment is very lax (Kreiss & Howard, 2010), in most Western democracies the use of data for political and campaign purposes is tightly regulated (Anstead, 2017), thus limiting political organizations' abilities and incentives to rely on these techniques.

Second, the distinction between mobilization efforts directly managed by political actors and the ones autonomously conducted by citizens is more blurred on social media than in face-to-face environments (Vaccari, 2017). Social media not only offer opportunities for citizen-initiated activities (Gibson, 2015) but also enable users to recirculate mobilization messages originally shared by political actors. When this happens, the original messages are augmented by the social cues discussed earlier in this chapter, and if diffusion reaches a certain threshold, the social endorsements highlighted previously may also enhance these messages' credibility.

In sum, social media offer activist citizens many avenues through which to informally mobilize members of their networks, and thus there is reason to believe that these nudges may, under certain circumstances, be consequential not only for voter turnout, but also for broader modes of participation. Accordingly, Aldrich and colleagues (2016) found that being targeted by mobilization messages online has an impact on citizens' participation in election campaigns in the United States and the United Kingdom, and Vaccari (2017) found similar patterns in Germany, Italy, and the United Kingdom. Thus, we expect that users who are targeted on social media by messages aimed at convincing them to vote for a party or candidate will also show richer repertoires of political participation.

One Outcome Does Not Fit All: Indirect Effects at the Individual Level

The hypotheses outlined earlier are only part of the story we aim to tell in this book. We have previously argued that the effects of digital media have too often been studied generically, based on the assumption that they should unfold similarly among all groups of users. To address this gap, we will test a second set of hypotheses that assess the differential effects of political experiences on social media on different groups of individuals based on two sets of political attitudes.

First, we focus on differential effects related to two specific individual dispositions that capture levels of political involvement: citizens' *interest in politics* and their *attentiveness to the latest general election campaign.* These factors have been theoretically and empirically connected to participation (e.g., Verba et al., 1995; Finkel, 1985). While interest in politics captures political involvement in its long-lasting, more stable dimension (Prior, 2010), attention to the latest election taps into the more context-specific involvement that may be enhanced, depressed, or revived as a result of particular features of the campaign, such as the closeness of the race, the personalities of the leaders, and the issues at stake.

Second, we shed light on the differential effects of ideology. Ideological preferences are an important driver not only of citizens' participation, but also of the goals that they may pursue while participating. This issue has been relatively neglected in studies on digital media and participation so far, but we argue it has important implications for political competition.

CITIZENS' POLITICAL INVOLVEMENT, SOCIAL MEDIA, AND PARTICIPATION: DO THE RICH GET RICHER?

In theory, one could expect that measures of political involvement should moderate the relationship between political experiences on social media and participation in two opposite ways. Scholars have contended that the increased information and discussion opportunities provided by digital media benefit almost exclusively those who are already politically engaged while having minimal effects on those who are less active and are thus less likely to experience politics online in any meaningful way (Bimber & Davis, 2003; Norris, 2003). This has been named the "rich get richer" hypothesis (Brundidge & Rice, 2009). In support of this theory, Xenos and Moy (2007) found that exposure to political information on the Internet increased participation, especially among citizens with higher levels of interest in politics. These studies, however, predate social media. As we discussed earlier, to the extent that social media occasionally expose vast amounts of users, many of whom are politically uninterested, to some political content, their effects on participation may not be confined to the most politically active segments of the population but may also encompass the less involved (Martin, 2015).

We take both these competing claims seriously and, consequently, we expect that the political experiences on social media we focus on should enrich the repertoires of *both* the usual suspects of, *and* the usually detached from, political participation. However, we also expect that *the relationship between these experiences and participation should be stronger for the less politically involved than for the highly involved.* Thus, overall, political experiences on social media should contribute to narrowing gaps in participation between citizens with higher and lower levels of political involvement.

Our argument stems from the premise that citizens with high and low involvement in politics start from different baseline levels of participation, have different potential to become more active, and can reap different, and differently consequential, benefits from political experiences on social media.

Let us examine the highly involved. Citizens who are interested in politics and pay attention to campaigns can be expected, all else being equal, to be more active in politics than average. As a result, there is less room for their levels of participation to grow than there is among citizens who are comparatively less politically involved. Highly involved voters are already quite embedded in political life and exposed to large amounts of political stimulation from various sources (not only social media but also mass media and interpersonal communication). Thus, any additional political message or participation opportunity they may encounter, on social media or elsewhere, should yield diminishing returns on their participation.

Now consider the less politically involved. While they may not be likely to search for political content, the network dynamics of social media discussed previously mean that some of them should see some political messages on these platforms some of the time. Because these voters are less politically active, they have more room to see their participation grow than their more involved counterparts. As they start from a very low level of participation, they have practically nowhere else to go but up. They are also less used to being exposed to political content and calls to action. Once they are reached by some political messages, however, these less involved users may reap disproportionate participatory gains. This is because political content lands on relatively virgin soil, where fewer seeds have been planted. No voter's political mind is a total blank slate, but the minds of less involved voters should be more of a blank slate than those of the more involved voters.

Our argument aims to update John Zaller's (1992) intuition, developed in the mass media age, that the probability that a message can cause attitude change is a function of the probability that it is, first, *received,* and, second, *accepted.* Normally, the more politically involved a citizen is, the more likely she is to be exposed to political messages (because politically engaged people seek out political news and campaign communication), but the less likely she is to accept them (because her beliefs are firmer and based on more information, and this stock of knowledge can also be marshaled to argue against messages she disagrees with). By contrast, the less politically involved someone is, the more likely he is to accept a message (because his ideas are fuzzier and held with less conviction), but the less likely he also is to receive it (because he tends to avoid politics). For Zaller, the logical conclusion was that, in the relatively low-choice mass media age, attitude change was most likely to occur among moderately involved citizens, who had sufficient probabilities of both receiving and accepting political messages, rather than among the most and the least involved groups of citizens. The most involved would be impermeable to persuasive messages, in spite of receiving plenty, and the least involved, while potentially highly persuadable, would not be in a position to receive such messages in the first place.

We argue that social media have not changed the logic of this equation but have altered the values of its terms. First, social media have broadened the audiences that *receive* political messages, as the three politically relevant experiences we focus on involve sizable amounts of the population who uses these platforms (as we will show in Chapter 3). Second, to the extent that at least part of the audiences that receive political messages on social media are politically less involved, they should have higher probabilities of *acceptance* of those messages. This is why we expect that most citizens who experience politics on social media in relevant ways will see their participation increase, but such increase should be relatively more pronounced among the less politically involved.

To fully articulate our logic, we will now outline how the differential effects we have theorized may play out with respect to the three political experiences on social media we focus on in this book.

With respect to engaging with agreeing viewpoints on social media, we have argued that citizens who are exposed to pro-attitudinal viewpoints see their political opinions confirmed and reinforced and as a result become more likely to act upon them. By the same logic, we should expect that the confidence boost deriving from exposure to like-minded others may yield stronger participatory returns among those who, being less politically involved, are more likely to have wavering political opinions and to be confused if exposed to conflicting information. From this standpoint, ideological echo chambers on social media, which are frequently blamed as detrimental for democracy (Sunstein, 2017), could have the bright side of providing people who are less confident in their political capabilities with some vital in-group support that propels them to participate in the political process. By contrast, users who are highly politically involved should benefit less from this confidence boost, as their convictions may already be stronger and, thus, less likely to be bolstered by engagement with agreeing viewpoints. Thus, we expect smaller increases in their levels of participation.

Similarly, citizens who are relatively less involved, and hence generally less informed, should disproportionately benefit from incidental exposure to political news on social media, because such accidentally encountered information stands out against a background of relatively low levels of knowledge and may thus be more consequential. By contrast, accidental exposure to political news on social media may make a smaller difference for citizens who already nourish themselves with rich political information diets, and for whom the beneficial effects of introducing new pieces of information may be smaller. Research shows that politically sophisticated citizens are also more likely to use digital media to seek out political information (Kaye & Johnson, 2002), and thus we can expect them to consume abundant political news online, as they would through other channels. Consequently, when highly informed and involved citizens stumble upon political news on social media, their levels of information and participation have less room to grow than is the case among those who are less engaged.

By the same token, an electoral mobilization message received on social media should entail stronger participatory benefits for citizens who, being less engaged with politics, are less likely to be targeted by such political messages elsewhere. Among those less politically connected voters, any single call to action is more likely to make a difference. Moreover, the social cues embedded in these messages may be more relevant for voters who are less involved in politics, and who may as a result pay more attention to the identity of the messenger (source cues) and the popularity of the message (social endorsements) than to its content. Political inputs by friends and acquaintances, and the idea of being part of a bandwagon of support, could be more influential for those who are less resolute in their political beliefs than for those who hold firmer, less malleable views.

IDEOLOGY AND THE WINNERS AND LOSERS OF SOCIAL MEDIA AND POLITICS

Political participation is important for democratic governance because it communicates information on citizens' preferences to public officials and party elites, because it enables individuals and groups to exercise political agency, and because it allows people to develop their political ideas and beliefs in interactions with other members of their communities. Broadly speaking, these are collective goods that strengthen democracy as a system of governance. They enhance what Dahl (1971) defines as the two pillars of democracy: *contestation*, which entails the ways in which citizens can formulate their preferences, convey them to public officials, and have them taken into account by the government, and *inclusiveness*, which comprises the mechanisms through which citizens can control the conduct of their government.

However, democracy is also based on fair and open competition among political elites in periodic and consequential elections for the popular vote (Schumpeter, 1942; Sartori, 1987). It is the possibility of a change in government via electoral competition that incentivizes elected officials to take into account citizens' preferences as expressed through the institutions and arrangements that make contestation and inclusiveness possible. In a democracy, who gets what, when, and how, as Harlod Lasswell (1936) famously defined the purpose of politics, depends to a great extent on which parties win elections and which politicians are elected to public office. While all adult citizens in a democracy enjoy the same rights to participate and exercise agency over policies, public officials, and other citizens, they do not all choose, or have the ability, to exercise these rights equally. As discussed earlier, these disparities in participation are mainly rooted in divides related to socioeconomic status, levels of political involvement, and networks of political recruitment (Verba et al., 1995). As we argue in this book, political experiences on social media can constitute a form of political recruitment—by providing relevant information on political issues, by alerting citizens of opportunities to participate, and by enabling them to engage with others around debates of public relevance. However, these experiences may not necessarily be equally powerful spurs to action among citizens who believe in different causes, parties, and ideologies. The widespread assumption that political experiences on social media equally benefit participation no matter the political values and beliefs of the individuals they reach is another example of the one-effect-fits-all fallacy that we aim to overcome.

There are at least two sets of reasons why we expect that political experiences on social media may not uniformly affect citizens of different political preferences. They are rooted in the supply side (what political elites do as they use social media to reach voters) and the demand side (what citizens do with political communication on social media) of online political communication (Vaccari, 2013).

On the supply side, although using a wide array of social media tools has become an imperative for contemporary political organizations, political elites of different persuasions may prefer to employ different features of social media and to spread different kinds of content on these spaces, which may have implications for the voters they reach and the behaviors they encourage. In an analysis of party and candidate websites in seven Western democracies between 2006 and 2010, Vaccari (2013) found that moderate leftist parties tended to produce more informative and engaging sites than both moderate right and radical parties on the left and right. Differences in party strategies and success, however, are heavily context specific. For instance, Kreiss (2012, 2016) documents how U.S. progressives in the 2000s built professional networks, tools, and infrastructures for digital campaigning that enabled them to maintain a superiority vis-à-vis conservatives that lasted at least until the re-election of President Barack Obama in 2012 (see also Vaccari, 2010; Karpf, 2012a). Subsequently, however, this gap was closed by the increasing importance of paid online advertising, which enabled well-funded campaigns to reach large numbers of voters without having to build substantial supporter networks. Another important development was the fact that digital platforms themselves were willing to directly provide their expertise to presidential campaigns—at least in the 2016 U.S. election cycle (Kreiss & McGregor, 2018). As we will argue later, the United States is a candidate-centric political system, where party organizations are skeletal and candidates build short-term organizations to run their election campaigns and usually disband them after the vote. In party-centric democracies where political elites are keen to preserve the centrality of party organizations (Plasser & Plasser, 2002), outsider parties, such as *La France insoumise* and *En Marche!* in France, the Five Star Movement in Italy, and *Podemos* in Spain, tend to use social media in a more aggressive and innovative way than established parties that can rely on legacy communication channels. Supporters of these parties, therefore, may be more likely to benefit from political experiences on social media.

On the demand side, it is possible that supporters of different parties have different styles and preferences for how to encounter political content online and how to participate in politics. For instance, Freelon et al. (2020: 1197) suggest that, in the United States, "left and right differ sharply in how they use digital media." While the left attempts to combine online and offline activism, the right tends to refrain from offline protests and directs its focus on influencing conversations on social media (sometimes via trolling and disinformation) and on criticizing and putting pressure on news organizations and technology companies so that they provide better conditions for their favored candidates and causes. While these patterns are probably U.S. specific, they highlight the possibility that social media users of different political ideologies may engage with, and respond to, political experiences on social media in different ways. After all, as highlighted by comparative research on party members and supporters, "different parties are expected to attract different kinds of people, and to shape them through different party cultures" (Heidar, 2006: 308). Thus, it is reasonable to expect that social media users of different political views may reap different participatory benefits from their political experiences on these platforms.

To shed light on these issues, we will assess the differential effects of political experiences on social media on levels of political participation based on a third moderating variable: *ideology*, measured as self-placement in the left–right axis.[7] The literature suggests various plausible hypotheses for how ideology may moderate our main relationships of interest. Because our main motivation for investigating these patterns is to assess the implications of social media for political competition, we have developed five distinct competitive scenarios derived from existing theories and research. We will use these scenarios to guide how we interpret our analyses.

Let us suppose that the relationship between political experiences on social media and participation is stronger among voters who locate themselves at the extreme left and the extreme right of the political spectrum. Since social media users can exercise some control over the content they see and the sources they interact with, and since people with more extreme views are both more likely to be highly involved in politics and less likely to see those views represented in ways they find satisfying in the mass media, citizens who place themselves at the extremes of the ideological spectrum may be especially likely to turn to social media to find political content that fulfills their preferences. In this situation, social media could be seen as disproportionately mobilizing voters with relatively more radical political views. To the extent that these voters become more vocal as a result, they may then disproportionately influence policies, policymakers, and other citizens, at the expense of more moderate voices. We call this the *polarization* scenario, as higher levels of participation among ideologically extreme voters may increase the distance between the left and the right. If more radical voters participate more intensely, they will put pressure on party elites to support more radical policies, and most party supporters are likely to update their preferences to match those conveyed by their standard-bearers (Achen & Bartels, 2017). More radical voters, disproportionately mobilized by social media, may also be able to directly influence other voters to support their more extreme positions, thus increasing attitudinal and affective polarization in the electorate (Lelkes, 2016).

Another possibility is that the relationship between political experiences on social media and participation is stronger only among voters who identify with either the left or the right writ large, without substantial differences between their moderate and extreme varieties. Past research on campaign communications and voting behavior has suggested that these types of patterns are possible. For instance, Duverger (1951) observed that left-wing parties in post–World War II Europe were thriving electorally because they were more efficiently adapting the organizational model of the mass bureaucratic party. At the dawn of the television age, Epstein (1967) claimed that conservative parties were reaping greater electoral benefits due to their more skillful use of professional communication techniques. In his earlier research on the Internet and party competition, one of the authors of this book found that, in many different countries, progressive voters were more likely to use the Web for political information (Vaccari, 2013). To the extent that a similar asymmetric scenario may repeat itself on social media, favoring either the right or the left, a set of political ideas would benefit from a stronger wind beneath its wings, potentially shaping public debate and electoral outcomes. We call this the *tilting-the-balance* scenario.

Suppose, instead, that quite the opposite occurs, and the relationship between political experiences on social media and political participation turns out to be stronger among those voters who refuse to identify with mainstream politics, as represented by traditional left–right divisions, than among the rest. In this case, social media may be aiding the populist challengers that have sent shock waves throughout many Western political systems, from the Five Star Movement in Italy to *Podemos* in Spain, from the *Front National* in France to Donald Trump in the United States. The populist ideology (Mudde, 2004) is flexible enough to be adopted by political actors advocating both left-wing and right-wing policies, and their leaders recurrently proclaim to proudly transcend traditional political categories such as left and right. Hence, elements of the populist ideology and style have been adopted by leaders and parties espousing both conservative and progressive ideas (della Porta et al., 2017; Zulianello et al., 2018). The differential mobilization of politically unaffiliated citizens may disproportionately benefit populist parties that challenge the validity of traditional left–right alignments.[8] Thus, we call this the *populist* scenario.

An alternative but related possibility is that the differential effects of political experiences on social media on participation are relatively stronger among respondents who locate themselves to the far right of the political spectrum. These citizens are more likely to support what Norris and Inglehart (2019) define as "authoritarian populism." The success of political leaders (such as Donald Trump in the United States), parties (such as Law and Justice in Poland), and causes (such as Brexit in the United Kingdom) that articulate these views has been one of the key developments in Western democracies over the past decade, with deep social roots and momentous political consequences (Gest, 2016; Clarke et al., 2017; Eatwell & Goodwin, 2018; Hochschild, 2018). Supporters of this particular incarnation of populism espouse authoritarian values that emphasize conformity, security, and loyalty to the in-group and its leaders. As such, Norris and Inglehart (2019) argue, authoritarian populists endanger democracies because they promote the weakening of institutional checks and balances and erode support for peaceful coexistence of and compromise between different groups. To be sure, the relationship between left–right alignments and this variety of populism is ambiguous, as many of its leaders and voters support traditionally left-wing economic policies (Cramer, 2016). However, if social media mostly mobilized voters from the far right, we could still reasonably infer that authoritarian populists might be among the greatest beneficiaries. We call this the *authoritarian populist* scenario.[9]

Finally, it is also possible that none of the scenarios discussed up to this point materializes, as ideology turns out to not moderate the relationship between political experiences on social media and participation. We call this possible configuration, which would support some aspects of the one-effect-fits-all approach, the *rising-tide* scenario, as in the proverbial rising tide (of political experiences) lifting all boats (of social media users' participation, regardless of their ideology).

Social Media and Participation in Context: Indirect Effects at the Country Level

As we have pointed out when discussing the "contextual vacuum" fallacy, one of the main arguments of this book is that social media can affect patterns of political participation in ways that depend on context. In particular, we contend that political and media institutions shape the ways in which different political experiences on social media are associated with political participation. Because we focus on three distinctive political experiences on social media— encountering agreeing viewpoints, accidental exposure to political news, and electoral mobilization—we develop specific theories on the systemic conditions that may accelerate or hinder the effects of each experience. We theorize that three institutional characteristics can moderate those relationships: patterns of *electoral competition*, types of *mass media systems*, and whether political systems are mainly *party-centric or candidate-centric*. Conceptually and empirically, each systemic characteristic is most relevant to one of the three political experiences on social media we focus on and, thus, more likely to moderate the relationship between that particular experience and participation.[10]

First, we argue that *patterns of electoral competition* matter. In this domain, political scientists usually distinguish between *majoritarian and proportional democracies* (Powell, 2000). Majoritarian democracies are characterized by greater levels of general consensus in the population on foundational principles and values than proportional democracies (Sartori, 1997). This may be because the electoral system causes polities to be more unified (at least at the elite level) by compressing latent conflicts, or because polities that are less unified avoid majoritarian systems and choose proportional systems that reflect rather than channel those differences. Regardless of the direction of these relationships, research shows that "majoritarian elections are associated with weaker cleavage politics" than proportional elections (Norris, 2004: 255). All else being equal, majoritarian systems incentivize parties to employ catch-all, "bridging" strategies and appeal to relatively broad and diverse segments of the electorate.[11] By contrast, proportional electoral systems incentivize parties to pursue niche, "bonding" strategies based on the mobilization of narrower segments of the population (Norris, 2004). The political spectrum in majoritarian democracies tends to be divided into a limited number of ideologically loose catch-all parties supported by broad electoral coalitions. By contrast, political competition in proportional democracies tends to be segmented across more ideologically entrenched and internally cohesive parties, each of which tends to cover a narrower spectrum of political views. As a result, voters generally develop stronger partisan identities and attachments in proportional systems than in majoritarian ones (Bowler et al., 1994). Starting from these premises, we argue that in majoritarian democracies citizens may be more sensitive to the degree of agreement they encounter on social media. Because their political attachments are weaker, the reassurance they receive from exposure to viewpoints they agree with may be a stronger catalyst toward political action for them. In comparison, citizens in proportional democracies have generally firmer political affiliations and may be less moved, comparatively speaking, by political content that supports their views. Social media users in proportional democracies may thus be less receptive to the partisan tone of the information they encounter on these platforms, and their levels of participation may thus be less affected by it. In sum, citizens in majoritarian democracies who engage with agreeing viewpoints on social media should see relatively greater increases in their participation compared with citizens in proportional democracies experiencing the same condition.

Second, *mass media systems* may play an important role in shaping the informational context in which political content acquired accidentally on social media affects participation. Although television is still the most important source of political news across Western democracies (Reuters Institute for the Study of Journalism, 2019), and even if Anstead and Chadwick convincingly argued that "internet campaigning does not exist in a media vacuum" (2009: 69), research has neglected the relationship between mass media and digital media in shaping citizens' participation. We argue that accidental exposure to political news on social media may yield greater participatory benefits for citizens in countries characterized by *Liberal mass media systems*, as defined by Hallin and Mancini (2004), than in *Polarized Pluralist* and *Democratic Corporatist media systems*. In Liberal systems, media and political actors are relatively autonomous from each other. In news organizations, commercial logics tend to prevail over party logics, and audience considerations tend to trump partisan agendas in the production of political coverage. Political parallelism, i.e., systematic relationships between individual media outlets and specific political parties or viewpoints, also tends to be weak in Liberal media systems. Rather than appeal to specific political and ideological audience subgroups, media tend to adopt "catch-all" politically balanced and centrist reporting styles. These systemic media characteristics have important implications for participation, as research suggests that citizens are more likely to be spurred into action by one-sided news that directly advocates for specific parties and viewpoints than by more neutral or two-sided content (Zaller, 1992). Accordingly, Van Kempen (2007) has shown that voter turnout tends to be higher in countries with high levels of media political parallelism than in countries with low levels of parallelism. Because information containing political cues and calls to action is more likely to mobilize audiences, citizens who acquire their news from the mass media in Liberal systems have fewer opportunities to encounter mobilizing content than those in Polarized Pluralist and Democratic Corporatist systems.[12] However, digital and social media have created opportunities for a more opinionated style of political communication in Liberal media systems as well (see, e.g., Davis, 2009, on the role of political blogs in the United States) and allow individuals to add their own interpretations to the news they share. Therefore, in these systems, citizens who accidentally encounter political news on social media can be expected, all else being equal, to read news that is more politically slanted, and thus more capable of activating their participation, when compared with the news they normally find in the mass media. We expect this to be less the case in other types of media systems, where political parallelism in the mass media is higher and where the political slant that may be present in news accidentally encountered on social media may not be substantially higher or different than what users normally find in the news on television or in newspapers. Our hypothesis, therefore, is that citizens in Liberal media systems who accidentally encounter political information on social media experience higher increases in their levels of participation compared with citizens in the same condition in other types of media systems.

The final systemic characteristic we consider is the *types of electoral organizations* that are prevalent in a country. The impact of electoral mobilization via social media on political participation may be contingent on whether a political system is *party-centric* or *candidate-centric*. Political parties provide important avenues and opportunities for citizens to participate in politics. As permanent structures that function during but also beyond elections, they build bridges between electoral and non-electoral participation. And because they operate in both physical and digital spaces, parties are well positioned to connect political participation that occurs online with face-to-face activities (Vaccari & Valeriani, 2016; Dommett, 2020). In party-centric systems, where party organizations are stronger, individuals aiming to influence politics can find more viable linkages to government and policymaking (Lawson, 1980). By contrast, in candidate-centric contexts where party organizations are weaker, people who wish to affect political outcomes may see limited value in working to influence political institutions and may pursue their goals by other means. Hence, citizens exposed to online mobilization in party-centric systems will have more opportunities, compared with their counterparts in candidate-centric systems, to participate in politics—because parties are there to provide them. Therefore, we hypothesize that electoral mobilization via social media may have comparatively stronger effects on political participation in countries where political organizations are predominantly party-centric than in those where they are mainly candidate-centric.

In this chapter, we have outlined various theories and hypotheses on the reasons why we expect political experiences on social media to be positively associated with political participation among different groups of citizens and in different contexts characterized by specific systemic characteristics. In the next chapter, we will conceptualize political participation, discuss how to measure it, and provide an overview of the comparative research design we developed to test our hypotheses.

2

Political Participation in the Digital Age

Tulsa, Oklahoma, June 2020. As the United States is struggling to contain the Covid-19 pandemic and while many cities and states are enforcing full or partial lockdowns, President Donald Trump's campaign machine is preparing for a mass rally in the largest indoor arena in town, the first of this kind during the 2020 election campaign. Several public health experts have expressed concerns about the planned event, which would see thousands of people sit side by side indoor while chanting slogans, waving flags, and possibly even not wearing masks—as polls are showing that many conservative Americans see the requirement to wear one as an attack on their freedom (McKelvey, 2020). Trump and his staff, however, have decided to use the event as an occasion to show the country, and the media, how widespread support was for the president and the way he was handling the Covid-19 crisis. Not coincidentally, Oklahoma is one of the most pro-Republican and pro-Trump states in the country, and the president would go on to carry it with almost two-thirds of the votes in November. Indeed, Trump's communication strategy has largely been based on constantly downplaying the Covid emergency and on repeating an upbeat message that while the pandemic is real and is hitting the United States, at the same time it is under control, and there is no need to undertake "exaggerated" precautionary measures that would damage the economy and limit individual freedom. Hence, in this context, a large turnout at the Tulsa rally has acquired an even greater significance for Trump's re-election effort than is usually the case for the inaugural event of a presidential campaign.

On June 15, five days before the rally, various news stories report that key officials in the Trump campaign are over the moon as more than one million people have filled out the online form to request an admission ticket—to be provided on a first-come, first-served basis—to the event. Brad Parscale, the (soon to be demoted) campaign manager, is all over Twitter sharing his enthusiasm for such an impressive result, thus making the news of the expected turnout public and

Outside the Bubble. Cristian Vaccari and Augusto Valeriani, Oxford University Press. © Oxford University Press 2021.
DOI: 10.1093/oso/9780190858476.003.0003

further raising expectations of the success of the event. It is nowadays common knowledge, not only among political insiders, that not all those who register online for an event will actually attend it. Online registration procedures themselves are first and foremost data capture operations. Citizens who have expressed interest for the event are—at least in theory—more likely to be receptive to future messages and requests from the campaign (Karpf, 2016; Kreiss, 2016). Furthermore, their contact details can be used for refining micro-targeting on social media as well (Kreiss & McGregor, 2019). Still, it is reasonable to expect that, among the million people who preregistered, at least nineteen thousand will be present at the Bank of Oklahoma Center Arena—enough to fully pack the venue. Indeed, the Trump campaign has started arranging outside facilities for those unlucky ticket holders who will not make it inside.

On June 20, the eyes of the nation's media are set on Tulsa to assess the size of the crowd attending the event. The reality, however, turns out to be shockingly disappointing for the president. According to the Tulsa Fire Department, only 6,200 people enter the arena, not counting the Trump campaign staff, media, and guests to the skybox suites, none of whom had needed to register online (Lorenz et al., 2020). Rally organizers try to blame protesters for physically impeding supporters from entering the venue, but the media that are present on-site report that anti-Trump demonstrators were few and far between. The president's frustration is evident when, at night, he is photographed while returning to the White House alone, his tie undone, a highly disappointed expression on his face, and a wrinkled "Make America Great Again" campaign cap hanging from his left hand.

On the very same day that the "TeamTrump" official Twitter account had posted instructions for how to book tickets online for the Tulsa rally, Mary Jo Laupp, a 51-year-old grandmother from Iowa, recorded a video on TikTok expressing her disdain for the choice to hold the rally on June 19, which in the United States is also known as "Juneteenth" and is dedicated to celebrating the emancipation of those who have been enslaved. (The Trump campaign subsequently moved the rally to the next day.) In the video, Laupp also launched what, in the TikTok sociotechnical environment, is known as a "challenge" to other users. Laupp encouraged her followers to book tickets for the event, even if they were never going to attend, and then immediately opt out from receiving further campaign-related messages. The intent was to prank the event organizers by artificially inflating its expected attendance.

Laupp's throwing of the gauntlet was very much in tune with the emerging culture among TikTok users at the time. This platform was the fastest-growing social media at the time, topping 800 million users in April 2020 (We Are Social, 2020). TikTok users often engage in challenges whereby people are requested to post videos of themselves doing something—sometimes funny, sometimes weird, sometimes difficult, sometimes dangerous. Several users took up and amplified Laupp's challenge, as ironic videos of people showing their "fake" reservations while mocking Trump started bubbling up on the platform (O'Sullivan, 2020). The idea to prank the president then spread across multiple other digital platforms, from Twitter to Instagram to Snapchat.

The plot then took another crucial twist when the initial pranksters were joined by a highly organized collective of unusual political suspects: K-pop fans. K-pop stands for "Korean Pop music" and refers to a genre born in South Korea that combines elements of Asian and Western cultures connected to music, dance, and fashion. K-pop has developed as a global phenomenon, especially among teenagers and young adults, and has become a global fandom subculture, albeit with local specificities (Han, 2017; Yoon, 2019). Some of our readers might remember the song "GanGam Style" by PSY, an example of a K-pop song that became a worldwide sensation in 2012 largely via shares of the video on YouTube.[1] Tech skills are a crucial component of K-pop fandom, as is the case for most contemporary fan cultures (Jenkins et al., 2018). K-pop fans employ digital platforms to engage in and coordinate actions such as mass streaming (repeatedly viewing some content online to increase its view count), buying and management of band-related merchandising and concert tickets, and individual and collective performances aimed at showing support for their idols. Moreover, K-pop musicians and fans have been heavily involved in charity initiatives around the world (Herman, 2018), and, in 2020, some of them endorsed the Black Lives Matter movement against systemic racism and encouraged their supporters to contribute to it. As well as making financial donations to the BLM movement, K-pop fans have hijacked white supremacist hashtags on social media to spread content related to their music idols, thus making the hashtags useless for those who were aiming to employ them to spread racist content (Lee, 2020).

We cannot quantify with certainty how much the loosely coordinated actions of TikTok (and social media) users in general, and of K-pop fans specifically, have contributed to inflating ticket reservations for the Trump Tulsa rally, and to the consequent frustration and embarrassment that this fiasco caused the organizers and the president. However, we can definitely say that, in joining the prank and in inviting others to do so, these TikTok users were participating in a political activity. Their actions were aimed, albeit indirectly, at impacting a politically relevant outcome, by expressing disappointment for Trump's presidency, exposing its unpopularity, and thus contributing to hindering his re-election. For instance, a *New York Times* (NYT) report (Lorenz et al., 2020) told the story of Erin Hoffman, an 18-year-old New Yorker who found out about the campaign on Instagram from a friend, shared it on Snapchat, reserved two tickets for Tulsa without any intention to attend, and convinced one of her parents to do the same. Hoffman is quoted in the NYT as saying: "Trump has been actively trying to disenfranchise millions of Americans in so many ways, and to me, this was the protest I was able to perform." The choice of words "the protest I was able to perform" is revealing. Even in normal circumstances, an 18-year-old from New York, no matter how passionate for politics and anxious about Trump's reelection, would be very unlikely to be able to travel 1,343 miles to Tulsa to participate in an on-site protest. But these were not normal circumstances, as the spread of Covid-19 had forced many if not most Americans inside their homes. In this context, online action was the only possible form of political action.

In their analysis of the impact of digital media on collective action, Bruce Bimber and colleagues (2012) highlight three types of effects any technology can have on organizations. *First-order* effects happen when individuals and organizations use new technologies to perform the same tasks and achieve the same goals as before, but in different ways, and possibly at lower costs. An example would be replacing mail with email, without aiming to change the frequency, content, and recipients of the messages being exchanged. *Second-order* effects take place when organizations realize that technologies can help them do different things and pursue different goals than before, as when the speed and low (monetary) costs of email communication lead to an exponential growth in the number of messages individuals exchange, as well as broaden participation in these communications and redefine their purposes. *Third-order* effects occur at a deeper level, when technology is so embedded in the lives of individuals and the functioning of organizations that they are taken for granted as part of the environment. Just as humans—apart from space travelers—hardly ever think about the fact that a certain concentration of oxygen is present in the air they breathe and appreciate that this makes it possible for them to stay alive, most people nowadays do not really consider how different life would be without email, smartphones, Google, or Facebook. At this stage, Bimber and colleagues write, "the ubiquity of the sociotechnical infrastructure changes normative expectations for what is and should be possible" (Bimber et al., 2012: 51–52).

The Tulsa prank is a compelling example of the third-order effects Bimber and colleagues discuss. Those who participated in it were deliberately engaging in a political act aimed at, first, expressing their discontent with Trump and, second, affecting the electoral outcome of the election by initiating a cycle of negative news for the president. However, in conceiving and undertaking such a complex political act, participants leveraged practices, cultural codes, and social dynamics that are typical of their networked lives (Papacharissi, 2011): taking part in a TikTok challenge, participating in a social media prank, inviting others to join a cause by moving across platforms, and using digital media to organize actions online and offline. This example stands for a broader set of phenomena. Digital technologies, and social media in particular, are now thoroughly integrated with the everyday lives of most individuals in Western democracies, including their political dimensions, bigger or smaller as those may be. As such, social media are changing the *context* of citizenship and participation, creating new ways of engaging with politics and redefining, to some degree, how people participate in activities that long predate the Internet.

As we have known for decades, political participation is seldom motivated by exclusively *instrumental* goals—the belief that one's actions are meaningfully, even decisively, contributing to social and political change. This belief is not rational most of the time, because the success or failure of any form of collective action almost never hinges on a single contribution (Downs, 1957; Olson, 1965). Instead, participation is most often driven by *expressive* goals—the desire to manifest one's views, values, and commitment to a certain audience, imagined or real (Fiorina, 1976; Klandermans, 2013). By providing individuals with new ways to express their views and display how they act upon those views, social media constitute a new channel to both learn about opportunities to participate and communicate one's participation to others (Theocharis, 2015). Thus, social media have changed the ways in which many people participate in political activities that have existed for centuries, as well as generating entirely new forms of action.

This book aims to tell a small but relevant part of the story of why and how social media are changing the context of contemporary political participation. In this chapter, we define and discuss what political participation is and what it is not. To do that, we take stock of the third-order effects that Bimber and colleagues talk about and assess how digital media have changed what we mean by political participation itself. The second half of this chapter discusses the research design we employed to reliably measure political participation and answer the questions we outlined in Chapter 1.

Why Study Political Participation?

In a democracy, citizens are free to employ various tools to influence the people who make decisions on their behalf and the processes that lead to the selection of those people. Examples include voting, signing petitions aiming to affect public officials on specific policies, or trying to influence other people's political views and behaviors so that they will also act to achieve the same goals, or, at a minimum, vote for parties and candidates pursuing them. Whichever way citizens choose to exercise their political rights, by making their voices heard rather than remaining silent they increase the likelihood that political elites take their preferences into account. Even the sheer possibility of political action by citizens can have important effects on politicians' behavior via the process known as anticipated reactions (Sartori, 1987). As long as elites know that voters may raise their voices if they do not feel political institutions are fulfilling their needs and desires, public officials are incentivized to behave more responsibly than they would if they thought their actions, or inactions, had no consequences on their ability to win and hold on to power. Mass uprisings and electoral upsets, albeit rare, remind politicians that they ignore the possibility of citizen action at their own risk.

Given how important participation is in a democracy, it is no surprise that many scholars have discussed how it should be conceptualized and measured. The diffusion of digital media has also expanded the modes and ways in which citizens can engage in political action, and created conditions that may stimulate them to increase their participation (as we show in the rest of this book). We begin by discussing the changing democratic norms and values that constitute the cultural and attitudinal background to citizens' propensities to participate and decisions to do so.

The Evolving Context of Democratic Citizenship

The nature of citizens' involvement in political life is strongly dependent on their individual and collective priorities, the way they evaluate and relate to institutions, and, more broadly, the systems of values that characterize a society at a given moment. Ronald Inglehart (1997: 28) argued that, starting from the 1970s, Western citizens' main concerns shifted from materialistic values, such as physical safety and sustenance, to postmaterialistic values, such as self-expression and quality of life. This transformation bred new ideological and policy cleavages and, consequently, new political subjects. More broadly, however, it has transformed citizens' orientations toward politics and political institutions. While trust in established political actors and in the functioning of democratic institutions has declined (Norris, 2011), attention to issues of public relevance and engagement in activities challenging elites has not. Citizens of Western democracies have become increasingly disenchanted with established institutions and the actors, such as political parties, that have traditionally dominated them (Dalton & Wattenberg, 2002; Coleman, 2012).

Changes in citizen attitudes toward politics and institutional actors have transformed norms and patterns of political participation. Russell Dalton argues that citizenship norms have shifted, especially among younger generations, from "dutiful" to "engaged" models. Whereas dutiful citizenship prioritizes social order, voting, and involvement with institutional actors, engaged citizenship emphasizes solidarity, participation in civil society beyond institutional arenas, and personal autonomy (Dalton, 2008a; 2008b). As citizens become less invested in long-established democratic institutions and more involved with personalized forms of political action, often promoted by civil society organizations, many are only prepared to engage with parties, politicians, and representative institutions when they believe they have to, while choosing other ways of expressing their voice whenever they can. Pierre Rosanvallon (2008) argues that widespread distrust for representative institutions has shifted the balance in democratic governance, as citizen input is more likely to be motivated by the desire to oppose ideas and policies than to propose them. At the same time, citizens are more willing to participate when they feel political actors and structures are failing them, and since they generally believe this to be the case, they remain in a suspecting "standby" mode even when they are not active (Amnå & Ekman, 2014). From a less pessimistic perspective, Michael Schudson (1998) has theorized the rise of "monitorial citizenship," whereby individuals pay only superficial attention to political institutions and actors but remain vigilant enough that they can occasionally engage and participate when they believe it is necessary to do so—for instance, during crises and scandals. A corollary to the increasingly situational, context-dependent nature of monitorial citizenship is the rise of what Bruce Bimber (2003) has called "event-based political organizations," which arise out of specific circumstances that stimulate citizens' participation in particular causes but may not necessarily last beyond them.

These trends in democratic citizenship have been accelerated by the emergence of digital technologies and especially of platforms for social networking. Within and through these online spaces, individuals encounter several opportunities for publicly and politically oriented self-expression and collective action. Even recreational activities—such as those occurring in fandom or gaming communities—may help citizens acquire expressive and collaborative skills that can subsequently increase their sense of individual and collective efficacy and, at some point, be marshaled for social and political action (Jenkins, 2015). K-pop fans' involvement in the Tulsa prank is an example of these dynamics. Another example is the role of the "gamer-gate" controversy in facilitating the emergence of a collection of loose networks and organizations that coalesced into the so-called "alt-right" in the United States, which would later become an important component of the reconfiguration of the Republican Party and the election of Donald Trump as president (Phillips, 2015; Nagle, 2017). Relatedly, Lance Bennett (2008) has argued that patterns of active citizenry have changed dramatically, especially among the youth, creating a hiatus between the older ideal of the "Dutiful Citizen" and a newer "Self-Actualizing" vision of citizenship. While the dutiful citizen participates out of a sense of obligation toward democratic institutions and is mobilized by the top-down efforts of parties and campaigns, self-actualizing citizens define the terms and extent of their involvement more autonomously. Self-actualizing citizens are part of "loose networks of community action" (Bennett, 2008:14), where strong and weak personal ties coexist thanks in part to digital technologies. These looser, often informal connections are better positioned to mobilize these groups of citizens than traditional one-way communication flows initiated by elites.

These cultural transformations, however, do not mean that established democratic actors such as parties no longer have any meaningful role to play and that citizens have completely turned their back on them as channels for participation in public life (Dommett, 2020). A careful reading of the contributions discussed so far suggests that the relationship between parties and citizens has only become more volatile, frequently based on single issues and often revolving around new cleavages such as support or opposition to postmaterialistic values. Such a new relationship resembles an *alliance* more than an *obligation*, with citizens taking policy cues from, and engaging in activities organized by, political parties on their own terms and on a case-by-case basis. Adapting to these changes, political activity is increasingly structured via temporary assemblages of different groups and individuals rather than permanent organizations with durable boundaries and memberships (Bimber et al., 2012; Nielsen, 2012). In response to these cultural and behavioral shifts, political actors have experimented with new organizational formats—chiefly revolving around the use of digital media—aimed at capturing new participatory forms, to which citizens respond by crafting highly personalized, fluid, and multifaceted styles of participation (Chadwick & Stromer-Galley, 2016).

This shift in the modes and motivations of participation entails at least two important implications. The first is related to participation to activities centering on parties and elections, which has been increasingly recast into what Rachel Gibson (2009, 2015) calls *citizen-initiated campaigning*, i.e., the emergence of a "self-directing, spontaneous and socially embedded (rather than institutionally driven) layer of political action" (Gibson, 2009: 293). Citizen campaigners perform electoral activities within a loose organizational framework enabled by digital media and provided by parties and candidates. However, they are not part of any formal chain of command and are not bound to follow any direct instructions from party or campaign staffers dictating when, where, or how to help. The second implication pertains to the profile of those who participate in political activities. The opportunity to get involved on their own terms without necessarily making a permanent commitment to a party or cause may lure relative newcomers into joining campaigns and other collective political efforts, thus broadening and diversifying the pool of participants (Vaccari & Valeriani, 2016). The result is a hybridization in roles and repertoires of action, as newcomers may contribute by bringing in expertise and styles developed in their previous nonpolitical or contentious activities online and offline—such as those conducted by social movements and civic groups (Heaney & Rojas, 2015).

Citizen campaigners frequently perform these self-directed actions within their extended social networks, which they leverage to recruit volunteers to their causes, mobilize resources, and spread the word about issues or candidates they care about. Because digital media, and especially social networking platforms, have become crucial spaces where individuals nurture and interact with their social networks (Rainie & Wellman, 2012), they also play an important role as infrastructures for citizen-initiated campaigning.

To conclude, active citizenship within democratic contexts has greatly evolved during the past decades. Far from being exclusively driven by techno-logical innovations, such transformation has been made possible by sweeping cultural shifts that affected not only citizens and institutions but, importantly, the relationship between the two. As a result, the ways in which we concep-tualize and measure political participation have been called into question, opening a lively debate among scholars and commentators. In the next sec-tion, we discuss how political participation should be defined to incorporate these insights.

Setting the Boundaries of Political Participation: An Ongoing Puzzle

The scholarly debate on political participation has often revolved around its borders. Which activities and behaviors should be counted as participation, and which ones should be excluded? This is not just a measurement puzzle that scholars have to confront when they design empirical research. It is also part of broader systemic debates on how democracy works and of normative discus-sions on how it should work. Democracy is a complex system of interactions and interdependencies between institutions, elites, and citizens (Schumpeter, 1942; Sartori, 1987; Dahl, 1989; Erikson et al., 2002; Achen & Bartels, 2017). As such, democracy is many things at once, and sometimes it struggles to reconcile the different pressures it faces, from above and from below; the different goals it aims to accomplish; and the different ideals it is supposed to fulfill (Bobbio, 1987). But if democracy is intended as—among other things—the government of the people, then "the more participation there is in decisions, the more democracy there is," as Verba and Nie (1972: 1) pointed out in their seminal work on par-ticipation in America (see also Norris, 2000). Thus, if we want to assess how healthy a democracy is, we need to estimate, among other things, how wide-spread participation is, how diverse the participants are, and how inclusive the main participatory practices are. To do that, we must first define what we mean by participation and establish how to measure it.

Most discussions on the boundaries of participation have taken stock of the progressive widening of what is conceptualized as "political" (Theocaris & Van Deth, 2018). This expansion derives from the above-mentioned shifts in political values, the emergence of citizen campaigners, and the multiplication of opportunities for political expression, contacting, and networking made possible by digital platforms. As a result, we have generally moved from highly restrictive definitions of participation, which characterized scholarship until the 1990s, to more inclusive ones developed in the last decades. Such a general move from parsimony to inclusiveness, however, was not completely linear. To the contrary, the emergence of social media has resulted in a heated debate. Some authors have adopted a skeptical stand toward political engagement online and have refused to consider any kind of expressive activity online as participation. Others have suggested a more inclusive approach that takes online political actions as seriously as those performed in physical settings.

To understand what is at stake in this debate, we will start from the very influential definition of participation as an "activity that has the intent or effect of influencing government action—either directly by affecting the making or implementation of public policy or indirectly by influencing the selection of people who make those policies," proposed by Verba and colleagues (1995: 38). Here, we can clearly recognize a *vertical* vision that considers as participation only those practices aimed at communicating citizens' preferences to political elites operating within representative institutions. Conversely, *horizontal* communication between citizens is excluded, even if it is performed by some citizens to influence others so that they will then engage in some forms of vertical communication aimed toward elites.[2] Under the classic definition proposed by Verba and colleagues, citizens who speak to others with the intention to affect their behavior so that they vote in a certain way, donate to a certain cause, or talk to other citizens to persuade them to do the same, would be treated as participants in the political process only if they performed those activities *because they have been recruited and instructed by an institutional political organization,* such as a party or candidate campaign. However, they would not be treated as participants if they engaged in the same actions by their own impulse or because a friend or acquaintance has motivated them to do so independently.

That the same activities, aiming at the same goals, should be treated differently solely on the basis of whether parties or campaigns organized them strikes us as unnecessarily reductive, especially in light of the changes, discussed earlier, from permanent to ad hoc approaches to political involvement. Thus, almost a decade after Verba and colleagues' work, Pippa Norris (2002) called for a "reinvention" of the concept of political activism. Norris (2002: 4) argued that to understand the evolution of participation in postindustrial societies, we must look outside of "traditional agencies," such as parliaments, governments, and parties, and include actions primarily aimed at influencing civil society and collective behavior at large. In other words, participation should be understood as horizontal communication among citizens as well as vertical communication between citizens and elites. As one of the core components of postmaterialistic values is the importance placed on self-expression, reflections on political participation also began to take informal political talk more seriously. In this vein, Delli Carpini and colleagues (2004: 319) argued that talking with other citizens in public about matters of public concerns should be considered as "discursive participation," a legitimate and relevant form of participation in its own right. One of the reasons for this proposed new conceptual expansion is that talking about politics can lead to many positive outcomes for democracy, such as helping individuals clarify their views, understand those of others, and reach some compromise between the two.

The emergence of digital environments, especially social networking websites, has further enriched this debate. Digital media enable citizens to perform various relevant political behaviors. If we combine Verba and colleagues' elite-focused approach and the more inclusive, citizen-focused definitions proposed by Norris and by Delli Carpini and colleagues, many online behaviors related to politics can be considered as vertical or horizontal forms of political participation. A non-exhaustive list may include expressing opinions and feelings, discussing public affairs, contacting public officials, organizing and signing up for activities on the Web and on the ground, communicating one's participation in those activities, protesting, raising and donating money, and campaigning for parties and candidates. However, the extent to which some of these activities are to be considered as participation has often been questioned. Critics have dismissed forms of political expression on social media simply as self-focused (and, according to some critics, self-indulgent) "feel good" actions lacking tangible political consequences (Christensen, 2011). By contrast, Zizi Papacharissi's (2015) idea of "affective publics" has offered a new vision of political participation and collective action centered on discursive and emotional connections developed through the affordances of digital platforms.

One of the most important contributions to this debate has been made by Yannis Theocharis (2015), who proposed a clear conceptualization of "digitally networked participation" and situated it vis-à-vis previous theorizations of participation. Theocharis contends that most citizens' political behaviors on social media can be considered as political participation without overstretching classic definitions of the concept. This is because many forms of political expression online are not self-referential and self-centric but are aimed at an audience and embedded in a network and, therefore, seek to raise awareness or exercise pressure around political issues (Theocharis, 2015: 6). In this vision, joining political groups, as well as posting, sharing, or commenting on political content on social media, should all be considered as forms of political participation tout court.[3]

There are limitations to both restrictive and expansive approaches to participation. If we adopt a narrow view of participation that focuses exclusively on elite-targeted and relatively demanding actions, possibly only performed in face-to-face contexts, we overlook many politically relevant activities that characterize citizens' lives and agency in contemporary democracies. Defining participation too narrowly means that, when we measure it, we find little of it. Conversely, if we define as participation any means by which citizens express opinions or engage with information that has some political relevance, without paying any attention to the reasons why they may perform these activities, we risk putting ourselves in a conceptual corner where almost everything related to politics that citizens see, or do, on social media or elsewhere, constitutes participation, and thus it becomes nearly impossible to distinguish between what we aim to explain (participation) and what we believe can at least in part explain it (politically relevant experiences on social media). In other words, one cannot argue that political expression and exposure to political content on social media are forms of political participation and then hypothesize that they may (or may not) enhance political participation *at the same time*. Arguing both that A is part of B and that A is causing B is a logical fallacy that leads to circular theory and flawed research. We are sympathetic to discussions of political expression and information acquisition on social media as legitimate and relevant forms of political engagement—especially if we understand engagement, as Ben Berger suggests, as any form of "attentive activity directly involving the polity" (2009: 341), where citizens can be seen as being either "engaged by" politics, because they are paying attention to it, or "engaged in" politics, because they are acting on it. However, for analytical purposes, forms of political self-expression and information acquisition need to be conceptually separated from other politically relevant behaviors, occurring both online and face to face, that are more directly aimed at exercising political influence. In order to clarify this point, we now introduce a conceptual distinction between *political experiences, citizenship,* and *participation* and show how these categories characterize different forms of political engagement on social media.

Political Experiences, Citizenship, and Participation on Social Media

How can we study political participation in contemporary media environments, and how should we understand politically relevant behaviors on social media?

To answer these questions, we need to examine and account for the specific features of different types of political endeavors enabled by digital media.

We propose that forms of political engagement on social media be grouped into three different families: *experiences* that involve exposure to political content but do not entail any action from the user; forms of digital *citizenship*, which are active behaviors related to politics that ostensibly lack a deliberate aim to exercise influence on others; and *participation*, which comprises actions that aim to affect politically relevant outcomes.

Political *experiences* on social media comprise the ways in which citizens *encounter* politics on online social networking services. The characteristics of these experiences—the political content individuals see, the sources that generate and distribute it, and the modes in which users receive, process, and act upon it—depend on various factors, such as platforms' affordances (i.e., what kinds of networks they encourage users to build and how they present information produced and shared by different members of such networks, including by filtering them through algorithms), users' individual choices in crafting their own digital networks, and attitudes toward politics (such as interest in politics, ideology, and partisanship). In this book, we will treat some of these experiences as our *independent variables*. In other words, we will assess the relationship between political participation and different types of political experiences—i.e., what kinds of political content and sources individuals encounter on social media, and in which context.

Our definition of political experiences on social media has two advantages. First, conceptualizing experiences as clearly differentiated from citizenship and participation enables us to separate what we believe is the predictor—political experiences on social media—and what we aim to explain—political participation—in our models. Second, by conceptualizing different types of politically relevant experiences on social media, we can escape the generic explanations of the relationship between social media and political participation that have so far been common in the literature. To date, most research (Boulianne, 2009, 2015) has asked "does *social media use* affect participation?" (and before that, "does *Internet use* affect participation?"). This question is far too broad, as there are many different ways to "use" the Internet and social media, and it is theoretically unclear how, for instance, using social media to share pictures of one's family, to complain about the weather, or to find out which restaurants to eat in while on holiday may have any systematic bearing on political participation. As these technologies have been nearly universally adopted in many Western democracies, it is also increasingly challenging to differentiate individuals simply based on whether they have access to them. Hence, to understand the relationship between social media and participation, we need to ask more precise questions such as: "do *specific types of politically relevant experiences resulting from social media use* affect participation?"

Our second category—political *citizenship*—includes activities that are more purposeful than those we classified as experiences but that are not aimed at generating, or facilitating, a specific political outcome. Examples include searching for political information or discussing matters of public relevance. We do not intend to define democratic digital citizenship simply as access to information or acquisition of technical skills—which are crucial preconditions for such citizenship to be exercised—but also as involvement in the public sphere through the informative and expressive opportunities enabled by digital technologies (Mossberger, 2009). We know that conversation and expression around topics of public interest on digital media are connected to political participation (Gil de Zúñiga et al., 2012; Shah, 2016). Expressive activities on social media have the potential to "affect the sender" of political messages, as argued by Raymond Pingree (2007), because participants in discussions modify some of their behaviors when they know that they will be expected to express and justify their views and anticipate that what they will say may be subsequently discussed by others. Nevertheless, we cannot put all expressive activities in the same conceptual basket as political participation, for the same reasons why we argued against doing that for political experiences—namely, that this conceptual move would preclude any understanding of the role political expression may play in promoting (or limiting) political participation. Even though they are not the focus of this book, practices of digital citizenship are an important part of the puzzle of social media's contribution to political participation, which is why the two dimensions should not be confounded, at least if we are to understand their mutual relationships. Thus, we include measures of political citizenship on social media—particularly, acquiring information and participating in discussions about politics—as control variables in our models predicting political participation. We expect these variables to be part of the story that explains participation, but this is not the story we aim to tell in this study.

Finally, we classify as forms of *political participation*—our *dependent variable*—those political actions that are deliberately aimed at achieving different types of political influence: on specific policies (which we define as *primary* influence), on the selection of public officials tasked to decide on such policies (which we define as *secondary* influence), and on other citizens' political preferences and behaviors (which we define as *tertiary* influence). Importantly, tertiary influence may then recursively affect the ways citizens targeted by these participatory behaviors subsequently attempt to exercise primary, secondary, or tertiary influence on their own.

Whether the different behaviors we classify as constituting political participation occur on digital media or in face-to-face environments is immaterial to our discussion. Political endeavors aiming at exercising primary, secondary, or tertiary influence should not be included or excluded from the spectrum of political participation based on where they occur. This consideration seems even more appropriate as we finalize this book, as both the major parties' 2020 presidential nominating conventions in the United States occurred entirely online, and citizens' participation in these events and most of the subsequent campaign was by and large limited to digital activities, due to the restrictions necessary to combat the spread of the Covid-19 virus. An objection may be that the costs of similar behaviors differ remarkably between face-to-face and digital environments. Indeed, for most social media users, retweeting a get-out-the-vote message from a political party requires less effort and entails lower risks than striking a random conversation with strangers on a bus and convincing them to get out and vote. However, this argument is overly simplistic for at least three reasons.

First, as emphasized by Theocharis (2015: 8), not even the most traditional and minimalist definitions of participation exclude behaviors based exclusively on the resources they require. For instance, it costs very little to acquire and wear a pin expressing support for a party or candidate, yet this behavior is normally treated as a form of participation, particularly in the United States.[4] It should also be noted that different digital activities entail different costs (Vaccari et al., 2015). Although it is very easy to simply recirculate content produced by others, many political activists use the Internet for more complex endeavors, such as trying to persuade other users, organizing meetings and rallies, and soliciting others to volunteer or donate money to campaigns (Penney, 2017). Although social media make it easier to take political stances in public and to communicate them to multitudes of others than was previously the case, these activities can entail costs beyond the simple transmission of the message, for instance in terms of one's reputation and relationships with other people in their network who will be exposed to such messages (Settle, 2018).

Second, there is a difference between informal political conversation writ large—which we previously proposed to classify as part of political citizenship—and political talk aiming to affect others' political views and behaviors. Whereas the former is not per se poised to achieve tertiary political influence, the latter is. Although social media have made it comparably less costly to talk about politics, they have not made the task of changing people's minds—including about whether they should care about politics at all—any more or any less difficult than it is in face-to-face environments (Druckman & Lupia, 2016). As argued by Arthur Lupia (2015), humans' neurological structures have essentially remained the same while technology has massively increased the quantity of stimuli, political or otherwise, that can potentially reach an individual. The mismatch between our unchanged cognitive abilities and the deluge of content we are supposed to process and interpret has made it harder to capture our attention and persuade us, all else being equal.

Finally, as argued by Andrew Chadwick (2017b), we inhabit hybrid media systems where the norms, affordances, and logics of older and newer media coexist and get conflated and remixed as elites and citizens leverage them to exercise political agency. In this context, influence travels across different communication environments—mass, digital, and face-to-face—and actors strive to exploit the interconnections between different milieux to multiply their power across different platforms. As a result, the boundaries between digital and face-to-face political action are increasingly porous. What Rasmus Kleis Nielsen (2012) calls "personalized political communication," i.e., the distribution of political messages by individuals, now takes place across online and face-to-face realms. When such communication is self-directed by citizen campaigners (Gibson, 2015), individuals use digital media to maintain and cultivate relationships, many of which also have a face-to-face component and may also involve mobile messaging apps (Valeriani & Vaccari, 2018), so that conversations constantly move from digital to physical spaces and vice versa. When parties and interest groups organize this communication, they strive to integrate digital conversations—and the data they generate—with face-to-face interactions (Nielsen, 2012; Karpf, 2016; Kreiss, 2016). Thus, in hybrid media systems various modes of political action take place across online and offline environments. Accordingly, individuals combine political activities occurring on the Web with those in physical settings rather than keep them separate (Oser et al., 2013; Ohme et al., 2018).

Political Participation: A Definition

Having established the conceptual and theoretical premises for how we think about political participation, we now offer a formal definition. For the purposes of this book, political participation is a fluid set of *repertoires of political action spanning across face-to-face and digitally enabled activities and aiming to exercise influence on politically relevant outcomes*. As anticipated earlier, we consider three types of political influence depending on its intended target: *policy decisions* (primary influence), the *selection of public officials* who make those decisions (secondary influence), or *other citizens' political preferences and actions* (tertiary influence). This definition advances the debate on political participation in various ways.

First, we overcome the elite-centric, vertical focus of classic definitions of participation (e.g., Verba et al., 1995), which included only citizens' behaviors communicating their preferences to, and aiming to affect, political elites. Based on our conceptualization, those types of actions aim to accomplish only what we call primary and secondary political influence, i.e., affecting policy decisions and the selection of public officials. Instead, we also include tertiary influence, which aims to affect other citizens' preferences and behaviors. Tertiary influence should be included in any definition of participation for two reasons. First, interpersonal communication has been proven to affect political behavior, such as the decision to vote and the content of vote choices (Katz & Lazarsfeld, 1955; Huckfeldt & Sprague, 1995; Zuckerman, 2005; Campus et al., 2008; Bond et al., 2012). Second, the effects of tertiary influence may be even more important than those of primary and secondary influence, as affecting others enables individuals to *multiply their political impact* by mobilizing other people to political action or changing the content of their political behaviors. For instance, each citizen can only (legally) vote once in every election, so the only way to increase one's agency after that vote has been cast is to influence the votes of others. A similar logic applies to other types of activities that can be performed more than once but may have diminishing returns unless others join in. For example, elected officials may be less likely to act on an issue if they receive a thousand letters by the same constituent than if they receive one letter each from a thousand different constituents. Including activities aiming to achieve tertiary influence in our definition of political participation thus enables us to more precisely conceptualize and measure citizens' attempts to exercise agency and power, as well as the interdependencies by which they are bound and through which they can multiply their influence or enhance others' agency.

Second, our definition takes into account the increasing integration of digital and face-to-face repertoires of political action, as opposed to arbitrarily excluding endeavors that do not require physical effort or movement across geographic space (Margetts, 2006). As discussed in the previous paragraph, these black-and-white characterizations have become untenable both empirically and normatively. Citizens combine online and offline modes of political action in their everyday lives, and there are no defensible reasons to argue that the same types of action, performed with the same intentions, should be treated differently solely based on whether they occur in digital or physical spaces.

Third, we define political participation as comprising activities that place different levels of emphasis on *action* and *communication*. In a sense, all forms of participation aim to communicate something to someone else. Voting conveys citizens' preferences to elites, as does contributing to an organized protest by either marching in the streets or spreading the word about it on social media. By the same token, communication is a form of social action, as its content can affect social and political relationships (Searle, 1969). However, some politically relevant activities are manifested as actions that, to a degree, speak by themselves, as with donating money to a party or candidate, while others are more closely reliant on the exchange of ideas, such as when one tries to convince someone else to vote a certain way. However, we do not consider all forms of political talk as constituting political action and, thus, participation. Instead, we treat as participation only those forms of political talk that aim to exercise political influence, as opposed to expressing one's views (which we classify as political citizenship) and being exposed to political content (which we consider as a political experience). This distinction avoids the risk of overstretching the concept of participation to the point that it becomes too broad to be helpful (Sartori, 1970).

Measuring Political Participation

Since we have argued that participation comprises endeavors that occur both online and in face-to-face settings and that aim to exercise primary, secondary, or tertiary influence on relevant political outcomes, we need to measure participation in a way that captures these behaviors as comprehensively as possible. In particular, we must do justice to the variety of endeavors our definition comprises, including the different types of efforts they require, the types of political influence they pursue, and the costs they entail. We also need to ensure that our measures accurately describe political behaviors that are relevant for contemporary citizens in Western democracies, at least within the time frame of our research (2015–2018). Our goal is to assess whether and how social media can contribute to societal patterns of political participation among the whole population, as opposed to simply mobilizing specific niches or publics that coalesce on social media around certain topics (Graham & Wright, 2015), social movements (Freelon et al., 2018), or events (Vaccari et al., 2015). Finally, we need measures that can safely travel across a variety of Western democracies, characterized by important differences in the functioning of their political and media institutions, in the types of political organizations that facilitate citizen action, and in the formal and informal norms that regulate campaigning, organizing, and political communication.

To achieve these goals, we measure political participation by asking people questions about whether they engaged in meaningful forms of political action. We rely on custom-built, online surveys of samples representative of the population with Internet access in the nine countries included in our research.[5] This method is not perfect, especially because it rests on the assumption that individuals are capable and willing to accurately recall past political behaviors—which we know is often not the case (Bernstein et al., 2001; Prior, 2009; de Vreese & Neijens, 2016). However, surveys have the unique advantage of enabling us to build a richly textured portrait of how contemporary citizens engage in different forms of political action spanning across different environments, both online and offline, while also providing measures of our independent variables (political experiences on social media) and a host of other variables, which we will employ as moderators or controls in multivariate regression models predicting political participation.[6]

We conceptualize participation as being constituted by *repertoires*, that is, a set of practices that individuals (and organizations) construct by choosing among a broader inventory of what they consider to be available, desirable, and effective forms of political action. In Charles Tilly's original definition of the concept, "The word *repertoire* identifies a limited set of routines that are learned, shared and acted out through a relatively deliberate process of choice" (Tilly, 1995: 26, cited in Chadwick, 2007: 285). We further conceptualize these repertoires as being fluid, changing over time to adapt to different political demands and opportunities, and hybrid, integrating digital and face-to-face endeavors. There are relevant differences in the ways in which individuals and groups in Western democracies construct their own repertoires. Some citizens, for instance, rely more heavily on activities that connect them with representative institutions, such as voting and volunteering for political parties, while others tend to focus more on contributing to the initiatives of civil society organizations, and others still prefer engaging with non-institutional actors such as social movements. In this book, we do not take up the important task of precisely identifying these clusters of preferences, let alone isolating what factors explain them. We are more specifically interested in measuring and understanding repertoires of participation that are, broadly speaking, relevant to citizens' ability to influence processes and outcomes occurring within representative institutions. We aim to establish how broad citizens' repertoires are, and to achieve this we assess how many activities each individual remembers performing in the past year. Our central assumption is that someone who has a broader repertoire, that is, engages in a greater number of political activities, can be understood as participating in politics more intensely than someone who has a narrower repertoire, that is, engages in a smaller number of endeavors. To perform this comparison, one needs to choose a well-defined set of activities against which to evaluate citizens' repertoires. We focus on six:

- Contacting a politician to support a cause
- Signing petitions and subscribing to referenda[7]
- Financing a party, candidate, political leader, or electoral campaign
- Taking part in public meetings and electoral rallies
- Distributing leaflets to support a political or social cause
- Trying to convince someone to vote for a party, leader, or candidate[8]

A general observation that pertains to all these endeavors is that they are not the kind of relatively low-cost, low-effort, and casual forms of online political expression that have been criticized as "low-quality participation" (Shulman, 2009). As discussed earlier, we consider such forms of engagement as important, but we classify them as political experiences and political citizenship, not political participation. This assessment is not based on how high or low we estimate their costs to be, but on whether we consider them to be ostensibly motivated to achieve primary, secondary, and tertiary political influence.

Table 2.1 summarizes the main characteristics of each activity we measure to capture citizens' repertoires of political participation. These six behaviors can be distinguished with respect to the level of influence they aim to achieve (primary, secondary, or tertiary), the environments within which the action can be performed (offline, online, or both), the main types of resources it requires (skills, time, and money), and the general diffusion of each activity within our nine-country sample of survey respondents. We note that the population to which our surveys refer, and to which our data should be generalized, is not the general voting-age population, but the subset of the population that, in each of the countries we studied, has Internet access.[9] This is because, by definition,

Table 2.1. **Classification of Different Forms of Political Participation**

Action	Influence	Main Resources	Environment	Diffusion
Contacting a politician to support a cause	primary	skills	online/offline	14.8%
Signing petitions and subscribing referenda	primary	skills	online/offline	46%
Financing a party, candidate, political leader, or electoral campaign	secondary	money	online/offline	8.1%
Taking part in public meetings and electoral rallies	secondary	time	offline	15.1%
Distributing leaflets to support a political or social cause	tertiary	time	offline	10.7%
Trying to convince someone to vote for a party, leader, or candidate	tertiary	skills	online/offline	42.6%

only citizens with Internet access could be included in the online panels from which we recruited our respondents. To the extent that Internet users tend to be better educated and more politically involved than nonusers (Norris, 2001; Van Dijk, 2005), the activities we measured may have been less common if we had surveyed the whole population, including Internet nonusers. However, it would have made little sense to ask people without access to digital media if they performed political activities that take place online, which is why we decided to focus on Internet users.

We now briefly discuss the six activities we chose to measure and comment on their key characteristics and diffusion.

Contacting politicians to support a cause and signing petitions or subscribing referenda are aimed at exercising a primary influence on policymaking processes, either by pushing representatives to act in a certain direction or by trying to enact policy change directly via popular vote. However, while signing a petition is an act that people can perform without engaging in any forms of interpersonal exchange, writing to a politician implies a substantial communicative effort, which contributes to explaining why it is a less common activity.

Financing a party or a candidate and taking part in electoral rallies are related to the selection of representatives and are thus aimed at exercising secondary influence on policymaking, by influencing who is to make decisions on citizens' behalf. These actions, however, clearly differ in terms of the resources they require. While donating to a party or campaign costs money, attending rallies might be financially inexpensive, apart from transportation costs, but is much more demanding in terms of time spent to reach the place of the event, attend it, and return to one's home or other destination afterward. If the event occurs on a working day, there may also be opportunity costs if participants have to abstain from work to be able to attend and may see their income reduced as a result.

Finally, leafleting to support a cause and trying to convince other people to vote for someone are relevant examples of what we have defined as tertiary influence, since they are directed at influencing other people's political opinions and behaviors. Similar to attending rallies and events, leafleting mainly requires time and does not necessarily involve in-depth personal exchanges. By contrast, trying to convince others to make a particular voting decision requires a broader set of resources. To be an effective political persuader one needs to master information, acquire argumentative skills, and dedicate time to political discussion. Engaging in political persuasion also entails risks to one's personal reputation. Talking to others, whether they be strangers or not, about something as sensitive as their vote choices requires overcoming people's reluctance to discuss politics (Schudson, 1997; Eliasoph, 1998), especially with those who have different political views (MacKuen, 1990; Wells et al., 2017). Moreover, not all political talk is equal, as individuals rely on cues such as perceived similarity, social capital, and respectability to assess the credibility of those who try to persuade them (Lupia & McCubbins, 1998). When citizens try to persuade others to vote in a certain way, they both rely on their reputation and put it on the line in case the interaction should not unfold as they planned and wished.

As explained in the previous section, our vision of political participation does not distinguish between different activities based on whether they occur in digital or face-to-face contexts. Instead, we adopt an inclusive approach that comprises actions occurring across both these domains. Among the six activities we consider, only two—attending rallies and leafleting—can be performed exclusively, or nearly so,[10] in physical spaces, while the remaining four can be undertaken both online and offline. For example, a donation to a party or campaign can be made in multiple ways, from writing and handing over a check to a politician to using digital applications, and the same is true for signing a petition, contacting a politician, and trying to convince others to vote for a certain party or candidate.

The descriptive statistics on the diffusion of the six activities presented in the last column of Table 2.1 suggest that signing petitions and trying to convince other people to vote for someone (undertaken by more than 40% of respondents) are substantially more popular than the others. This pattern holds across all the nine democracies included in our study. The remaining four activities are still reasonably common in our samples: around 15% of our respondents have contacted a politician to support a cause and participated in electoral meetings or rallies, while about 10% have been involved in leafleting, and 8% have donated money to fund a politician, a party, or a campaign. Our measures of political participation thus include actions with different levels of diffusion. None of the activities we measured are so common that they are not useful for differentiating politically active citizens from the rest of the population, or so rare that they are effectively irrelevant as examples of mass political behavior. Hence, the measures of participation we employ in this study are broad and diverse enough that they provide a comprehensive portrait of citizens' repertoires of political action aimed at influencing representative democratic politics and policies.

Before we discuss these issues further, we must address one potential objection: why is voting not included among our measures of political participation? The main reason is that voting is by far the most common form of political participation in Western democracies. As Table 2.1 shows, none of the activities we measured were performed by half or more of our respondents during the previous year. By contrast, voter turnout in all the national elections we studied was substantially higher, and roughly 80% of our survey respondents claimed they voted in the previous general election. Moreover, the factors affecting the choice of whether to vote or not differ to a substantial degree from the determinants of other modes of political participation (Verba et al., 1995; Blais, 2000; Leighley & Nagler, 2013).

WHY ARE SOME FORMS OF PARTICIPATION MORE POPULAR THAN OTHERS?

The descriptive data presented in Table 2.1 provide an opportunity to reflect on the state of political participation repertoires in the digital age. As already noted, signing petitions and trying to influence other people's votes are largely more popular than the other four activities we measured. As can be seen by examining the classification presented in Table 2.1, the popularity of different forms of participation cannot be explained solely based on one of their three properties we have outlined (type of political influence pursued, online vs. offline environments, and prevalent costs). However, if we consider such properties in combination, we can at least begin to understand the reasons that make different kinds of political actions more or less popular among citizens of contemporary Western democracies.

First, both signing petitions and engaging in discussions aimed at influencing others' vote can be undertaken both in digital spaces and in offline environments, and citizens, indeed, take advantage of both settings. Only 43% of our respondents who tried to influence others' voting choices did so exclusively offline. Similarly, only 28% of respondents who signed a petition or subscribed a referendum did so only in physical spaces, signing a piece of paper with a pen. Thus, the majority of our respondents (and a supermajority of two-thirds when it comes to signing petitions) who undertook these actions did so either exclusively online or in both digital and offline environments. These patterns suggest that digital media have contributed to expanding the opportunities for at least some relevant types of citizen participation. Obviously, we cannot know if those who conduct these activities solely online would avoid them altogether if the Internet did not exist or if they did not have Internet access. Some may still engage in these practices in physical spaces and may have switched to their online equivalents only because they are more convenient. Others might have got acquainted with these practices online and subsequently performed similar activities offline. Without knowing precisely what a world without the Internet would look like for these participants, it seems plausible that, when it comes to petition signing and interpersonal proselytizing, the Internet and social media may have strengthened patterns of political participation across online and offline realms.

However, the fact that citizens can perform some activities both online and offline does not alone explain their popularity. A case in point is making financial contributions to parties and campaigns, which is the least popular activity among those we measured. To explain this, it is worth considering an additional characteristic, i.e., the degree to which an activity requires direct contact with political organizations. Donating money and leafleting, contacting politicians to support a cause, and taking part in political rallies all require interacting with institutional political actors at some point. Candidates and parties are in charge of producing and distributing leaflets to activists, are the beneficiaries of financial donations, are the main organizers of most (though by no means all) rallies, and are the recipients of the emails and letters written by citizens to support political causes (given that in our question we specifically referred to messages addressing politicians). By contrast, signing petitions and trying to influence others' votes, albeit aimed at influencing institutional politics, do not necessarily require direct contact with parties or candidates. Such absence of party mediation could increase the appeal of these activities, especially in a context of generalized decline of trust in political institutions and of volatile identification with parties characterizing citizens across Western democracies. Going back to the distinction between dutiful and engaged citizenship norms proposed by Dalton (2008), trying to influence other people's votes and signing petitions share qualities, such as personal autonomy and involvement with civil society actors, that are typical of engaged citizenship, whereas the other four, less popular activities are more congruent with the norms of dutiful citizenship, being tied in one way or another to institutional political actors. Trying to influence others' votes is an activity that can be definitely performed by "citizen campaigners" (Gibson, 2009) acting on their own terms, without any direct exchanges with parties or candidates. Similarly, signing a petition can be considered a typical action by "monitorial citizens" (Schudson, 1998), who do not feel any obligation to be permanently active in politics but can on occasion decide to make their voice heard for a cause they deem worthy.

It might also be argued that the popularity of signing petitions and trying to influence others is simply a function of their lower cost, measured according to traditional parameters such as time or money. However, the evolution of political participation and the transformations characterizing contemporary political communication environments require a more nuanced vision of the costs of participation. For example, as contended, among others, by Zizi Papacharissi (2011) and danah boyd (2014), social media have complicated the ways in which individuals manage their self-presentation vis-à-vis others. Most social media encourage users to build audiences that span across different networks, which they may otherwise want to keep separate—for instance, family, friends, work colleagues, and distant acquaintances. Whereas individuals would normally present themselves in (slightly but noticeably) different ways when engaging with these different groups in isolation, on social media they address multiple and vaguely defined audiences (in the sense that users never really know with certainty who will see their messages), now collapsed into a hodgepodge of digital "friends" or "followers" (Marwick & boyd, 2011). Trying to convince someone to vote for a party on a platform where conversations are almost public and aimed at a broad, imperfectly controlled, and partially unknown audience may thus become a risky endeavor that could jeopardize some relationships and, thus, individuals' social capital.[11] While some of one's contacts on social media might cheer when they see them articulating their political views, others, who connected with that person for different reasons and may have different political views, could be less pleased, and the relationship with those people may be damaged as a result (Settle, 2018). By contrast, donating a minimal amount of money—a practice nowadays highly encouraged by political actors in most democracies—can be done very easily online and without necessarily making a public statement on this action. However, in spite of the potential social cost of expressing a political preference by trying to influence others' votes, as many as 19% of the respondents in our sample reported to have performed this action specifically on social media. This finding confirms that messaging people to influence their vote and subscribing petitions or referenda are popular not only due to their low costs, but also because they fit well with contemporary citizenship norms and participatory styles.

The Context of Our Research: A Note on Country Selection

The theories we outlined in the final section of Chapter 1 can only be tested with a comparative research design. We tackle this challenge by studying nine Western democracies: Denmark, France, Germany, Greece, Italy, Poland, Spain, the United Kingdom, and the United States. This group of countries fulfills the main criteria identified by Seawright and Gerring (2008: 296) to ensure that the findings drawn from a set of cases can be extended, at least tentatively, to a broader population of which they can be considered representative. We argue that our nine cases are representative of the broader realm of Western democracies for two reasons: their size and the diversity of characteristics they encompass.

Let us start from size. If we take estimates related to 2016,[12] the nine countries we covered in this book hosted a total 570.796 million Internet users, while the sum of their populations was 695.646 million (Internet Live Stats, 2017). This means that about 82% of the populations in these countries had Internet access. By comparison, in 2016 there were an estimated 3.366 billion Internet users in the world, but only 1.663 billion lived in one of the eighty-seven countries that Freedom House classified as "free" in the same year, which we can take as a rough indicator that they are functioning democracies (Freedom House, 2017).

This means that more than one-third (precisely, 34.32%) of Internet users in democracies around the world lived in one of the nine countries included in our research.

Let us now conduct a similar exercise with data on social media use. In this case, we employ 2018 market research figures (We Are Social, 2019), which show that the total number of active social media users in the world was 3.484 billion, and of these, roughly 436 million (or 14.9% of the global population of active social media users) lived in 8 of the 9 countries included in this study (there were no data for Greece). The report included 44 countries, 26 of which were classified as "free" by Freedom House[13] and 18 as less than free. In the twenty-six free countries, active social media users were estimated at 1.179 billion, so the eight countries (all but Greece) included in our research and in the cited report comprise 36.91% of the population of active social media users in a diverse sample including the largest democracies in the world. In sum, the countries we study comprise a sizable proportion of Internet users and social media users worldwide, and this is especially true when we focus solely on relatively well-functioning democracies—to which our theories and questions pertain.

The countries we chose feature theoretically relevant differences that enable us to test theories, outlined in Chapter 1, about how systemic characteristics moderate the relationship between political experiences on social media and participation. However, the nine countries also share important similarities that enable us to discount characteristics that are common, in broad terms, across all cases. This combination of similarities and differences is the main goal of the *diverse case selection strategy*, whose main purpose is "the achievement of maximum variance along relevant dimensions" within a defined population (Seawright & Gerring, 2008: 300). In other words, the nine countries we focus on here are similar enough with respect to certain features that we can safely discard such features as sources of variation, and different enough on other characteristics that we can attempt to estimate how they shape the relationship between political experiences on social media and participation.

Let us start from the features the nine countries share. First, they are functioning liberal democracies.[14] In spite of their particular problems and difficulties— for instance, the attack on liberal institutions by the Polish government in office after the 2015 elections; the fractious center–periphery relationships in Italy, Spain and the United Kingdom; the near-collapse of Greece's public finances and the political and social crises it caused; legislative gridlock and the erosion of democratic norms in the United States; and the electoral rise of the populist right almost everywhere—they can all be considered stable, if not perfect, democratic regimes, and they have been consistently classified as such by international organizations and academic research. Second, they are relatively wealthy countries, and, as discussed earlier, they show comparably high, though by no means even, levels of Internet and social media diffusion in their populations. Digital platforms in these countries have become widespread enough to be part of most of the population's everyday lives and, thus, to play an important role in the fabric of their societies and polities.

We now briefly highlight the main theoretically relevant differences between the democracies we focus on. When classifying countries' differences in comparative research, scholars need to strike the right balance between doing justice to the nuances and complexities that characterize each country and devising measures of relevant systemic features that can travel across countries. Each country is a complex combination of different properties, and whether countries can be considered similar or different from one another depends on what phenomena researchers want to understand and what factors they believe may explain them. In other words, "Comparability is a quality that is not inherent in any given set of objects; rather it is a quality important to them by the observer's perspective" (Rustow, 1968, cited in Lijphart, 1971). Such perspective can only derive from theory, which provides a rational basis for meaningfully *simplifying* the space of attributes of a set of countries so as to identify those that really matter for the research. In his seminal essay on the use of the comparative method in political science, Arend Lijphart makes a strong case for *theoretical parsimony*: "Comparative analysis must avoid the danger of being overwhelmed by large numbers of variables [...] and it must therefore judiciously restrict itself to the really key variables, omitting those of only marginal importance" (Lijphart, 1971: 690). In a nutshell, this research strategy aims to sacrifice some empirical breadth to gain analytical depth.

As discussed in Chapter 1, we have identified three systemic characteristics, each of which, we theorize, may moderate the relationship between one of the political experiences on social media we study and political participation: patterns of electoral competition, mass media systems, and types of political organizations. In our analysis, we chose to treat these complex concepts as simple categorical variables, classifying patterns of electoral competition as either majoritarian or proportional; mass media systems as either liberal, democratic corporatist, or polarized pluralist; and political organizations as either party-centric or candidate-centric.

This level of simplification is not uncommon in comparative research, where a certain degree of complexity reduction is often necessary for the reasons highlighted previously. However, we could have taken specific numeric indicators to operationalize some aspects of the concepts we are interested in, and use those values, rather than the country groupings we created, in our multivariate models. We chose not to take this route for three reasons. First, any numeric indicator, or group of numeric indicators, would be a useful but imperfect simplification of the reality we aim to capture and may also be contingent on the timing of data collection. As an example, we could use data on party membership as a proxy for the strength of party organizations. Such data are to some degree available (e.g., Van Biezen et al., 2012), but they are notoriously noisy, as different parties in different countries enroll, count, and report members in different ways. Second, while we applaud efforts by scholars such as Brüggemann and colleagues (2014) in collecting, systematizing, and analyzing a variety of empirical indicators to classify complex realities such as mass media systems, conducting such an empirical enterprise, or updating the results of others, on all our countries and for all our key systemic variables would have exceeded the scope of our research. Finally, even if we could collect a number of valid and reliable indicators on each dimension of our comparative analysis to generate empirically driven classifications of our nine countries, this greater granularity would yield few analytical benefits given the theories we aim to test. For example, consider patterns of electoral competition. A well-known indicator of the number of competitive actors in a party system is the Effective Number of Electoral Parties (Laakso & Taagepera, 1979). Thanks to data compiled by Michael Gallagher (2017), we know the value of this indicator for all recent elections in the countries included in our study. The United States normally score about 2, while the United Kingdom hovers around 3.5, reflecting important differences between the party systems in those two countries. Yet, when it comes to the theory we aim to test, what matters is how electoral competition plays out, and in particular, to what extent the major parties cultivate niches or try to appeal to broad sectors of the population—employing bonding versus bridging strategies, in Norris's (2004) terminology. From this standpoint, we argue that electoral competition in the United Kingdom, the United States, and France (which we also classify as majoritarian) functions according to the same bridging strategy, at least as far as the main parties are concerned. To us, this is the crux of the theoretical matter, and as a result we choose to rely on qualitative classifications rather than employ quantitative measures of the key systemic characteristics we investigate.

The fact that we chose qualitative classifications over quantitative indicators, however, does not mean that our classifications are evidence free. To the contrary, we took into account both quantitative and qualitative data to make our decisions. In Chapter 6 we provide evidence of how we classified each country with respect to the systemic characteristics we are interested in. Table 2.2 summarizes these decisions, as well as provides some background information on the elections about which we conducted the surveys our analyses are based on.

As can be seen from the table, we conducted our surveys between June 2015 and March 2018. More precisely, we completed four surveys in 2015, one in 2016, three in 2017, and one in 2018. This is because we collected data immediately after the last general election that took place in each country during the period in which our project ran. Our fieldwork dates were, therefore, bound by the differences in the timing of elections in every country. There are different benefits and costs to this choice.

On the one hand, national general elections are crucial moments in democratic governance as well as important opportunities for citizens to engage with politics and for political actors to reach out to voters. While outside of general elections most voters pay scant attention to politics, campaigns provide an opportunity for citizens who are less involved in politics to learn about and participate in the political process (Zaller, 1992; Arcenaux, 2006). One of the key arguments we aim to test in this book is that citizens who are less politically involved stand to reap larger participatory gains from political experiences on social media. Studying elections offers the best opportunity to observe this phenomenon because campaigns are particularly important for this group of voters. If one is to conduct comparative research on elections, there is no alternative to collecting data when (or right after) elections are held.

On the other hand, social media change constantly, and so do their political uses. For one, digital platform companies constantly experiment with, tweak, and overhaul their algorithms and interfaces in pursuit of a complex combination of commercial, normative, and reputational goals (Bucher, 2018). For instance, in June 2016 Facebook announced that it would change the algorithm that ranks the content a user sees in her news feed, so that posts from "friends and family" would be more likely to appear than posts from public pages, such as politicians, celebrities, or news organizations (Mosseri, 2016). This led to a steep decline in the traffic that news outlets' websites received from Facebook (Vogelstein, 2018). Two years later, the company updated its policy again to prioritize "posts that spark conversations and meaningful interactions between people" (Mosseri, 2018). Platforms also change the rules and processes underlying advertising, which can affect the kinds of paid messages citizens see. For instance, in October 2019 Twitter prohibited any advertising that "references a candidate, political party, elected or appointed government official, election, referendum, ballot measure, legislation, regulation, directive, or judicial outcome" (Twitter, 2019). Although as far as we know there were no such substantial changes in the major platforms' advertising policies during the period in which we collected our data, it is possible that some important developments may have occurred behind the scenes (see, e.g., Kreiss & McGregor, 2019). The popularity and reputation of different platforms also change over time. For instance, after the 2016 U.S. presidential elections and the Cambridge Analytica scandal that unfolded two years later, Facebook's public image worsened substantially (Weisbaum, 2018), although its user base continued to grow at the rate of around 100,000 per year (Statista, 2020a). At the same time, Instagram's user base grew massively, jumping from 400,000 in 2015 to one billion in 2018 (Statista, 2020b). Furthermore, as readers will recall from the vignette that introduced

Table 2.2. **Summary of the Main Systemic Characteristics of the Nine Countries Covered in This Book**

Country	Electoral Competition	Mass Media System	Political Organizations	Election Covered	Voter Turnout (Highest Office)	Resulting Government
Denmark	Proportional	Democratic Corporatist	Party-centric	2015	85.8%	Center-right-led coalition
France	Majoritarian	Polarized Pluralist	Candidate-centric	2017	77.7%	Independent/Center-liberal one-party government
Germany	Proportional	Democratic Corporatist	Party-centric	2017	76.2%	Center-right-led coalition
Greece	Proportional	Polarized Pluralist	Candidate-centric	2015 (September)	56.6%	Left-led coalition
Italy	Proportional	Polarized Pluralist	Candidate-centric	2018	72.9%	Coalition of Five Stars Movement and League
Poland	Proportional	Polarized Pluralist	Candidate-centric	2015	55.3%	Center-right one-party government
Spain	Proportional	Polarized Pluralist	Candidate-centric	2015	69.7%	Political stalemate; new elections in 2016
U.K.	Majoritarian	Liberal	Party-centric	2017	68.7%	Center-right-led coalition
U.S.A.	Majoritarian	Liberal	Candidate-centric	2016	59.3%	Center-right one-party government

this chapter, new platforms, such as TikTok, have also emerged, though its global rise began in 2019, after we finished collecting our data (Sherman, 2020). All these dynamic patterns mean that the way social media function and the way citizens and politicians use them change more frequently than most social science research methods assume and are able to capture empirically. Hence, the validity of our measures and findings over time should never be taken for granted (Karpf, 2012b; Bimber & Copeland, 2013; Munger, 2019).

As is often the case in comparative research, scholars are faced with trade-offs between competing values where there is no perfect solution that accomplishes all desirable goals and, thus, need to decide which side to err on. In this project, we considered the uniqueness of elections as moments of democratic decision-making, participation, and mobilization. We reasoned that the value of consistently studying elections taking place at different moments across different political systems outweighs the loss of precision that derives from staggering the data collection to follow each country's electoral calendar, even if it means partly overlooking constant developments in the social media environment we study. It is important, however, to acknowledge that this choice comes at the potential cost of using a fixed method and a set of standardized measures to capture what is effectively a set of moving targets.

3

Of Arguments, Accidents, and Asks

How and Why Political Experiences Occur on Social Media

In 2014, Scotland voted in a historic referendum to decide whether to remain part of the United Kingdom or to form an independent state. In launching the Scottish National Party's campaign for independence, First Minister Alex Salmond claimed that the key ingredients would be community activism and "online wizardry" (BBC News Online, 2012). Supporters of independence mobilized around popular hashtags such as #yesbecause (Molloy, 2014), to which the unionist campaign responded with its own #nobecause. According to the UK Electoral Commission, the Internet closely rivaled television (52% versus 56%) as the main source of information on the referendum (UK Electoral Commission, 2014). A plurality of respondents (39%) to a survey claimed that social media had been the most helpful source of information to make up their minds on the referendum, ahead of newspapers (34%) (Haggerty, 2014). On election day, 84.6% of registered voters turned out—more than 20% higher than in the 2010 general election—giving "No" a comfortable victory by 55.3% to 44.7%.

As social media became one of the key battlegrounds in the referendum, many voters were exposed to political messages on these platforms, whether they liked it or not. Activists and supporters of both camps took to social media to make their case in this once-in-a-generation choice. The outcome was a vibrant—and at times vicious—multiplication of online claims and counterclaims around this fundamental question of national identity. According to news reports, undecided voters in focus groups conducted by the "No" campaign expressed irritation and fatigue over the constant flow of online propaganda, and this sentiment was effectively summarized by the refrain "I want my Facebook back!" (Behr, 2014).

In the heat of an election, "I want my Facebook back" may be a widespread grievance. Most citizens in Western democracies are happy to ignore politics

Outside the Bubble. Cristian Vaccari and Augusto Valeriani, Oxford University Press. © Oxford University Press 2021.
DOI: 10.1093/oso/9780190858476.003.0004

most of the time, unless a pivotal decision needs to be made or a crisis must be faced (Hibbing & Thesis-Morse, 2002; Zaller, 2003). However, the fact that, in certain moments, many users claim they want their Facebook back clashes with the increasingly popular representation of social media users as self-entrapped in cocoons where they have (nearly) full control over the information they are exposed to. Underlying these portrayals are popular metaphors that describe social media as "echo chambers" (Sunstein, 2009) or "filter bubbles" (Pariser, 2011). The evocative power of these images has contributed to the diffusion, especially in public debate, of a generalized perception that social media are fostering higher levels of political self-segregation and information asymmetries than other media, thus accelerating the march toward what Markus Prior (2007) has termed "post-broadcast democracy," characterized by increasing levels of polarization and political inequality. However, if this were really the case, hardly anyone would ever complain that their social media feed has been hijacked, against their will, by political actors and political junkies, as some Scottish voters did in 2014.

Echo chambers and filter bubbles are frequently employed as quasi-synonymous terms, even by some social scientists (e.g., Flaxman et al., 2016). Although both terms refer to the fact that Internet users experience information selectively, the two metaphors actually capture two different types of digital (self-)segregation (Bruns, 2019). With "echo chambers," Cass Sunstein (2009, 2015, 2017) describes conversational cocoons where netizens almost exclusively congregate with like-minded others, as a result of both individual choices and algorithmic personalization. According to Sunstein, this process fosters political polarization by leaving individuals safe within their political comfort zone. Conversely, with "filter bubbles," Eli Pariser (2011) more broadly refers to a narrowing in the types of content and views we are exposed to while on the Internet, mainly due to algorithmic filtering affordances. As a result, opportunities for serendipitous encounters with information that falls out of our interests—and the positive implications that may result from such exposure—are highly reduced. In Pariser's vision, users' previously expressed interest for specific subjects (political or otherwise) narrows the breadth of their online experience because digital platforms rely on these revealed preferences to offer them more of the same type of content as they have already interacted with. While the nature of echo chambers is intrinsically ideological, in the form of prevalent exposure to and engagement with agreeing viewpoints, filter bubbles are mainly rooted in individuals' interests for different kinds of content—in particular, for our purposes, their interest in news and politics—and the ways in which they manifest such interest in their online behavior.

This book aims to develop a more granular understanding of both echo chambers and filter bubbles. For this reason, we will differentiate the two concepts—possibly even more than what a comparative reading of Sunstein's and Pariser's original works suggests. The social media experiences we consider, and whose relationships with political participation we investigate, allow us to estimate how widespread both echo chambers and filter bubbles are in the context of Western democracies.

As we discussed in Chapter 1, we should reconsider the idea that social media affordances and algorithms create an unavoidable destiny of selective exposure to agreeing viewpoints and of deliberately filtered content that isolates people from politics if they so wish. We pointed out several reasons for this, mainly pertaining to how social media affordances actually work (Colleoni et al., 2014), different individual motivations behind the uses of these platforms (Vaccari et al., 2016), and the nature and focus of specific conversational situations (Barberá et al., 2015). The analyses we present in this chapter aim to move a step further in this direction. By describing and explaining Western citizens' experiences with agreeing opinions, their incidental encounters with political information, and their exposure to electoral mobilization on social media, we show that, to the extent that echo chambers and filter bubbles exist, they are less widespread and more permeable than is often assumed. As we will show, the specific configurations described by these terms are not the norm but characterize the experiences of a rather specific, and politically unrepresentative, set of users.

Echo Chambers, Open Windows?

Two limitations characterize the research that has supported what could be defined as a "strong vision" of political self-segregation on social media. First, many of these studies (e.g., Bakshy et al., 2015; Del Vicario et al., 2017) have almost exclusively focused on users' active behaviors such as sharing, commenting, or following links, without considering the content to which users are exposed. We know from political psychology (e.g., Festinger, 1962; Taber & Lodge, 2006) that individuals tend to pay more attention to, and prefer to engage with, content that is consistent with their political views. However, just because individuals may prefer to actively *engage* with agreeing political views on social media, as they do in any communication environment, this does not necessarily mean that they are not *exposed* to disagreeing ideas as well. Indeed, most of the time we spend on social media is dedicated to reading and observing, rather than acting upon, content (Crawford, 2009), and, while confirmation bias could be one of the main drivers guiding the way we process information (Nickerson, 1998), this does not mean that we do not also encounter attitude-divergent content (Huckfeldt et al., 2004). This idea finds empirical support in a study by Song and colleagues (2020) on online political discussion forums. By combining behavioral and survey data, the authors show that partisan selectivity is highly reduced when reading choices, instead of more active behaviors such as replies, are considered. These findings suggest that exposure to disagreeing content in online environments might be more frequent than indicated by studies solely considering users' active engagement with political content. To understand whether social media users are (self-)segregated in hermetically sealed echo chambers, we should not only study whether users *actively interact* with political content they agree or disagree with. The amount of *sheer exposure* to consonant versus adversarial views should also be considered.

The second limitation characterizing most research that describes social media as echo chambers is that it has tended to focus on social media in isolation from other channels of political communication. Scholars often assumed, or implied, that digital platforms make citizens more politically isolated or segregated *by comparison with other channels* through which they learn about and discuss public affairs (Sunstein, 2017). However, whether social media are more likely to expose people to consonant political ideas than face-to-face interactions or news in the mass media is an empirical question that cannot be assumed away. To answer it, we need to estimate levels of pluralism on social media as well as in other relevant channels of political communication.

THE EXPERIENCE OF POLITICAL AGREEMENT AND DISAGREEMENT ON SOCIAL MEDIA

Agreement and disagreement can coexist in the political experiences of social media users. Even though many users prefer to engage with politically consonant views, they may still also be exposed to diverging opinions and information, especially if such information comes from contacts established on the basis of commonalities other than political orientations. With this in mind, William Eveland and Myiah Hively (2009) criticized one-dimensional models that characterize many studies of network heterogeneity in political interactions. They argued that a correct understanding and operationalization of the concept should address not only whether individuals agree or disagree with each person they discuss politics with, but also how people position their views via-à-vis those of the whole network of citizens they interact with. What uniquely defines the nature of citizens' political conversations is not only the *frequency* of discussion with like-minded and/or disagreeing partners, but also the *ratio* between the two. Accordingly, as already discussed in Chapter 1, Lilach Nir (2011) has contended that the extent to which citizens encounter disagreement in their political conversations entails two different dimensions: "opposition" (i.e., the distance between citizens' views and those of their discussion partners) and "competition" (i.e., heterogeneity of views among all discussants). Nir (2011) further argues that networks of political conversation should be defined as "supportive" when citizens engage predominantly with agreeing others, "oppositional" when they mainly interact with contrarian partners, and "mixed" when the frequency of conversations with like-minded and disagreeing discussants is more or less evenly balanced. This approach can also help describe how citizens encounter different types of political opinions on social media.

As we have discussed, to assess to what extent and for how many people social media constitute echo chambers, we should look not only at actual engagement with agreeing and/or disagreeing viewpoints but, more fundamentally, at exposure to them. Hence, in our analyses we combine answers to two different questions that ask respondents how frequently they agree and disagree with the political opinions and messages they see on social media. For each question, respondents were offered the following response modes: "Always," "Often," "Sometimes," "Never," and "I don't know" (which we treated as a missing value). Echoing the terminology adopted by John Zaller (1992) in his work on how citizens' opinions are affected by information, we define our respondents' exposure to political views on social media as "two-sided" if they claim to encounter agreement and disagreement with the same frequency (whether it be "always," "often," or "sometimes"), "one-sided supportive" if they see consonant views more frequently than dissonant views, and "one-sided oppositional" if the reverse pattern applies.[1] Finally, we classify as "never exposed to political messages" those individuals who chose the option "never" for both questions.[2]

Figure 3.1 shows how many respondents fall into each of these categories. The figure also provides a comparison between social media and face-to-face conversations, for which we asked similar questions and recoded the answers based on the same logic presented for social media.

The upper bar in Figure 3.1 shows that, far from predominantly encountering information and opinions they agree with, most social media users report that they are exposed to either politically balanced content (as more than half of our respondents mainly see two-sided messages) or to politically skewed but mainly disagreeing content (as roughly 1 in 3 among our respondents are exposed to one-sided oppositional messages). Conversely, only a minority (15% in our sample) inhabit an echo chamber environment where they more often agree than disagree with the political messages they see, which we define as one-sided supportive.

It might be argued that this finding, which is strongly at odds with the echo chamber narrative, is an artifact of our use of self-reported measures. Self-segregation in politically homophilic bubbles could be perceived as normatively undesirable, leading respondents to overreport disagreement and underreport agreement. However, if that were the case, then we would observe similar

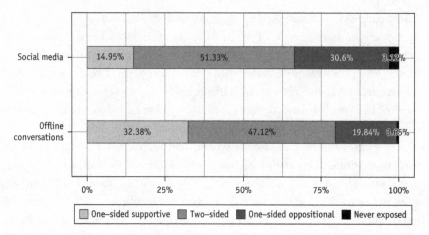

Figure 3.1. Encounters with Agreeing and Disagreeing Information and Opinions on Social Media and in Offline Conversations

Note: Percentages refer exclusively to social media users; only respondents who answered all questions (excluding "don't know" answers) are included (*N* = 13,038).

patterns in answers to questions regarding face-to-face conversations. Instead, as shown by the lower bar of Figure 3.1, less than 1 in 5 respondents reported participating in face-to-face discussions that mainly involved people they disagree with.

The findings reported in Figure 3.1 suggest that social media should not be blamed for increasing levels of political self-segregation in contemporary Western democracies, at least when compared with other forms of interpersonal communication (see also Fletcher & Nielsen, 2017, 2020). If echo chambers exist, they are much more easily found in face-to-face conversations than on social media (Barnidge, 2017).

In six countries (France, Germany, Italy, Spain, the United Kingdom, and the United States), we also asked questions measuring exposure to agreement and disagreement with political information encountered in two other important political communication environments: the mass media (newspapers and television) and mobile instant messaging services such as WhatsApp and Facebook Messenger. Following the procedure discussed earlier, we classified respondents' experiences of agreement and disagreement in these two additional realms. Figure 3.2 compares the four settings, considering exclusively respondents who are both social media and mobile instant messaging services (MIMS) users.

As Figure 3.2 shows (prevalent) exposure to disagreeing opinions (one-sided oppositional messages) is much more common on social media (28%) and, especially, mass media (38%) than in offline discussions (20%) and MIMS

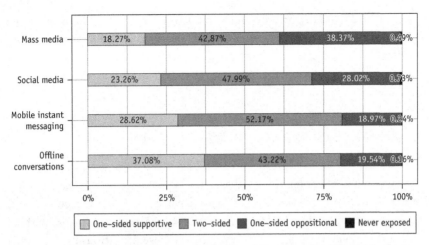

Figure 3.2. Encounters with Political Agreement and Disagreement in Multiple Settings
Note: Data include respondents who are users of both social media and mobile instant messaging
services and refer exclusively to Spain, the United Kingdom, the United States, France, Germany, and
Italy; only respondents who answered all questions (excluding "don't know" answers) are included
($N = 3,711$).

(19%). On the other hand, face-to-face conversation (37%) and MIMS (27%)
are most likely to expose people to one-sided supportive views.

When compared with social media and mass media, offline conversation and
MIMS are more likely to involve strong than weak ties. Because politics is considered a highly divisive topic, most people prefer avoiding political conversations in face-to-face public settings, especially when facing the possibility that
they may disagree with their discussants (Eliasoph, 1998; Wells et al., 2017).
Hence, most people talk about politics more frequently with family members
and close friends, whose political views are known and are more likely to be
similar to their own. By the same token, MIMS are mainly used for one-to-one
or small-group conversations with strong ties (O'Hara et al., 2014; Utz et al.,
2015; Vaterlaus et al., 2016; Kligler-Vilenchik, 2021).[3] Consequently, individuals who are less comfortable with, and thus tend to avoid, political disagreement on social media are more likely to feel at ease discussing politics on MIMS
(Valeriani & Vaccari, 2018). By contrast, despite the multiplication of outlets
offering citizens political content tailored around their ideological preferences
(Prior, 2007), television and newspapers still provide the greatest opportunities to encounter political disagreement (Mutz, 2001). Interestingly, our data
indicate that, in aggregate terms, social media fall in between face-to-face conversations and mass media in facilitating exposure to one-sided messages, both
supportive and oppositional.

This general pattern could be more or less true for different kinds of people and for users of different social media platforms. In the following pages, we investigate individual characteristics and dispositions that make users more likely to encounter supportive, oppositional, or two-sided political messages on social media.

ECHO CHAMBERS AND WHERE TO FIND THEM

Most studies that have addressed social media users' engagement with consonant and dissonant content have either treated all kinds of users as having similar experiences (e.g., Bakshy et al., 2015) or have focused almost exclusively on differences related to ideological preferences or discussed topics (e.g., Barberá et al., 2015; Colleoni et al., 2014).[4] We address these limitations by investigating how a large number of variables related to sociodemographic characteristics, political attitudes, social media use, and country of residence predict the likelihood that users encounter supportive, oppositional, or two-sided political messages on social media.

To flesh out these differences, we ran multinomial logistic regressions[5] where the dependent variable is exposure to supportive or oppositional political messages, relative to encountering a two-sided, politically balanced combination of messages (which we treat as the reference category).[6] Among sociodemographic characteristics, we consider gender, age, age squared, education, occupational condition, and income.[7] With respect to political attitudes, we have included interest in politics, attention to the latest political campaign, sense of political efficacy, trust in various institutions, political ideology, satisfaction for democracy, frequency of acquiring political information via multiple sources (newspapers, websites, radio, television, and face-to-face conversations), and frequency of political talk offline. Regarding social media use, we consider frequency of use of Facebook, Twitter, Instagram, and YouTube, as well as frequency of political talk on social media.[8] Finally, since we conducted the analyses on a pooled data set aggregating data from the nine countries we consider, we cluster our respondents according to their country of residence (setting the United States as the reference category) to control for national differences.[9]

Table 3.1 presents four multinomial logistic models predicting the likelihood of encountering one-sided supportive and one-sided oppositional messages relative to the likelihood of encountering two-sided messages. In each model, we have incrementally added sets of predictors related to sociodemographic characteristics (Model 1), political attitudes and behaviors (Model 2), social media use (Model 3), and country of residence (Model 4). This choice enables us to observe potentially interesting correlations that may wash away when all variables are included in the model. As shown by the decreasing values

Table 3.1. **Models Predicting the Likelihood of Encountering One-Sided Supportive and One-Sided Oppositional Messages on Social Media**

	Model 1 (Sociodemo.)		Model 2 (Political Attitudes)		Model 3 (SNS Usage)		Model 4 (Country)	
	Supp.	*Opp.*	*Supp.*	*Opp.*	*Supp.*	*Opp.*	*Supp.*	*Opp.*
Gender (Male)	0.178***	0.115**	-0.054	0.096*	-0.166**	0.085	-0.153*	0.066
Age	-0.059***	-0.045***	-0.041**	-0.056***	-0.036**	-0.053***	-0.035*	-0.060***
Age squared	0.001***	0.000***	0.000*	0.001***	0.000*	0.001***	0.000*	0.001***
Education	0.102**	-0.102***	-0.033	-0.101**	-0.047	-0.107**	-0.033	-0.075*
Working condition	0.083	0.001	0.019	0.024	-0.026	0.028	-0.040	0.042
Income	0.000	-0.017	-0.040**	-0.001	-0.027*	-0.001	-0.031*	0.004
Ideology (reference = Center)								
Left			0.398***	-0.189*	0.359**	-0.195*	0.424***	-0.186
Center-left			0.265**	-0.017	0.322***	-0.023	0.343***	-0.035
Center-right			0.171	0.060	0.175	0.058	0.186*	0.044
Right			0.319**	0.050	0.208	0.072	0.244*	0.070
Unaligned			-0.009	-0.006	0.016	0.000	0.031	-0.020

Continued

Table 3.1 Continued

	Model 1 (Sociodemo.)		Model 2 (Political Attitudes)		Model 3 (SNS Usage)		Model 4 (Country)	
	Supp.	Opp.	Supp.	Opp.	Supp.	Opp.	Supp.	Opp.
Attention to the campaign			0.180***	-0.054	0.142**	-0.048	0.082	0.010
Interest in politics			0.100*	-0.017	0.071	-0.025	0.053	-0.050
Efficacy index			0.032	0.010	0.030	0.012	0.034*	0.009
Institutional trust index			0.027**	-0.023**	0.024*	-0.023**	0.025*	-0.025**
Satisfaction with democracy			-0.023	-0.228***	-0.024	-0.228***	-0.045	-0.181***
Political information via …								
Newspapers			0.126***	0.037*	0.068**	0.041*	0.063**	0.047**
Websites			0.105***	0.016	0.041	0.022	0.045	0.008
Radio			-0.025	0.014	-0.032	0.014	-0.036	0.009
Television			-0.073**	0.004	-0.057*	0.002	-0.050	-0.005
Offline conversation			0.107**	-0.001	0.033	0.006	0.050	0.000
Political talk offline			0.092*	0.023	-0.046	0.042	-0.044	0.028
Political talk on SNSs					0.445***	-0.088**	0.457***	-0.085**

	Model 1 Supp	Model 1 Opp	Model 2 Supp	Model 2 Opp	Model 3 Supp	Model 3 Opp	Model 4 Supp	Model 4 Opp
Frequency of SNS use								
Facebook					0.016	−0.062***	0.027	−0.063***
Twitter					0.048*	−0.003	0.056**	0.009
YouTube					0.088***	0.029	0.088***	0.016
Instagram					−0.005	0.013	−0.023	0.016
Country (reference = U.S.)								
Greece							−0.365**	0.559***
Poland							−0.075	0.368***
Denmark							−0.462**	0.385***
Spain							−0.234*	0.242*
U.K.							−0.141	0.163
France							−0.261*	0.216*
Germany							0.299**	0.248*
Italy							0.002	0.477***
Intercept	−0.059	0.626***	−1.914***	1.091***	−2.093***	1.184***	−1.967***	0.984***
Log-likelihood (d.f.)	−17,176 (43,488)		−13,346 (35,433)		−11,566 (34,998)		−11,473 (34,974)	
N	14,504		11,835		11,695		11,695	

Note: SNS = social networking site. Entries are multinomial log-odds for One-sided supportive ("Supp.") and One-sided oppositional ("Opp.") experiences relative to Two-sided experiences. Standard errors and *p*-values are provided in Tables A8–A11 of the Online Appendix. d.f. = degrees of freedom.

*p ≤ .05.
**p ≤ .01.
***p ≤ .001.

of the log-likelihood, each time we better specify the model, its goodness of fit improves substantially.

Model 1 shows that, among sociodemographic variables, age and education have a significant relationship with the experience of supportive and oppositional messages on social media. Older people are more likely than youths to encounter two-sided political content on social media, and this probability increases more strongly as people get older (as indicated by the positive coefficient for age squared). The strength of this association is confirmed by the fact that coefficients for age and age squared are statistically significant in all the models in Table 3.1, which control for a variety of other factors. Conversely, while highly educated respondents are more likely to mainly encounter supportive messages, education depresses the probability of one-sided oppositional experiences, and such negative association persists even when all other blocks of variables are included. Model 1 in Table 3.1 also shows that women are more likely than men to be exposed to two-sided content on social media, while men encounter both mainly supportive and mainly oppositional mixes of political messages. However, once we include variables measuring digital behaviors (Models 3 and 4), the pattern is reversed, as male respondents are significantly less likely to inhabit social media echo chambers than women.

In Model 2 (Table 3.1) we add variables measuring political attitudes and behaviors. Attention for the campaign, interest in politics, trust in political institutions, frequency of political information via newspapers, websites and face-to-face conversation, and frequency of offline political discussion all increase the likelihood that citizens encounter one-sided supportive political messages on social media. Institutional trust and satisfaction for democracy reduce the odds of engaging with one-sided oppositional messages. Looking at political orientations, respondents with more extreme positions have higher probabilities of being exposed to mainly supportive political messages, and left-wing respondents are less likely to encounter oppositional content. In sum, these results suggest that political junkies—i.e., those who are more interested and informed, and who frequently talk about politics—and citizens who are more ideologically extreme are much more likely to encounter agreement on social media than their less engaged fellow citizens. The more politically involved people are, the more likely they are to be part of political echo chambers on social media.[10]

Different habits in social media usage also have strong relationships with the experience of political agreement and disagreement. As can be observed in Model 3 of Table 3.1, once we introduce predictors related to social media use, some coefficients related to political attitudes, such as interest in politics and attention to the campaign, become weaker and often not significant. The frequency of political talk on social media significantly increases the likelihood of being exposed to one-sided supportive messages while it decreases the probability of encountering one-sided oppositional content. The more people discuss politics on social media, the more occasions and incentives they have to carve their networks and experiences according to their political proclivities. Moreover, by actively engaging with political content and expressing their views, political talkers on social media feed algorithms with more information on their orientations, which might result in a higher probability of being exposed to politically congruent content (Bakshy et al., 2015).

These findings help us understand why studies measuring levels of political homophily on social media based on digital traces of active behaviors such as sharing, liking, or commenting might overestimate levels of ideological segregation in the online population. Those "power users" who avidly discuss politics on social media are logically among those who contribute the most to the flow of political information online, which researchers employing digital trace data rely on. However, power users are unrepresentative of the broader user base of a platform, particularly those who may produce little or no content but consume much of it (Bright et al., 2020). While studies of online political conversations and interactions help understand how people talk about politics online, our approach enables us to capture a broader realm of users and behaviors, and to compare the experiences of those users who are more likely to leave large data trails of political behavior with those who are less likely to heavily feature in data sets representing active online behaviors. A study by Andrew Guess (2020) based on behavioral data capturing the media diets of samples of U.S. citizens confirms that those who inhabit digital echo chambers represent a highly active, vocal, and visible minority of engaged partisans. As Guess (2020: 28) points out, while the experience of the majority of citizens is characterized by ideologically moderate media diets, with significant overlaps in news consumption across the ideological spectrum, the small group of people that exclusively gets ideologically consonant news is more likely to discuss politics.

To provide a clearer representation of the relationship between frequency of political conversation on social media and users' encounters with similar and different political views, we construct four respondents who have values equal to the mean (for numeric variables), median (for ordinal variables), or mode (for categorical variables) for all the variables in our models. The only difference between these four imaginary average respondents is that they report different frequencies of political talk on SNSs. Based on the coefficients in Model 4 of Table 3.1 (which includes the full set of predictors), we estimate the likelihood that each respondent is exposed to mainly supportive, mainly oppositional, or two-sided political messages on social media. For the sake of completeness, we have also included effect sizes for respondents who reported to never encounter agreeing and disagreeing political views on social media (whom we grouped together with those who do not use these platforms).

As can be seen in Figure 3.3, the likelihood of encountering one-sided supportive political messages on social media increases in lockstep with frequency of political talk on these platforms. While an average respondent who never discusses politics on SNSs has a 10.6% probability of mainly encountering politically agreeable content, the same probability triples to 34% for a similar respondent who talks about politics on social media on a daily basis. Conversely, frequency of political conversation on social media reduces the likelihood of being exposed to adversarial messages, as the probability of experiencing one-sided oppositional content falls from 26.1% for someone who never discusses politics on social media to 16.5% for someone who does that every day. Finally, while an average respondent who does not engage in political conversation on social media has a 60.8% probability of being equally exposed to agreeing and disagreeing messages, this probability declines to 49.5% if the same kind of user discusses politics daily on these platforms.

Model 3 in Table 3.1 also reveals that platforms matter when it comes to the experience of agreement and disagreement. Frequent use of Twitter and YouTube is positively associated with the probability of encountering one-sided supportive messages. Conversely, habitual users of Facebook are less likely to be exposed to one-sided oppositional content. These findings, which persist after we include country coefficients in Model 4, can be linked to the different affordances of these platforms and to how users decide to take advantage of them. While Facebook tends to function as a "generalist" environment where

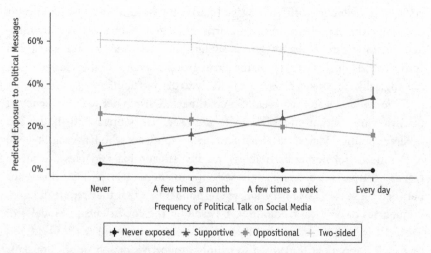

Figure 3.3. Exposure to Agreeing and Disagreeing Political Messages as a Function of Political Talk on Social Media

Note: The values are simulated quantities of interest based on Model 4 in Table 3.1 for respondents with values equal to the sample mean, median, or mode (depending on the nature of the variables) for all variables apart from frequency of political talk on social media. Vertical lines show 95% confidence intervals.

users connect with their broader social networks, Twitter users are more likely to carefully craft their networks based on specific interests and attitudes rather than preexisting social relations (Huberman et al., 2008; Hughes et al., 2012; boyd, 2014). YouTube is often employed as a search engine for video content (Rieder et al., 2018), a use that is much more goal oriented than those of other social media, along with feeding relevant information to the platform's algorithm regarding users' political preferences. Recent research also shows that most users encounter political YouTube videos because they select a specific channel within the platform or because they found the video on an external website, which again suggests that YouTube usage is highly intentional (Hosseinmardi et al., 2020; see also Munger & Phillips, 2020). These patterns may explain why we found that frequent Facebook users have a lower probability of experiencing oppositional than two-sided political content, while heavy Twitter and YouTube users are more likely to encounter one-sided supportive messages. However, the small magnitude of these relationships suggests that we should not overestimate the role of specific platforms in facilitating encounters with agreeing and disagreeing political information.

Finally, the likelihood that social media users inhabit political echo chambers or their opposite, which we previously called "contrarian clubs" (Vaccari et al., 2016), varies across national settings. Model 4 in Table 3.1 shows that U.S. citizens (the reference category) are less likely to experience oppositional political messages on social media than respondents from all other countries in our sample, and the relevant coefficients are significant in all cases apart from Britain. American respondents are also significantly more likely to experience one-sided supportive content on social media than Greek, Danish, Spanish, and French citizens, while only Germans have a stronger probability than U.S. respondents of being predominantly exposed to messages they agree with. If we construct a hypothetical average respondent, the probability that she engages with supportive content on social media, as predicted by Model 4 in Table 3.1, is 15.9% for a U.S. resident and lower than that in all other countries apart from Germany (19.1%), and as low as 9.8% in Greece and 9.6% in Denmark. Conversely, U.S. respondents are the least likely to encounter oppositional content on social media, with predicted probabilities of 23.8%, compared with 36.9% in Greece and 33.6% in Italy. Still, even among American respondents, and notwithstanding all the concerns among U.S. scholars for polarization (Finkel et al., 2020) and the role of social media in exacerbating it (Tucker et al., 2018), the likelihood that an average American respondent is enveloped in an echo chamber is substantially lower (15.9%) than the probability that she is part of a contrarian club (23.8%).

These results suggest that the United States cannot be taken as a typical case when it comes to social media users' experiences with supportive and adversarial views. A similar indication comes from a study by Pablo Barberá (2014), who estimated levels of ideological homogeneity within networks of Twitter users and found greater homophily in the United States than in Germany and Spain. In the same vein, Fletcher and colleagues (2020) showed that the United States features the highest levels of news audience polarization among twelve diverse Western democracies across the globe. The authors cautioned against treating the United States "as a microcosm of the rest of the world" (Fletcher et al., 2020: 171). This is a compelling exhibit in support of the relevance of comparative research. General theories on and assumptions about the political implications of social media that are grounded exclusively on U.S. data may lead scholars to confound national specificities with universal patterns.

To summarize, echo chambers, which we have operationalized as predominantly exposing social media users to one-sided supportive content, are much rarer than is often assumed—even in the United States, where they are relatively more common compared with other Western democracies—and contingent on specific political attitudes, patterns of social media use, and national characteristics.

What if the Filter Bubble Had a Hole?

Several authors (e.g., Sunstein, 2002; Prior, 2007; Beniger, 2009) have contended that digital technologies, by offering their users vast opportunities to choose what they see and who they connect with, have enabled citizens to craft tailor-made online experiences reflecting their interests, passions, and proclivities while avoiding unwanted content. This process started well before the advent of the Internet, with the transformation of television production and consumption as a result of the diffusion of cable and satellite channels (Iyengar & Hahn, 2009; Hollander, 2008). However, the World Wide Web made it much easier for citizens to encounter the kinds of content they prefer. As a result of this transformation, some authors (e.g., Prior, 2005, 2007) have argued that increased choice would widen the differences in media diets between those who are highly interested in politics and those who dislike it or simply prefer nonpolitical content.

During the pre-social-media era of the Web, most scholars who emphasized the selective nature of the Internet generally concluded that gaps between information "haves" and "have nots" would increase (Norris, 2003). These authors argued that, while the information-rich can get even better informed thanks to the Internet, the politically uninterested can easily avoid the news (Bimber & Davis, 2003; Brundidge & Rice, 2009). In low-choice media environments— such as those dominated by newspapers or broadcast radio and television—most citizens were likely to be exposed to some political news "by default," as a result of the general fruition of those media (Neuman et al., 1992). By contrast, in the digital high-choice environment, citizens were presumed to consume politics mainly "by choice" (Prior, 2007; Hollander, 2008). According to this line of scholarship, the increasing diffusion of the Internet would amplify the differences between the avid "news seekers" and the uninterested "news avoiders" (Ksiazek et al., 2010). Importantly, these differences are rooted in individuals' preferences, not in their ability to access different types of content, and so would not be evened out by increased adoption of digital media in the population.

However, during the same period, other studies (e.g., Tewksbury et al., 2001) showed that most users experienced the (pre-social-media) Internet mainly through generalist portals where political information was integrated with nonpolitical news. Although the Internet presented users with a higher spectrum of consumption choices, the way content was offered to them also facilitated unintended exposure to politics.

With the emergence of social media, the debate around selectivity and its consequences has further intensified. In his *Republic* trilogy (Sunstein, 2009, 2015, 2017), Cass Sunstein argued that social media facilitate citizens' self-segregation in cocoons where counter-attitudinal information is sealed off. According to Sunstein, this happens both as a result of algorithms exposing people to content and sources they have previously shown to enjoy, and as a consequence of practices such as the use of hashtags, which channel people toward their interests and inclinations. Similarly, Eli Pariser (2011) argued that search engines and social media are hiding from us most if not all of the content that falls outside of our interests. As we have contended in the chapter's opening, Pariser's metaphor of the online "filter bubble" broadly refers to reduced exposure to information that is not in line with our predispositions: if we are not interested in politics, we will not be shown political news. This is why we take Pariser's term as our reference point in investigating patterns of citizens' incidental exposure to politics on social media—irrespective of the supportive or adversarial nature of such information.

In spite of the theoretical claims and assumptions we have just summarized, several empirical studies have shown that incidental exposure to news and political information, far from being an exceptional event, is a common experience for many social media users (Valeriani & Vaccari, 2016; Bode, 2016; Karnowski et al., 2017; Fletcher & Nielsen, 2018; Boczkowski et al., 2018). While these studies are not unanimous in describing the *effects* of incidental exposure to politics on social media, all reject the idea that users of digital platforms encounter politics *exclusively or mainly by choice*. To the contrary, most research suggests that social media are, to a substantial degree, the realm of *politics by chance* (Chadwick, 2012).

While selectivity is an important affordance of the Internet and social media, it is not the sole "physical law" governing the Web. Instead, there is evidence that selective and incidental exposure coexist on social media (Weeks et al., 2017). On social media, users deliberately craft their networks by establishing connections with offline strong and weak ties, with previously unknown ordinary people, and with public figures, groups, and organizations (boyd & Ellison, 2007; Marwick & boyd, 2011). This enables users to select the primary sources of their information diets on these platforms. Selectivity of *sources* and *networks*, however, does not necessarily mean actual selection of *content*. In fact, many, possibly most, of the nodes in our digital networks are ordinary users with whom we connect for multiple reasons related to our offline and online lives—and many of these reasons have little to do with politics. What we see on our social media timelines is thus the result of the multiple actions of all these users, which we cannot fully predict or control (Anspach, 2017).

The content social media users get exposed to results from the curation activities of different types of actors, which include individual users, their social contacts, and algorithms, but also journalists and "strategic communicators" such as parties and candidates (Thorson & Wells, 2015). In particular, social media offer targeting opportunities to actors—including news organizations, interest groups, parties, and candidates—aiming to reach users via sponsored content and other forms of promotion. This means that even social media users who do not express a specific interest for political information could be exposed to politics because someone has paid to reach them with advertised content related to news and politics. For instance, in the 2016 U.S. presidential election (Chadwick, 2017b, Chapter 10), campaigns took advantage of so-called Facebook "dark posts," i.e., content that does not appear on any public page while being showed exclusively as advertisements to specific target audiences. Such political messages could not be deliberately searched by users and were thus encountered exclusively by accident by those who were targeted by campaign advertisers. Even though Facebook subsequently eliminated this feature and promised to enable every user to search for and view any sponsored content by parties and candidates, it is plausible that most social media users—especially those who are not interested in politics—will not take advantage of these opportunities, and that exposure to political information conveyed by social media advertisements will remain incidental for many users.

It could be argued that the algorithms that curate social media users' feeds are precisely focused on fine-tuning the kinds of content users see based on their preferences (Turow, 2012), and, in spite of the heterogeneity of sources that might characterize users' networks, algorithms will prevent them from encountering information they are not interested in (Kümpel, 2020). In principle, social media platforms may arrange their algorithms so that, no matter what others share, a user who is defined as not interested in public affairs will see no news whatsoever. However, as Möller and colleagues (2018) have demonstrated, algorithms based on users' previous history do not necessarily decrease the diversity of news content users see. Moreover, the idea that algorithms necessarily create highly personalized information diets for each user may be exaggerated. For instance, Bechmann and Nielbo (2018) analyzed the newsfeeds of a representative sample of Danish Facebook users and found that a large majority saw similar news items (see also Nechushtai & Lewis, 2019).[11] Social media's choice affordances and profiling apparatuses are not so deterministic and pervasive that they completely block out political news for those who do not regularly seek it out or consume it. Thus, there might be holes in the filter bubbles supposedly enveloping social media users, and some political and news content may be able to pass through by accident. In the next sections, we investigate how big these holes are for different types of individuals across Western democracies.

POLITICS BY CHANCE ON SOCIAL MEDIA

To quantify the extent to which selectivity and serendipity shape social media users' exposure to political information, we consider and quantify unsearched encounters with political news on these platforms. We aim to understand the degree to which social media function as a context where information is physiologically in the air (Hermida, 2010). Hence, we ask whether social media's affordances and dynamics promoting accidental encounters with politics can counterbalance features enhancing users' control and fostering political segmentation of the audience.

To understand these phenomena, we asked our respondents[12] to report the frequency with which they come across news and information on current events, public affairs, or politics when they may have been going on social media for a purpose other than to get the news. As shown in the lower bar in Figure 3.4, almost one in two respondents "frequently" or "always" encounters unsearched political news on social media, while only 14% report that they "never" have such an experience.

Our data thus confirm that the extent to which social media enable us to selectively establish our digital networks, as well as the role of algorithms in enhancing visibility of the content that we seem to like the most, still allow substantial opportunities for unplanned encounters with political news. A first explanation for this finding is that most users do not employ social media to exclusively gratify a single appetite, political or otherwise. To the contrary, they employ these platforms, and especially the most popular ones, for multiple reasons linked to a variety of interests, habits, and relationships. The social media experience described by our respondents thus has similarities with the pre-social-media Web as characterized by Tewskbury et al. (2001): an environment where current affairs news

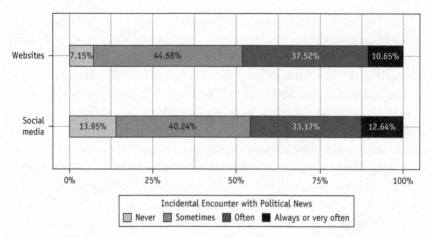

Figure 3.4. Incidental Exposure to Political News on Social Media and Websites
Note: To make the results more comparable, only respondents who answered both questions (excluding "don't know") are included (*N* = 15,308).

is sprinkled together with other types of content, so that users can get exposed to them irrespective of their contingent will. According to our data (see upper bar in Figure 3.4), patterns of incidental encounters with politics on social media and on websites and portals are actually quite similar. However, the small minority of respondents who report never getting incidentally exposed to politics on social media is double (14%) that for browsing websites (7%). Such a difference might indicate that people who use social media for very specific—and nonpolitical— reasons can effectively leverage the selective affordances of these platforms to iso- late themselves from politics more tightly than they can when they surf websites. However, as Figure 3.4 shows, users who never encounter news accidentally rep- resent a small minority (about 1 in 7) among social media users. Conversely, for about half of our respondents, politics appears to be a "pop-up" experience that is often unplanned when they log into digital platforms.

In conclusion, our descriptive findings confirm that the kinds of filter bubbles through which social media users can seal themselves off political content are softer than many have argued. Our next goal is to understand for what types of citizens these bubbles are more tightly sealed or porous.

DO ONLY THE INFORMATION-RICH GET (INCIDENTALLY) RICHER?

Since the emergence of the Internet, scholars have considered its potential to widen or bridge inequalities in political information and engagement across dif- ferent groups of citizens. The core idea guiding these debates was that, behind a "first-level" digital divide rooted in different opportunities to access the Internet

(Compaine, 2001; Norris, 2001), there is also a "second-level" divide connected to differences in specific usages of the Web, and thus to the potential political gains different types of users can make as a result of their online activity (Hargittai, 2002; Min, 2010).

Key to this issue is whether and how the Internet can impact the "democratic divide" between those who care, are informed about, and engage with politics, and those who by and large do not (Norris, 2001). Some authors argued that the Internet was creating a "new information environment" (Delli Carpini, 2000) whose key features—e.g., interactivity, flexibility, ubiquity—make political information easier to encounter and more appealing for less attentive citizens like, for example, the youth. Skeptic voices, however, countered with compelling evidence. Various scholars contended that the Internet did not have any strong transformative potential on existing balances of political power (Margolis & Resnick, 2000). To the contrary, according to this perspective the Web was not only reproducing, but sometimes even reinforcing, political inequalities. For example, in their study of the U.S. 2000 presidential campaign, Bimber and Davis (2003) found that citizens who more frequently got political information through newspapers and television were also more likely to get exposed to political content on the Internet. As a result, the more informed (usually the most affluent, literate, and politically engaged) were becoming even better informed while the less informed did not substantially benefit from the Internet (see Brundidge & Rice, 2009). The theoretical basis of such claims was mainly that, since the Internet offered opportunities for a highly diverse spectrum of uses, individuals selected content that really mattered to them to fulfill specific interests and needs (Katz & Rice, 2002; Kaye & Johnson, 2002). When those interests and needs did not include politics, the Internet enabled users to avoid it and gave them ample opportunities to spend their time and focus their attention on other domains of life.

More recent studies confirm this idea (Min, 2010). Those who *deliberately* engage with political content on social media are more likely to be male, better educated, highly interested in politics, and heavily engaged in offline political talk and action (e.g., Vaccari et al., 2013). However, the same pattern may not necessarily apply to citizens who *accidentally* encounter politics on social media. As pointed out by Fletcher and Nielsen (2018: 2454), politically disengaged users are less likely to curate their social media experiences based on political criteria, and they may thus leave some doors open to incidental encounters with political content on social media. Indeed, an analysis of survey data from thirty-six countries showed that "news-limiting curation" behaviors, such as deleting or blocking a user or organization because of the news they had shared, or changing one's settings on a digital platform to see less news from a user or organization, are substantially more common among those who are more engaged with the news and more politically extreme (Merten, 2020).

To estimate which factors predict individuals' likelihood of accidentally encountering political news on social media, we recoded the ordinal variable whose distribution we have commented on and discussed in the previous paragraph into a dichotomous one.[13] The new variable clusters together respondents who answered that they "never" or "rarely" stumble into unsearched political content on social media (recoded as 0) and combines those who report to "frequently" or "always" have such experience (recoded as 1). We thus employed logistic regression and, following the same approach adopted to explain experiences with agreement and disagreement on social media, we ran four different models by incrementally adding sets of variables related to sociodemographic characteristics, political attitudes and behaviors, use of different social media platforms, and country of residence (Table 3.2). As can be inferred from the Nagelkerke R^2 coefficients at the bottom of the table, the models' goodness of fit improves substantially when we add new variable blocks, and this is particularly the case in the move from Model 1 (which only predicts about 7% of the total variance of the dependent variable) to Model 2 (which predicts about 44%). When we add variables measuring social media usage, in Model 3, the model's predictive power further jumps beyond 51%. Adding country coefficients, by contrast, increases the model's goodness of fit only marginally, thus suggesting that accidental exposure to news on social media does not vary substantially across countries once all the other variables in the model are controlled for.

Model 1 in Table 3.2 shows that the sociodemographic characteristics of respondents who are more exposed to unsearched political information on social media do not resemble those typically associated with textbook political junkies, usually characterized by higher socioeconomic status (Verba et al., 1995). Female, younger, unemployed, and less affluent respondents are significantly more likely to frequently encounter politics on social media by accident. While the explanatory power of Model 1 is low as shown by the Nagelkerke R^2 coefficient at the bottom of the table, many of these associations hold even after all other predictors are included in Models 2–4. Similarly, attitudes usually associated with an active orientation toward public affairs—such as interest in politics and attention to the campaign—do not significantly predict (Model 2 in Table 3.2) incidental exposure, while sense of efficacy and satisfaction for democracy are negatively and significantly associated with this outcome across all models. The only political attitude that stands out is trust in political institutions, which is positively and significantly associated with accidental exposure in Model 2. However, the relationship is no longer significant when measures of activity on social media are controlled for (Model 3). Overall, citizens who are more likely to incidentally encounter political information on social media do not fit with the profile of highly engaged political "usual suspects." The idea that incidental exposure to political messages on social media may reduce historically

Table 3.2. **Models Predicting Accidental Exposure to Political News on Social Media**

	Model 1 (Sociodemo.)	Model 2 (Political Attitudes)	Model 3 (SNS Usage)	Model 4 (Country)
Gender (Male)	−0.089**	−0.183***	−0.181***	−0.207***
Age	−0.020**	−0.028**	−0.021*	−0.028**
Age squared	0.000	0.000	0.000	0.000
Education	0.040	−0.041	−0.010	−0.026
Working condition	−0.080*	−0.103*	−0.115*	−0.096
Income	−0.022**	−0.025**	−0.017	−0.008
Ideology (reference = Center)				
Left		0.143	0.055	0.038
Center-left		−0.023	−0.033	−0.038
Center-right		−0.025	−0.059	−0.066
Right		0.144	0.032	0.053
Unaligned		−0.003	−0.014	−0.011
Attention to the campaign		−0.003	−0.038	0.038
Interest in politics		−0.013	0.017	0.006
Efficacy index		−0.025*	−0.024*	−0.037**
Institutional trust index		0.024***	0.011	0.007
Satisfaction with democracy		−0.160***	−0.158***	−0.112***
Political information via ...				
Newspapers		−0.070***	−0.110***	−0.097***
Websites		0.204***	0.133***	0.107***
Radio		−0.003	0.000	0.011
Television		−0.074***	−0.067***	−0.063***
Offline conversation		0.144***	0.094***	0.081***
Political talk offline		0.241***	0.179***	0.153***
Political talk on SNSs			0.253***	0.252***
Frequency of SNS use				
Facebook			0.288***	0.279***
Twitter			0.016	0.024

Continued

Table 3.2 Continued

	Model 1 (Sociodemo.)	Model 2 (Political Attitudes)	Model 3 (SNS Usage)	Model 4 (Country)
YouTube			0.105***	0.098***
Instagram			0.004	0.009
Country (reference = U.S.)				
Greece				0.454***
Poland				−0.152
Denmark				0.175
Spain				0.029
U.K.				−0.328***
France				−0.482***
Germany				−0.321***
Italy				−0.016
Intercept	1.103***	0.299	−1.203***	−0.977***
AIC	20,670	15,943	14,696	14,563
Nagelkerke R^2	0.069	0.439	0.516	0.525
N	15,587	12,512	12,335	12,335

Note: SNS = Social networking site. Entries are log-odds. Standard errors and p-values for coefficients are provided in Tables A12–A15 of the Online Appendix. AIC = Akaike information criterion.
  *$p \leq .05$.
  **$p \leq .01$.
  ***$p \leq .001$.

rooted information gaps is also supported by the negative and significant coefficients for information acquired via legacy media (newspapers and television). Conversely, the coefficient for frequency of information via websites is positive and significant. While we cannot disentangle the causal dynamics behind this association, it is possible that accidental exposure to news on social media may lead users to follow links to the websites of news organizations.

The coefficients related to different forms of political talk, however, complicate this picture. Models 2 and 3 in Table 3.2 reveal positive and significant associations between frequent incidental exposure to politics on social media and frequency of political conversation both offline and on social media. Figure 3.5 shows the probabilities of frequent incidental exposure to politics on social media for four hypothetical respondents with typical values (mean,

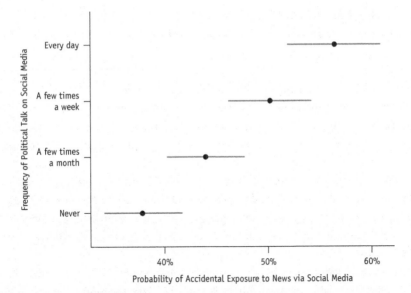

Figure 3.5. Frequent Incidental Exposure to Political News as a Function of Political Talk on Social Media

Note: The values are simulated quantities of interest based on Model 4 in Table 3.2 for respondents with values equal to the sample mean, median, or mode (depending on the nature of the variables) for all variables apart from frequency of political discussion on social media. Horizontal lines show 95% confidence intervals.

median, or mode, depending on the variable) for all the variables included in Model 4 of Table 3.2 apart from frequency of political discussion on social media. The likelihood that an average respondent who discusses politics on social media just a few times a month frequently stumbles into political news is 43.9%, while the same probability jumps to 56.5% for a similarly average respondent who engages in political discussion every day.

Of course, if someone is willing to talk about politics, whether offline or online, that person cannot be construed as being completely detached from public affairs. At the same time, at least on social media, political discussions can occur informally and spontaneously rather than because a user has planned or particularly desires to engage in them. The association between political talk on social media and accidental exposure suggests that these discussions might lead users to learn information about politics that they had not intended to acquire, thus highlighting a potentially valuable outcome of online political talk (Gil de Zúñiga et al., 2014; Shah, 2016).

Consistent with our findings on agreement and disagreement, platforms matter for accidental exposure, too. As shown by Model 3 (Table 3.2), frequency of use of Facebook and YouTube is positively associated with inadvertent exposure to politics, while frequency of use of Twitter and Instagram is not. While on Facebook individuals tend to establish connections with other users on the basis of existing relationships of multiple natures, Twitter networks are more frequently based on specific interests. As a result, Facebook users are likely be connected with some compulsive posters of political information with whom they have personal relationships unrelated to politics. Conversely, for a Twitter user it is less common to follow an avid political tweeter if getting political content is not among the main reasons for her use of the platform. The positive association between frequent YouTube use and accidental exposure to political content can also be understood based on the common use of this platform as a search engine for visual content. For most YouTube users, these searches have less to do with politics than with sports, music, DIY, or even their kids' cartoon preferences. However, the home page and the suggestion column of the average YouTube user usually features a potpourri of different subjects that could also include political matters, especially if politics has been previously consumed. Hence, stumbling onto political videos is possible even for a YouTube user who rarely consumes politics on the platform. Accordingly, Barnidge (2020: 13) found that incidental exposure to news on social media is more common on social networking sites such as Facebook, followed by video-sharing platforms like YouTube. He also found that users report lower frequency of unsearched encounters with news on microblogging sites such as Twitter and photo-sharing apps like Instagram.

To illustrate our findings on platform use, Figure 3.6 plots the predicted probability of frequent exposure to unsearched political content for average respondents in our sample with different frequencies of Facebook and YouTube use. The figure shows that the gap between occasional and habitual users is much larger on the former than the latter platform. While moving from a sporadic to a massive use of Facebook gives our average respondent a large boost (from 24.5% to 55.9%) in the probability of accidentally encountering political news, the same difference in the frequency of YouTube use results in a more limited, albeit still statistically significant, increase (from 40.6% to 52.5%).

Finally, Model 4 in Table 3.2 shows that accidental encounters with political messages on social media are unevenly widespread in the different countries we surveyed. As was the case for exposure to one-sided supportive messages, U.S. social media users are more likely to frequently encounter unsearched political content than users in most of the other countries we studied. The regression coefficient comparing each country to the United States is negative and significant for the United Kingdom, France, and Germany, and negative but not significant for Poland and Italy.

However, Greece stands out as the country where accidental exposure is the most frequent. If we construct a respondent who has values equal to the mean, median, or mode for all variables apart from country of residence, the predicted probability of accidentally encountering political news on social media,

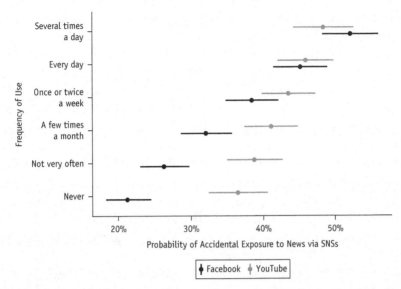

Figure 3.6. Accidental Exposure to Political News on Social Media as a Function of Frequency of Facebook and YouTube Use

Note: SNS = social networking site. The values are simulated quantities of interest based on Model 4 in Table 3.2 for respondents with values equal to the sample mean, median, or mode (depending on the nature of the variables) for all variables apart from frequency of Facebook and YouTube use. Horizontal lines show 95% confidence intervals.

derived from Model 4 in Table 3.2, is 54.5% for Greek respondents, 43.2% for U.S. respondents, and as low as 32% for French respondents. While we can only speculate about the underlying causes of these difference, the particular context in which we collected our data in Greece offers some clues. The Greek general elections of September 2015, after which we conducted our survey, were held amid exceptional instability and apprehension. Indeed, as described by Tsatsanis and Teperoglu (2016: 427), the first nine months of 2015 were "anything but ordinary, even by the standard of the Greek 2010s." On January 25, a first parliamentary election resulted in the formation of an unprecedented coalition government combining the radical-left party SYRIZA (Greek abbreviation for "Coalition of the Radical Left") with the right-wing populist ANEL (abbreviation for "Independent Greeks"). The newborn government was immediately absorbed in cliffhanger negotiations with international financial creditors, whose outcome was then placed on the ballot in a national referendum, held on July 5. Although a large majority voted against the proposal, an alternative plan that accepted most of the creditors' demands was eventually ratified by the Greek parliament. The process was accompanied by massive street demonstrations and a split within SYRIZA, many of whose representatives voted against the new plan in Parliament. As a result of this escalation, the SYRIZA-ANEL coalition lost a parliamentary motion of no confidence and new general elections were called. Despite being shorter and less intense than the campaigns preceding the January elections and the referendum (Tsatsanis & Teperoglu, 2016), the September campaign came right after a prolonged period of political turmoil, with political matters occupying the interests and everyday conversations of most Greek citizens, understandably worried for their uncertain future. This unusual political effervescence may contribute to explaining why our Greek respondents were the most likely, across the nine countries we studied, to accidentally encounter news on social media.

In this section, we have shown that accidental exposure to political news on social media is quite widespread in Western democracies, and it is experienced by users whose demographic profile and political attitudes do not closely resemble those of the kinds of citizens who are typically more involved in politics. However, these findings do not necessarily imply that accidental exposure should automatically increase citizens' political knowledge. While Fletcher and Nielsen (2018) found that those who are incidentally exposed to news on social media display richer media diets, other studies (e.g., Bode, 2016b; Shehata & Strömbäck, 2021; Feezell & Ortiz, 2019) demonstrate that exposure to political information on social media (whether incidental or not) has a very limited effect on political knowledge compared with news consumption via traditional media. At the same time, incidental encounters with political information may benefit political participation even without substantially contributing to political knowledge, especially if such knowledge is measured with civic textbook questions that may not necessarily be relevant to political action.

I Am (Posting) Here to Recruit You

This chapter started with a discussion of some Scottish social media users' complaints that their profiles had been hijacked by referendum campaign messages. This anecdote suggests that social media are a fertile environment for electoral mobilization, as users can be targeted by messages asking them to vote for a specific candidate, party, or cause. On social media, a diverse plethora of subjects—parties, candidates, party members, and activists—can be involved in the production and circulation of messages aimed at influencing other users' political choices. Such efforts may not necessarily be coordinated, but they can reinforce each other, potentially generating pervasive cascades.

For political actors, social media represent an important opportunity to reduce the distribution costs of mobilization messages, following a trend that started with email campaigning (Nickerson, 2007; Krueger, 2006). Both organic activity and paid targeted messages on social media are less expensive in economic and organizational terms than door-to-door, street, telephone, and postal canvassing. Moreover, politicians and parties can take advantage of built-in pro-filing tools that digital platforms provide for advertisers (Kreiss & McGregor, 2019). In some cases, social media companies have also offered direct assistance to campaigns on how best to employ their technologies to reach voters (Kreiss & McGregor, 2018). On top of this, parties and politicians can ask their supporters to become social media campaigners, delivering messages to users that politi-cal actors cannot reach directly. Since social media users who follow parties and candidates tend to be vocal and influential in their online (Karlsen, 2015) and offline (Vaccari et al., 2013) communities, social media can help political actors create and maintain a two-step flow process of digital mobilization, whereby activists leverage their online networks to reach voters who are less involved in politics (Vissers, 2009).

This could be especially true for newborn political organizations that lack or deliberately neglect building a traditional organization on the ground, and that elect the Internet as their favorite campaigning battlefield (Lilleker & Jackson, 2013). For these "cyber-parties" (Margetts, 2006), social media represent one of the most important environments for establishing and maintaining their bonds with supporters and asking their help for campaigning activities. On the demand side, users who do not feel a strong and permanent bond with a party or are not inclined to interact with political organizations may find it easier to use social media to join the campaign on their own terms (Gibson, 2015; Vaccari & Valeriani, 2016). In our sample, 19% of social media users reported that they tried to influence someone else's voting choices by sending messages on social media, and two-thirds of those users are not members of any political party.

In the final sections of this chapter, we investigate how pervasive electoral mobilization is on social media. We also uncover the characteristics of social media users who are more likely to receive invitations to vote for a specific candidate or party on these platforms. As the data show that large numbers of social media users are targeted by electoral mobilization and that the probability of seeing these messages is not strongly correlated with their lev-els of political involvement, our vision of filter bubbles as highly permeable is broadly confirmed. If social media users who do not want to be bothered by campaigners could effectively seal themselves off from their persuasion attempts, we should observe much lower levels of reported exposure to elec-toral mobilization.

THE SCOPE OF ELECTORAL MOBILIZATION ON SOCIAL MEDIA

A robust line of research has addressed electoral mobilization on the ground and its effects on turnout and participation writ large (e.g., Huckfeldt & Sprague,

1992; McClurg, 2004; Nickerson, 2007, 2008). More recent studies have addressed online mobilization, especially focusing on get-out-the-vote messages (Bond et al., 2012; Aldrich et al., 2016). Though based on a variety of different research designs employing both experimental and survey data, all these studies tend to distinguish between messages delivered by political and institutional actors and those channeled by common citizens. Rosenstone and Hansen (1993) classify the former as "direct" and the latter as "indirect" mobilization. Most authors (e.g., Nickerson, 2008; Bond et al., 2012) highlight that interpersonal influence, rooted in existing social relationships, plays an important role in making indirect mobilization effective.

Although direct and indirect mobilization might have different effects in theory, this distinction becomes more blurred on social media. As we have contended, these platforms potentially enable a variety of subjects and organizations to engineer mobilization efforts or, more broadly, to produce and circulate campaign content. In such environments, hybrid assemblages of actors and messages combining direct and indirect mobilization frequently emerge (Penney, 2017). Users can relay messages originally created by institutional actors, adding to them a specific call to action targeting their own digital network or a specific subgroup thereof; they can simply tag some of their contacts while circulating mobilization messages produced by a candidate; and they can craft original messages by reshaping and remixing digital campaign material initially created by party actors. These messages could also convey social cues, e.g., the information that someone in the target's network has previously interacted with the content or with its sender. As discussed in Chapter 1, these cues can make an important contribution to the effects of social media messages. All these possibilities for hybrid forms of electioneering confirm how problematic it is to maintain a clearcut distinction between direct and indirect mobilization on social media, as relevant and helpful as this classification still is when studying mobilization on the ground (Vaccari, 2017).[14] Hence, to measure exposure to mobilization messages on social media we asked our respondents whether, during the six months preceding the interview, they had received messages on social media inviting them to vote for a party or candidate, without distinguishing between direct and indirect mobilization. Respondents could only answer "Yes," "No," or "I don't know" to this question. Those who answered "I don't know" were excluded from the analysis.[15]

Our data indicate that the experience of online mobilization is quite common, as roughly 1 in 3 (32.2%) social media users in our sample report seeing electoral mobilization messages aiming to influence their vote. In the next sections, we identify the factors that predict this experience.

MOBILIZING THE MOBILIZED?

In a well-known article from the pre-social-media era, Pippa Norris (2003) proposed the incisive metaphor of "preaching to the converted" to describe how party websites mainly attracted users whose sociodemographic and attitudinal profiles were similar, if not identical, to those of citizens who were politically informed, interested, and engaged. Based on these findings, Norris concluded that the Internet enabled political actors to cater to citizens who were already active and likely to support them in the first place but was not going to help parties reach beyond this already engaged pool of voters. In the next pages, we aim to understand whether a similar pattern, and thus a similar metaphor of "mobilizing the mobilized," also applies to citizens who are targeted by electoral mobilization on social media.

To answer this question, we employ logistic regressions predicting respondents' likelihood of being targeted by social media messages aimed at influencing their vote choices.[16] Based on the same approach adopted in the rest of this chapter, we built our models incrementally by adding four blocks of independent variables: sociodemographic characteristics, political attitudes and behaviors, social media use, and country of residence. Similar to our analyses of accidental exposure (Table 3.2), the predictive power of the models explaining electoral mobilization increases substantially between Models 1 and 2 (from 6% to 41% of the total variance in the index of political participation) and then is further enhanced when we add variables measuring social media use (with almost 50% of the variance explained by Model 3). Adding country dummy variables, as we do in Model 4, only leads to a marginal improvement.

The coefficients reported in Table 3.3 paint a complex picture of the profile of social media users who are targeted by digital mobilizers. If we look at sociodemographic characteristics (Model 1) and political attitudes (Model 2), we see many indications that citizens exposed to electoral mobilization on social media fit the profile of politically active citizens: they are male, with high educational credentials, employed, attentive to the campaign, and confident in political institutions. They also tend to have rich political information diets, which, however, in line with previous research (Newton, 1999), do not include a massive amount of television news. Finally, they frequently engage in political talk face to face. These findings suggest that parties, candidates, and their supporters mainly reach social media users who are likely to have already activated their political radar and to have a generally positive orientation toward political institutions. To some degree, it therefore seems that campaigners on social media actually try to mobilize citizens who are, if not already mobilized, at least potentially mobilizable.

Table 3.3. **Models Predicting the Likelihood of Being Exposed to Electoral Mobilization Messages on Social Media**

	Model 1 (Sociodemo.)	*Model 2 (Political Attitudes)*	*Model 3 (SNS Usage)*	*Model 4 (Country)*
Gender (Male)	0.443***	0.197***	0.185***	0.185***
Age	−0.060***	−0.041***	−0.034***	−0.027**
Age squared	0.001***	0.000**	0.000***	0.000**
Education	0.330***	0.212***	0.234***	0.127***
Working condition	0.183***	0.113*	0.080	0.087
Income	0.012	−0.037***	−0.023*	−0.015
Ideology (reference = Center)				
Left		0.147	0.046	0.061
Center-left		−0.020	0.015	0.066
Center-right		0.179**	0.175**	0.184**
Right		0.318***	0.202*	0.185
Unaligned		−0.198**	−0.155*	−0.167*
Attention to the campaign		0.148***	0.092*	0.044
Interest in politics		−0.021	−0.024	0.018
Efficacy index		−0.003	−0.005	−0.011
Institutional trust index		0.027***	0.016*	0.017*
Satisfaction with democracy		0.036	0.040	0.014
Political information via . . .				
Newspapers		0.168***	0.113***	0.133***
Websites		0.164***	0.070***	0.056**
Radio		0.018	0.015	0.036*
Television		−0.109***	−0.100***	−0.071***
Offline conversation		0.170***	0.083**	0.055*
Political talk offline		0.155***	0.013	0.032
Political talk on SNSs			0.543***	0.542***
Frequency of SNS use				
Facebook			0.173***	0.169***

Table 3.3 Continued

	Model 1 (Sociodemo.)	Model 2 (Political Attitudes)	Model 3 (SNS Usage)	Model 4 (Country)
Twitter			0.057***	0.050**
YouTube			0.052**	0.068***
Instagram			0.043**	0.041**
Country (reference = U.S.)				
Greece				−0.411***
Poland				−0.799***
Denmark				−0.725***
Spain				−0.802***
U.K.				−0.562***
France				−0.717***
Germany				−1.007***
Italy				−0.838***
Intercept	−0.104	−2.035***	−2.943***	−2.414***
AIC	18,335	14,202	12,963	12,798
Nagelkerke R^2	0.059	0.410	0.495	0.506
N	15,571	12,497	12,343	12,343

Note: SNS = social networking site. Entries are log-odds. Standard errors and p-values for coefficients are provided in the Online Appendix section, Tables A17–A20. AIC = Akaike information criterion.

*$p \le .05$.
**$p \le .01$.
***$p \le .001$.

However, this is just one side of the story, as other findings paint a more nuanced picture. For example, interest in politics—a robust and stable indicator of political involvement (Prior, 2010)—is not a significant predictor of being targeted by electoral mobilization, and the same is true for political efficacy and satisfaction with democracy (Model 2). Similarly, the negative coefficient for age and the positive one for quadratic age in Model 1 indicate the now familiar pattern of younger voters being substantially more likely to be targeted than older voters—in spite of the fact that younger voters, all else being equal, tend to

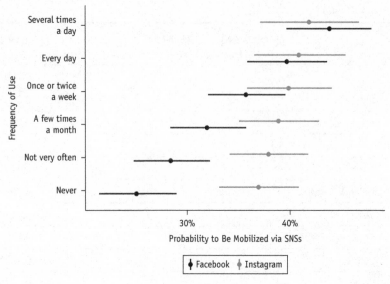

Figure 3.7. Exposure to Electoral Mobilization Messages as a Function of Facebook and Instagram Uses

Note: SNS = social networking site. The values are simulated quantities of interest based on Models 4 in Table 3.3 for respondents with values equal to the sample mean, median, or mode (depending on the nature of the variables) for all variables apart from frequency of Facebook and Instagram use. Horizontal lines show 95% confidence intervals.

be less politically involved (Verba et al., 1995). To the extent that mobilization via social media also reaches some users who typically lack a strong and long-standing commitment to political life—because they are not highly interested in politics or because they are young—at least some of the mobilization efforts of digital pastors may preach to the outcasts as well as the converted.

Whether or not users are exposed to electoral mobilization on social media also depends on how frequently they employ different platforms. As shown in Model 3 in Table 3.3, frequency of use of all the main social media platforms increases the likelihood of being targeted by a message supporting a party or candidate. This finding differs from those pertaining to encounters with agreement (Table 3.1) and accidental exposure to political news (Table 3.2), where the patterns differed by platform. The more uniform, positive associations we found for electoral mobilization suggest that none of the social media we included in our questions constitute a completely apolitical ground and that every platform is patrolled by campaigners in search of votes, so that the more frequently one accesses any social media, the more likely she is to be reached by electoral mobilization. At the same time, our estimates indicate that not all battlefields are equal and that Facebook, once again, plays a larger role than other platforms.

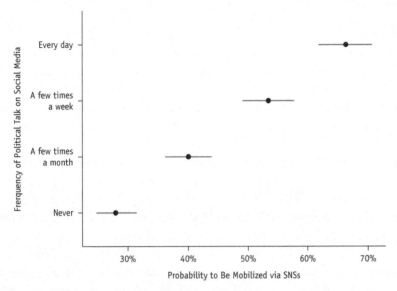

Figure 3.8. Exposure to Electoral Mobilization Messages as a Function of Frequency of Political Discussion on Social Media

Note: SNS = social networking site. The values are simulated quantities of interest based calculated on Model 4 in Table 3.3 for respondents with values equal to the sample mean, median, or mode (depending on the nature of the variables) for all covariates apart from frequency of political talk on SNSs. Horizontal lines show 95% confidence intervals.

To illustrate these patterns, we once again construct hypothetical respondents who have values equal to the sample mean, median, or mode on all covariates (based on Model 4 in Table 3.3) apart from usage of Facebook (which has the strongest coefficient among social media platforms in the model) and Instagram (which has the weakest coefficient). Based on these estimates, accessing Facebook several times a day yields a 43.8% predicted probability of experiencing electoral mobilization compared with 35.8% for an identical respondent who uses Facebook a few times a week. The difference is statistically significant as shown in Figure 3.7. Conversely, the probability of receiving mobilizing messages grows much less markedly when frequency of Instagram use increases. To summarize, while the direction and significance of model coefficients tell us that political preachers can be found at every social media corner, their magnitudes and effect sizes reveal that some platforms are more crowded with political mobilizers than others, and once again Facebook emerges as a particularly relevant arena.

Political talk on social media is also strongly and significantly associated with exposure to electoral mobilization. It should be noted that when the variable measuring frequency of political talk on social media is introduced in the model (together with the others included for the first time in Model 3), the coefficient for offline political conversation is no longer significant. Online political conversation creates opportunities for being mobilized on social media. Users who frequently talk about politics have a higher probability of encountering someone who wants to convince them to vote in a certain way. At the same time, engaging in political discussion generates digital footprints of one's political involvement and preferences, which makes it easier for political actors to reach these users with advertisements tailored to them based on these data. The predicted probability of being targeted by electoral mobilization for an average respondent who very rarely discusses political matters on social media is 40%, which jumps to 53.4% if the same average respondent engages in political conversation on a weekly basis. The difference is statistically significant as shown in Figure 3.8.

Finally, the country coefficients (Model 4 in Table 3.3) show that systemic differences are associated with the probability of experiencing electoral mobilization on social media. Once again, the United States markedly stands out. When compared with American citizens, residents in all other Western democracies we consider in this book are significantly less likely to be targeted by mobilization messages on social media. Based on Model 4 in Table 3.3, a hypothetical average respondent who lives in the United States has a 38.3% probability of being targeted by electoral mobilization on social media. In all other countries, predicted probabilities range from 29.1% (Greece) to 18.5% (Germany), and the differences between the United States and all other countries are statistically significant.

Here we have encountered yet another form of American exceptionalism in terms of the diffusion of political experiences on social media. What factors could explain it? In the United States, where turnout is historically low (Powell, 1986; Lijphart, 1997), door-to-door canvassing represents a crucial component of electoral campaigning (Nielsen, 2012). Candidates who lack the support of strong party infrastructures have always needed help from legions of volunteers to persuade undecided citizens or to ensure that their supporters turn out (Green & Gerber, 2015). Our data suggest that social media has become a new environment for prosecuting the American "ground wars" (Nielsen, 2012) by other means. Moreover, the fact that the United States has been the first laboratory where political actors have executed well-resourced digital campaigns aiming to precisely target voters (Issenberg, 2012a, 2012b; Kreiss & McGregor, 2018), combined with the huge, and comparatively unmatched, financial resources available to American campaigns (Norris & Van Es, 2016), has contributed to supercharging electoral mobilization on social media in the United States compared with other Western countries. The 2020 presidential campaign, conducted in the exceptional context of the Covid-19 pandemic, confirmed this trend: both Joe Biden and Donald Trump spent more on Facebook ads between January 2019 and October 2020 (94 and 107 million dollars, respectively) than the sum of Trump's and Hillary Clinton's combined spending in 2016 (81 million dollars; Leigh & Manthey, 2020).

By contrast, it seems notable that German citizens are the least likely to report receiving messages aiming to convince them to vote for any party or candidate, as the negative coefficient for Germany in Model 4 (Table 3.3) is the largest and the predicted probability of being targeted by electoral mobilization is the lowest. Bearing in mind that German respondents were also the most likely to encounter one-sided supportive political content on social media (see the discussion of Model 4 in Table 3.1), these low levels of electoral mobilization may indicate a general reluctance among Germans to cross political lines on social media, whether it be to argue with people of different views or to invite others to take a political stand. The value that Germans give to online privacy has been confirmed by studies on, for instance, consumer marketing (Singh & Hill, 2003) and access to digital services (Hoerbst et al., 2010). When it comes to political matters, such general sensitivity for privacy dovetails with a historically rooted reluctance among Germans, especially those who experienced the pervasive surveillance system of the former German Democratic Republic (Völker & Flap, 2001), to discuss politics in public environments offline and online (Valeriani & Vaccari, 2016). These factors could also contribute to explaining why the German social media sphere appears to be less permeable to the circulation of potentially dispute-provoking messages and mobilization calls.

There Is Life Outside the Bubble

In this chapter, we have shown that exposure to attitude-divergent political content, accidental encounters with political news, and being targeted by electoral mobilization are far from residual experiences for social media users across Western democracies. Our findings highlight that the explanatory potential of the "echo chamber" and "filter bubble" metaphors, in spite of their strong suggestive power, is more limited than is often assumed. Political homophily and self-segregation from public affairs are not a destiny inscribed in the sociotechnical affordances of social media. Instead, they are outcomes that different types of users experience with highly variable, and sometimes quite low, intensity. In other words, there is (political) life *outside of the* (filter) *bubble*!

One of the key findings of this chapter is that political junkies and heavy social media users are more likely to encounter predominantly supportive political messages. This is by no means surprising, but it should be understood in light of the fact that *most social media users are not political junkies*. Because they are more vocal on social media, and more likely to discuss the role of social media in democracy, politically active users constitute a strong and vocal minority that has greatly contributed to popularizing the notion of social media as all-encompassing echo chambers. Based on our data, this is what, indeed, social media look like to them most of the time. But while political junkies are more right than wrong in characterizing *their own* experience of social media as echo chambers, they are more wrong than right in projecting their own experience of social media into that of *the majority of users*, among whom two-sided and oppositional messages are much more commonly experienced.

Another key finding is that specific social networking platforms have different implications for the kinds of political experience their users have. Overall, frequent Facebook use is more likely to facilitate most of the political experiences on social media we study. Other social media platforms also have elective affinities with different outcomes, but they seem to make a smaller difference. These findings confirm the dominance of Facebook in facilitating politically relevant outcomes among its users and highlight how critical it is to better understand the (constantly evolving) functioning of this platform and its democratic implications. However, the role and importance of one platform can hardly be understood in isolation: only by simultaneously studying different social media can we properly situate them in the complex digital environments that users inhabit.

Our findings also speak to the issue of political equality, which is central to this book. We have shown that differences in socioeconomic status and political involvement do not massively bear upon the likelihood that social media users encounter supportive content, nor that they get accidentally exposed to political information they were not looking for. The story was less clear-cut for electoral mobilization, which reaches users whose profiles more closely resemble those of typically active citizens, albeit with some relevant exceptions. These findings are important for our argument because, as we will show in Chapter 5, the relationship between political experiences on social media and political participation is stronger among respondents with lower levels of political involvement. For these stronger statistical correlations to substantively matter in the real world, political experiences must empirically reach some of those low-involvement voters. In this chapter, we have shown that they have the potential to do so.

Moreover, we have observed that frequency of political talk on social media has a strong positive relationship with all the three experiences we considered. As we have argued, this finding suggests that, more than—usually stable—political attitudes such as interest in politics or ideology, specific digital behaviors may play a decisive role in facilitating relevant political experiences on social media. Behaviors such as online political talk are partly habitual, but they can also be activated by particular circumstances. For example, a user may start intensely discussing politics on social media because an issue has suddenly risen to prominence and attracted her attention, or because she has been intrigued by the kind of effervescence that results from multiple concurrent mobilization endeavors, as in the Scottish referendum discussed earlier. Political talk, both online and offline, can, of course, also become an inconvenient and unpleasant activity, especially at times when divisions and animosities grow within communities (Wells et al., 2017). What our findings show is that when political talk occurs on social media, it facilitates engagement with supportive views, accidental encounters with political news, and exposure to electoral mobilization. As we will show in the next chapter, all three experiences are, in turn, positively associated with levels of political participation.

More broadly, our results show that different users have specific political experiences on social media, and that there are stark differences between the United States and other countries. These findings should caution researchers not to assume that social media usage yields uniform political outcomes in a given population, and that patterns identified in one country—particularly the United States—should never be automatically generalized elsewhere. In the next chapter, we will investigate whether and to what extent citizens' experiences with political agreement, accidentally encountered political content, and electoral mobilization on social media are associated with their levels of political participation.

4

Do Social Media Matter?

Direct Effects of Agreement, Accidental Exposure, and Electoral
Mobilization on Political Participation

Teresa Shook was an Indiana-born retired lawyer in her sixties who lived on the island of Maui, Hawaii, and had four grandchildren. She hardly fit the profile of the habitual political agitator and lived in a U.S. state better known for its beaches and flower garlands than for campaigning and street demonstrations. But on November 9, 2016, the day after Donald Trump had been elected president, Theresa Shook was upset. She had been a supporter of Democratic candidate Hillary Clinton, who had won the popular vote but lost to Trump in the electoral college. Theresa Shook was disappointed with Clinton's defeat and worried about Trump's attitude toward women. So, she went to a four-million-strong Facebook group of Clinton supporters, called "Pantsuit Nation," and wrote a post where she argued that women should march to stand for their rights on the day of Trump's inauguration. After receiving one encouraging response from a member of the group, Shook asked her online contacts to help her use a popular feature of Facebook through which users can say they are going to attend or are interested in an event. She created the event page for the march, sent it to about forty contacts, and went to sleep.

When Shook woke up the next morning, more than ten thousand Facebook users had responded that they would attend the march, and the page of the event had been forwarded to countless public and private Facebook profiles and groups, including Pantsuit Nation, as well as having been noticed and endorsed by various civil society organizations (Stein & Somashekhar, 2017). Many other similar pages had been created on Facebook and elsewhere online. By the end of 2016, more than three hundred thousand people had expressed interest in the event on Facebook, and many political activists and groups had gotten involved to consolidate the movement and help organize the march, which was

Outside the Bubble. Cristian Vaccari and Augusto Valeriani, Oxford University Press. © Oxford University Press 2021.
DOI: 10.1093/oso/9780190858476.003.0005

scheduled to take place in Washington, D.C., and in many other cities across the country on January 21, 2017—the day after Trump was to be sworn in. A network of public interest groups, social movements, activist organizations, and ordinary citizens assembled around the event, not without friction, as some felt the stances of minority groups were not sufficiently included (Women's March on Washington, 2016). As what came to be known as the "Women's March" turned into a national demonstration, Teresa Shook happily got on board as a participant and speaker, still incredulous that her idea had become real so quickly and effectively. The march was now a highly professionalized effort, with a twenty-one-member-strong organizing committee, five strategic advisors, two campaign operatives, seven communication officers, sixteen staffers overseeing social media, and official support from large interest groups and more than five hundred partner organizations (Women's March on Washington, 2018a). Hundreds of thousands of people took part in the main march on the National Mall in Washington. There were also 673 sister marches across the United States and in ninety-four countries around the world (Women's March on Washington, 2018b). Based on pictures of the events in Washington, experts estimated the size of the crowd at the march in Washington to be about three times as large as that of the crowd that attended Trump's inauguration the previous day—around 470,000 who marched against Trump versus 160,000 who gathered to witness his swearing-in (Wallace & Parlapiano, 2017). The total estimated number of participants to all the events across the country was more than four million, as many of the sister marches in large cities registered crowds of more than a hundred thousand (Pressmann & Chenoweth, 2018). The demonstrations were heavily covered by the news media and widely discussed on social media, with nearly the same number of tweets posted about the Women's March as were posted about Trump's inauguration the day before—11.5 million versus 12 million (Cohen, 2017). As the incoming Trump administration was struggling to argue that the size of Trump's inauguration crowd was the largest in the history of presidential inaugurations (it clearly was not), the Women's March provided a "counter-inauguration" to Trump's (Chadwick, 2017b, Chapter 10), plastically showing the strength of opposition to the incoming president and throwing a massive spanner in the works of the administration's attempt to set the tone for its crucial first days in office.

In commenting on the implications of the Women's March, Zeynep Tufekci (2017a) argued that the size of the crowds attending a demonstration is no longer as reliable a signal of movement strength as it used to be considered in the past (Tilly & Wood, 2013). Digital media have dramatically reduced coordination costs and have made it easier to spread the word about an initiative, so the time and effort it takes to gather crowds of the size of the Women's March is now much smaller than in the predigital age (see also Tufekci, 2017b). While one-off demonstrations are by no means sufficient to generate meaningful and lasting political change, the speed and scale at which the Women's March took place and the role it came to play in the early days of the Trump administration should not be dismissed. Social media enabled amateur activists (starting from Teresa Shook), professional campaigners, civil society groups, institutional political actors, and journalists to raise awareness of the march, mobilize participants, and create an effective narrative during and after the event. No demonstration of this magnitude owes its success entirely to the means of communication its organizers employ, of course. The protest clearly resonated with the mood of a large part of the country—more than half the electorate, considering the outcome of the 2016 popular vote—and followed a bitter campaign where Trump had repeatedly insulted women and had even been caught on tape bragging that, as a celebrity, he could harass women without paying any price. Yet, the potential of such a resonant call for action could only generate real mass-scale participation if enough people for whom the message struck a chord could learn about it, over and above the cacophony of other media content competing for their attention. This, we argue, is where the power of social media lies in bolstering political participation.

As we saw in Chapter 3, political information reaches many people on social media, whether they deliberately seek it out or not. These messages, even when produced by political actors, might not directly ask people to get involved, as was the case in the episode we have just sketched. However, different types of political encounters on social media can encourage participation in various ways. In the following pages, we will assess whether the political experiences described in the previous chapter actually matter for political participation. Before we dive into these analyses, we provide a brief summary and description of our dependent variable and how we constructed our statistical models to predict it.

How We Study Social Media and Political Participation

In Chapter 1, we have argued that different types of political experiences on social media—seeing content one agrees with, accidentally encountering political news, and being targeted by electoral mobilization—may enhance citizens' political participation. In Chapter 3, we examined an important objection to our argument—that these experiences are rare because most people avoid politics on social media—and found that, even though the extent to which individuals experience politics online varies based on their characteristics, attitudes, and behaviors, political content reaches a large percentage of social media users. In this chapter, we assess whether these political experiences are associated with higher levels of political participation. Here, we provide statistical estimates of *direct effects*, as we consider the relationships between the independent variables (political experiences on social media) and the dependent variable (political participation) across all our respondents. In the next two chapters, we will look at *differential effects*, comparing these relationships across different types of individuals (Chapter 5) and countries (Chapter 6).

As readers may recall, in Chapter 2 we conceptualized political participation in the digital age and described how we measured its different facets to construct our *dependent variable*—an additive index, ranging from 0 to 6, of modes of political participation occurring both online and offline, that our respondents reported engaging in during the previous year. These activities are:

- Contacting a politician to support a cause
- Signing petitions and subscribing to referenda
- Financing a party, candidate, political leader, or electoral campaign
- Taking part in public meetings and electoral rallies
- Distributing leaflets to support a political or social cause
- Trying to convince someone to vote for a party, leader, or candidate

Among our respondents, 37.1% claimed they did not perform any of these activities, and this group of inactive citizens is the most numerous in our sample. 25.9% respondents recalled engaging in only one form of action, 18.3% performed 2 out of the 6 activities we measured, 9.5% participated in 3 different ways, and the remaining 9.2% conducted 4 or more activities. The mean across all our respondents is 1.34, the median is 1, and the standard deviation is 1.45. These values provide a baseline against which we can evaluate the size of the effects our models will estimate.

In Chapter 3, we described the questions we used to measure our *independent variables*: encountering agreement, accidental exposure to political news, and electoral mobilization on social media. In our models, these variables predict respondents' levels of political participation, together with a set of controls that theory and previous research suggest may also explain participation and, thus, potentially confound our relationships of interests if our models did not account for them. These include sociodemographic characteristics (gender, age, age squared, education, occupational condition, and income), political attitudes and behaviors (interest in politics, attention to the latest election campaign, sense of political efficacy, trust in political institutions, political ideology, satisfaction for democracy, frequency of political information via multiple sources, and frequency of political talk offline), social media use (frequency of use of Facebook, Twitter, Instagram, and YouTube, and frequency of political talk on social media), and country of residence.[1] Our Online Appendix (Table A3) reports extensive information on the questions we used to create the variables included in our analyses.

To understand the relationship between political experiences on social media and political participation, we ran Poisson regressions, which are best suited to deal with count variables such as the cumulative index of participation whose values our models predict. As in Chapter 3, we employed a pooled data set combining all respondents across the nine countries we studied, and to take this into account the models included a variable that clusters respondents by country of residence (taking the United States as reference category).

Before running our regressions, we preprocessed the data with Coarsened Exact Matching (CEM; Iacus et al., 2012) to improve the balance on some key characteristics between respondents included in our analysis who did and did not report the political experiences on social media that constitute our independent variables. This procedure increases our confidence that the relationships we found between political experiences on social media and political participation are not confounded by any of the covariates on which we balanced our data. As an example, we saw in Chapter 3 that people with higher levels of education are more likely to be targeted by electoral mobilization on social media, and we account for this fact by controlling for education in our regressions. With this simple set-up, however, if our models suggested that both education and exposure to electoral mobilization are positively associated with participation, we could not confidently conclude that mobilization may enhance participation *over and above* the effects of education—because education predicts mobilization as well. CEM addresses this problem. Before we run a regression analysis, CEM preselects a subset of respondents who look exactly the same on covariates such as education, while differing from each other in terms of being or not being mobilized on social media. Thus, in our example, CEM enables us to include similar numbers of respondents at all levels of education who received and did not receive mobilization messages. This will enable us to draw firmer conclusions on the effects of political experiences on social media—within the limits of employing survey data taken at only one point in time. Because we executed the CEM algorithm on each of our three key independent variables (exposure to agreement, accidentally encountering political news, and being targeted by electoral mobilization) and because the variables based on which we matched respondents (gender, age, education, interest in politics, attention to the campaign, and sense of political efficacy) were associated with political experiences on social media in different ways, CEM was able to match a different number of respondents depending on which independent variable we considered. In particular, we were able to match 8,318 respondents for agreement and disagreement (57.3% of the total sample), 10,150 for accidental exposure (65.1%), and

14,001 for exposure to mobilization (89.9%). In our multivariate analyses, we used the weights generated by CEM to account for the fact that the different strata that resulted from the matching procedures include unequal numbers of treated and untreated units. CEM assigns a weight of 0 to units that are not matched, effectively excluding them from subsequent analyses.[2] This is why, in the regression models that we will present in this and the next two chapters, the number of respondents included varies depending on whether the models aim to test hypotheses focusing on agreement, accidental exposure, or electoral mobilization. The reason why the Ns reported in the tables in this and the next two chapters are lower than the total numbers of units matched based on CEM, reported earlier, is that some of the independent variables had missing data and we removed those respondents based on listwise deletion.[3]

In the following pages, we present the results of models assessing the relationship between political participation and the different types of political experiences on social media we are studying.[4] Following the same order as in Chapter 3, we start from exposure to supportive political views, then move on to accidental exposure to political news, and finally focus on electoral mobilization.

Better to Join the Herd Than the Fight: Echo Chambers, Contrarian Clubs, and Political Participation

The first question we answer is whether exposure to different levels of agreement and disagreement on social media is associated with higher or lower levels of political participation. In Chapter 3, we showed that most social media users encounter viewpoints they both agree and disagree with (we call these configurations *two-sided*). We also showed that the percentage of users who mainly see content they agree with (i.e., those who receive *one-sided supportive* information) is roughly half the percentage of users who disagree more often than agree with the political messages they see on social media (a pattern we define as *one-sided oppositional*). Social media, therefore, do not resemble the kinds of political "echo chambers" described by critics. There is much to be said about the democratic value of engaging with a variety of opinions and being exposed to a healthy diet of viewpoints, including many different to one's own (Delli Carpini et al., 2004). However, research on face-to-face conversations shows that the confidence boost that individuals receive from engaging with supportive viewpoints can embolden and motivate them to act upon their beliefs, thus stimulating participation (Mutz, 2002, 2006). Is this also true for social media?

To answer this question, we first estimate a multivariate Poisson regression where our key independent variable distinguishes between respondents predominantly exposed to one-sided supportive, one-sided oppositional, and two-sided messages. Our classification also includes "never exposed" respondents, i.e., those who do not encounter political content on social media (clustered with nonusers of social media; see Chapter 3), whom we expect to participate the least of all. Table 4.1 presents the results of these models, which are based on data matched by CEM and include all the control variables listed in the previous section. As shown by the pseudo-R^2 coefficient, our model explains a little more than one-fourth of the overall variance in levels of participation.

From Table 4.1 we can see that, taking as reference respondents who equally encounter agreeing and disagreeing political messages, there is a positive and significant association between being in a one-sided supportive political environment on social media and levels of political participation. By contrast, those who do not see political messages or do not use social media report significantly lower levels of participation. In other words, all else being equal, respondents who find themselves in political echo chambers on social media engage in a significantly higher number of political activities than those who inhabit two-sided environments on these platforms. Conversely, there is no substantial difference, in terms of political participation, between being exposed to two-sided political content and being immersed in a one-sided oppositional milieu (as the relevant coefficient is not statistically significant). This latter finding is somehow coherent with the results of the meta-analysis conducted by Matthes and colleagues (2019) on the effects of exposure to crosscutting views on political engagement. Considering forty-eight studies and seventy independent samples, the authors found no significant relationship between exposure to crosscutting views (online and offline) and political participation.

What are the substantive implications of the associations we found in the data? To answer this question, we calculate estimates of the predicted levels of political participation for statistically average respondents who experience different combinations of agreement and disagreement on social media, based on the results of our model and the characteristics of our sample. We construct four hypothetical respondents who have values equal to the means, the medians, or the modes in the sample (depending on whether a variable is numeric, ordinal, or categorical) on all control variables, apart from our independent variable, i.e., the mix of political agreement and disagreement in the messages one sees on social media. On this variable, each of our four hypothetical respondents has different values: one tends to see supportive messages, one tends to see oppositional messages, one generally views a mixture of supportive and oppositional messages, and one does not see political content (or is not a social media user). We then calculate the values of the index of political participation that the model in Table 4.1 predicts

Table 4.1. **Poisson Regression Predicting Levels of Political Participation (0–6 Index): Direct Effects for Agreement on Social Media**

	Coefficient	Standard Error	p-value
Political messages seen on social media (reference = Two-sided)			
Never exposed	−0.206	0.046	0.000
One-sided supportive	0.170	0.026	0.000
One-sided oppositional	0.023	0.023	0.324
Gender (Male)	0.069	0.021	0.001
Age	−0.033	0.005	0.000
Age squared	0.000	0.000	0.000
Education	0.038	0.015	0.013
Working condition	0.008	0.024	0.747
Income	−0.014	0.005	0.003
Ideology (reference = Center)			
Left	0.292	0.038	0.000
Center-left	0.259	0.030	0.000
Center-right	0.141	0.031	0.000
Right	0.166	0.042	0.000
Unaligned	−0.027	0.036	0.460
Attention to the campaign	0.041	0.022	0.069
Interest in politics	0.093	0.021	0.000
Efficacy index	0.038	0.006	0.000
Institutional trust index	0.010	0.003	0.003
Satisfaction with democracy	−0.043	0.015	0.004
Political information via . . .			
Newspapers	0.054	0.007	0.000
Websites	−0.005	0.009	0.555
Radio	0.026	0.007	0.000
Television	−0.060	0.009	0.000
Offline conversation	0.090	0.012	0.000
Political talk offline	0.107	0.016	0.000
Political talk on SNSs	0.208	0.011	0.000

Table 4.1 Continued

	Coefficient	Standard Error	p-value
Frequency of SNS use			
Facebook	−0.014	0.007	0.039
Twitter	−0.002	0.007	0.748
YouTube	0.018	0.007	0.013
Instagram	0.017	0.008	0.035
Country (reference = U.S.)			
Greece	−0.179	0.043	0.000
Poland	−0.080	0.043	0.060
Denmark	−0.181	0.044	0.000
Spain	−0.304	0.041	0.000
U.K.	−0.160	0.038	0.000
France	−0.107	0.039	0.006
Germany	−0.236	0.038	0.000
Italy	−0.143	0.039	0.000
Intercept	−0.193	0.140	0.169
AIC	21,220		
Pseudo-R^2	0.265		
N	7,205		

Note: SNS = social networking site. AIC = Akaike information criterion.

for these four average respondents. The differences between them, shown in
Figure 4.1, are useful summary estimates of how different balances of political
agreement and disagreement on social media are related to political participation.

All else being equal, our models estimate that an average respondent who
mainly encounters supportive viewpoints on social media should engage in two
modes of political action per year. By contrast, an average respondent who is
mostly exposed to two-sided messages should participate in 1.7 political activities, and this difference is statistically significant as can be seen from the lack of
overlap in the relevant error bars in Figure 4.1. The predicted value of political
participation for social media users who see one-sided oppositional messages
is also 1.7, and the difference in levels of participation between these respondents and those who mainly encounter one-sided supportive messages is almost
significant, as the 95% confidence intervals only slightly overlap (1.59–1.86 for

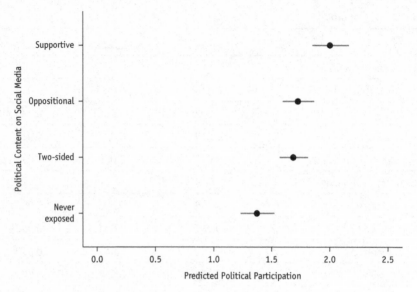

Figure 4.1. Estimated Effects of Different Levels of Agreement on Social Media on Political Participation, with 95% Confidence Intervals

Note: Estimates are count values of a 0–6 index and are based on the coefficients in Table 4.1 for respondents with values equal to the sample means, medians, or modes (depending on whether variables were entered in the model as numeric, ordinal, or categorical) for all variables apart from agreement and disagreement with political content seen on social media.

one-sided oppositional vs. 1.85–2.16 for one-sided supportive). Finally, and unsurprisingly, respondents who do not see much political content on social media participate in the lowest number of activities (1.3).

These are, of course, average estimates, as one can either participate or not participate in any of the six modes of political actions we measured. In practical terms, we can imagine that almost all social media users who are exposed to supportive political content participate in about two activities per year. By contrast, among those who see two-sided or oppositional political content, only about 70% engage in two activities per year while the others participate in only one activity. Finally, only 3 out of 10 of those who do not see political content on social media participate in two activities while the rest engage in just one political activity per year.

Knowing that, partly as a result of encountering supportive political content on social media, someone may perform zero, one, two, or more political activities per year is interesting, but it does not tell us anything about *which* activities one performed. Our index combines six relevant and diverse modes of political action, but what happens when we consider how each of these activities is associated with engaging with supportive, oppositional, and two-sided political content on social media?

To answer this question, we ran six logistic regression models, one for each mode of political action we consider. We measured individual activities with yes-or-no questions; thus, the resulting variables take only two values: 0 when respondents did not recall engaging in the measured activity, and 1 when they did. (When respondents answered that they did not remember, they were excluded from the analysis.) Hence, we use logistic regressions to estimate the relationship between each form of political action, levels of agreement and disagreement on social media (setting two-sided messages as the reference category), and the control variables mentioned earlier and used in the model in Table 4.1. We present the full results of these regressions in the Online Appendix (Tables A21–A26). Here, we focus only on respondents who mainly encounter one-sided supportive content on social media, as we previously found they are those who receive the greatest participatory boost.

In all the models, the coefficient for supportive content (compared with two-sided content) is positive and significant, apart from the model that predicts contacting a politician. To illustrate the implications of these results, we construct two imaginary average respondents: one who mostly engages with supportive viewpoints on social media and one who is exposed to two-sided messages. This set-up enables us to estimate the probabilities that these two imaginary average respondents may participate in each activity. Figure 4.2 shows how likely it is that an average respondent encountering politically supportive content performs each of the six actions we measured when compared against an average respondent who experiences similar levels of agreement and disagreement on social media.

To clarify the implications of our estimates, we will discuss each step of our analysis for one participatory mode: leafleting to support a political or social cause. The estimates suggest that our first average respondent, who predominantly sees supportive political content on social media, should have a 9% probability to distribute leaflets, while the probability is only 5% for our second average respondent, who mainly sees two-sided political content. The difference (4%) between the higher (9%) and lower (5%) probabilities is our measure of the effect of encountering supportive political messages compared with two-sided messages. This is the number we plotted next to "Leafleting" in the left panel of Figure 4.2, where we report "Absolute Values" of predicted changes in the probability to perform each action. Since the horizontal bar plotting confidence intervals for these estimates in the figure does not cross the 0% vertical line, we can be confident that the difference in these predicted probabilities is robust enough to be statistically significant.

However, knowing that the probability of an event may increase by a certain amount (in this case, 4%) under a certain condition (engaging with supportive content on social media) is more meaningful if we also know how likely it is that

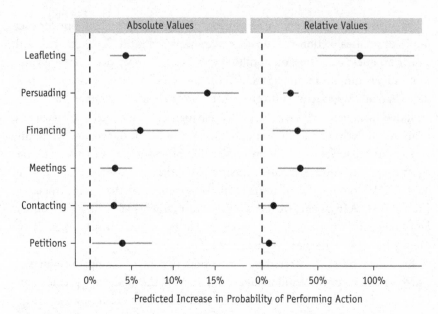

Figure 4.2. Estimated Effects of Supportive Political Messages on Social Media on Six Modes of Political Participation, with 95% Confidence Intervals

Note: Estimates are first differences of the predicted probabilities to perform each action when comparing average respondents experiencing one-sided supportive and two-sided political content on social media. Estimates are based on the coefficients in the logistic regression models reported in the Online Appendix (Tables A21–A26) for individuals with values equal to the sample means, medians, or modes (depending on whether variables were entered in the model as numeric, ordinal, or categorical) for all variables apart from agreement and disagreement with political content seen on social media.

such event may happen in a different condition (such as engaging with two-sided messages). A 5% increase has different implications if the alternative outcome is 4% or 40%. We know that those who see two-sided content on social media have a 5% probability of distributing leaflets. Hence, if we divide 4% (the increase) by 5% (the alternative outcome), we obtain 80%, which means that, roughly, we can expect people exposed to supportive messages on social media to be 80% more likely to engage in leafleting compared with those who see two-sided messages. This is the meaning of the "Relative Value" estimates for "Leafleting" in the right panel of Figure 4.2.[5] Substantively, then, exposure to supportive viewpoints on social media is associated with an 80% increase in an average respondent's predicted probability of distributing political leaflets, compared with exposure to a balanced mix of agreement and disagreement.[6]

Let us now use the estimates in Figure 4.2 to compare how exposure to supportive content may benefit different modes of participation. Looking at the absolute values (left panel of Figure 4.2), we can see that, first, all activities increase by a significant margin, as the error bars do not overlap with 0. The only exception, again, is contacting a politician to support a cause, consistent with the fact that the coefficient for supportive content is not significant in the model predicting this activity. Second, the participatory form that shows the highest absolute boost is trying to convince others to vote for a specific candidate or party, which we predict should increase by about 14% when a respondent sees supportive political content on social media. Financing parties or candidates is estimated to increase by 6%. Leafleting, signing a petition, and attending a meeting all see increases of 3–4%.

As can be observed in the left panel of Figure 4.2, the growth in the predicted probability of trying to influence others' voting choices is significantly larger than those of all the other activities. How should we interpret this finding? Recall that trying to persuade others to vote for a candidate is one of the most popular activities among respondents (see Table 2.1 in Chapter 2). Moreover, it could be argued that this action requires fewer resources than others, such as leafleting and participating in rallies. One could contend that the most popular and the less costly activities are more strongly affected by the energizing implications of supportive content on social media. However, when it comes to signing petitions (which is the most popular action among our respondents and is also not particularly resource intensive), our estimates show that it makes little difference whether someone experiences supportive or two-sided content. Hence, the fact that an action is popular and relatively low-cost does not explain, at least on its own, the degree to which supportive political content enhances its probability. Another possible explanation is that exposure to supportive political content on social media may convince people that their opinions are not in the minority, giving them the nerve to directly approach and try to influence others. It is worth recalling that our measure of political persuasion encompasses multiple settings where it may occur, including face-to-face conversations, email, and social media. For someone who is immersed in a dominantly supportive environment on social media, persuading others on these platforms might be superfluous, as they already share the same worldview. However, those who experience supportive environments on social media may receive the necessary confidence boost to try to persuade people in other, potentially less friendly, environments.

When we look at the right panel of Figure 4.2, however, the *relative* contribution that supportive messages seen on social media make to individuals' participatory efforts turns out to be much more relevant for distributing leaflets than for persuasion, or any other activity for that matter. As discussed earlier, respondents exposed to supportive content on social media are 80% more likely to engage in this activity compared with individuals exposed to a balanced mix of agreeing and disagreeing messages. Attending political meetings and financing political actors follow at a distance, with a predicted relative growth of, respectively, 34%

and 32%. Trying to influence others' vote is fourth, with a relative increase of around 26%, while signing petitions occupies by far the last position with an expected relative probability increase of less than 7%. The main lesson we can learn from looking at relative rather than absolute predicted increases is that the activities that are less popular and more resource intensive—because they cannot be conducted online, as in the case of leafleting and attending rallies, or because they require money, as with financing parties or candidates—benefit the most, in relative terms, from exposure to politically supportive content on social media. By contrast, signing petitions and trying to persuade others to vote can be conducted online as well as offline and do not require financial resources, which makes them more accessible. However, we must be cautious in interpreting these results because, as shown in Figure 4.2, the confidence intervals tend to be large, and thus most estimates of the participatory boost associated with exposure to supportive content on social media overlap with others. This means we cannot be sure, with 95% certainty, that the differences between the estimated relative growth in the probability to conduct each action are real and not random.

The results of our analysis on the relationship between agreement on social media and political participation have at least three important implications.

First, exposure to political messages on social media plays an important role in stimulating participation. No matter whether you agree, disagree, or split the difference between the messages and users you encounter online, if some political content does not reach you (because you do not see political messages on social media or because you do not use social media at all), your participation will be substantially lower than if it does.

Second, encountering politically supportive views on social media may lead to noticeably—albeit perhaps not dramatically—higher levels of participation than engaging with oppositional or two-sided messages. Even though social media are fertile grounds for exposure to contrarian and balanced mixes of opinions (as shown in Chapter 3), those experiences are actually less fruitful, in terms of spurring political participation, than the—less common—condition of predominantly encountering views one agrees with. Social media have expanded opportunities for engaging with different views compared to face-to-face communication. Yet, they have not changed the functioning of users' political brains. Even though most of us may not want, or manage, to isolate ourselves from views different from our own, we scan our social environments—including digital platforms—in search for indicators of how popular and widespread our political beliefs are. If we encounter supportive views, we receive positive feedback and increase our propensity to act upon those views. If we experience oppositional or two-sided views, we receive negative or mixed feedback, respectively. We may not abandon our beliefs as a result, but we do not increase our participation as much as we do when we enjoy social validation (Mutz, 2002, 2006). While there are potential democratic benefits to citizens' engaging with diverse and dissenting viewpoints on social media (but see Bail et al., 2018), overall levels of political action grow more if users join political herds rather than fights.

Finally, social media appear to make a contradictory contribution to political pluralism in contemporary democracies. On the one hand, as we saw in Chapter 3, they strengthen rather than weaken pluralism by predominantly exposing most users to views they disagree with or with a mixture of views they agree and disagree with. On the other hand, to the extent that users who mainly see supportive political content are more likely to act upon their views than those who encounter two-sided or oppositional messages, these differential levels of activation imply that the views from the minority of echo chamber inhabitants will be more visible, and possibly more influential, than the opinions of the majority of users, whose social media feeds are more politically diverse. Some of what social media giveth, in terms of enhancing exposure to pluralistic debate, they taketh away, as they disproportionately activate the minorities that are less likely to encounter political disagreement on these platforms.

Participation by Accident? Inadvertent Exposure to News on Social Media and Political Participation

Irrespective of whether they agree or disagree with it, many people encounter political content on social media accidentally, when they had accessed these platforms for other reasons—for instance, checking what their friends were doing, keeping tabs on sports scores, looking for celebrity gossip, or simply to kill time. As you may recall from Chapter 3, almost half our respondents report to frequently come across political information by accident when they use social media. Do these causal encounters make a difference for political participation? It may be that only purposive exposure to political content increases political activity, as in these cases whatever information is acquired gets channeled into preexisting motivations and may, thus, more easily result in concrete action. However, it may also be that unplanned exposure to political news results in higher levels of participation—precisely because it was not planned.

Suppose that a social media user reads about a new exciting recipe for a cake based on honey posted by a home-cooking account he follows. He may save the recipe, go shopping, and bake a delicious cake. Everything went according to plan, and nothing changed in this person's political horizons. Suppose, however, that the post linking to the recipe also included the hashtag "#savethebees," which is used by campaigners against bee-killing pesticides. Suppose, moreover, that the user clicked on the hashtag out of curiosity and got exposed to a cascade of advocacy posts as a result. Alternatively, suppose that the original post containing the recipe explicitly referenced the issue, reminding readers that if we want to enjoy honey-based cakes we need to protect bees, and that the post also provided a link to learn more about the issue. Or suppose that no such references were included in the recipe but that, after reading it, our imaginary social media user began to search social media for "honey" to find out which brands and flavors to buy, and that in performing such search he came across a post by one of his contacts that denounces the killing of millions of bees due to pesticides. In all three scenarios, the original plan may still be carried out, and a delicious honey-based cake may be baked, but the baker may also have incidentally learned about bee-killing pesticides. Our imaginary user may then be persuaded that bee-killing pesticides must be abandoned or drastically reduced, and he may even have decided to get involved—perhaps by signing an online petition found on social media, or by writing to a public official urging action on the topic.[7]

The moral of this story is that social media users spend a lot of time on these platforms, sometimes with no particular purpose, other times with a goal they hope to achieve. If a user already knew what she was looking for and she simply finds it, her plan will not change, irrespective of whether the goal was to find a new recipe or learn about a political cause. If, however, that user does not find what she was looking for, or if she finds something else on top of what she was looking for, then the plan might change—and if that something else has to do with politics, so might the user's levels of political participation.

As we did with agreement and disagreement, we assess the relationship between accidental exposure to news on social media and political participation with a multivariate Poisson regression. Our key independent variable is the measure of accidental exposure we introduced in Chapter 3. There, however, we treated this variable as dichotomous, clustering together respondents who "never" and "sometimes" encounter political content by accident on social media and similarly combining those who "often" and "always" report such experience. For the purposes of the analysis in Chapter 3, treating accidental exposure as dichotomous helped us clearly differentiate between users who do and do not frequently encounter political news by accident on social media. Conversely, here we aim to understand whether even a small increase in the frequency of serendipitous exposure to political messages on social media corresponds to higher levels of participation. To achieve this goal, we need to retain as much granularity as possible in our measure of incidental exposure. Hence, in the independent variable we employ for the analyses in this chapter, as well as in Chapters 5 and 6, we code as 0 respondents who are "never" incidentally exposed to politics on social media, as 1 individuals who are exposed "only sometimes," as 2 those who "often" have such experience, and as 3 those who "always or very often" stumble into political news by accident when accessing their social media profiles. Our model includes the same control variables—demographic characteristics, political attitudes and behaviors, social media use, and country—as the previous one. The data have been preprocessed with CEM (as discussed in the opening of this chapter and, more extensively, in the Online Appendix), and the matching has been conducted on each of the four levels at which we measured accidental exposure. Table 4.2 shows the results of our model. The pseudo-R^2 coefficient suggests that the model accounts for slightly over one-fourth of the total variance in participation.

The coefficient for accidental exposure to political news in Table 4.2 is positive and significant. Thus, even if we account for respondents' levels of political involvement and the extent to which they acquire information from a variety of sources, unplanned encounters with political content on social media still enhance participation. But what difference does it make in practice? How much does accidental exposure move the needle of participation?

As we did in the previous paragraph, we provide a more precise assessment of the relationship between accidental exposure and participation by plotting estimates derived from the model reported in Table 4.2 for four average respondents, each reporting a different frequency (from "never" to "always") of casual encounters with political news on social media. Figure 4.3 plots the number of political activities we predict these four average respondents should undertake.

When estimated on average respondents, the direct effects of accidental exposure look smaller than those we found for supportive political messages (Figure 4.1). We predict that an average respondent who never experiences accidental exposure to news on social media should engage in 1.1 political activities. A similarly average respondent who always comes across political content on social media should, according to our model, participate in 1.2 activities per year, which corresponds to a growth of about 9%. Undoubtedly, this is a small difference, so small that the confidence intervals between all estimates in Figure 4.3 overlap. This means that we cannot be sure, at the 95% confidence level, that the differences between these estimates are real rather than due to random noise in the data. Thus, even though we found a positive correlation between frequency of accidental exposure and participation when we ran our overall model (Table 4.2), when we estimated the effect sizes underlying this relationship at meaningful values of all the other variables included in our model, we found no significant difference. This is a useful reminder that the results of multivariate models should always be read in conjunction with estimates of the effect sizes of key variables (King et al., 2000).

For now, we have an answer to the question of whether accidental exposure to news on social media boosts participation: not much. Recall, however, that

Table 4.2. **Poisson Regression Predicting Levels of Political Participation (0–6 Index): Direct Effects for Accidental Exposure to Political News on Social Media**

	Coefficient	Standard Error	p-value
Accidental exposure to political news on SNSs	0.037	0.011	0.001
Gender (Male)	0.038	0.019	0.049
Age	−0.033	0.004	0.000
Age squared	0.000	0.000	0.000
Education	0.030	0.016	0.057
Working condition	0.062	0.024	0.009
Income	−0.016	0.004	0.000
Ideology (reference = Center)			
Left	0.266	0.035	0.000
Center-left	0.193	0.028	0.000
Center-right	0.112	0.028	0.000
Right	0.184	0.036	0.000
Unaligned	−0.083	0.032	0.010
Attention to the campaign	0.063	0.022	0.004
Interest in politics	0.119	0.021	0.000
Efficacy index	0.026	0.006	0.000
Institutional trust index	0.011	0.003	0.000
Satisfaction with democracy	−0.035	0.013	0.009
Political information via . . .			
Newspapers	0.072	0.007	0.000
Websites	0.013	0.009	0.147
Radio	0.029	0.007	0.000
Television	−0.066	0.008	0.000
Offline conversation	0.082	0.011	0.000
Political talk offline	0.067	0.015	0.000
Political talk on SNSs	0.215	0.011	0.000

Table 4.2 Continued

	Coefficient	Standard Error	p-value
Frequency of SNS use			
Facebook	−0.011	0.007	0.084
Twitter	0.017	0.006	0.005
YouTube	0.018	0.007	0.015
Instagram	0.025	0.006	0.000
Country (reference = U.S.)			
Greece	−0.125	0.038	0.001
Poland	−0.056	0.037	0.131
Denmark	−0.167	0.043	0.000
Spain	−0.267	0.037	0.000
U.K.	−0.097	0.035	0.005
France	−0.142	0.037	0.000
Germany	−0.257	0.036	0.000
Italy	−0.106	0.036	0.003
Intercept	−0.447	0.105	0.000
AIC	25,320		
Pseudo-R^2	0.286		
N	8,639		

Note: SNS = social networking site. AIC = Akaike information criterion.

we are estimating direct effects, i.e., effects averaged across all respondents. Estimating these relationships across different types of respondents—which we will do in Chapter 5—may tell a different story.

We may also hear a different story if we look at specific modes of political participation. To this end, we now assess the relationship between accidental exposure and each of the six participatory modes we included in our overall index. The procedure we followed is the same as illustrated earlier when introducing Figure 4.2, and the underlying logistic regression models are all reported in the Online Appendix (Tables A27–A32). Based on these models, we estimated predicted probabilities for two average respondents: the first "never" accidentally encounters news on social media while the second does that "always or very

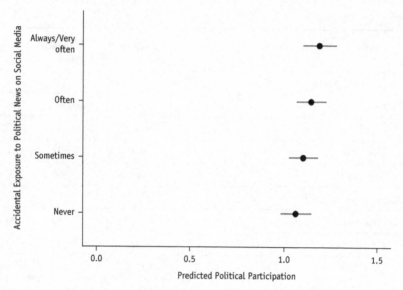

Figure 4.3. Estimated Effects of Accidentally Encountering Political News on Social Media on Political Participation, with 95% Confidence Intervals

Note: Estimates are count values of a 0–6 index calculated based on the coefficients in Table 4.2 for respondents with values equal to the sample means, medians, or modes (depending on whether variables were entered in the model as numeric, ordinal, or categorical) for all variables apart from accidental exposure to political news on social media.

often." Figure 4.4 shows the differences in the predicted probabilities of participating in each of the six actions.

When we disaggregate participation into specific activities, accidental exposure to news on social media is associated with significant increases in the probability of undertaking three activities: signing petitions, attending meetings, and trying to persuade others to vote in a certain way. It is also associated with declines in the probability of leafleting, while there is no significant relationship with contacting a politician and financing a party. This is shown graphically by the vertical line corresponding to 0 on the horizontal axis in Figure 4.4: when the error bars for our estimates cross this vertical line, we cannot be sure, with 95% certainty, that the predicted effects are different from 0—in other words, that there is any relationship distinguishable from noise and random variation. Here, the results from the overall models (summarized earlier, and reported in full in the Online Appendix) and the effect size estimates converge.

Signing petitions, trying to persuade others to vote in a certain way, and attending meetings and rallies are the three most popular activities in our sample (Table 2.1; Chapter 2), which again suggests that the more common an activity is, the greater the likelihood that political experiences on social media may boost

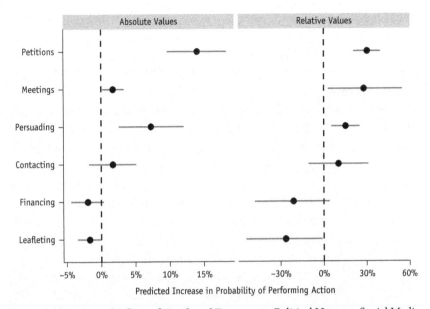

Figure 4.4. Estimated Effects of Accidental Exposure to Political News on Social Media on Six Modes of Political Participation, with 95% Confidence Intervals

Note: Estimates are first differences in predicted probabilities to perform each action. Values are based on the coefficients in the logistic regression models reported in the Online Appendix (Tables A27–A32) for two respondents with values equal to the sample means, medians, or modes (depending on whether variables were entered in the model as numeric, ordinal, or categorical) for all variables apart from accidental exposure to political news on social media, where they respectively score 0 ("never") and 3 ("always or very often").

it. Conversely, the negative effect of incidental exposure on leafleting is not easy to interpret, but it is also small in absolute terms.

In the right panel of Figure 4.4, we compare predicted effect sizes of accidental exposure for an average respondent against our baseline—the probability that a similar average respondent who does not accidentally encounter political news on social media will engage in the same activity. Here, we see a reversal akin to what we observed for engagement with supportive content in Figure 4.2. While accidental exposure does not increase the probability of attending meetings by a large margin in absolute terms, it does in relative terms: a 1.7% absolute boost goes a long way (a 28% increase) when the baseline level is only 6.1%. By contrast, the growth in a popular activity such as trying to persuade others, albeit larger in absolute terms (7.3%), is smaller in relative terms (15.1%). Similarly, if we compare absolute and relative gains (left and right panels, Figure 4.4) in the probability of signing petitions, we see that, in spite of registering the highest predicted growth in both absolute (14%) and relative terms (30.3%), the difference with other actions is much starker in the former than in the latter case.

Once again, however, we interpret these results with caution because the differences between the relative effect sizes are not statistically significant, as shown by the overlapping error bars in the right panel of Figure 4.4.

The conclusion we draw from these findings is that accidental exposure to news on social media seems to matter for political participation, but in a limited way. Granted, the fact that we controlled for a wide variety of variables, as well as matching observations before running the regressions, means that our estimates are likely to be lower than they would otherwise have been. Still, these are the estimates we believe are the most accurate. When we focus on the average social media user, unplanned encounters with political information move the needle of participation a bit, but the difference is small and is limited to more popular forms of political action such as persuading others, signing petitions, and attending meetings and rallies. This is not entirely surprising, as accidental exposure entails a milder level of political stimulation and is experienced by broader user constituencies than the other types of political experiences we are studying here.

Before moving forward, we want to acknowledge once again that the cross-sectional nature of our data prevents us from making strong claims of causality. Lee and Xenos (2020) employed longitudinal data and found reciprocal effects between unsearched exposure to news on social media and offline political participation, with a stronger effect of the latter on the former than the other way round, as well as mediation by purposeful political actions on social media. These findings suggest that incidental exposure to politics on social media is not completely incidental but results at least in part from users' deliberate political behaviors on these platforms and, indirectly, from offline actions. The complexity of these relationships confirms the importance of investigating, as we do in the next chapter, whether accidental exposure to news on social media closes or widens participatory gaps between more and less engaged citizens.

From Digital Mobilization to Political Participation

The third political experience we focus on is exposure to messages aiming to persuade one to vote for a candidate or party. Much political action does not happen spontaneously but is stimulated by social pressure by friends, colleagues, acquaintances, civic groups, and political organizations (Rosenstone & Hansen, 1993). As Verba and colleagues (1995) eloquently put it, one of the main reasons people do not participate in politics is that nobody ever asked them to.

Social media may contribute to reducing the number of citizens who are not asked to participate in the political process. First, these platforms enable ordinary citizens who are willing to mobilize other citizens to communicate with them easily and efficiently, as well as allow political actors to reach interested users with targeted messages. Second, social media facilitate communication that is fast and embedded in people's everyday lives, which explains why it has been found to encourage attending protests (Larson et al., 2019). Third, social media enable users to embed opportunities for participation in their calls to action, as when someone posts a message promoting a cause, shares a petition supporting it, and asks her contacts to sign it, all within the same communication. Finally, social media combine content from ordinary citizens and political elites and organizations, so that individuals can share and comment on messages by parties and candidates. This enables political actors to indirectly reach voters via their supporters, who are more likely to be influential on their social media contacts (Karlsen, 2015).

As a result, social media are fertile grounds for electoral mobilization by political actors and activist citizens. In Chapter 3, we saw that more than 30% of our respondents claimed that they had been encouraged to vote for a party or a candidate by someone else on social media in the past year. We now ask whether these invitations spill over into other forms of political participation. By alerting their recipients that there is an election and that their vote matters to someone else, these messages may increase their awareness of the possibility of participating and, potentially, prime individuals' sense of civic duty and willingness to get involved. Mobilization on social media may also prompt citizens to develop contacts and relationships with political organizations, civic groups, and activists, which may subsequently result in exposure to further opportunities and appeals to participate.

As in the rest of this chapter, we assess the relationship between participation and mobilization via social media by running a multivariate Poisson regression that includes several controls. This time, our key independent variable derives from a simple yes/no question that asked respondents whether someone else tried to convince them to vote for a particular party or candidate on social media during the 12 months preceding the interview. Therefore, the coefficient for this variable in Table 4.3 represents the estimated difference between respondents who did and did not recall receiving such invitations in the previous year. The data were preprocessed with CEM, with cases matched based on whether respondents recalled being mobilized on social media or not. Based on the pseudo-R^2 coefficient reported at the bottom of the table, we can estimate that our model predicts about 30% of the total variation in levels of participation across our sample.

The coefficient for electoral mobilization via social media in Table 4.3 is positive and significant, which means that individuals who receive social media messages inviting them to vote for a party or candidate participate in a higher

Table 4.3. **Poisson Regression Predicting Levels of Political Participation (0–6 Index): Direct Effects for Exposure to Electoral Mobilization via Social Media**

	Coefficient	Standard Error	p-value
Exposure to electoral mobilization via SNSs	0.457	0.016	0.000
Gender (Male)	0.017	0.016	0.300
Age	−0.030	0.003	0.000
Age squared	0.000	0.000	0.000
Education	0.008	0.012	0.500
Working condition	0.049	0.020	0.014
Income	−0.011	0.004	0.001
Ideology (reference = Center)			
Left	0.260	0.029	0.000
Center-left	0.165	0.023	0.000
Center-right	0.098	0.023	0.000
Right	0.141	0.029	0.000
Unaligned	−0.117	0.028	0.000
Attention to the campaign	0.050	0.015	0.001
Interest in politics	0.073	0.014	0.000
Efficacy index	0.025	0.004	0.000
Institutional trust index	0.010	0.003	0.000
Satisfaction with democracy	−0.047	0.011	0.000
Political information via . . .			
Newspapers	0.062	0.006	0.000
Websites	−0.012	0.008	0.110
Radio	0.023	0.006	0.000
Television	−0.051	0.007	0.000
Offline conversation	0.080	0.009	0.000
Political talk offline	0.068	0.012	0.000
Political talk on SNSs	0.179	0.009	0.000

Table 4.3 *Continued*

	Coefficient	Standard Error	p-value
Frequency of SNS use			
Facebook	−0.018	0.005	0.001
Twitter	0.025	0.005	0.000
YouTube	0.012	0.006	0.053
Instagram	0.018	0.005	0.001
Country (reference = U.S.)			
Greece	−0.094	0.032	0.003
Poland	0.082	0.030	0.007
Denmark	−0.047	0.036	0.194
Spain	−0.197	0.030	0.000
U.K.	−0.082	0.028	0.004
France	−0.027	0.029	0.363
Germany	−0.143	0.030	0.000
Italy	−0.052	0.030	0.087
Intercept	−0.310	0.083	0.000
AIC	34,727		
Pseudo-R^2	0.300		
N	11,488		

Note: SNS = social networking site. AIC = Akaike information criterion.

number of political activities, even after controlling for a host of other relevant covariates that predict participation.

To better estimate the implications of this finding, Figure 4.5 plots estimates derived from the model in Table 4.3. As we did for encountering supportive messages and accidental exposure to news, we construct two imaginary average respondents that only differ in terms of whether they did or did not see a message on social media inviting them to vote for a party or candidate. Our models estimate starkly different levels of political participation for these two hypothetical respondents: 1.8 versus 1.2 political activities per year. This is a larger difference than the ones we observed for supportive messages and incidental exposure, and it is statistically significant, as shown by the fact that the error bars in Figure 4.5 do not overlap.

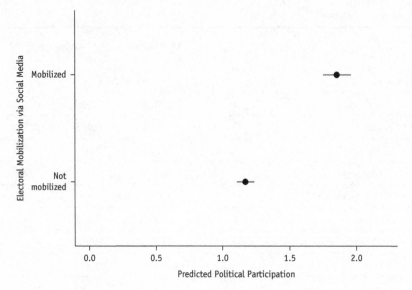

Figure 4.5. Estimated Effects of Exposure to Electoral Mobilization via Social Media on Political Participation, with 95% Confidence Intervals

Note: Estimates are count values of a 0–6 index based on the coefficients in Table 4.3 for respondents with values equal to the sample means, medians, or modes (depending on whether variables were entered in the model as numeric, ordinal, or categorical) for all variables apart from exposure to electoral mobilization via social media.

Let us now assess the relationships between electoral mobilization and each of the six modes of participation that our index combines. All six individual logistic regressions predicting each of these activities, reported in the Online Appendix (Tables A33–A38), show positive and significant coefficients for electoral mobilization. As we did for supportive messages and accidental exposure, we use these models to calculate the predicted probabilities that two average respondents, targeted and not targeted by electoral mobilization, engaged in each activity. Figure 4.6 shows estimates of the absolute and relative differences between these two respondents in the probability to perform each of the actions.

Let us first discuss the absolute values of our estimates (left panel of Figure 4.6), taking financing a party or a candidate as an example. The model estimates that an average respondent who was not mobilized via social media has a 6.3% probability of funding a campaign. This probability grows to 16.7% for an average respondent who was mobilized on social media, hence the difference between the two is 10.4%. This is a rather large increase compared with most of those we estimated for exposure to supportive political messages (see Figure 4.2) and frequent accidental exposure to political news (see Figure 4.4). As shown in the left panel of Figure 4.6, receiving invitations to vote for a candidate is predicted to boost the absolute probabilities of two activities—financing a political initiative

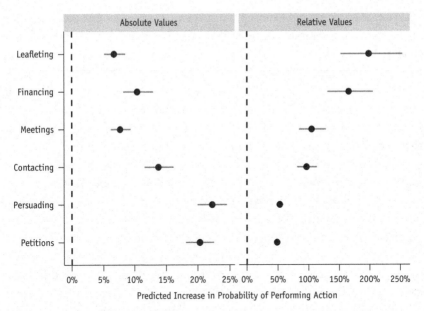

Figure 4.6. Estimated Effects of Electoral Mobilization on Social Media on Six Modes of Political Participation, with 95% Confidence Intervals

Note: Estimates are first differences in predicted probabilities to perform each action based on the coefficients in the logistic regression models reported in the Online Appendix (Tables A33–A38) for respondents with values equal to the sample means, medians, or modes (depending on whether variables were entered in the model as numeric, ordinal, or categorical) apart from electoral mobilization on social media.

and contacting a politician—by more than 10% and of two other activities— persuading others and signing petitions—by more than 20%. Apart from these overall larger effects, the extent to which mobilization enhances different activities seems to follow similar patterns as observed before, with the most popular activities receiving the largest boost.

If we focus on relative increases, in the right panel of Figure 4.6, the first thing to look at are the values of the horizontal scale. As in Figures 4.2 and 4.4, the scales are different between the right and left panel, but unlike in Figures 4.2 and 4.4, we are now dealing with ratios that are often higher than 100%. Let us again look at financing parties and candidates. The ratio between the predicted effect of mobilization (16.7%) and the baseline (6.3%) is 165%. Similarly, the estimated probability of distributing leaflets almost trebles if an average respondent is mobilized on social media. To put things in perspective, the highest estimates of relative effects for supportive messages was about 80% (for leafleting, see Figure 4.2) and for accidental exposure it was about 30% (for signing petitions, see Figure 4.4). The relative magnitude of the predicted effects of mobilization shows patterns similar to (and even clearer than) those observed for other experiences, with the most popular activities (persuading others and signing petitions) receiving smaller relative boosts. However, in this case even these smaller increases hover around 50%, by no means a negligible figure. Attending meetings and contacting politicians are predicted to grow by about 100%, while financing parties and leafleting increase by between 150% and 200%. While in our previous estimates for supportive content and accidental exposure most of the error bars overlapped, here the differences between the predicted growth in the probability of these three pairs of actions are statistically significant. Thus, we can say with 95% certainty that mobilization via social media has a larger relative impact on leafleting and donating money than it does on contacting politicians, attending meetings, signing petitions, and persuading others. Mobilization also has a stronger relative effect on attending political meetings and contacting politicians than on persuading others and signing petitions. In sum, electoral mobilization via social media seems to especially boost activities that channel resources toward political actors—such as financing them and distributing their campaign literature. This, in turn, suggests that parties and campaigns may reap considerable dividends if they manage to mobilize supporters on social media, as these targets might then become party donors and canvassers.

In Chapter 2, we argued that any definition of political participation should include *tertiary influence*, that is, trying to affect other citizens' political preferences and actions. We noted that, by attempting to exercise influence on others, citizens can multiply their capacity to provide input into the system, thus acquiring more voice and, possibly, power than if they just acted on their own to affect policy decisions (primary influence) and the selection of public officials (secondary influence). Trying to convince others to vote for a party or candidate is one of the ways in which citizens can pursue tertiary influence, and social media are viable channels through which to do that. Hence, when we set out to estimate levels of political participation, we included a measure of whether respondents had tried to convince someone else to vote for a party or candidate. In this section, we have looked at what happens to people when they are targeted by these efforts because someone else has tried to influence them, by inviting them to vote for a party or candidate. We have shown that these efforts generally increase levels of participation by a substantial margin—the highest among the three types of political experiences we are studying. In our survey, we did not ask respondents to discriminate between messages they received based on whether they came from organized political actors or citizens, and, therefore, we cannot disentangle the effects of different sources of electoral mobilization—though, as noted earlier, the boundaries between them are blurrier on social media than elsewhere. Even if we could meaningfully discriminate between direct (campaign-driven) and indirect (citizen-driven) online contacting (Aldrich et al., 2016), it is reasonable to assume that some of the messages our respondents recalled seeing on social media came from ordinary people like themselves. Our estimates suggest that a social media user trying to convince others to vote for a party or candidate may prompt them to participate in a variety of online and offline activities, including, once again, trying to persuade others to vote in a certain way. In particular, people who are mobilized on social media can be expected to be 22% more likely to become mobilizers themselves. Note, too, that when we measured whether respondents had tried to convince other people to vote in a certain way, we combined attempts performed on social media, via email, and in face-to-face conversations. Hence, the positive association we found between being targeted by mobilization and persuading others means that some of the mobilization attempts performed on social media may spill over into other domains, both on the Web and offline, thus potentially reaching broader audiences. In sum, social media may generate *hybrid chains of electoral mobilization*, whereby mobilizers, when successful, breed other mobilizers operating in and outside of the Web.

All of these patterns might explain why, in the heat of a contested campaign, social media users may feel overwhelmed by the volume of persuasive messages posted by parties, candidates, activists, and citizens. Personalized political communication, when individuals distribute messages to others (Nielsen, 2012), can be an effective tool for fostering participation. Social media enable users to (attempt to) persuade and mobilize citizens at large scale and relatively low cost, which explains why they have become one of the most important channels for personalized political communication. It is no surprise that organized political actors and their supporters take to social media for electoral mobilization— even if at times clumsily and, for some, irritatingly, as the Scottish anecdote that opened Chapter 3 suggests.

Is the Glass Half-Empty, or Half-Full?

We now summarize the main findings presented in this chapter. Based on our estimates, exposure to mobilization on social media increases overall levels of participation by about 50% (Figure 4.5), engagement with supportive views increases participation by about 18% when compared against two-sided content (Figure 4.1), and frequent accidental exposure to political news boosts participation by about 9% (Figure 4.3). In the grand scheme of the many factors that affect participation, are these substantial increases, or just a little nudge?

The answer depends on how large the influence of social media looks when compared with the influence of other factors that affect participation. In their classic study of participation in the United States, Verba and colleagues (1995) showed that three sets of factors explain participation: resources, political involvement, and recruitment networks. We will now present some simple estimates of the direct effects of three important variables that at least partially capture each of the explanatory factors proposed by Verba and colleagues (1995): education (as a proxy for resources), interest in politics (as a proxy for political involvement), and frequency of face-to-face political conversation (as a proxy for offline mobilization networks).

To this end, we estimate a simple model predicting our index of participation as a function of education, political interest, and face-to-face political talk. To avoid diluting the effects of these variables we only include a small number of controls: gender, age, age squared, and income (see Online Appendix, Table A39). Here, we focus only on the estimated effect sizes derived from the model and based on hypothetical respondents who have average values on all variables apart from those whose effects we aim to estimate. First, we compare an average respondent with at least a university degree with another average respondent who only went to primary school. The absolute difference in our 0–6 index of participation between these two respondents is 1.3 versus 1.1, which corresponds to a relative increase of about 18% from primary to tertiary education. Second, we compare an average respondent who claims to be very interested in politics with another average respondent who claims to be only slightly interested. Here, the absolute difference is larger: 1.5 versus 1, an increase of about 50%. If we compare a highly interested respondent with one who claims no interest at all, the gap grows to 1.5 versus 0.8, or an 87.5% increase. Finally, we compare an average respondent who talks about politics "every day or almost every day" with an average respondent who talks about politics "a few times a week." The estimated levels of participation are 1.8 versus 1.3, or a 38% increase. If we compare respondents who talk about politics every day with those who never do that, the difference grows to 1.8 versus 0.7, a 157% relative increase.

We are not suggesting that readers compare these estimates directly, as they are based on models that employ different sets of control variables. However, these figures provide suggestive evidence that political experiences on social media may play a role that is quantitively comparable to that of some "fundamentals" of participation as described by Verba and colleagues (1995).

Any effects political experiences on social media may have on political behavior should always be seen in the broader context of factors that contribute to shaping citizens' practices. This does not necessarily mean that readers who thought the glass was half-full before reading this paragraph should now think it is half-empty. First, the glass of social media may look differently full, or empty, depending on which type of political experience is filling it. Second, while social media are important factors in shaping citizens' participatory repertoires, they sit alongside other, more enduring individual and contextual factors.

Summary: Do Social Media Matter?

Political experiences on social media—such as being targeted by electoral mobilization, seeing politically supportive messages, and accidentally encountering news—contribute, to a larger or smaller degree, to citizens' repertoires of political participation. In this chapter, we have shown that these associations are, on average, stronger for mobilization than for accidental exposure. Exposure to supportive political content lies in between.

The different strength of these relationships confirms the validity of one of our conceptual and theoretical starting points—that social media use does not matter per se, but specific political experiences resulting from social media use can enhance political participation with different intensity. The more direct and explicit the political signal is in these experiences—as with exposure to electoral mobilization and politically supportive content—the stronger the effect. Vice versa, the more mixed and unfocused the experience is—as with accidental encounters with news—the weaker the effect. When arguing that "social media" play any (positive or negative) democratic role, we should always specify which type of "political experience on social media" we are referring to.

When we zoomed in on specific modes of political action, we saw that the more popular activities (i.e., trying to persuade others and signing petitions) tend to grow more in absolute terms as a result of the political experiences we studied. However, when it comes to relative growth, it is the least popular activities (such as donating money, distributing leaflets, and taking part in rallies) that on average receive the highest boost. Overall, political experiences on social media do not seem to disproportionally encourage participation in relatively easier, less resource-intensive (at least in conventional terms) activities, nor in activities primarily occurring in digital spaces. Instead, they foster hybrid repertoires that combine higher-threshold and lower-threshold endeavors occurring both on the Web and face to face.

However, there is more to political life—and participation—than political experiences on social media. When seen amid the array of factors that affect participation, political experiences on social media play a distinctive and important role, but their impact may be weaker than that of long-standing differences in resources, motivations, and recruitment networks. To understand how political experiences on social media shape political behaviors, we need to bear in mind that they do not operate in a vacuum. Whatever political stimulations, incentives, and opportunities for action social media may help disseminate do not fall on blank slates, but on individuals characterized by specific personal and political histories, preferences, and contexts. Individuals differ from one another in meaningful ways that matter for participation over, above, and beyond whatever happens to them on social media. In the next chapter, we will see that some of these differences also play a role in shaping the ways in which, and the groups among whom, social media enhance participation.

5

Picking Winners or Helping Losers?

Social Media and Political Equality

On April 7, 2017, a very unusual video was published on the highly popular YouTube channel of Jean-Luc Mélenchon, the left-wing candidate in the French 2017 presidential election. It was titled "Mélenchon Gaming: Fiscal Kombat" and showcased a video game released by *La France Insoumise* ("Unbowed France"), the organization Mélenchon launched in 2016 to support his presidential bid. Fiscal Kombat, a game that can be played online, deliberately parroted the cult video gaming series "Mortal Kombat" and featured Mélenchon himself as the hero. The mission was to guide the candidate in an urban raid, punching around squads of rich and corrupt businessmen, literally shaking them to get back the money they had snatched from state coffers and taxpayers. The game also featured some obvious villains such as the managing director of the International Monetary Fund, Christine Lagarde, and the former French president, Nicolas Sarkozy (Saeed, 2017).

The website hosting the game prominently featured various "share on social media" buttons and enabled users to download the full manifesto of the candidate, to visit his campaign website, and, most importantly, to jump to a page where users could easily calculate the exact amount of taxes any citizen would pay if the fiscal reforms proposed by Mélenchon were implemented. This page also offered information on how to get involved in the campaign. For instance, users could request electioneering material, donate money, join a local group of activists, find or organize a campaign-related event, and see practical examples of actions one could take to support the candidate on social media and on the ground. The YouTube video showcasing the game quickly gathered thousands of visualizations online, and news about the launch was shared by Mélenchon's official accounts on other social media platforms. In turn, national and international media covered the release of the game extensively. This was just one extravagant enterprise by a tech-savvy campaign that deployed multiple digital

Outside the Bubble. Cristian Vaccari and Augusto Valeriani, Oxford University Press. © Oxford University Press 2021. DOI: 10.1093/oso/9780190858476.003.0006

tools to reach, mobilize, and organize supporters. Such efforts included a dedicated platform for creating campaign-related memes and the organization of simultaneous rallies in multiple cities where a hologram of Mélenchon appeared on stage.

Let us now imagine a French Internet user in her thirties who, on April 7, 2017, was hanging around on Facebook without any precise goal and suddenly stumbled upon Fiscal Kombat because a friend had shared its launching video. This imaginary user may or may not have been interested in the campaign, but, as most of her peers around the globe, she had been a Mortal Kombat maniac as a kid and, out of curiosity, decided to try Mélenchon's video game. In this way, she ended up getting exposed to abundant gamified information on the candidate's economic views and fiscal program. If she wandered around the website after playing the game, she may also have had the opportunity to calculate the potential impact on her pocketbook of Mélenchon's proposals to reform the French fiscal system. At that point, our imaginary user was just one step away from receiving multiple requests to participate in the campaign. Assuming that this scenario materialized in whole or in part, a few questions arise: Was the Fiscal Kombat experience a turning point for our imaginary character's orientation to participate in the 2017 presidential campaign? Was she previously disengaged but changed her mind after learning, via the online game shared by a friend on Facebook, about fiscal injustices, the need for reform, and the possibility to advance this program by supporting Mélenchon? Did the information and opportunities for action she stumbled upon while on social media activate some latent predispositions and encourage her to get more involved? Or was she already active in politics, but the gaming experience enlightened her about forms of participation that she had not previously considered? Obviously, we cannot answer these questions with certainty. However, we know that one of the cornerstones of Mélenchon's strategy was to encourage people to join the campaign online and offline, and that the campaign was overall quite successful in these endeavors. According to media reports (Fouquet, 2017), Sophia Chikirou, Mélenchon's head of communications, had previously been sent to the United States to study the Bernie Sanders 2016 presidential campaign, which had used the Web effectively to mobilize grassroots support (Penney, 2017). Moreover, we know that at the beginning of the campaign Mélenchon was considered a second-tier candidate at best, but he surprisingly received more than 19% of the vote.

In this chapter, we address systematically the kinds of questions we asked about the main character in our French vignette: Can political experiences on social media engage the relatively less engaged, or do they mostly boost participation among those who are already active? In other words, are political experiences on social media more likely to enhance political equality or to exacerbate existing inequalities? There are various reasons why political experiences on social media may be beneficial for participation among most voters, and in Chapter 4 we have shown that this is actually the case. Getting in contact with supportive opinions, accidentally encountering political news, and receiving a suggestion to vote for a certain party may convey helpful information on candidates, parties, and issues; remind recipients of their own social and political identities; reinforce their political predispositions; and offer practical information about how to get involved, both online and in physical settings. However, in Chapter 1 we also theorized that the marginal utility—the benefit that may result from any additional political stimulation—of political experiences on social media may be higher among those users who are less involved in politics than among those who are more involved. Regardless of the particular type of politically relevant content that is exchanged, these interactions should yield the greatest returns among the relatively less involved, who tend to have weaker political convictions and enjoy fewer opportunities to get exposed to news and campaign communications, than among the more involved, who tend to have stronger political allegiances and can be expected to encounter higher quantities of political content, not only on social media but also elsewhere in their everyday lives. As we saw in Chapter 3, political experiences on social media have the capacity to reach beyond the highly involved. If our argument is right that the less involved, once they engage in political experiences, receive a greater participatory boost from them than the highly involved do, we expect that the political experiences we study in this book, while benefiting users across the board, will yield higher participatory returns among the less involved.

To test this theory, we need to differentiate between the more and the less politically involved of our respondents. Hence, in our models we will use as moderators two political attitudes that are among the most reliable predictors of participation and that effectively capture both long-term and short-term political involvement: *interest in politics* and *attention to the campaign* (see Chapter 1). We will show that, overall, political experiences on social media increase participation among those who are less involved in politics (i.e., citizens who describe themselves as less interested and attentive) more than among those who are more involved. Hence, political experiences on social media contribute to reducing important attitude-driven participatory inequalities among citizens.[1]

Moreover, as discussed in Chapter 1, if political experiences on social media have differential effects among citizens with different political attitudes, it is possible that some of these differences may be related to political ideologies. This, in turn, may contribute to reshaping patterns of electoral competition, to the extent that citizens who support different types of leaders, parties, and causes may be more likely to be prompted to participate, and thus to advance those same leaders, parties, and causes, as a result of political experiences on social media. To assess the implications of political experiences on social media for electoral competition, we estimate whether *ideology* (one of the most reliable predictors of voting behavior) moderates their relationship with political participation.

To measure ideology, we asked respondents a standard question about left–right placement that is used in most studies of voting behavior in Western democracies.[2] Moreover, as readers may recall, some of the scenarios we theorized in Chapter 1 when discussing differential effects related to ideology addressed the debate on the relationship between digital media and populism. Although we cannot use established measures of populist attitudes to differentiate our respondents, we can tap into a useful behavioral measure—their vote in the last election. To this end, we classified all the parties or presidential candidates that respondents reported voting for in the most recent and most relevant election in their country in two ways: a binary division between populist and non-populist and a three-way distinction between left-wing populist, right-wing populist, and non-populist. Because classifying parties and leaders as populist or not is far from a settled question (see, e.g., Bergman, 2019; Margulies, 2018; Norris & Inglehart, 2019; Rooduijn, 2019), we have run different models based on different classifications, from the most expansive to the most restrictive. Overall, we compiled eight different variables classifying respondents based on their populist vote, four of which comprise two categories and four comprise three categories. Our Online Appendix provides a detailed discussion of these classifications.

Based on these analyses, we evaluate the plausibility of different competitive scenarios: a stronger effect for extremists on both sides, potentially leading to increased polarization; a tilting of the balance in favor of one ideological tendency; a boost for authoritarian populists or for populists in general; or, finally, a roughly even distribution of participatory gains irrespective of ideological alignments. As this chapter will show, our results suggest that the rising tide of political experiences on social media by and large evenly lifts all ideological boats.

A Voice, Not an Echo, Can Reach Beyond the Front Rows

In Chapter 4, we saw that social media users who are exposed to viewpoints they predominantly agree with are substantially more active in politics than those who are exposed to either two-sided or mainly oppositional content, let alone those who barely see any political messages on these platforms. As readers may recall, our models predicted that an average respondent who mostly sees politically supportive content on social media should engage in about two political activities per year, compared with about 1.7 for average respondents who see oppositional or two-sided content. While these estimates apply to the population in general, do they differ among users with different levels of political involvement, and if so, how?

To answer this question, we augmented the Poisson regression models presented in Chapter 4 with interaction terms that capture the differential relationships between agreement on social media and political participation at different levels of the three political attitudes we use as moderators (interest, attention, and ideology). To avoid the risk of multicollinearity, which would reduce the precision of our estimates, we ran three separate models, each with one interaction term.

Table 5.1 shows the results of the models with interaction terms for interest and attention. To make the table easier to read, we only present the coefficients

Table 5.1. **Poisson Regressions Predicting Levels of Political Participation (0–6 Index): Differential Effects of Agreement on Social Media by Interest in Politics and Attention to the Campaign**

	Model 1: Interest		Model 2: Attention	
	Coefficient	*Std. Error*	*Coefficient*	*Std. Error*
Political content on social media (reference = Two-sided)				
One-sided supportive	0.648***	0.092	0.492***	0.099
One-sided oppositional	0.208*	0.089	0.238*	0.093
No political content	−0.827***	0.170	−0.645***	0.169
Interest in politics	0.141***	0.027	0.094***	0.021
Attention to the campaign	0.043	0.022	0.082**	0.028
Interactions (reference = Two-sided)				
One-sided supportive × Interest	−0.194***	0.036		
One-sided oppositional × Interest	−0.073*	0.034		
No political content × Interest	0.247***	0.064		
One-sided supportive × Attention			−0.130***	0.039
One-sided oppositional × Attention			−0.086*	0.036
No political content × Attention			0.175**	0.064

Note: N = 7,205. Cell entries are unstandardized coefficients for Poisson regressions. Coefficients for all control variables are omitted for simplicity. Full model results are available in the Online Appendix (Table A40).

*$p \leq 0.05$.
**$p \leq 0.01$.
***$p \leq 0.001$.

for the variables of interest and their interactions. We note that the goodness of fit of these models increases only marginally compared with models without interaction coefficients: the pseudo-R^2 for the model with direct effects (Table 4.1) was 0.265, and it is 0.271 for Model 1 and 0.268 for Model 2 in Table 5.1. This means that, although the differential effects we estimate are large enough to be significant, accounting for these factors does not massively increase our ability to explain the extent to which levels of participation vary in our sample. The full models are available in the Online Appendix (Table A40).

The results are similar across both models. The coefficients for exposure to supportive political content are all positive and significant, and much larger than those for exposure to oppositional content, consistent with the results presented in Chapter 4. In Table 5.1, these coefficients now represent the strength of the relationship between exposure to political content and participation when interest in politics (Model 1) and attention to the campaign (Model 2) are at their lowest levels. The coefficients for the interaction terms are a mirror image of those for their main constitutive variables: for exposure to supportive views, they are all negative and significant; for exposure to oppositional views, they are also negative and significant, but noticeably smaller; for lack of exposure to political content, instead, the interaction terms are all positive and significant.

These results mean that *the strength of the positive relationship between exposure to supportive (and, to a lesser degree, oppositional) political content on social media declines as levels of both long-term (interest) and short-term (attention) political involvement increase.* In other words, social media users who engage with supportive political content and are less politically interested and attentive receive a higher participatory boost than social media users who are more interested and attentive. Conversely, when individuals are not exposed to any meaningful political content coming from social media, they are left to their own attitudinal devices, so to speak, and their participation repertoires depend much more on their levels of interest and attention. These findings support our theory that citizens who are less politically involved gain higher marginal participatory utility from political experiences on social media.

To better gauge the implications of these results, we estimated the levels of political participations that our models predict for respondents who exhibit average values for all the variables we included, apart from agreement and disagreement on social media and levels of political involvement. Given that the results in Table 5.1 are similar across the two models, we focus on the interaction with interest in politics for simplicity. Figure 5.1 shows the predicted levels of political participation for average respondents exposed to different combinations of agreement and disagreement on social media and who have the highest and lowest levels of interest in politics.

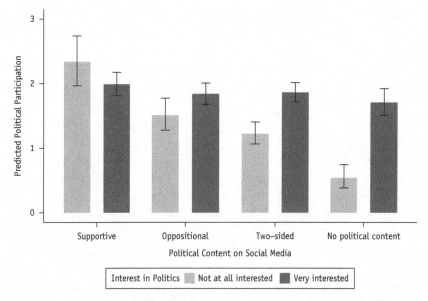

Figure 5.1. Predicted Levels of Political Participation Among Average Respondents with High and Low Levels of Interest in Politics Exposed to Different Levels of Agreement on Social Media

Note: Estimates are count values of a 0–6 index and are based on the coefficients in Table 5.1, Model 1, for respondents with values equal to the sample means (for numeric variables), medians (for ordinal variables), and modes (for categorical variables) apart from agreement and disagreement with political content seen on social media and interest in politics.

If we compare the bars in light gray, which represent average respondents with no interest in politics, we see the same pattern as we showed in Chapter 4 for the whole sample: users who mainly engage with supportive views on social media participate in significantly more activities (2.34) than those who engage with oppositional (1.51) and two-sided views (1.22), and all three groups participate significantly more than those who do not see any political content on social media (0.54). However, this pattern disappears if we look at the dark-gray bars, which represent respondents with the highest levels of interest in politics. Even though these respondents still participate in more political activities if they predominantly encounter supportive messages (1.99) rather than two-sided content (1.86), oppositional messages (1.84), or no political content at all (1.71), all the error bars associated with these four configurations overlap, which means that the estimates are statistically indistinguishable once we take into account the uncertainty around them. Moreover, if we compare the light- and dark-gray bars for each type of political content seen on social media, there is no significant difference in predicted levels of participation between respondents with the highest and lowest levels of interest in politics, as long as they encounter supportive and oppositional political views on social media. Instead, there are significant differences between users with high and low interest in politics who encounter both two-sided views and no political content. In other words, all else being equal, *exposure to supportive and* (to a lesser degree) *oppositional political views on social media eliminates the participatory gap between voters with high and low levels of interest in politics.* The same holds true if we look at differences rooted in attention to the campaign.

Another way to explore the relationships highlighted in Table 5.1 is to estimate marginal effects, that is, the predicted changes in levels of participation resulting from exposure to supportive versus two-sided political content on social media across citizens with different levels of political involvement. From the previous example, we already know that, among respondents who are not interested in politics at all, those who encounter supportive views on social media are predicted to participate in 2.34 activities, nearly twice as many as those who encounter two-sided views (1.22 activities). The difference between these two predicted outcomes is the marginal effect of predominant exposure to supportive content among respondents with no interest in politics. This is a sizable gap, as 2.34 is nearly double 1.22. By contrast, among respondents who are very interested in politics, those who engage with supportive viewpoints on social media are predicted to participate in 1.99 activities, while those who are exposed to two-sided political content are predicted to participate in 1.86 activities. Thus, the marginal effect of supportive versus two-sided political content is nearly nine times as large for respondents with no interest in politics (2.34 − 1.22 = 1.12) than for respondents with high interest in politics (1.99 − 1.86 = 0.13). Figure 5.2 shows these differences and their confidence intervals for all the relevant values of interest in politics (in the left panel) and attention to the campaign (in the right panel). If estimates are lower than 0, the predicted effect within that group is a reduction in the index of political participation. If confidence intervals include 0, the predicted effect within that group is not statistically distinguishable from 0, so there is no significant marginal effect. To facilitate these comparisons, the two panels in Figure 5.2 feature vertical dashed lines corresponding to 0, which means no increase.

Figure 5.2 shows that, for both indicators of political involvement we analyze as moderators, the predicted increase in political participation associated with exposure to supportive content on social media is substantially larger among the least politically involved (who are "not at all interested" in politics and followed the last general election campaign "not at all closely") than among the most politically involved (who are "very interested" in politics and followed the campaign "very closely"). While the confidence intervals of some estimates overlap (for instance, between those who are "slightly" and "not at all" interested), the marginal effects for the lowest categories of political involvement are always significantly stronger

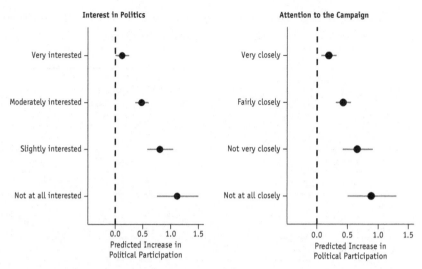

Figure 5.2. Marginal Effects of Exposure to Supportive Versus Two-Sided Political Content on Social Media at Different Levels of Interest in Politics and Attention to the Campaign

Note: Estimates are changes in count values of a 0–6 index and are based on the coefficients in Table 5.1, Model 1 (interest in politics) and Model 2 (attention to the campaign), for respondents with values equal to the sample means (for numeric variables), medians (for ordinal variables), and modes (for categorical variables) apart from agreement with political content seen on social media (comparing respondents who predominantly see supportive and two-sided messages), interest in politics (left panel), and attention to the campaign (right panel).

than those for the highest categories. In sum, participation increases among most social media users who encounter supportive political content on these platforms, but the least involved experience the highest gains. The absolute values of such differences are greater for political interest (where, as shown earlier, the least interested gain nearly 9 times as much as the most interested) than for attention to the campaign (where participation increases about 4.5 times as much among the least attentive as among the most attentive). In sum, exposure to supportive political content on social media is associated with substantially higher participatory gains among the least politically involved citizens than among the most involved.

Let us now assess the differential effects of exposure to supportive political content on social media and participation based on respondents' ideology. To this end, we added to our Poisson regression models an interaction term that captures the differential effects of exposure to varying degrees of agreement and disagreement on social media among citizens with different ideological alignments. Table 5.2 displays the simplified results of our regression models with interaction terms for ideology. As was the case for the models in Table 5.1, the pseudo-R^2 only increased marginally compared with the model without interactions (0.269 versus 0.265), again suggesting that taking these differential effects

Table 5.2. **Poisson Regressions Predicting Levels of Political Participation (0–6 Index): Differential Effects of Agreement on Social Media by Ideology**

	Coefficient	Std. Error
Political content on social media (reference = Two-sided)		
One-sided supportive	0.256 ***	0.071
One-sided oppositional	0.025	0.055
No political content	−0.295**	0.096
Ideology (reference = Center)		
Left	0.346***	0.054
Center-left	0.260***	0.044
Center-right	0.123**	0.045
Right	0.197***	0.060
Unaligned	−0.019	0.052
Interactions (reference = Two-sided, Center)		
One-sided supportive × Left	−0.247*	0.099
One-sided oppositional × Left	−0.058	0.090
No political content × Left	0.345*	0.169
One-sided supportive × Center-left	−0.086	0.085
One-sided oppositional × Center-left	−0.019	0.071
No political content × Center-left	0.229	0.118
One-sided supportive × Center-right	−0.038	0.089
One-sided oppositional × Center-right	0.040	0.073
No political content × Center-right	0.130	0.120
One-sided supportive × Right	−0.139	0.111
One-sided oppositional × Right	−0.067	0.099
No political content × Right	0.144	0.163
One-sided supportive × Unaligned	−0.036	0.099
One-sided oppositional × Unaligned	0.044	0.083
No political content × Unaligned	−0.263	0.147

Note: $N = 7,205$. Cell entries are unstandardized coefficients for Poisson regressions. Coefficients for all control variables are omitted for simplicity. Full model results are available in the Online Appendix (Table A41).

*$p \leq 0.05$.

**$p \leq 0.01$.

***$p \leq 0.001$.

into account does not greatly enhance the model's explanatory power. Full results of the model are available in Table A41 in our Online Appendix.

In Table 5.2, the coefficients for exposure to supportive, oppositional, and no political content now refer to participants who are in the reference category for ideology (center) and confirm that encountering supportive political content on social media is positively and significantly associated with participation, while lack of exposure to political content is negatively and significantly associated with it. By the same token, the coefficients for ideology refer to respondents who encounter two-sided political content on social media (the reference category) and imply that, among respondents who see both agreeing and disagreeing content in similar proportions, those who align with a particular position, whether left or right, participate in politics significantly more than those who locate themselves at the center. This is not surprising, as people who locate themselves to the left or the right of the spectrum tend to have stronger allegiances, and thus participate more intensely to voice them, than those who describe themselves as centrists. The coefficients for the interaction terms between agreement and disagreement on social media and ideology, however, are all non-significant apart from two, both pertaining to respondents who place themselves to the left. All else being equal, leftists receive a smaller participatory boost than centrists from engaging with supportive views, and, at the same time, their participation is less markedly depressed by lack of exposure to political content on social media—in both cases, when compared against encountering two-sided content.

To clarify the substantive implications of these results, Figure 5.3 plots the marginal effects of exposure to supportive versus two-sided political content on social media among respondents with different ideologies. Our estimates suggest that average respondents who place themselves around relatively more moderate parts of the spectrum (center-left, center, and center-right) experience statistically significant increases in their levels of participation if they predominantly see political content they agree with on social media—compared with an alternative situation in which they see a two-sided mix of messages. The same is true for respondents who refuse to locate themselves anywhere in the left–right spectrum. This is shown by the fact that the point estimates and error bars for all these groups do not overlap with 0 (which is marked with a dashed line in the figure). The size of this predicted increase in participation is comparable across all of these four ideological groups, and the differences in the marginal effects between them are not statistically distinguishable, as shown by the fact that the respective error bars overlap with one another. The only two ideological groups in our sample that do not receive a statistically significant participatory boost from encountering supportive content on social media are those who locate themselves at the extremes of the spectrum, both on the left and on the right.

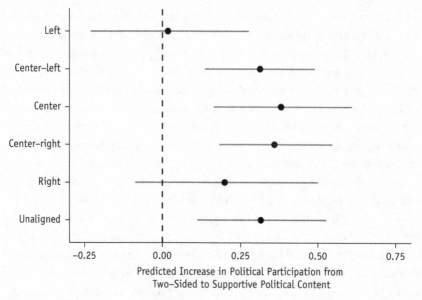

Figure 5.3. Marginal Effects of Exposure to Supportive Versus Two-Sided Political Content on Social Media Among Respondents with Different Ideologies

Note: Estimates are changes in count values of a 0–6 index and are based on the coefficients in Table A41 (available in the Online Appendix) for respondents with values equal to the sample means (for numeric variables), medians (for ordinal variables), and modes (for categorical variables) apart from respondents' self-placement in the left–right ideological spectrum and exposure to supportive views (versus two-sided ones).

This is shown by the fact that the error bars for those estimates in Figure 5.3 overlap with 0.

These findings strikingly refute the idea that exposure to politically congruent information on social media disproportionately mobilizes users with the most radical views and, thus, contributes to polarizing society. Quite the contrary. Unlike the rest of the population, the most ideologically extreme members of the electorate—on both the left and the right—do not experience any significant participatory gains when they engage with supportive viewpoints on social media. Instead, it is the more moderate sectors of the electorate, as well as the ideologically unaligned, that see their participation increase.

When compared against the five scenarios discussed in Chapter 1, these results refute the one we termed "polarization," as respondents located to the extremes were the only ones to not receive a participatory boost. The most ideologically radical users may be so strong in their beliefs that their levels of participation do not significantly increase when their views are reinforced by agreeing others. Results also fail to support the "tilting-the-balance" scenario, as center-right and center-left identifiers experienced very similar increases, statistically indistinguishable from one another. Nor is there evidence for an "authoritarian-populist" scenario, because those located to the right did not experience significant gains. Moreover, additional analyses that estimated differential effects based on whether respondents voted for a party classified as right-wing populist did not yield any significant results with respect to exposure to supportive content (see Tables A42–A45 in the Online Appendix).[3] The fact that unaligned respondents experienced a significant increase in their levels of participation when they saw supportive political content on social media could provide some grounds for the broader "populist" scenario, i.e., a stronger participatory boost for supporters of populist parties, who frequently refuse right–left identifications as a frill of establishment parties. However, such increase was statistically indistinguishable from the one we estimated for centrist, center-right, and center-left voters—hardly evidence of a populist digital tide. Moreover, when we estimated differential effects based on whether respondents had voted for a party classified as populist (regardless of whether that party mainly articulates the left-wing or right-wing variant of populism), our models did not yield any significant results for this interaction (see Tables A46–A49 in the Online Appendix for full results). Thus, when it comes to the participatory gains associated with exposure to supportive viewpoints on social media, our findings mostly corroborate the "rising-tide" scenario, with the caveat that the tide does not include ideologically more extreme voters.

Accidents Matter—Where You Least Expect It

We now shift our focus to accidental exposure to political news on social media. In Chapter 4, we saw that, overall, there is a positive and significant relationship between this experience and political participation, but the association is weaker than those for predominant exposure to agreeing viewpoints and electoral mobilization. We now assess whether this relationship varies according to respondents' levels of interest in politics and attention to the last election campaign. Our expectation is that the interaction terms we will use to estimate these differential effects should have negative coefficients, indicating that the positive relationship between accidental exposure and participation is stronger among the less politically involved than among the more involved. Table 5.3 shows the relevant coefficients for these models. As was the case for agreement and disagreement, adding these interaction terms does not lead to substantial increases in our model's explanatory power, as the goodness of fit grows marginally from a Pseudo-R^2 of 0.286 for the model without interaction terms (Table 4.2) to 0.287 for both models in Table 5.3. This means that, similarly as before, estimating

Table 5.3. **Poisson Regressions Predicting Levels of Political Participation (0–6 Index): Differential Effects of Accidental Exposure to Political News on Social Media by Interest in Politics and Attention to the Campaign**

	Model 1: Interest		Model 2: Attention	
	Coeff.	*Std. Err.*	*Coeff.*	*Std. Err.*
Accidental exposure to political news on SNSs	0.154***	0.040	0.189***	0.041
Interest in politics	0.193***	0.032	0.118***	0.021
Attention to the campaign	0.063**	0.022	0.159***	0.034
Accidental exposure × Interest	−0.047**	0.015		
Accidental exposure × Attention			−0.061***	0.016

Note: SNS = social networking site. N = 8,639. Cell entries are unstandardized coefficients for Poisson regressions. Coefficients for all control variables are omitted for simplicity. Full model results are available in the Online Appendix (Table A50).

 *$p \leq 0.05$.
 **$p \leq 0.01$.
 ***$p \leq 0.001$.

differential effects does not substantially increase our ability to explain variation in participation, even though it helps highlight relevant differences between subgroups. The full models are reported in the Online Appendix (Table A50).

The results confirm our expectations. Similar to exposure to agreeing views, accidental encounters with political news on social media are more strongly associated with participation among the less politically involved than among the more involved. In Figure 5.4 we plot estimated levels of political participation among hypothetical average respondents who claimed to incidentally encounter political news on social media at different frequencies and who followed the campaign either not closely at all or very closely.

Let us start by inspecting the darker bars, which represent respondents who claimed to follow the campaign very closely. Among these hyper-attentive citizens, accidental exposure made no difference whatsoever, as all four groups participated in about 1.2 activities irrespective of how frequently they accidentally encountered news online. In a sense, this is not surprising, as those who already paid close attention to the campaign were in a position to intentionally obtain enough information to motivate them to participate and may thus not benefit from further, accidental encounters with news on social media. However, if we focus on the least attentive, represented by the lighter-gray bars, a different pattern emerges that confirms our expectations. The more frequently these respondents

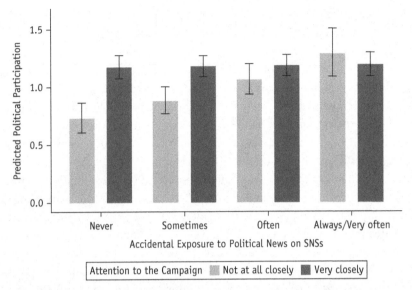

Figure 5.4. Predicted Levels of Political Participation Among Average Respondents with High and Low Levels of Attention to the Campaign and Different Frequencies of Accidental Exposure to Political News on Social Media

Note: Estimates are count values of a 0–6 index and are based on the coefficients in Table 5.3, Model 2, for respondents with values equal to the sample means (for numeric variables), medians (for ordinal variables), and modes (for categorical variables) apart from accidental exposure to political news on social media and attention to the campaign.

claimed to incidentally bump into news online, the more they participated. Although overall predicted levels of participation are low, the differences are quite stark in relative terms. An average respondent who paid no attention at all to the campaign and never claimed to accidentally see political news on social media is estimated to take part in 0.73 political activities. Contrast this with a similarly average inattentive respondent who, crucially, said she very often came across news on social media without seeking it out. Our model predicts this second respondent participated in 1.28 political activities—almost twice as many as the first. As the error bars in Figure 5.4 show, the differences in predicted levels of participation among the inattentive are significant if we compare those who encountered political news by accident "always or very often" and those who did so "sometimes" or "never." Interestingly, the error bars for attentive and inattentive respondents overlap if they reported accidental exposure either "often" or "always or very often." Hence, high levels of accidental exposure eliminate participatory inequalities based on attentiveness to the campaign. Recall from Chapter 3 that nearly half of our respondents claimed to "often" or "always or very often" run into news on social media that they were not seeking. These findings suggest that the pervasiveness of political content on social media may make a small but important participatory difference among the less politically involved who encounter information on these platforms by accident. Rather than being merely the icing on the cake of political junkies' information diets, accidentally encountered political news on social media contributes to closing participatory gaps between the attentive and the inattentive.

Our results add to a growing body of research on the political implications of accidental exposure to news online. For instance, a study based on both cross-sectional and longitudinal surveys of Austrian voters shows both converging and diverging results from ours (Heiss & Matthes, 2019). When the authors modeled the relationship between accidental exposure and participation using cross-sectional data, they found similar patterns to those we found, with stronger affects among voters with lower levels of interest in politics. However, when they estimated their models using panel data, the authors found that the relationship between accidental exposure and participation was actually slightly stronger among the highly interested than the less interested. Another study by Weeks and colleagues (2021) also employs longitudinal data from two different panel surveys of U.S. citizens and shows that online incidental exposure to news results in larger political knowledge gains for individuals with lower levels of interest in politics. While longitudinal surveys are better suited than cross-sectional data to establish one aspect of causality—temporal antecedence—our research covers a broader range of countries and thus provides more robust findings on these patterns across different political systems. Our study, however, is definitely not the final word on these topics, and we hope scholars will continue shedding light on these phenomena by employing richer data sets and considering different national contexts in which to assess whether and to what extent accidental exposure to news on social media can reduce important political inequalities.

To illustrate our findings more systematically, Figure 5.5 shows how much our estimates of political participation (calculated based on the models in Table 5.3) change when comparing an average respondent who "never" accidentally encounters news on social media to another who does so "always or very often." First, the error bars for the estimates corresponding to the most interested and attentive respondents consistently overlap with 0, which means that these highly involved groups do not experience any significant participatory gains when they very frequently encounter political news by accident on social media. Second, the least politically interested and attentive respondents benefit the most, and significantly so when compared with the most involved. In particular, the least interested are predicted to increase their levels of participation by 0.4 activities and the least attentive by 0.55.

In sum, our analysis confirms our expectation that accidental exposure to news on social media yields a higher marginal participatory utility among the least involved than among the most involved. Hence, accidental exposure is another

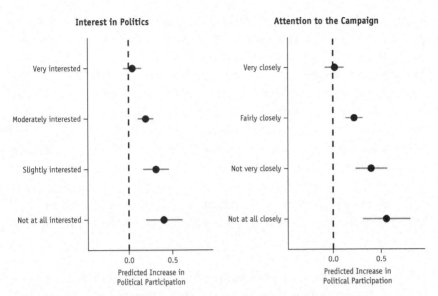

Figure 5.5. Marginal Effects of Accidental Exposure to Political News on Social Media at Different Levels of Interest in Politics and Attention to the Campaign

Note: Estimates are changes in count values of a 0–6 index and are based on the coefficients in Table 5.2, Model 1 (interest in politics) and Model 2 (attention to the campaign), for respondents with values equal to the sample means (for numeric variables), medians (for ordinal variables), and modes (for categorical variables) apart from accidental exposure to political news on social media (comparing those who answered "Never" with those who answered "Always or very often"), interest in politics (left panel), and attention to the campaign (right panel).

mechanism that may help level participatory gaps rooted in different levels of political interest and campaign attentiveness. If accidental exposure was a residual experience that very few social media users report, then this finding could be safely dismissed as statistically valid but practically inconsequential. However, we know from Chapter 3 that substantial percentages of social media users encounter news online by accident. The case for the importance of accidental exposure for political equality thus becomes stronger, although the magnitude of the relationship is weaker than for other political experiences on social media.

We now focus on the differential effects of accidental exposure to political news on social media by ideology. We summarize the results of these analyses in Table 5.4 (see Table A51 in our Online Appendix for full model results). Once again, the explanatory power of this model is only marginally higher (pseudo-$R^2 = 0.288$) than that of the model without interaction terms (0.286, see Table 4.2). The coefficient for accidental exposure, which now refers to respondents who place themselves at the center of the left–right spectrum, is positive but fails to reach statistical significance. The coefficients for ideology, which now refer to respondents who never encounter news on social media accidentally, suggest that these citizens tend to participate significantly more if they align with the left, center-left, and right compared with those who situate themselves at the center. The coefficients for the interaction terms all fail to reach conventional levels of statistical significance, apart from leftist respondents, whose participation increases significantly less, compared with centrists, when the frequency with which they accidentally encounter news on social media increases. These predominantly null findings suggest that the relationship between accidental exposure and participation, which is overall relatively weak, does not differ substantially based on ideology.

To clarify the implications of our results, Figure 5.6 plots estimates derived from our model for average respondents aligned with different ideologies. The change in levels of political participation associated with frequently

Table 5.4. **Poisson Regressions Predicting Levels of Political Participation (0–6 Index): Differential Effects of Accidental Exposure to Political News on Social Media by Ideology**

	Coefficient	Std. Error
Accidental exposure to political news on SNSs	0.045	0.025
Ideology (reference = Center)		
Left	0.405***	0.072
Center-left	0.256***	0.056
Center-right	0.017	0.059
Right	0.257***	0.076
Unaligned	−0.102	0.064
Interactions (reference = Center)		
Accidental exposure × Left	−0.084*	0.039
Accidental exposure × Center-left	−0.040	0.031
Accidental exposure × Center-right	0.060	0.032
Accidental exposure × Right	−0.043	0.040
Accidental exposure × Unaligned	0.012	0.035

Note: SNS = social networking site. $N = 8,639$. Cell entries are unstandardized coefficients for Poisson regressions. Coefficients for all control variables are omitted for simplicity. Full model results are available in the Online Appendix (Table A51).

$*p \leq 0.05$.

$**p \leq 0.01$.

$***p \leq 0.001$.

encountering news on social media by accident is statistically distinguishable from 0 for only two groups: those espousing center-right positions and— minimally—those who refuse to locate themselves between left and right. For all the other ideological groups, the predicted increases in participation associated with accidental exposure to news on social media cannot be distinguished from 0. Centrist respondents come closest to registering a significant effect, but they still fall short.

When we consider the implications for political competition, these results border on endorsing the "tilting-the-balance" scenario, as accidental exposure boosts participation among center-right respondents by a statistically significant, albeit relatively small, margin (0.43 on a 0–6 scale). By contrast, voters who identify with the center-left do not record any significant increase. The results could also be seen as lending some support to the "populism" scenario, a participatory boost mostly concentrated among those who eschew the right-left identification. Ideologically unaligned voters, indeed, experience a significant (but even smaller, equaling only 0.19 activities) participatory gain when they often encounter news on social media by accident. However, when we estimated

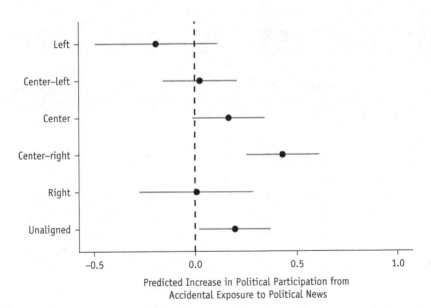

Figure 5.6. Marginal Effects of Accidental Exposure to Political News on Social Media Among Respondents with Different Ideologies

Note: Estimates are changes in count values of a 0–6 index and are based on the coefficients in Table A51 (available in the Online Appendix) for respondents with values equal to the sample means (for numeric variables), medians (for ordinal variables), and modes (for categorical variables) apart from respondents' self-placement in the left–right ideological spectrum and accidental exposure to political news on social media (comparing those who "Never" encounter news accidentally and those who do so "Always or very often").

the differential effects of accidental exposure based on whether respondents had, in fact, voted for a populist party, we found no significant coefficients in all the eight models we ran (see Tables A52–A59 in the Online Appendix). Hence, there is no evidence that accidental exposure to news on social media is associated with disproportionately larger levels of participation among citizens who voted for populist parties. Overall, given the weakness of the relationships we identified and the small magnitude of the predicted effect sizes, these results can mainly be interpreted as supporting the "rising-tide" scenario, with the qualification that the participatory tide resulting from accidental exposure is not particularly high regardless of respondents' ideology, and marginally higher among center-right and unaligned voters.

Mobilizing the Un-Mobilized

Finally, we turn to the third political experience on social media this book focuses on—being targeted by electoral mobilization. We know from Chapter 3 that about one-third of our respondents reported receiving at least one message on social media inviting them to support a candidate or party. We also know from Chapter 4 that this experience has the strongest direct relationship, among the three we are studying, with political participation. We now ask whether, similar to encountering supportive views and accidental exposure to news, the participatory benefits associated with electoral mobilization on social media are marginally higher for citizens with lower levels of political involvement. To this end, Table 5.5 shows the coefficients for models that predict levels of political participation and that include, together with the same right-hand-side variables as in the models presented in Chapter 4, interaction terms between exposure to mobilization and interest in politics and attention to the campaign. Once again, here we only report coefficients for the main independent variables of interest and their interaction terms. The full models are available in our Online Appendix (Table A60). Similar to other analyses presented in this chapter, including these interaction terms did not substantially improve the model's goodness of fit, as the pseudo-R^2 increased minimally, from 0.300 (Table 4.3) without interactions to 0.302 with interactions (both models in Table 5.5). Hence, we must acknowledge that estimating these differential effects does not increase the precision with which our models predict levels of political participation.

The pattern emerging from the results should look familiar by now. In both models, the coefficients for exposure to electoral mobilization, which now represent respondents with the lowest levels of interest (Model 1) and attention

Table 5.5. **Poisson Regressions Predicting Levels of Political Participation (0–6 Index): Differential Effects of Exposure to Electoral Mobilization on Social Media by Interest in Politics and Attention to the Campaign**

	Model 1: Interest		Model 2: Attention	
	Coeff.	*Std. Err.*	*Coeff.*	*Std. Err.*
Exposure to electoral mobilization on SNSs	0.774***	0.055	0.784***	0.060
Interest in politics	0.139***	0.018	0.073***	0.014
Attention to the campaign	0.051***	0.015	0.117***	0.020
Mobilization × Interest	−0.128***	0.021		
Mobilization × Attention			−0.129***	0.023

Note: SNS = social networking site. $N = 11{,}488$. Cell entries are unstandardized coefficients for Poisson regressions. Coefficients for all control variables are omitted for simplicity. Full model results are available in the Online Appendix (Table A60).
*$p \leq 0.05$.
**$p \leq 0.01$.
***$p \leq 0.001$.

(Model 2), are almost twice as large as those in Table 4.3, suggesting that the relationship between electoral mobilization and participation is stronger among these groups than among the rest of the sample. The coefficients for both interaction terms are negative and significant, indicating that the strength of the positive relationship between exposure to electoral mobilization on social media and political participation declines as interest and attention increase. As shown by the estimates plotted in Figure 5.7, an average respondent who has no interest at all in politics and does not recall being exposed to electoral mobilization on social media (or is not a social media user) is predicted to engage in 0.85 political activities per year. By contrast, a similar average respondent who is uninterested in politics and remembers being mobilized on social media is predicted to participate in 1.85 activities—more than twice as many, and a significant difference. Predicted levels of participation among respondents who are highly interested in politics and were mobilized (1.91) are also significantly higher than among highly interested respondents who were not mobilized (1.29), but the gap is noticeably smaller. Finally, the difference between two average respondents who were mobilized and reported the highest and lowest levels of interest in politics is not significant (1.91 vs. 1.85). Hence, similar to supportive political messages and accidental exposure, electoral mobilization boosts participation among the least involved while making a smaller difference among the most involved. Thus,

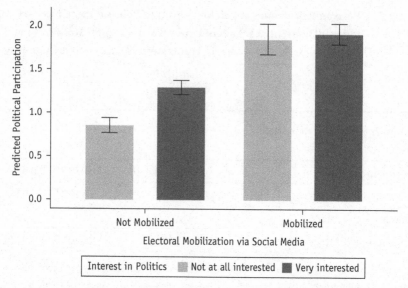

Figure 5.7. Predicted Levels of Political Participation Among Average Respondents with High and Low Levels of Interest in Politics and Who Were and Were Not Exposed to Electoral Mobilization on Social Media

Note: Estimates are count values of a 0–6 index and are based on the coefficients in Table 5.3, Model 1, for respondents with values equal to the sample means (for numeric variables), medians (for ordinal variables), and modes (for categorical variables) apart from exposure to electoral mobilization on social media and interest in politics.

electoral mobilization on social media levels the participation gap that normally exists between these groups.

Figure 5.8 presents our findings more systematically. If we estimate changes in levels of participation between average respondents who were and were not mobilized, predicted participation increases significantly among respondents reporting both high and low levels of interest and attentiveness. This is shown by the fact that all the dots representing our point estimates and the error bars representing 95% confidence intervals are way over the dashed line that corresponds to a null effect. However, the predicted increases in participation are much higher for respondents who reported the lowest levels of interest and attention than for those who reported the highest values. For instance, an average respondent who followed the campaign very closely is predicted to engage in an additional 0.61 activities per year if she was mobilized on social media, but a similarly average respondent who did not follow the campaign sees her estimated participation increase by 1.06 activities—nearly twice as many.

Moreover, in both panels of Figure 5.8 the error bars of the estimates do not overlap in at least one case, indicating that differences in predicted participatory increases between average respondents who were and were not mobilized are statistically significant across different levels of involvement. In particular, the marginal

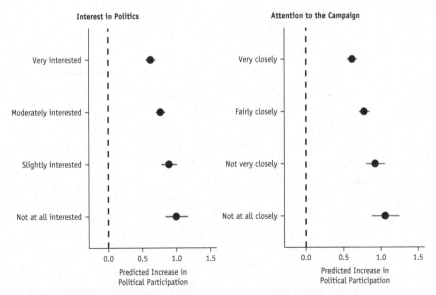

Figure 5.8. Marginal Effects of Exposure to Electoral Mobilization on Social Media at Different Levels of Interest in Politics and Attention to the Campaign

Note: Estimates are changes in count values of a 0–6 index and are based on the coefficients in Table 5.3, Model 1 (interest in politics) and Model 2 (attention to the campaign), for respondents with values equal to the sample means (for numeric variables), medians (for ordinal variables), and modes (for categorical variables) apart from exposure to electoral mobilization on social media (comparing those who were and were not mobilized), interest in politics (left panel), and attention to the campaign (right panel).

effects of electoral mobilization are significantly higher among respondents who are "not at all interested" in politics than among those who are "very interested," as well as among those who followed the election "not at all closely" compared with those who followed it "very closely." In sum, unlike engagement with supportive messages and accidental exposure to news, electoral mobilization is associated with significantly higher levels of participation among all voters, irrespective of their levels of political involvement. However, similar to the other two experiences, the marginal participatory yields of electoral mobilization via social media are substantially higher for voters who are relatively less interested in and less attentive to politics than among respondents with higher levels of political involvement.

Do the participatory gains associated with exposure to electoral mobilization on social media vary among respondents with different ideologies? As in the rest of this chapter, to answer this question we estimated models with interaction terms between electoral mobilization and ideology. Although the predictive power of our model did not increase substantially (with a pseudo-R^2 of 0.302), the results, reported in simplified form in Table 5.6, still provide some helpful indications (see Table A61 in the Online Appendix for full results). Exposure to mobilization on social media is positively and significantly correlated with participation among centrist voters (the reference category for ideology). Moreover, voters who locate themselves to the left, center-left, center-right, and right tend to participate more in politics than centrist voters when they do not receive mobilizing messages on social media, while unaligned voters in the same situation tend to participate even less than centrist voters. The negative and significant interaction coefficients suggest that, among the more ideologically extreme voters (both left and right) as well as center-left voters, electoral mobilization via social media is associated with significantly lower increases in participation than among centrist voters. This is not the case for center-right and unaligned voters, as the coefficients for the interaction terms involving these groups, albeit also negative, are not statistically significant.

Table 5.6. **Poisson Regressions Predicting Levels of Political Participation (0–6 Index): Differential Effects of Exposure to Electoral Mobilization on Social Media by Ideology**

	Coefficient	Std. Error
Exposure to electoral mobilization on SNSs	0.575***	0.035
Ideology (reference = Center)		
Left	0.403***	0.040
Center-left	0.259***	0.032
Center-right	0.119***	0.034
Right	0.226***	0.044
Unaligned	−0.082*	0.037
Interactions (reference = Center)		
Mobilization × Left	−0.288***	0.057
Mobilization × Center-left	−0.198***	0.046
Mobilization × Center-right	−0.051	0.046
Mobilization × Right	−0.162**	0.058
Mobilization × Unaligned	−0.061	0.054

Note: SNS = social networking site. $N = 11,488$. Cell entries are unstandardized coefficients for Poisson regressions. Coefficients for all control variables are omitted for simplicity. Full model results are available in the Online Appendix (Table A61).
 *$p \leq 0.05$.
 **$p \leq 0.01$.
 ***$p \leq 0.001$.

To better gauge the substantive implications of these findings, Figure 5.9 plots the changes in levels of participation resulting from exposure to electoral mobilization on social media, as predicted by our models for average respondents with different ideologies. All the point estimates and their error bars do not overlap with the dashed line that corresponds to 0 in the horizontal axis. This suggests that all respondents who recalled seeing messages on social media inviting them to vote for a party or candidate reported higher levels of political participation than those who did not, irrespective of their ideology. Hence, the rising tide of electoral mobilization lifts all ideological boats, and the strength of the tide is stronger than it is for engagement with supportive content and accidental exposure to political news. Voters locating themselves to the center and the center-right experience the highest participatory gains, but the increases of each ideological group are not statistically distinguishable from those of the other groups, as shown by the overlapping error bars. The only exception to this pattern involves voters who placed themselves to the left of the spectrum. Among this group the participatory gains, while respectable (0.46 on a 0–6 scale), are significantly smaller than those registered by center and center-right voters (0.73 for both subsets). Combined with the fact that right-wing voters

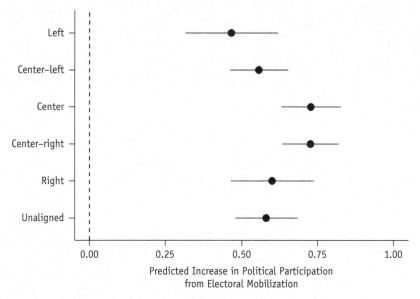

Figure 5.9. Marginal Effects of Exposure to Electoral Mobilization on Social Media Among Respondents with Different Ideologies

Note: Estimates are changes in count values of a 0–6 index and are based on the coefficients in Table A61 in the Online Appendix for respondents with values equal to the sample means (for numeric variables), medians (for ordinal variables), and modes (for categorical variables) apart from respondents' self-placement in the left–right ideological spectrum and electoral mobilization.

register increases that are statistically indistinguishable from those reported by other ideological groups, this finding further confirms that political experiences on social media do not seem to be disproportionally motivating the most extreme voters to become more engaged, thus disproving the "polarization" scenario outlined in Chapter 1.

Consistent with previous analyses in this chapter, we find little evidence of disproportional effects on populist voters. When we assessed the differential effects of electoral mobilization based on whether respondents had voted for a populist party, we once again found very little evidence of significant differences. None of the eight interaction coefficients we estimated based on different classifications of populist parties reached the conventional p-value of 0.05. Three coefficients for the interaction terms between exposure to electoral mobilization on social media and populist voting behavior meet the looser threshold of $p = 0.10$, but they are all negative, thus suggesting that voters of populist parties may experience slightly lower participatory gains than voters of non-populist parties when they are exposed to electoral mobilization on social media. Overall, then, the results yield no support to the "authoritarian populist" and "populist" scenarios. (See Tables A62–A69 in the Online Appendix for full model results.)

In sum, once again our findings mostly corroborate the "rising-tide" scenario, as all ideological groups participate significantly more when they are exposed to electoral mobilization via social media and most of the differences between voters of different persuasions are not significant. The fact that center and center-right voters report a significantly higher increase than left-wing (but not center-left) voters also lends some qualified support to the "tilting-the-balance" scenario.

Summary: A Rising Tide Lifts All Boats— Especially the Smaller Ones

Overall, the analyses presented in this chapter support our theory that political experiences on social media enhance participation among the relatively less involved more than among the highly involved. With respect to electoral mobilization, both groups see their participation grow significantly, but this is more the case for the less involved than for the highly involved. Accidental exposure to political news shows a different pattern, as only the less involved reap participatory rewards while the highly involved do not show significant gains. Exposure to supportive political content stands somewhere in between, with some highly involved groups (those who closely followed the campaign) experiencing significant increases and others (those who are very interested in politics) failing to do so, while the less involved groups receive larger and significant participatory boosts.

The main argument we evidenced in this chapter is that political experiences on social media—such as engaging with supportive viewpoints, accidentally encountering news, and being exposed to electoral mobilization—help boost participatory repertoires among relatively less politically involved users more than they encourage the already involved to further increase their participation. While both groups benefit, the less involved benefit more, and, as a result, some participatory gaps rooted in different levels of political motivation are narrowed substantially or even disappear. To paraphrase Verba and colleagues (1995), citizens who "do not want to" engage with politics can be persuaded by the right political content, and social media provide a fertile environment for compelling political experiences that prod relatively uninvolved voters into becoming more active. To be sure, lack of motivation is only one of the three key reasons why people do not participate in politics, the other two being socioeconomic inequalities and networks of recruitment (Verba et al., 1995). Still, the fact that some aspects of social media use can functionally substitute for long-standing and often unchanging (Prior, 2010) political motivations highlights the importance of these platforms as incubators of contemporary participation.

If one adopts the view that, overall, citizen participation is beneficial for democratic governance and that relatively less unequal participation is even more beneficial, then the findings presented here suggest a cautiously positive outlook. However, representative democracy entails competition by political elites for the popular vote, and mass political participation can affect the outcomes of that competition and, thus, the distribution of electorally derived power in a political system. Hence, it is conceivable that the leveling of the participatory gaps we observed may contribute to altering the landscape of electoral competition by disproportionately encouraging specific ideological groups to participate in politics. To the extent that citizens with different political values, ideas, and beliefs may pursue different goals as they participate in public life, the electoral prospects of different leaders, parties, and coalitions may be enhanced or diminished, and certain policy outcomes may become more and less likely as a result. In a political system, the inputs have some bearing on the outputs, and citizen participation is an important component of such inputs (Easton, 1965).

Our analyses of differential effects based on citizens' ideology, however, suggest that the participatory gains associated with political experiences on social media are rather evenly distributed across voters of different political views. First, engaging with politically supportive content boosted participation among all ideological groups apart from the most extreme ones, thus amplifying the more moderate voices in society. Second, accidental exposure to news on social media was associated with participatory gains among center-right and unaligned citizens, but the differences across groups were small. Third, electoral mobilization via social media was associated with relatively large and similar gains across all ideological groups, though the increases were slightly higher among center and center-right respondents.

Overall, then, our findings suggest that political experiences on social media are not contributing to political polarization, at least in the specific sense of disproportionately enhancing participation among ideologically more extreme voters. We also found no compelling evidence that social media are yielding greater participatory benefits for those who vote for populist parties and leaders, or substantially tilting the competitive balance in favor of one particular set of political actors to the left or the right. The scenario that is most clearly supported by our data is one of a "rising tide" whereby, broadly speaking, political experiences on social media result in similar participatory gains among voters irrespective of their ideological persuasions.

These results, however, can be seen in a different light if compared with those of earlier research on digital politics. Writing about online campaigning in the first decade of the twenty-first century, one of us argued that progressive parties and citizens had reaped the greatest benefits from digital media (Vaccari, 2013). This does not seem to be the case anymore. Although the differential effects related to ideology that we uncovered are very small, more often than not, political experiences on social media seem to yield slightly greater participatory benefits for moderate conservatives (i.e., center-right identifiers) than for progressives (i.e., those aligned with the center-left). While in most cases these differences are too small to be statistically significant or substantively relevant, this pattern suggests that the landscape of digital political competition may have undergone a correction compared with the previous decade. Conservatives are now at least as well positioned as progressives to harvest the participatory gains of political experiences on social media.

In the next chapter, we shift our focus to country-level differential effects. In doing that, we add an important layer to our theory and analysis by assessing how different systemic characteristics shape the relationship between political experiences on social media and political participation.

6

Does Context Matter?

Political Experiences on Social Media in Comparative Perspective

Imagine a group of fifty women of all ages who had never met before driving in the night to a secret location in a rural area, where they gather in a barn located at the end of a dark alley to discuss how to change politics in their state and in their country. This is more or less what the first meeting of a secret grassroots organization of Trump opponents, held in November 2016 in the traditionally Republican state of Texas, looked like. Emily Van Duyn (2018) analyzes the birth of this unlikely assemblage, inconspicuously called "Community Women's Group" (CWG), the motivations behind its foundation, and the implications for its members' political activism. Some of our non-American readers might find it difficult to understand why secrecy was required for the meeting and why these women chose not to work with the local Democratic party. However, especially in rural areas of the United States characterized by small and isolated communities, those who have minority political views might feel particularly uncomfortable, or even unsafe, openly expressing them, particularly if they are women. By the same token, they may also end up abstaining from other forms of political action. CWG members originally came together thanks to a call circulated via email, and their activity was sustained through digital tools including closed Facebook groups. As Van Duyn (2018) points out, the group was crucial for breaking the sense of isolation that most of its members were experiencing, and for giving them greater confidence and willingness to act in public. A member of the group is quoted in the study (Van Duyn, 2018: 979) as saying:

> At the last meeting I presented this thing called "Knock Every Door." When I introduced the idea I said "if I had known, if somebody had told me eight months ago that I would be willing to knock on doors in this county, I would have said no way. I would have been terrified." And I'm still nervous about it, but because of the support of the group and

Outside the Bubble. Cristian Vaccari and Augusto Valeriani, Oxford University Press. © Oxford University Press 2021.
DOI: 10.1093/oso/9780190858476.003.0007

because I think it's going to do a lot of good, I'll do it. It [CWG] has given me courage."

Thus, the creation and functioning of CWG were specific responses to the challenges to political expression and activism that the particular context of 2016 rural Texas posed for those women who were concerned with the turn American politics was taking. While Van Duyn (2018) focuses on the differences between the urban and rural United States, some features of this case resonate with some of the theories we discussed in Chapter 1. For example, only a few CWG members self-identified as Democrats, while most considered themselves as independent and presented the group as nonpartisan. The weaker relationship between parties and voters typical of majoritarian systems such as the United States (Bowler et al., 1994) and the limited permanent presence of parties on the ground characterizing the U.S. context could have meant that CWG members did not feel strong enough attachments to the Democratic party and that they did not find strong enough party organizational networks on the ground to operate within. For these Texan progressive women, then, the possibility of encountering like-minded people and discussing politics with them was much more relevant, as a catalyst of political action, than if they had lived in a context where parties inspired stronger attachments and provided more viable and constant opportunities to get involved.

Social media are global platforms that, at least within the boundaries of Western liberal democracies, function based on very similar, if not identical, technological principles, business models, and (hitherto permissive) legal frameworks. Yet, political institutions and political communication differ widely around the Western world (Esser & Pfetsch, 2004). As we have shown so far, social media play important roles in how citizens learn about, communicate around, and participate in the political process, but politics is also deeply contextual. The conditions under which citizens exercise agency are, to a certain degree, shaped by the political institutions they inhabit. These include historically determined features that are unlikely to be swept away by the global surge of social media. For one, most citizens are still more engaged with national than global politics, not least because key institutions of democratic governance have so far failed to expand outside of the boundaries of nation-states. And while the affordances of social media may be creating a global vernacular that has popularized and redefined the meaning of words such as "friending," "liking," "snapping," and "sharing," political communication is still by and large conducted based on national languages and cultures. Moreover, in spite of the rise of global policy challenges such as climate change, income inequalities, terrorism, automation, migration, and pandemics, the cleavages that dominate national politics are the result of complex, context-sensitive interactions between social structures, citizen preferences, and elite strategies (Sartori, 1976).

Yet, most research on social media and political participation has tended to focus on individual countries—mostly the United States. In a sweeping meta-analysis of twenty years of research on digital media and politics, Shelley Boulianne (2020: 955) found that, out of 243 studies conducted between 1995 and 2016 across fifty different countries, more than half (127) covered the United States. The second most studied country was China (14 studies), followed by Germany and Hong Kong (13), the United Kingdom (12), and South Korea (10). Many of the countries covered in this book have been the subjects of few, if any, systematic studies of the relationship between social media and participation. While single-country studies have overwhelmingly focused on a handful of political systems, there has been little cross-country research on these phenomena. We hope this chapter begins to address this gap. Comparing different political systems is important not only to widen the geographical scope of our knowledge, but also to shed light on how context shapes digital politics. To guide this part of our inquiry, we identify some hypotheses, outlined in Chapter 1, and test them with our data.

Why Context Matters: A Summary of Our Theoretical Approach

A general question revolves around whether systemic characteristics play any role in shaping patterns of political communication, and the relationship between political experiences on social media and participation among them. In previous research, this problem has been framed in terms of standardization or differentiation.

Studies of global election campaigning, for instance, debated the merits of the so-called "Americanization" hypothesis, according to which methods and techniques pioneered in the United States would gradually spread throughout Western democracies and even non-democratic regimes (Scammell, 1998; Negrine & Papathanassopoulos, 1996; Swanson & Mancini, 1996). Other models of the development of campaigns suggested a linear evolutionary process from premodern to modern to postmodern styles (Norris, 2001), which, albeit mediated by domestic factors such as electoral rules, party system, media system, and characteristics of the electorate, were understood as unfolding in a similar way across liberal democracies. These models portrayed the United States either as an exporter of the technologies and techniques introduced by its politicians and their media advisors, or as a pioneer in a modernization tide that would eventually wash up on the shores of most other countries (Pasquino, 2005). As documented earlier, the U.S. case has remained central in the study of digital politics. Previously, one of us (Vaccari, 2013) argued against the premise, implicit in most Internet politics research, that models and findings developed in and for the United States should necessarily constitute a starting point for studying online political communication in other liberal democracies. Still, the underlying theme and implicit assumption of much digital politics scholarship has been *standardization*, i.e., the expectation that relevant patterns and relationships would be broadly similar across different countries and anticipated, or magnified, by the peculiar position and characteristics of the United States. Critiques of the Americanization and modernization paradigms, however, emphasized that not all new forms of political communication are seamlessly and uncritically imported from the United States into other democracies and that national characteristics matter. Thus, Plasser and Plasser (2002) proposed a "shopping" model, whereby national actors selectively incorporate only those techniques that are relevant to their domestic context. Along these lines, Anstead and Chadwick (2009) identified five country-specific characteristics of political and media systems that explain why parties adopt different tools of digital political communication. If we consider how peculiar the institutions of American democracy are when compared with other Western democracies (Taylor et al., 2014), it should be no surprise that the patterns that can be observed in political communication in the United States are not seamlessly and uniformly applied in other democratic regimes (Vaccari, 2013). The key theoretical insight of this line of research is that *differentiation* across countries characterizes at least some of the links between digital media and relevant political outcomes.

The first question we ask, therefore, is whether the relationship between political experiences on social media and citizens' political participation across Western democracies is best described by standardization or differentiation. The concept of differentiation, however, requires some further unpacking.

In its most extreme version, differentiation suggests that the relationship between social media and participation should vary so much across different democracies that its direction may change—i.e., that in some countries the relationship is positive while in others it is negative. Based on her comprehensive cross-country and longitudinal meta-analysis, Boulianne (2020) finds that most studies inside and outside the United States have found stronger relationships between Internet use and participation over time. Hence, she argues, "results do not suggest that the United States is distinctive in its digital media effects" (Boulianne, 2020: 962). At least within the Western democracies we study, we do not expect such extreme forms of differentiation to apply. We do not theorize, for instance, that citizens exposed to electoral mobilization via social media should increase their participation in some countries and reduce it in others.

A milder, but still relevant form of differentiation entails that the positive association between certain political experiences on social media and political participation may be significantly weakened, or strengthened, in the presence or absence of particular contextual characteristics. In Boulianne's meta-analysis (2020), the strength of the relationship between Internet use and participation is shown to increase significantly in U.S.-based studies but not in non-U.S. studies (Boulianne, 2020: 960, Table 3). Moreover, the average size of the predicted effects of digital media use on participation between 2003 and 2016 was higher inside than outside the United States in nine years, lower in four years, and indistinguishable in one year (Boulianne, 2020: 961). That a relationship is positive everywhere but stronger in a particular country or set of countries still constitutes evidence that these patterns are differentiated.

Thus, in this chapter we investigate whether the strength of the positive relationship between political experiences on social media and political participation varies across different groups of countries. Even if the direction of the relationship remains the same across different political systems, significant differences in the strength of this relationship would constitute evidence of differentiation, while lack of such differences would constitute evidence of standardization.

What differences, then, do we expect to find in the strength of the relationship between political experiences on social media and political participation in the nine countries we are studying, and what factors should explain them?

Our starting point is that political and media institutions are likely to play an important role. As discussed in Chapter 1, our theories build on existing concepts, classifications, and research in political science and political communication. While we hope our theoretical approach will help guide further and broader studies, the paucity of established theories in comparative digital politics and the limitations of our data suggest a parsimonious approach. The hypotheses we test are admittedly partial and only capture some facets of a more complex set of relationships. Moreover, we are conscious of the fact that our nine-country data set, while rare in a field that is still dominated by single-country studies, only allows us to investigate a limited number of systemic variables. As discussed in Chapter 1, the three factors we consider are *electoral competition, mass media systems,* and *political organizations.* Our key premise is that specific systemic characteristics should not be relevant per se, but only with respect to particular political experiences on social media. Thus, we argue that each of these systemic features should moderate the relationship between political participation and one of the three political experiences on social media we study.

To test our hypotheses, we ran multivariate Poisson regression models predicting levels of political participation among our respondents, with data preprocessed with Coarsened Exact Matching (CEM) as discussed in Chapter 4.[1]

We included the same independent variables as in the models in Chapter 4, with three important differences.

First, to test the differential effects of political experiences on social media in countries with different institutional characteristics, we included an interaction term between the relevant political experience (for instance, exposure to political agreement on social media) and a variable that classifies respondents based on the systemic characteristic of their countries of residence (for instance, patterns of electoral competition). Consistent with our parsimonious theoretical approach, for each political experience on social media we only model one interaction term with a country grouping variable at a time. This is because simultaneously testing interaction terms with more systemic variables would result in high levels of multicollinearity, thus making our estimates unreliable.[2] However, our Online Appendix (Tables A70–A75) shows additional models that test all possible interactions between the three political experiences on social media and the three types of systemic characteristics we focus on in this chapter. That these additional models consistently yield null findings suggests that alternative hypotheses combining different systemic characteristics with different political experiences on social media than those we theorized would not shed further light on the phenomena we are studying.

Second, because these models consider groups of countries based on their systemic features, we omit the country dummy variables that were included in the models in Chapters 4 and 5. Keeping these dummy variables in the models would yield uninterpretable results because there would not be enough degrees of freedom in the data to disentangle the meaning of the coefficients for systemic country characteristics and of the coefficients representing individual countries. Instead, as discussed previously, we include additional variables classifying countries based on their institutional characteristics, both as predictors and as components of the two-way interactions described earlier. We acknowledge that this setup means that the models presented in this chapter are slightly different from those discussed in Chapters 4 and 5, and thus the results reported in this chapter cannot be fully compared with those shown in previous chapters. However, in Tables A76–A84 in the Online Appendix, we demonstrate that if we run the same models as in Chapters 4 and 5 but with country groupings based on institutional characteristics rather than country dummy variables, with standard errors clustered by country as we do in this chapter, the results are substantively consistent with those shown in those two chapters.

Third, to take into account that responses may still exhibit country-specific patterns above and beyond those captured by grouping countries based on their systemic characteristics, we ran a different type of Poisson regression that accounts for dependence within clusters, with clusters defined as corresponding to countries.[3] This solution enables us to capture cross-country variations while accounting for within-country similarities between respondents. We are cognizant that multilevel modeling is generally preferable for modeling these types of cross-country relationships. However, simulations suggest that at least twenty-five countries—way more than the nine we include here—are needed to obtain reliable estimates in multilevel models (Bryan & Jenkins, 2016).

The rest of this chapter is organized as follows. For each theory we test, first we summarize our expectations, then we discuss how we classified the countries included in our research with respect to the systemic characteristic relevant to the theory, and finally we present our empirical findings.

Electoral Competition and Supportive Political Content

In majoritarian democracies, the most relevant[4] parties appeal to broader swaths of the electorate than in proportional democracies. All else being equal, this should lead parties to pursue more inclusive policies aimed at bridging and bringing together different sectors of the electorate. These broader, centripetal strategies, in turn, shape the development of political identities, as parties' "catch-all" approaches and flexible policy offerings, while potentially appealing for ideologically malleable median voters (Downs, 1957), are less likely to satisfy ardent supporters, who tend to prefer ideological coherence to electoral expediency. As a result, in majoritarian democracies social cleavages play a smaller role in predicting how citizens vote, and party identifications are weaker than in proportional democracies (Norris, 2004).

This difference should have implications for the extent to which encountering supportive views on social media encourages citizens to participate in politics. Such a relationship should be stronger in majoritarian democracies where, all else being equal, parties represent broader constituencies and therefore inspire weaker loyalties among voters. For citizens with looser political affiliations, the sense of social validation that results from engaging with politically supportive content on social media may constitute a stronger participatory catalyst than for citizens whose political attachments run deeper, and who are thus less likely to be moved by confirmatory information and more likely to resist and counter-argue oppositional messages seen online (Zaller, 1992). Therefore, prevalently encountering political agreement on social media should be more strongly correlated with participation in majoritarian democracies, where citizens' political loyalties are weaker, than in proportional democracies, where political affiliations, all else being equal, are stronger.

COUNTRY CLASSIFICATION

We classify 3 of our 9 countries as featuring majoritarian patterns of electoral competition: France, the United Kingdom, and the United States.

The United Kingdom and United States employ first-past-the-post electoral systems to elect members of parliament in single-member districts with a plurality of the votes. In the United States, the president is also elected with a majoritarian system, albeit a more complex one. In France, both parliamentary and presidential candidates are elected with majoritarian systems that require runoffs if no candidate achieves a majority of first-round votes.

Largely as a result of the electoral incentives created by the electoral system, the United States features what is arguably the purest two-party system in the Western world, with only the Republican and Democratic parties credibly contending and alternating in power (Bowler et al., 2005; Rosenstone et al., 2018).

The United Kingdom is a more complex case, with relevant sub-national parties in Scotland, Wales, and Northern Ireland, but at the national level the Labour and Conservative Parties have governed on their own and alternated in office for most of the postwar period, with some exceptions such as the 2010–2015 coalition between the Conservatives and the Liberal-Democrats. In the 2017 elections, after which we fielded our survey, the two major parties garnered 82.4% of the popular vote and 89.1% of the seats in the House of Commons, even though no party had a working majority on its own and the Conservatives depended on the votes of the Northern Irish Democratic Unionist Party to govern.[5] Overall, while conflict around center–periphery relationships and Britain's exit from the European Union have severely challenged the two main parties, their hegemony on national politics has remained intact.

France is a more nuanced case. After the creation of the Fifth Republic (1958–), one of whose key innovations was the majoritarian electoral rules, party competition revolved around two blocs, each dominated by one main party—the Gaullists and the Socialists. While this was generally the case for the first fifty years of the Republic, support for these parties in the 2017 elections collapsed. The candidates who accessed the runoff were Emmanuel Macron, who had founded his new party *En Marche!* just a year before, and Marine Le Pen, the leader of the right-wing *Front National*. Competition maintained a bipolar structure in the subsequent parliamentary elections, as Macron's new venture *La Republique En Marche!* garnered a majority of seats and the center-right coalition, led by the heirs to the Gaullist party, emerged as the main opposition. While the French electoral rules constrain voters' choices and parties' opportunities less than the British and American ones, the majoritarian push is still sufficiently strong in both parliamentary and, especially, presidential elections to structure political competition around catch-all parties, often linked to presidential candidates as was the case with Macron (Grunberg & Haegel, 2007).

In sum, while featuring different varieties of majoritarian electoral systems and different contextual conditions, France, the United Kingdom, and the United States all present majoritarian patterns of electoral competition.

The other countries in our study—Denmark, Germany, Greece, Italy, Poland, and Spain—all feature purely or predominantly proportional electoral systems and, partly as a result, patterns of party competition where more than two parties can be considered as relevant (Benoit, 2006). More numerous parties compete for relatively smaller sectors of the electorate than the main parties do in majoritarian systems.

Denmark is a straightforward case of party list proportional system, where voters choose between lists of candidates compiled by parties, with a low threshold (2%) for access to parliamentary representation. These arrangements result in a multiparty system where governments typically involve coalitions of parties and there are at least six relevant parties.[6]

The German electoral law entails a mixed system where citizens vote for both party lists and candidates in single-member districts, but the allocation of seats is entirely proportional unless parties win more seats in single-member districts than they gained with the proportional vote, in which case the winners of majoritarian races receive additional seats (Zittel, 2018). Coalition governments have been the norm since the return to democracy in 1949, and six parties can currently be considered as relevant. What is more, "grand coalitions" between the two main parties (Christian Democrats and Socialists) supported the government in 3 of the last 4 legislatures (2005–2009, 2013–2017, and 2017–2021). These grand coalitions are nearly impossible in majoritarian democracies, apart from extraordinary circumstances such as large-scale wars.

Greece employs a "reinforced proportional" system (Gallagher & Mitchell, 2018) that, while assigning parliamentary seats on a proportional basis, provides advantages to the largest parties. After democracy was restored in 1975, Greece effectively had a two-party system, as only the Socialists and the conservative New Democracy alternated in government. However, the landscape changed dramatically with the post-2007 economic crisis and the severe austerity measures implemented by successive governments from both major parties. The Socialists and New Democracy also governed together in emergency grand coalitions from 2011 until 2015. Successive general elections in January and September 2015 then led to a dramatic overhaul of the party system, with the emergence of the left-wing SYRIZA (Greek abbreviation for "Coalition of the Radical Left"), the collapse of the Socialist Party, and the appearance of new relevant parties both at the center and the right of the spectrum. The new government was supported by a coalition between SYRIZA, the Independent Greeks, and the Greens, none of which had ever governed before.[7] Hence, Greece is currently functioning as a proportional multiparty democracy, with five or six relevant parties.

Italy is a fragmented multiparty system, which functioned according to a bipolar logic from 1994 to 2013 (Bardi, 2004) and subsequently evolved into a tripolar system. The 2018 electoral law allocates about two-thirds of seats in both chambers proportionally, while about one-third is assigned in single-member districts based on first-past-the-post rules (Chiaramonte et al., 2018). In previous electoral cycles, a proportional law with a majority bonus was in place (Passarelli, 2018). The 2013 and 2018 general elections saw the emergence of a tripolar system, with two large but internally differentiated coalitions (the center-right dominated by Let's Go Italy first and the League later, and the center-left led by the Democratic Party) and the Five Star Movement standing alone. In 2018, since no coalition or individual actor had enough votes to secure a working majority, the League and the Five Star Movement formed an unprecedented "populist" government coalition. Although the center-left was hugely weakened in 2018, electoral competition still revolves around three main poles, some including more than one party, in a system historically prone to high levels of fragmentation, which is further encouraged by the proportional electoral rules. The tripolar nature of the system was confirmed in the summer of 2019, when the populist coalition fell apart and the Five Star Movement formed a new government with the Democratic Party.

Poland is a semi-presidential system like France, but with a less powerful president. Similar to France, Polish presidential elections require a runoff between the two most voted-for candidates if no one achieves a majority in the first round. By contrast, parliamentary elections employ a proportional system with a 5% threshold for inclusion in the House (Rose & Munro, 2003), while the Senate, which has less power, is elected based on first-past-the-post in single-member districts. There are currently six relevant parties, and it has been difficult for a single party to win a majority of seats. While this happened to the Law and Justice Party in 2015, theirs was the first single-party government since democratic elections began in 1991.[8] The Polish party system is arguably still consolidating after the democratic transition, which means mass party loyalties are comparatively weaker (Mainwaring & Torcal, 2006).

Spain is another example of a reinforced proportional system, as seats in the House are allocated proportionally, but the magnitude of districts and the counting rules have historically favored the two largest parties, the Socialist Workers Party (*Partido Socialista Obrero Español* in Spanish, abbreviated in PSOE) and the People's Party (Hopkin, 2005). From the return to democracy in 1976 until 2018, all Spanish governments were formed by either of these parties, although some cabinets required the external support of some regionalist parties (Heller,

2002). Since 2015, however, the party system has undergone massive changes, with the surge of three new relevant national parties: left-wing *Podemos*, center-right *Ciudadanos* (Orriols & Cordero, 2016; Rodon & Hierro, 2016), and, in the 2019 elections, right-wing *Vox* (Turnbull-Dugarte, 2019). While the two major parties did not see their support collapse as in Greece, the success of their new competitors drastically increased the fragmentation of the system. As a result, in 2016 the People's Party–led government needed the external support of *Ciudadanos*, as well as the Canary Island regional party, to maintain a working majority. After the government lost its majority, a minority Socialist-led government was formed, which lasted for a year and a half, after which general elections were called that resulted in a victory for the Socialists but required the formation of a new parliamentary coalition. It took PSOE and *Podemos* more than eight months to reach an agreement, which resulted in the first nationwide coalition government in Spain, sworn in at the beginning of 2020. In sum, while Spain features the least proportional patterns of electoral competition among the six countries we include in this group, the fact that as many as five national parties are now relevant suggests it can be classified as a proportional political system.

ANALYSIS

Our hypothesis is that exposure to supportive political messages on social media is more strongly associated with participation in majoritarian (France, the United Kingdom, and the United States) than proportional democracies (all other countries included in this study). To test our hypothesis, Table 6.1 presents the results of a multivariate Poisson regression model that predicts levels of political participation and, besides all the control variables included in the other models in this book, features an interaction term between the country-level patterns of electoral competition (majoritarian, with proportional serving as the reference category) and the individual-level experience of encountering supportive, oppositional, or no political content on social media (with exposure to two-sided political content serving as the reference category). Overall, the model predicts a little over one-fourth of the total variance in the index of political participation, a performance that is comparable with that of the other models presented in this book.[9]

In Table 6.1, the coefficient for encountering supportive political content on social media is positively and significantly associated with levels of political participation, as was the case when no interactions with country-level variables were specified (Chapter 4, Table 4.1). The interaction term between individual-level exposure to supportive content and country-level majoritarian electoral competition is also positive and significant, which means that the positive relationship between supportive content seen on social media and participation is

Table 6.1. **Poisson Regression Predicting Levels of Political Participation (0–6 Index): Indirect Effects of Agreement on Social Media in Majoritarian and Proportional Democracies**

	Coefficient	Standard Error	p-value
Political messages seen on SNSs (reference = Two-sided)			
Never exposed	−0.234	0.069	0.001
One-sided supportive	0.129	0.027	0.000
One-sided oppositional	−0.005	0.023	0.820
Type of democracy (reference = Proportional)			
Majoritarian democracy (FR, U.K., U.S.A.)	0.074	0.050	0.144
Interaction between political messages and type of democracy (reference = Two-sided, Proportional)			
Never exposed × Majoritarian	0.047	0.086	0.589
One-sided supportive × Majoritarian	0.109	0.046	0.018
One-sided oppositional × Majoritarian	0.073	0.047	0.126
Gender (Male)	0.070	0.016	0.000
Age	−0.034	0.007	0.000
Age squared	0.000	0.000	0.000
Education	0.048	0.012	0.000
Working condition	0.017	0.023	0.461
Income	−0.013	0.005	0.014
Ideology (reference = Center)			
Left	0.283	0.034	0.000
Center-left	0.248	0.048	0.000
Center-right	0.140	0.033	0.000
Right	0.188	0.066	0.004
Unaligned	−0.016	0.036	0.663
Attention to the campaign	0.051	0.049	0.292
Interest in politics	0.084	0.055	0.126
Efficacy index	0.039	0.006	0.000

Table 6.1 Continued

	Coefficient	Standard Error	p-value
Institutional trust index	0.008	0.009	0.345
Satisfaction with democracy	−0.036	0.020	0.070
Political information via . . .			
Newspapers	0.049	0.012	0.000
Websites	0.000	0.017	0.996
Radio	0.025	0.006	0.000
Television	−0.061	0.011	0.000
Offline conversation	0.096	0.017	0.000
Political talk offline	0.100	0.031	0.001
Political talk on SNSs	0.206	0.018	0.000
Frequency of SNS use			
Facebook	−0.014	0.010	0.187
Twitter	−0.008	0.007	0.243
YouTube	0.018	0.009	0.053
Instagram	0.020	0.011	0.068
Intercept	−0.391	0.130	0.003
Pseudo R^2	0.262		
N	7,205		

Note: SNS = social networking site. The pseudo R^2 coefficient reported in the table was calculated based on a Poisson regression model that did not cluster standard errors by country because the Zelig package we used to estimate this model in R did not generate the values of the model's null deviance and deviance.

relatively stronger in political systems that feature majoritarian electoral competition compared with those characterized by proportional competition. All the other relevant coefficients in the model are not statistically significant, apart from the one designating respondents who never encounter political content on social media (or who do not use social media at all), whose levels of participation are significantly lower. However, the non-significant interaction term shows that there is no difference in the strength of this relationship between majoritarian and proportional democracies. Consistent with Chapter 4, these respondents participate significantly less, regardless of how electoral competition is structured in their country. Our hypothesis that exposure to supportive political content on social media provides a greater boost to participation in majoritarian than proportional countries is thus confirmed.

To illustrate the substantive implications of our findings, we have plotted the increases in political participation predicted by the model in Table 6.1 for two respondents who exhibit average values in all the independent variables in the model, apart from encountering politically supportive content on social media (compared with encountering two-sided content) and the type of electoral competition in the country they live in. As shown in Figure 6.1, respondents who mainly encounter supportive political views on social media and live in countries with proportional electoral competition engage in an average 0.19 additional political activities compared with similar respondents who mainly encounter two-sided political views on social media. By contrast, average respondents in majoritarian countries are predicted to engage in 0.41 additional political activities when they are exposed to supportive political content on social media when compared with similar respondents who encounter two-sided content. As shown by the lack of overlaps in the error bars in Figure 6.1, the gains experienced by social media users exposed to supportive content are significantly higher in majoritarian than proportional political systems.

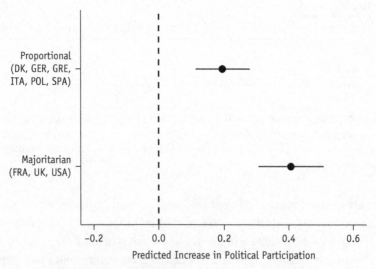

Figure 6.1. Marginal Effects of Exposure to Supportive Versus Two-Sided Political Content on Social Media in Majoritarian and Proportional Democracies

Note: estimates are changes in count values of a 0–6 index and are based on the coefficients in Table 6.1 for respondents with values equal to the sample means (for numeric variables), medians (for ordinal variables), and modes (for categorical variables) apart from agreement and disagreement with political content seen on social media (comparing respondents who predominantly see supportive and two-sided messages) and whether respondents reside in majoritarian (France, United Kingdom, and United States) or proportional (Denmark, Germany, Greece, Italy, Poland, and Spain) democracies.

To put these numbers in context, recall from Chapter 4 that the mean level of political participation recorded across all our respondents is 1.34 and the standard deviation is 1.45, and that, overall, social media users exposed to supportive content are predicted to engage in about 0.3 additional activities compared with those exposed to two-sided political content (2 versus 1.7 activities, see Figure 4.1). Now, we have shown that these small but important participatory gains are unevenly distributed across countries with different types of electoral competition, with citizens in majoritarian political systems experiencing participatory gains that are twice as large as their counterparts in proportional systems.

The results thus support our theory that the differential participatory gains associated with exposure to one-sided supportive political views on social media are significantly higher in majoritarian than proportional democracies. We have therefore uncovered initial evidence that political institutions contribute to shaping the relationship between political experiences on social media and participation.

Mass Media Systems and Incidental Exposure to News on Social Media

In hybrid media systems, the effects of political messages encountered in a sector of the media ecology may be contingent on the types of messages encountered in other sectors. Hence, we theorize that the relationship between accidental exposure to news on social media and political participation may vary depending on the kinds of news citizens prevalently encounter in the mass media. In particular, we argue that the extent to which political journalism in a given country tends to cover the news in a relatively more neutral or more partisan way may be relevant. This is because news shared on social media tends to exhibit a relatively partisan character, as the organizations that publish and distribute news online are likely to be ideologically more diverse than those operating in the more restricted environment of the mass media, and the actors posting news online include not only journalists, but also political parties and candidates, interest groups, social movements, civil society organizations, agents of foreign influence operations, and activist citizens, all of whom tend to engage in political advocacy more than most journalists and news organizations normally do.

Our theoretical starting point is that all else being equal, what should matter the most for citizens' participation is the difference between the level of partisanship in the news they (accidentally) encounter on social media and the level of partisanship in the news they see in the mass media. We know from studies of television and newspapers that the more partisan the news, the higher citizens' levels of participation (van Kempen, 2007), as partisan news is more likely to strengthen voters' confidence in their opinions and, thus, their willingness to act upon them. Hence, citizens in systems where mass media are less likely to explicitly advocate for specific parties or ideological orientations should receive a smaller participatory boost from the mass media than those who get their news in systems where the news tends to more forcefully espouse particular political actors and agendas. Hence, social media users in media systems where the news tends to be more neutral may be less used to seeing partisan journalism in the mass media and, thus, may experience greater participatory increases when they accidentally encounter more explicitly partisan news on social media. By contrast, citizens in mass media systems where news tends to be less neutral should receive a relatively smaller participatory boost from serendipitous exposure to political news on social media. For them, such news may not feature substantially more partisan cues than the kinds of news they already see in the mass media. Hence, accidentally encountered news on social media may have a relatively smaller impact on their desire to make their voices heard.

COUNTRY CLASSIFICATION

The comparative political communication literature provides many useful classifications of media systems in Western democracies. A milestone in the field is Hallin and Mancini's work (2004), which identifies four key systemic variables: development of media markets (in particular, the historical strength of a mass circulation press), political parallelism (the relationship between individual media outlets and political parties or ideological orientations), journalistic professionalism (the degree of autonomy journalists enjoy in doing their job), and the role of the state (with respect to media regulation, subsidies, and public service broadcasting). On this basis, Hallin and Mancini propose three models of media systems. Liberal media systems, best exemplified by the United States, feature a historically strong mass circulation press, high levels of journalistic professionalism, low levels of political parallelism, and low state intervention. In Liberal media systems, news is more strongly linked to market forces than to political actors and journalism is more oriented to the interests of the audience (and, to a certain degree, corporations) than those of politicians. Polarized Pluralist media systems, best represented by Italy, are a mirror image of Liberal ones, as they are characterized by weak newspaper circulation, low levels of professionalism, high levels of parallelism, and substantial state intervention. Here, media respond more strongly to political than business imperatives, and news tends to pursue political agendas more than it caters to the interests of the audience. Finally, Democratic Corporatist media systems, exemplified by Germany, feature high levels in all four key variables. Journalism in these countries is tied to both political and market logics, and news tends to strike a balance between both imperatives.

Hallin and Mancini's (2004) analysis covers 8 of the 9 countries included in this study. The United Kingdom and the United States are Liberal Media systems, although the United Kingdom exhibits stronger levels of political parallelism in its press and a marked degree of state intervention, particularly as it features a strong and well-respected public service broadcaster. France, Greece, Italy, and Spain are Polarized Pluralist media systems, but France partly diverges from the model in that its newspaper industry tends to be stronger and levels of journalistic professionalism are higher. Finally, Denmark and Germany are Democratic Corporatist media systems. To apply Hallin and Mancini's model, we only need to classify Poland, which was not included in their original analysis. Early research presented media systems in post-communist Eastern European democracies as "transitory" (Tenscher, 2008), due to the fluidity that characterized their initial development (see also Downey & Mihelj, 2012). However, subsequent work inspired by Hallin and Mancini's framework (Dobek-Ostrowska, 2012) highlighted many similarities between the Polish media system as it emerged in the first decade after the democratic transition and the Polarized Pluralist model, as Polish media featured high levels of political parallelism, low journalistic professionalism, and high state interventionism. The policies of the Law and Justice Party, which shortly after gaining a majority in 2015 brought all public service media under the control of the government and put one of its former political consultants in charge of public television (Fomina & Kucharczyk, 2016), entail the kind of political instrumentalization of media that characterizes Polarized Pluralist systems (Surowiec et al., 2020). Hence, we classify Poland as a Polarized Pluralist media system.

Before we apply this classification to our analysis, we must briefly address two potential concerns. The first is that Hallin and Mancini's ideal types may not adequately represent the empirical characteristics of the media systems they included. The three models do not fit all Western democracies equally well, as hinted earlier when discussing how the United Kingdom and France differ from their model's purest specimens. The second concern is that changes in contemporary media ecologies have dramatically reshaped media systems. This has been especially the case in the United States, where the primacy of objective, two-sided journalism has been challenged by the rise of partisan media, in particular cable news, talk radio, and blogs (Baum & Groeling, 2008). Accordingly, Nechushtai (2018) has suggested that scholars should now classify the United States as a hybrid "Polarized Liberal" media system, as the decline of mass circulation newspapers, increase in political parallelism, and challenges to journalistic autonomy do not fit squarely with the Liberal model outlined by Hallin and Mancini (2004). Moreover, there is evidence that partisan journalism declined substantially in Democratic Corporatist countries, as the party press experienced a stark decline in favor of more neutral, commercial outlets (van Kempen, 2007).

With respect to the first issue, Brüggemann and colleagues (2014) revisited Hallin and Mancini's typology based on a wide array of indicators covering the same seventeen Western democracies analyzed in their book (Hallin & Mancini, 2004). Based on statistical analyses of the correlations between these indicators, Brüggemann et al. (2014) identify four empirical clusters of countries, in contrast with the three proposed by Hallin and Mancini: Northern, Western, Central, and Southern. Importantly, Brüggemann and colleagues (2014) also come to different conclusions in terms of the classification of specific countries. In particular, they position the United Kingdom in a different cluster (Central) than the United States (Western) and split the countries identified by Hallin and Mancini as Democratic Corporatist into three different clusters (with Germany classified as Central and Denmark as Northern). By contrast, the authors concur with Hallin and Mancini on the clustering of France, Greece, Italy, and Spain in the same group (Southern). While Brüggemann and colleagues' classification has substantial merits, it would be difficult to apply it to our data as we only cover one country—Denmark—in their category of Northern media systems and only one—the United States—in their category of Western media systems. Hence, adopting this classification for our analysis would enable very weak generalizations on two out of the four groups of media systems they identified, as we only have one country representing each. Thus, we leave this challenge for future research comprising a larger and wider variety of countries spanning all four models of media systems as identified by Brüggemann and colleagues (2014).

The increasing role of partisan media in the United States and the decline of the partisan press in Democratic Corporatist countries are important developments that occurred, or fully unfolded, after Hallin and Mancini's (2004) book, and the vast body of research the authors employed to develop their models, was published. In a study of twelve Western democracies, Fletcher and colleagues (2020) show that levels of polarization in both online and offline news is highest in the United States and, within Europe, higher in Polarized Pluralist than Democratic Corporatist countries. Audience polarization is an indicator of high levels of political parallelism, signaling that audiences' news choices are more strongly shaped by their political preferences. In Brüggemann et al.'s (2014) analysis, the United States is assessed as featuring slightly lower than average levels of press market strength and political parallelism, markedly lower than average levels of state intervention, and higher than average levels of journalistic professionalism. To the extent that the key driving factor in our theory is the degree to which consumers of news in the mass media are likely to find objective versus partisan news, political parallelism should be the key criterion in deciding how to group different countries. Based on the measures reported by Brüggemann and colleagues (2014), levels of political parallelism in the countries we classified as Liberal (the United States and the United Kingdom) are still medium to low in comparative perspective. Interestingly, however, estimated levels of parallelism are even lower in Democratic Corporatist countries (Denmark and Germany). This suggests that Liberal and Democratic Corporatist countries may exhibit similar patterns, but we would still expect to find substantial differences with Polarized Pluralist media systems, where levels of political parallelism are substantially higher.

In light of these considerations, if we are to test our theory that higher levels of relatively two-sided news in the mass media may lead to a stronger correlation between accidental exposure to news on social media and political participation, we have two options. The first is to still rely on Hallin and Mancini's classification of mass media systems, which suggests that audiences in Liberal media systems should be exposed to higher levels of ideologically balanced news in the mass media. This choice would lead us to hypothesize that respondents in the United Kingdom and the United States should experience higher participatory gains from accidental exposure than respondents in other countries. The second option is to maintain Hallin and Mancini's classification, but, in light of more recent evidence that political parallelism is lower in some Democratic Corporatist countries than it is in some Liberal countries, hypothesize that differential effects should be higher in Denmark and Germany than in other countries. While there are merits to both hypotheses, the next section will show that neither is supported by the data.

ANALYSIS

Table 6.2 presents a model that predicts levels of political participation based on the usual set of independent variables, plus our media system country classification (with Democratic Corporatist countries serving as the reference category) and an interaction term between accidental exposure and type of media system. The model explains around 28% of the overall variance in the dependent variable. The coefficients for the interaction terms are both negative, suggesting that the association between accidental exposure and participation may be weaker in both Liberal and Polarized Pluralist media systems than in Democratic Corporatist media systems. However, both coefficients are very close to zero and very far from conventional thresholds of statistical significance. The coefficient for accidental exposure remains positive and significant, as in Chapter 4 (Table 4.2), and so are the coefficients identifying Liberal and Polarized Pluralist media systems, suggesting that levels of participation in these countries are overall higher than in Democratic Corporatist systems among citizens who do not accidentally encounter news on social media.

Table 6.2. **Poisson Regression Predicting Levels of Political Participation (0–6 Index): Indirect Effects of Accidental Exposure to News on Social Media in Different Types of Media Systems**

	Coefficient	Standard Error	p-value
Accidental exposure to political news on SNSs	0.048	0.012	0.000
Type of media system (reference = Democratic Corporatist)			
Liberal (U.K., U.S.A.)	0.227	0.088	0.010
Polarized Pluralist (FRA, GRE, ITA, POL, SPA)	0.091	0.042	0.030
Interaction between accidental exposure and media system (reference = Democratic Corporatist)			
Accidental exposure × Liberal	−0.025	0.033	0.450
Accidental exposure × Polarized Pluralist	−0.002	0.017	0.884
Gender (Male)	0.041	0.019	0.027
Age	−0.034	0.007	0.000
Age squared	0.000	0.000	0.000
Education	0.033	0.024	0.160
Working condition	0.064	0.016	0.000
Income	−0.015	0.007	0.027
Ideology (reference = Center)			
Left	0.264	0.053	0.000
Center-left	0.184	0.035	0.000
Center-right	0.121	0.044	0.006
Right	0.207	0.031	0.000
Unaligned	−0.071	0.028	0.009
Attention to the campaign	0.063	0.024	0.009
Interest in politics	0.122	0.029	0.000
Efficacy index	0.026	0.007	0.000
Institutional trust index	0.010	0.004	0.013
Satisfaction with democracy	−0.026	0.013	0.048

Table 6.2 Continued

	Coefficient	Standard Error	p-value
Political information via ...			
Newspapers	0.066	0.010	0.000
Websites	0.018	0.006	0.001
Radio	0.030	0.006	0.000
Television	−0.067	0.007	0.000
Offline conversation	0.087	0.013	0.000
Political talk offline	0.057	0.018	0.002
Political talk on SNSs	0.214	0.015	0.000
Frequency of SNS use			
Facebook	−0.010	0.006	0.098
Twitter	0.012	0.010	0.258
YouTube	0.018	0.007	0.010
Instagram	0.026	0.008	0.002
Intercept	−0.695	0.151	0.000
Pseudo R^2	0.283		
N	8,639		

Note: SNS = social networking site. The pseudo R^2 coefficient reported in the table was calculated based on a Poisson regression model that did not cluster standard errors by country because the Zelig package we used to estimate this model in R did not generate the values of the model's null deviance and deviance.

The estimates plotted in Figure 6.2 confirm the lack of any noticeable differential effects across different types of mass media systems. When projected on three average respondents each living in a different media system, the increases in participation associated with accidental exposure to news on social media do not differ significantly, and, indeed, remain very low, across Liberal, Democratic Corporatist, and Polarized Pluralist media systems. If anything, these relationships are weaker in Liberal media systems, as the error bars overlap with 0 for respondents living in these countries but not for those residing in other types of media systems.

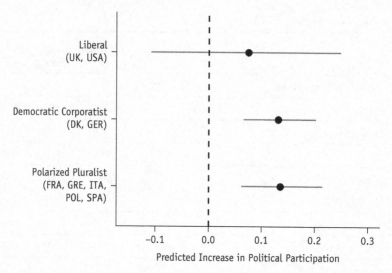

Figure 6.2. Marginal Effects of Accidental Exposure to Political News on Social Media in Different Types of Media Systems

Note: estimates are changes in count values of a 0–6 index and are based on the coefficients in Table 6.2 for respondents with values equal to the sample means (for numeric variables), medians (for ordinal variables), and modes (for categorical variables) apart from accidental exposure to political news on social media (comparing respondents who "never" see it and those who see it "always or nearly always") and whether respondents reside in countries with Democratic Corporatist (Denmark, Germany), Liberal (United Kingdom, United States), or Polarized Pluralist (France, Greece, Italy, Poland, Spain) media systems.

Unlike for electoral competition, we have therefore not been able to find any support for our hypothesis that the characteristics of mass media systems shape the relationship between accidental exposure to news on social media and political participation.

There may be various explanations for this null finding. First, as readers may recall from Chapter 4, of the three political experiences studied here, accidental exposure is the one that is most weakly correlated with participation. While this does not in and of itself rule out the possibility that the strength of such a correlation may differ across different groups (as we showed in Chapter 5 for at least some individual-level political attitudes), it may reduce the likelihood of statistically detecting such differences. Second, our theory could be poorly specified, as we may have not considered other systemic factors shaping this relationship. Third, our classifications may be incorrect even if our theory was accurate, especially considering that, for reasons explained earlier, the small number of countries for which we have data compels us to rely on coarse measures of the systemic features we are studying. Fourth, it may be that the reality on the ground has changed and that we should have classified the media systems in a completely different way, perhaps as suggested by Brüggemann and colleagues (2014), and possibly incorporating Fletcher and colleagues' (2020) finding that audience polarization is higher in the United States than in all other democracies we investigate. Both choices would lead us to consider the United States as a media system of its own (either as the lone example, in our data set, of a "Western" media system as classified by Brüggemann and colleagues, or as the country with the highest levels of audience polarization based on Fletcher and colleagues' analysis). However, as discussed previously, this would place severe limitations on the generalizability of our analysis. The problem is therefore best left to future research, hopefully covering a larger number of countries to assess the merits of different classifications of media systems and alternative measures of their key characteristics.

Political Organizations and Electoral Mobilization

Finally, we examine cross-country differences in the strength of the relationship between exposure to electoral mobilization via social media and participation. Electoral mobilization is aimed at prompting citizens to take part in elections, one of the key institutions of representative democracy. As discussed in Chapter 1, we theorize that the extent to which mobilization via social media contributes to participation depends on the functioning of another key institution of representative democracy—political parties. We follow Anstead and Chadwick's (2009) seminal contribution and distinguish between *party-centric* political systems, where parties maintain a relatively strong and permanent presence on the ground, and *candidate-centric* political systems, where political organizations are mostly temporary committees solely focused on winning elections. All else being equal, party-centric systems should offer individuals more opportunities to participate both during and outside campaigns, whereas candidate-centric systems should provide weaker and more ephemeral structures for political participation that only cover electioneering activities and vanish once votes have been cast. Therefore, electoral mobilization via social media should have a stronger relationship with participation in party-centric systems, where citizens can rely on some permanent catalysts and conduits for participation, than in candidate-centric systems, where political organizations channeling citizens' engagement are less readily available and function more intermittently. To the extent that encountering mobilizing messages on social media spurs people's interest in participating beyond the vote, as we showed in Chapter 4, party-centric systems should provide them with better opportunities to act upon such interest.

COUNTRY CLASSIFICATION

Based on the history of, and recent empirical evidence on, political parties in the nine countries we study, we classify three of them—Denmark, Germany, and the United Kingdom—as party-centric and the remaining six—France, Greece, Italy, Poland, Spain, and the United States—as candidate-centric. In deciding how to classify countries, we took into account not only quantitative indicators such as the number of party members, but also parties' political centrality and the degree of stability of the party system. In fluid contexts where new parties often emerge and replace older ones, parties may amass substantial numbers of members in the short term, but their organizations are unlikely to be as strong as in systems where parties are more stable and, thus, have more time to build and consolidate their structures, which, in turn, enable them to effectively channel citizen participation during and outside of elections.

The main political parties in Denmark, Germany, and the United Kingdom feature characteristics that we consider indicative of a party-centric system. They recruit relatively high numbers of members and have maintained rather stable and central roles over the past three decades. German major parties still pursue the model of the *Volkspartei*, which is "mainly concerned with the integration of . . . at least a large share of citizens into the political decision-making process" (Jun, 2011: 204). Recruiting substantial memberships is an important component of this model. Although enrollment faltered over the last two decades (Van Biezen et al., 2012), the six major German parties still had a total of 1.23 million members in 2019 (Niedermayer, 2020). Moreover, German parties receive public funding based on the contributions they raise from members and thus have a particular incentive to recruit them. While new entrants such as Alternative for Germany began challenging the major parties in the 2017 elections, the key actors have remained the same over the past two decades, enabling them to maintain strong ties in society.

The Danish case is relatively similar, as party membership is strong (Van Biezen et al., 2012), and the two main parties—the Social Democratic Party and the Liberal Party—maintain a strong commitment to nurture their membership organizations (Bille & Pedersen, 2004).

The United Kingdom is, among the three systems we characterized as party-centric, the one where party membership was hit hardest by the decline that started across most of Western Europe in the 1990s and continued in the 2000s (Van Biezen et al., 2012; Webb, 2002). However, this dip in party enrollment has been partly contrasted by the surge in the membership of the Labour Party, which in 2015 recruited more than one hundred thousand registered supporters (not formally treated as members, but allowed to vote in leadership elections) and then, following the election of Jeremy Corbyn as leader, nearly doubled its membership (see Vaccari & Valeriani, 2016, for a discussion). As of April 2018, Labour had 540,000 members—the most since 1980—and the membership of most parties had risen substantially since 2013 (House of Commons Library, 2018). Political parties are still central to many aspects of British political life, from candiate selection to policymaking, and the Labour and Conservative parties remain the dominant actors in the national political system.

The other countries in our research—France, Greece, Italy, Poland, Spain, and the United States—are all classified as candidate-centric. Some of them—France and the United States—feature historically weak party organizations (Green, 2002; Knapp, 2002), to some degree accompanied by a political culture suspicious of their institutionalization (Ignazi, 1996; Schudson, 1998). The two major American parties do not even formally enroll members (Anstead & Chadwick, 2009). Together with the direct election of a president with strong powers, these arrangements have meant that leaders and candidates dominate politics in France and the United States, while parties mostly serve as temporary electoral committees for individual politicians, particularly presidential aspirants.

The Polish system is also candidate-centric because the relatively recent transition to democracy in the 1990s meant that party organizations developed amid weak incentives to create mass memberships. As in other countries that democratized in the same period, voting behavior in Poland is mostly driven by candidates' and leaders' personalities rather than party loyalties (Mainwaring & Torcal, 2006). The personalization of politics is also incentivized by the direct election of the president, which focuses electoral competition on candidates rather than organizations (Bucar & McMenamin, 2015). While parties in the post-communist transition fulfilled the functions of structuring elections and recruiting elites, they did not develop strong societal ties, nor any substantial mass memberships (Szczerbiak, 2001). The most recent data on party membership suggest that none of the main parties exceed one hundred thousand members, which is rather low in a country with nearly 40 million residents and about 30 million eligible voters. As the authors of these estimates report, "Nowadays . . . parties are not expected to have large membership bases. . . . In practice, parties do not use members to their full potential" (Borowiec et al., 2017: 314–315). Similarly, Gherghina (2014) identifies a general trend of "loose mobilizing networks" and "small membership organizations" across all Central and Eastern European parties.

In Spain, democratization in the 1970s did not result in strong parties because it happened at a time when television enabled elites to quickly and easily reach voters. Hence, political organizations had little interest in recruiting mass memberships and "leap-frogged" to developing lean, professionalized, electorally oriented organizations (Pasquino, 2001; Gunther, 2005; Bosco & Morlino, 2007).

While Spanish parties recruit a substantial number of members (Van Biezen et al., 2012; Bosco & Morlino, 2007), they never took root as organizations with strong societal ties, partly out of suspicion for the kind of ingrained and uncompromising partisanship that most Spaniards considered as one of the causes of the collapse of democracy and the resulting civil war in the 1930s. Hence, Spanish parties have been described as "synthetic" (Halliday, 2002: 248), as they mostly serve as vehicles for elite coordination rather than as mass organizations aimed at mobilizing large numbers of members and supporters. A recent new entrant into the Spanish party system, *Podemos*, complicates this scenario, as it is rooted in the legacy of anti-austerity movements and tied to grassroots civic groups. However, these bottom-up legacies coexist with a personalized structure centered around *Podemos's* leader, Pablo Iglesias, whose televised visibility is as central to the party's communication as its grassroots participatory tools (della Porta et al., 2017; Casero-Ripollés et al., 2016).

Finally, we classify both Italy and Greece as candidate-centric systems. However, these two cases are less clear-cut than the ones we have discussed so far.

Greek parties developed slowly after the return to democracy in 1974, but by the mid-1980s they recruited a sizable number of members, comparable with those in other countries that we classified as party-centric (Van Biezen et al., 2012; Bosco & Morlino, 2007). However, the membership organizations maintained by the two dominant parties historically served patronage rather than mass mobilization purposes and as a result were neither strongly rooted in society nor geared toward faciliating participation (Pappas, 2009). Moreover, most party organizations were swept away in the aftermath of the 2007–2008 financial crisis, as the Panhellenic Socialist Movement (whose Greek acronym is PASOK) was all but wiped out at the ballot box and new parties emerged such as SYRIZA, originally founded as a coalition of small traditional leftist parties that subsequently embraced left-wing populism (Stavrakakis & Katsambekis, 2014) and became the dominant actor in Greek politics under the leadership of Alexis Tsipras. The party was initially rooted in grassroots movements engaged in anti-austerity mobilizations, but once it achieved electoral success it neglected to acquire and organize a large membership (della Porta et al., 2017; Kouki & González, 2018). Thus, while until the tumultuous developments of the 2010s Greek parties were more robust channels of electoral mobilization than French, Polish, or U.S. parties, their organizations were massively weakened in the past decade, and, importantly, they remained in that comatose state at the time when we collected our data.

The Italian case is characterized by moderately high but declining levels of party membership, combined with high electoral fluidity and party volatility. Similar to Greece, membership in Italian parties was historically robust by Western standards (Van Biezen et al., 2012), but it collapsed over the last decade. The country's main center-right party (Let's Go Italy) never set out to formally enroll members and the main center-left party (Democratic Party) saw its membership decline from one million upon its founding in 2007 to a reported 100,000 in 2014 (Vaccari & Valeriani, 2016), to then partially rebound to about 370,000 in 2018, far from initial levels (Partito Democratico, 2019). The party that replaced Let's Go Italy as the leading center-right force, the League (formerly Northern League), has a stronger organizational tradition of mass membership, but mostly limited to the Northern regions of the country, with the latest, albeit slightly outdated, estimates suggesting it counted little over one hundred thousand members (Passarelli & Tuorto, 2012). The Five Star Movement, which mostly organized online in its early days, does not formally enroll members but allows those who register online to vote in primaries and internal referenda[10] (Mosca et al., 2015). In sum, the high turnover of relevant parties and the lackluster investment in party membership and organization by many, if not all, political actors make Italian parties relatively weak and poorly equipped to systematically channel citizen participation.

In sum, parties in Greece and Italy can look back to a relatively recent history of organizational strength, supported by reasonably large memberships. However, this legacy is hard to recognize in the contemporary political lansdcape. As of 2015 and 2018, when the elections in Greece and Italy during which we collected our data took place, the organizational strength of political parties in both countries resembled that of parties in other candidate-centric systems more than party-centric systems. A sign of the parties' lackluster mobilization efforts was the historically low voter turnout recorded in both elections: 56.57% in Greece and 69.35% in Italy. At the time, these levels of electoral participation were the lowest in both countries' democratic elections in a century. For these reasons, we classify Greek and Italian systems as candidate-centric, together with those in France, Poland, Spain, and the United States. However, to better account for the possible role of historical legacies of party organizational strength in these countries, we also ran our analyses based on a three-way classification of parties: party-centric (Denmark, Germany, and the United Kingdom), candidate-centric (France, Poland, Spain, and the United States), and a third category that we call "legacy party-centric" (Greece and Italy) to emphasize the role parties used to play in those countries in a relatively recent past.

ANALYSIS

To test our hypothesis that electoral mobilization via social media is more strongly associated to participation in party-centric than candidate-centric systems, we ran two models that predict levels of political participation based on exposure to electoral mobilization on social media and a host of controls, to which we added our two classifications of party systems (a two-way version in Model 1 and a three-way version in Model 2) and interaction terms between exposure to electoral mobilization and type of party system. Both models predict around 30% of the total variance in the dependent variable, similar to other models discussed in the book. As shown in Table 6.3, the Poisson regression coefficients for exposure to mobilization are positive and significant in both Models 1 and 2. The negative coefficients for party-centric systems (significant in Model 1 and very close to the conventional threshold in Model 2) suggest that, among respondents who were not mobilized, participation was lower in party-centric systems than in candidate-centric systems. The interaction terms between mobilization and party-centric systems are positive in both models, which indicates that the strength of the relationship between mobilization and participation is stronger in party-centric systems than in candidate-centric ones, as we hypothesized. However, while the coefficient is significant at conventional levels of $p \leq 0.05$ in Model 1, it fails to meet this threshold in Model 2. The fact that the sizes of the two coefficients for this interaction term are very similar in the two models signifies that our estimate of the strength of the relationship is not substantially different. However, because in Model 2 we have fewer observations for candidate-centric systems, the standard errors associated with our estimate of the difference in the strength of our main relationship of interest (between party-centric and candidate-centric systems) are higher than in Model 1. Thus, the reduction of statistical power that derives from adopting a more granular classification of party characteristics is an important reason why we could not reject the null hypothesis in Model 2 while we were able to do so in Model 1.

In sum, the results provide some qualified support for our hypothesis. When we differentiate between party-centric and candidate-centric systems based on their configuration at the time our data were collected, we find evidence that exposure to electoral mobilization has a stronger relationship with participation in party-centric systems than in candidate-centric systems. However, when we incorporate parties' organizational history and add a third category of legacy party-centric systems, the direction and the magnitude of the coefficients does not change at all, but we cannot detect this relationship with sufficient statistical power to support our hypothesis. While both classifications of party organizations and both analyses in Table 6.3 have merit, we contend that the simpler distinction between party-centric and candidate-centric systems has the benefit of better capturing the situation on the ground at the time of our data collection than the more complex one, which incorporates historical realities that may not have been particularly relevant to voters when we fielded our surveys.

Table 6.3. **Poisson Regression Predicting Levels of Political Participation (0–6 Index): Indirect Effects of Exposure to Electoral Mobilization on Social Media in Party-Centric, Candidate-Centric, and Legacy Party-Centric Political Systems**

	Model 1 (2-way classification)			Model 2 (3-way classification)		
	Coefficient	S.E.	p-value	Coefficient	S.E.	p-value
Exposure to electoral mobilization via SNSs	0.427	0.032	0.000	0.440	0.037	0.000
Type of political system (reference = Candidate-centric)						
Party-centric (DK, GER, U.K.)	−0.125	0.053	0.019	−0.125	0.064	0.052
Legacy party-centric (GRE, ITA)				−0.006	0.062	0.925
Interactions (reference = Candidate-centric)						
Mobilization × Party-centric system	0.130	0.064	0.043	0.118	0.067	0.078
Mobilization × Legacy party-centric system				−0.043	0.068	0.531
Gender (Male)	0.015	0.012	0.196	0.016	0.014	0.231
Age	−0.033	0.006	0.000	−0.032	0.006	0.000
Age squared	0.000	0.000	0.000	0.000	0.000	0.000
Education	0.013	0.007	0.081	0.011	0.010	0.265
Working condition	0.055	0.026	0.031	0.055	0.026	0.036
Income	−0.008	0.003	0.024	−0.008	0.003	0.002
Ideology (reference = Center)						
Left	0.245	0.046	0.000	0.244	0.045	0.000
Center-left	0.146	0.028	0.000	0.147	0.028	0.000
Center-right	0.100	0.026	0.000	0.100	0.026	0.000
Right	0.164	0.035	0.000	0.163	0.034	0.000
Unaligned	−0.111	0.035	0.002	−0.110	0.034	0.001
Attention to the campaign	0.056	0.015	0.000	0.055	0.015	0.000
Interest in politics	0.073	0.017	0.000	0.074	0.016	0.000
Efficacy index	0.025	0.005	0.000	0.025	0.005	0.000

(continued)

Table 6.3 Continued

	Model 1 (2-way classification)			Model 2 (3-way classification)		
	Coefficient	S.E.	p-value	Coefficient	S.E.	p-value
Institutional trust index	0.008	0.005	0.081	0.009	0.005	0.063
Satisfaction with democracy	−0.024	0.016	0.127	−0.027	0.015	0.079
Political information via . . .						
Newspapers	0.059	0.010	0.000	0.058	0.009	0.000
Websites	−0.009	0.005	0.041	−0.009	0.005	0.074
Radio	0.025	0.006	0.000	0.025	0.006	0.000
Television	−0.055	0.012	0.000	−0.055	0.011	0.000
Offline conversation	0.085	0.011	0.000	0.085	0.011	0.000
Political talk offline	0.055	0.021	0.008	0.056	0.022	0.011
Political talk on SNSs	0.177	0.011	0.000	0.177	0.011	0.000
Frequency of SNS use						
Facebook	−0.017	0.007	0.018	−0.017	0.007	0.018
Twitter	0.020	0.006	0.001	0.019	0.006	0.002
YouTube	0.011	0.005	0.018	0.012	0.006	0.034
Instagram	0.019	0.008	0.023	0.019	0.008	0.013
Intercept	−0.322	0.119	0.007	−0.327	0.125	0.009
Pseudo R^2	0.296			0.296		
N	11,488			11,488		

Note: SNS = social networking site. The pseudo R^2 coefficient reported in the table was calculated based on a Poisson regression model that did not cluster standard errors by country because the Zelig package we used to estimate this model in R did not generate the values of the model's null deviance and deviance.

Figure 6.3 shows the marginal effects of electoral mobilization on participation, estimated on average respondents residing in different types of political systems based on Model 1 in Table 6.3. Here, participation is predicted to increase by 0.73 (on a 0–6 scale) in party-centric systems and by 0.59 in candidate-centric systems when voters are exposed to electoral mobilization on social media. The difference in the predicted effects across different types of party systems is relatively small, and the overlapping error bars suggest that it is not statistically significant at conventional 95% confidence levels. Hence, while the overall relationship between mobilization and participation is significantly stronger in party-centric political systems, such differences are not substantial enough when projecting them on a typical respondent in each group of countries.

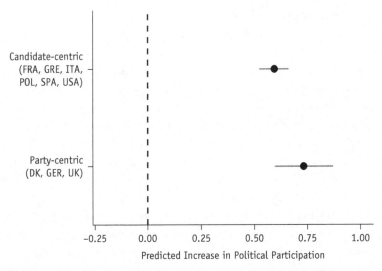

Figure 6.3. Marginal Effects of Exposure to Electoral Mobilization on Social Media in Party-Centric and Candidate-Centric Political Systems

Note: estimates are changes in count values of a 0–6 index and are based on the coefficients in Model 1 in Table 6.3 for respondents with values equal to the sample means (for numeric variables), medians (for ordinal variables), and modes (for categorical variables) apart from exposure to electoral mobilization on social media (comparing respondents who were and were not exposed) and whether respondents reside in countries with party-centric (Denmark, Germany, United Kingdom) or candidate-centric (France, Greece, Italy, Poland, Spain, United States) political systems.

In conclusion, our comparative analysis highlights the continuing importance of political parties in the digital age, as well as the potentially virtuous circles that can arise between informal interactions on social media and more structured participatory endeavors enabled by consolidated political actors— or at least occurring in systems where party organizations are still comparably stronger and, thus, potentially facilitate a more diffuse and continuous participatory culture. However, the statistical support we found for our hypothesis was mixed, as the relationship is strong enough to be observed in a general regression model, but not when comparing predicted levels of participation among average respondents, nor when adopting a more granular distinction between party-centric, legacy party-centric, and candidate-centric systems.

Conclusion: The Power and Limits of Differentiation

We started our comparative inquiry with two competing theoretical perspectives on how the relationship between political experiences on social media and participation may vary in different contexts: standardization and differentiation.

We argued in favor of a moderate version of differentiation, according to which the direction of these relationships should not change across contexts, but their strength should. On this basis we tested three hypotheses on how different systemic factors that vary in the nine countries included in our study may moderate the relationship between specific political experiences on social media and political participation.

We were able to confirm the hypothesis that exposure to agreement on social media is more strongly related to participation in majoritarian than proportional systems. We also found partial support for the hypothesis that exposure to electoral mobilization on social media is more strongly associated with participation in party-centric than candidate-centric political systems. Instead, the data led us to reject the hypothesis that accidental exposure to news on social media is more strongly correlated with participation in media systems where journalism tends to be more neutral than in media systems characterized by more partisan reporting styles. When we found support for our hypotheses, the estimated marginal effects we could attribute to systemic differences were relatively small. When the country characteristics we examined mattered, they did so in a limited way.

Where do these findings leave us? One could say we found support for the standardization theory, or for the differentiation theory, or both. If we look at the regression models, we can reject two out of three null hypotheses, and thus the evidence is in favor of differentiation. But if we look at the marginal effects on average respondents derived from these models, we can only reject one of three null hypotheses, so the balance would shift toward standardization. It may be that we did not test the right hypotheses and that future research needs to go back to the theoretical drawing board and think again about which systemic characteristics may shape the relationships we studied. It may be that we did not include enough countries, which limited our ability to test better specified theories and to include more nuanced measures of the characteristics of their political and media systems. Still, the findings reported in this chapter contribute to our knowledge about digital media and politics in various ways.

First, we have shown signs that contextual features can play a relevant role in shaping the relationship between political experiences on social media and participation. While the differential effects we investigated in this chapter were not very strong, overall, our analyses suggest that we should always take into account the role of context when we analyze the political implications of social media. Although we did not find smoking-gun evidence for full-fledged differentiation, our findings suggest that standardization is not the default pattern either. We cannot assume that any country or small group of countries, even within the realm of Western democracies, can offer conclusive evidence on the strength of these relationships. This is why we need comparative research on social media and politics.

Second, we have highlighted that constructing fine-grained theories on the relationship between specific political experiences on social media and types of systemic characteristics can be fruitful. So far, comparative research on social media and political behavior has mostly focused on generic uses of social media, or more active political endeavors (such as acquiring news and discussing politics) rather than specific and less demanding experiences such as those we studied. However, political experiences on social media are diverse, and each of them potentially involves different types of users (as we showed in Chapter 3) and may have different implications for political behavior (as we showed in Chapter 4). Hence, scholars who aim to understand the role that systemic characteristics play in shaping these relationships should be mindful of these specificities and develop theories that consider their interactions with specific institutional features.

Third and finally, we have provided evidence that some characteristics of political systems contribute to boosting or weakening the relationships between some political experiences on social media and participation, while we could not find any evidence that mass media systems shaped our relationships of interest. While our findings should by no means be treated as the last word on these issues, they suggest that political structures and logics may be central in shaping the connection between social media and citizens' political behavior.

Conclusion

London, June 23, 2016. The date that history will remember for the Brexit referendum started under very particular auspices for us. We spent most of that day
locked in a room of an almost empty Senate House, a University library building
in Central London. Our goal was to develop the first draft of a book proposal on
social media and political participation in Western democracies, which we had
been researching since 2012. We spent the day brainstorming, sketching dozens
of mind maps, discussing alternative book outlines, and refining key arguments.
After a very intense and productive day of work, we finally left the building and
had dinner together while watching the news on TV as polls were closing. Since
we had a second day of hard work ahead of us, we resisted the temptation to
stay up until the results were called. Instead, we said goodbye and went to sleep
unaware of the huge electoral upset that British voters had been delivering while
we discussed what our book should look like.

The day after, we woke up in a city, a country, and a continent left shocked and
incredulous by the Leave victory. Day Two of our book workshop was definitely
less productive than Day One, as we were constantly distracted by news alerts,
posts that our contacts were publishing on social media, messages from friends,
and even calls from journalists asking for comments. The idea that one of the reasons for the success of the Leave campaign was an aggressive and efficient digital
campaign began to gain momentum from that very day. This narrative would
reach its peak almost two years later, when the Facebook–Cambridge Analytica
scandal exploded, revealing that the U.K.-based consulting firm employed by
the Leave campaign (and subsequently by the Donald Trump campaign in the
United States) had illicitly acquired massive amounts of personal data without
consent from 87 million Facebook users and had employed such information
to profile and target voters online with specifically crafted messages invisible to
others (Cadwallar & Graham-Harrison, 2018). In November 2016, the election
of Donald Trump as president of the United States provided another, even bigger
shock. Like the Leave victory in Britain, Trump's success was also accompanied

Outside the Bubble. Cristian Vaccari and Augusto Valeriani, Oxford University Press. © Oxford University Press 2021.
DOI: 10.1093/oso/9780190858476.003.0008

by concerns for unscrupulous use of personal social media data for stealth political targeting and the mass spread of disinformation online.

As we have already argued in the Introduction to this book, it was on the night between June 23 and June 24, 2016, that the dominant narrative around social media and politics started changing. After that watershed moment, digital platforms were much more likely to be presented as poisoning agents for democratic societies than as the liberal champions they had often been considered, way too optimistically, in previous years (Tucker et al., 2017; Miller & Vaccari, 2020). Similarly, scholars are reappraising the notion—almost an assumption in earlier research—that citizens tend to act earnestly and fairly when they meet and interact online (Hedrich et al., 2018). The Internet is no longer presented as a freewheeling marketplace where the power of ideas and the ingenuity of outsiders working from their garages can bring down corporate giants (Benkler, 2006), but as a concentrated and hierarchical marketplace of attention controlled by a few, seemingly unassailable, digital monopolies (Wu, 2017; Hindman, 2018). Granted, some scholarly critiques of the Internet and its role in social and political life predate 2016 (e.g., Howard, 2006; Tufekci, 2014; Vaidhyanathan, 2012; Zuboff, 2015), but the tide in public and academic discourse turned between June and November of that momentous year (Chadwick, 2019).

Digital Politics and Cycles of Opinion

The post-2016 tidal shift was arguably the strongest observed in the relatively short history of digital media and politics so far, but it was by no means the first. Since the ancient times, philosophers and historians have debated whether history is cyclical or progressive. By the same token, in the last few decades public narratives on the state of democracy, including how digital media contribute to it, have alternated moments of enthusiasm and pessimism.

In introducing his study of public opinion and parties in Western democracies, Russell Dalton (2018) observed that in previous decades, public debate on the state of democracy had fluctuated between optimism and despair. Against the backdrop of such alternating black-or-white narratives, Dalton argued that systematic research must resist "the winds of punditry" (Dalton, 2018: xiii) and strive to understand reality in all its complexities.

Similarly, a few years before the post-2016 reckoning, Andrew Chadwick (2009: 11) pointed out that multiple waves of enthusiasm and pessimism had characterized academic and popular discourse on the Internet's potential to transform and improve democratic life. A few years later, Scott Wright (2012) argued against the "schism" between cyber-optimists (e.g., Davis, 2009) and cyber-pessimists (e.g., Margolis & Resnick, 2000). Adherence to the simplistic narratives of "everything has changed" or "nothing has changed," wrote Wright, affected the questions scholars had asked and obscured many important ways in which the Internet was transforming democracy.

The 2016 upheavals definitely sparked a new "everything has changed" moment that is still unfolding as we write these lines. The democratic role of social media has been called into question like never before. The digital platforms that were once hailed for making citizens' lives richer and more connected are now blamed for facilitating sinister activities such as discriminatory profiling, shady micro-targeting, voter suppression, foreign electoral interference, hate speech, and the mass spread of disinformation. The title of an article published in the British newspaper *The Guardian* in February 2019 called Facebook "A digital gangster destroying democracy" (Cadwalladr, 2019). This was not an editorial from a fringe commentator, but a news story that quoted the final report of an inquiry by the U.K. Parliament's Digital, Culture, Media and Sport Committee into the role of social media in democracy (House of Commons Digital, Culture, Media and Sport Committee, 2019). The report called for unprecedentedly restrictive regulation of digital platforms, as did the U.K. government's "Online Harms White Paper," released two months later (U.K. Government, 2019).

The current, broadly pessimistic, reckoning around the role of social media in democratic life is clearly rooted in valid concerns and real, important facts on the ground that scholars have a duty to investigate—and many, including us, are doing just that (e.g., Chadwick et al., 2018; Giglietto et al., 2019; Tucker et al., 2018; Miller & Vaccari, 2020; Vaccari & Chadwick, 2020). Studies have shed light on the role of social media in the spread of misinformation and disinformation, the propagation of hate speech and intolerance, and the empowering of shadowy and unaccountable groups who aim to manipulate public discourse (see Phillips, 2015; Persily, 2017; Allcott & Gentzkow, 2017; Bennett & Livingston, 2018; Kim et al., 2018; Waisbord, 2018; Bastos & Mercea, 2019; Rossini, 2020).

It is therefore somehow ironic that the two of us came together to draft the structure of this book exactly on the cusp of such a momentous turning point in public debate around the democratic role of social media. If we had to follow the predominant opinion tide, until June 23, 2016, we should have written this book in the form of a fairy tale. Conversely, from the day after, we should have progressively turned it into a tragedy. As our readers already know by this point, this volume is neither a fairytale nor a tragedy.

In this book, we have striven to provide a nuanced, empirically grounded account of the relationship between social media and political participation in Western democracies. We have shown that social media can contribute to the quality of democratic life, at least to the extent that the breadth of citizens' political participation, and the diversity in the types of citizens who participate, is an important component of the complex, delicate, and constantly evolving machinery of democracy. However, we have also shown that the relationship between specific political experiences on social media and political participation is not so strong as to justify unmitigated enthusiasm. Social media cannot and will not "save democracy," at least not on their own, from citizens' political apathy, distrust, and disconnection. Social media are also not well placed to help mitigate the damages caused to democracy by norm-breaking political elites and failing government policies (Przeworski, 2019). Whatever social media might do to help some citizens exercise their political voice, that voice may not even be decisive in swaying elections and determining policies, as Achen and Bartels (2017) have argued. And while we also showed that political experiences on social media do not seem to disproportionately stimulate participation among ideologically extremist citizens, nor among those who voted for populist political actors, we refrain from drawing sweeping conclusions about the normative desirability of *any* kind of citizen participation, irrespective of the aims it pursues and the means it employs.

What is more, evaluating the democratic contribution of social media mainly or exclusively based on the color of the sails they fill in a given moment and in a given context would effectively prevent us from exiting the cycles of optimism and despair described earlier. As we are putting the final touches on this manuscript, Joe Biden has won a U.S. presidential election in the midst of a pandemic. To ensure the safety of volunteers and voters, Biden strongly limited door-to-door canvassing and get-out-the-vote efforts (Alter, 2020) while making social media the centerpiece of his campaign (Suciu, 2020). And yet, organized political actors and ordinary voters also used social media during and after the election to spread falsehoods on the fairness and legality of the vote, which ended up being the last, desperate peg on which President Trump decided to hang his re-election hopes (Benkler et al., 2020). In sum, technology is far from neutral, and so is political participation, but disentangling democratically desirable and undesirable relationships between social media and participation was not among the goals of this project. We hope readers keep these caveats in mind when interpreting our results, but we equally trust they will deem our findings relevant for how we understand, and enhance, democratic participation and governance.

In the next pages, we summarize our main theoretical and empirical contributions, suggest some avenues for future research, and discuss how our study relates to broader contemporary debates on social media and democracy.

Affordances Matter, but so Do Individuals' Experiences

We have argued that platforms and their affordances matter, but so do individuals and their concrete political experiences on social media. Digital platforms' affordances shape the kinds of content people are exposed to, the users they interact with, and the activities they are encouraged to undertake. These nudges are very important and are rightly the focus of research, public debate, and, possibly, regulation. However, they do not fully determine the kinds of political content and interactions people experience online. As we have shown in Chapters 3–5, different users approach and employ platforms' affordances in different ways, which results in distinctive political experiences that in turn shape behaviors in different ways among different groups. For instance, while most social media platforms have some built-in mechanisms that prioritize affinity (of backgrounds, interests, and, often, political views) over encounters with difference, in the aggregate most social media users report that they are exposed to roughly equal proportions of political content they agree and disagree with. Similarly, although social media may be designed to let users indulge their preferences and escape their nemeses, it is not only political junkies who encounter news on social media. Instead, as many as half of our respondents claimed to accidentally stumble upon political news, and one-third received direct encouragement to vote for a party or candidate on these platforms.

These findings stand in contrast—but not necessarily in contradiction—to the much bleaker figures on Web traffic reported by Hindman (2018: 134), who showed that "news sites get only about 3% of web traffic." Three percent surely entails a small amount of time and effort compared with the cumbersome requirements of an informed citizenry. Hindman (2018) demonstrates that most Web traffic is directed toward search engines, social media, email, and pornographic sites. What people see on social media is therefore crucial. Even if the actual amount of news and political content users see is limited compared with other types of messages (Fletcher et al., 2020), we have shown that rather large portions of social media users in a variety of Western democracies encounter politics as part of their everyday experience of these platforms. It is possible that our survey questions may have overestimated the frequency with which these experiences occur or the number of users they involve (Prior, 2009), but at a minimum our results suggest that we should not write off social media as sources of meaningful encounters with political content for large sectors of the population. Since most people are not spending much time actively looking for news online, social media may serve as a partial but helpful supplement to news diets that would otherwise be even more devoid of public affairs information.

To understand whether social media may contribute to citizens' participatory repertoires, we need to assess concrete and politically relevant outcomes of social media use at the individual level. In this research, we have focused on three such outcomes: encountering political agreement, accidental exposure to news, and being targeted by electoral mobilization. These are by no means the only relevant experiences scholars can and should study. Exposure to disinformation, targeted political advertisements, uncivil political talk, and hate speech, just to name a few examples, are equally as relevant. It should also be noted that our measures gauged the kinds of content users encountered but did not discriminate between different sources (for instance, strong ties versus weak ties, individual users versus news media or political actors, and accounts exhibiting authentic or inauthentic behavior). The quality of the content that users are exposed to should also matter. For instance, future research may investigate the effects of political experiences on social media that include different types of content, such as candidate biographies, issue positions, social and partisan identities, or horse race coverage of the campaign. And while in our analyses we did not differentiate political experiences based on the social media where they occurred, future research should disentangle whether they are more or less likely to occur and have different effects across different platforms.

Political Experiences on Social Media Have Positive Implications for Political Participation

We have shown that political experiences on social media are positively associated with the breadth of citizens' repertoires of participation. Users who predominantly see political content they agree with on social media tend to participate more. The more often people accidentally encounter political news on social media, the more they participate. And citizens who are targeted by messages trying to persuade them to vote for a party or a candidate also participate more. Our research design does not warrant strong causal statements, although we enhanced our analyses with all available statistical techniques to bring us as close as possible to that goal. Yet, these topline findings confirm and specify a vast body of research, which we summarized in Chapter 1. In absolute terms, the magnitude of the relationships we uncovered is not so strong as to justify claims that social media can in and of themselves lead most of their users to become massively more active. Our results suggest that the effects of social media on participation are more appropriately compared to a light but steady breeze than to a wind gust. Yet, the breeze does blow, and it is felt by substantial numbers of citizens in a variety of Western democracies.

Political Experiences on Social Media Bridge Participation Gaps

We have demonstrated that political experiences on social media enhance participation among the less politically involved more than the highly involved. Most early work on digital media and politics argued that the Internet may eventually reinforce existing inequalities, so that the more active would become even more engaged and the less involved would, at best, fail to notice the new opportunities afforded by the Web and, at worst, become even more distracted by the panoply of entertainment available online. We took a different approach and argued that political content encountered on social media may be more impactful on less involved citizens, who should be less interested in it but are also less likely to see it elsewhere, than on more involved citizens, who may be more interested in it but are more likely to have already been exposed to it. First, while political junkies are definitely the main target of political content on social media, they are by no means the only one, as less involved users do experience some meaningful encounters with news and campaigns on these platforms. Second, when these encounters happen, they tend to have stronger, positive relationships with participation among less politically involved citizens than among more involved ones. Thus, instead of deepening political inequalities, social media can bridge at least some of them.

This is by no means the final word in this important debate. While social media may help reduce participatory inequalities between those with high and low levels of political involvement, they may be exacerbating other forms of inequality rooted in gender, education, and social class, as argued by Schradie (2019) and Schlozman and colleagues (2010). We only explored one of the reasons why people do not participate, as theorized by Verba and colleagues (1995): they "do not want to" because they are not sufficiently involved in politics. We partially addressed another reason, that "nobody asked them to," in our investigation of electoral mobilization via social media. We showed that such mobilization is widespread and that it has the strongest relationship with participation among the three experiences we analyzed. Hence, social media enable many organized and unorganized actors to "ask" others to get involved, and when that happens, levels of participation among those who are asked increase. However, we did not investigate the first reason identified by Verba and colleagues (1995): citizens "cannot" participate because they lack the time, knowledge, and resources that are necessary to bear the individual costs of participating.[1] In an age of growing economic and social inequalities, which are arguably reshaping political cleavages and patterns of electoral competition, this is a relevant issue for future research.

That being said, the implications of our finding that political experiences on social media reduce involvement-based gaps in participation merit some further reflections. Beside the already involved "usual suspects," who eagerly take advantage of social media to get informed about, discuss, and find opportunities to participate in politics, less familiar faces are joining the political arena as a result of their politically relevant experiences on social media, whether they encounter news by accident, because someone else prompted them to support a party or candidate, or because they find comfort in engaging with sympathetic discussants online.

This quantitative expansion of the pool of participants may entail a more profound, and potentially more consequential, qualitative change. Possibilities for political self-expression and serendipitous encounters with political content have become part of many social media users' habits. Thus, social media have contributed to changing what it means and what it takes to participate in politics—particularly, our data show, among people who are less involved in politics. This is an example of technologies' ability to *transform the context of participation* once they become so embedded in people's lives that they are no longer noticed as new (Bimber et al., 2012). The relatively new entrants who, according to our analyses, social media more strongly draw into politics, are not cut from the same cloth as the people we normally expect to undertake political action. They are less interested in public affairs and pay less attention to elections. While our study could only shed some partial light on these users' political preferences and values, it is possible that they may be different from those of textbook political activists who feature prominently in scholarly accounts of participation. It is also conceivable that such "unusual suspects" may respond to, and contribute to the success of, unconventional types of political leaders, organizations, and ideologies, thus facilitating the surge and success of outsiders at the expense of established political actors. Social media may thus be contributing to some of the vivid examples of political disruption that we have witnessed over the past few years across and beyond the Western world. Our analysis thus highlights some of the factors that explain the "political turbulence" described by Margetts and colleagues (2016). Some of the volatility in contemporary mass political behavior may be related to a qualitative expansion of the pool of participants in politics—a story in which we show that social media play an important role. But is such expansion of citizens' voice democratically desirable in and of itself?

Political Participation and Democratic Values

Theorists and empirical researchers of political participation do not always assume that more participation is always beneficial for democracy, or for most of its citizens. One contrarian position maintains that increased citizen participation can impede democratic governance by overloading overstretched political systems with excessive demands (Lipset, 1960; Huntington, 1975). According to this perspective, the solution to some of the challenges faced by contemporary democracies is to restrict participatory spaces or to leave citizens alone in their apathy, so that elites can guide a docile public toward what is best. The limits of this elitist approach are evident. While politicians and technocrats may enjoy "ruling the void," in Peter Mair's (2013) eloquent formulation, the legitimacy of this arrangement is weak and its sustainability doubtful. We concur with Russell Dalton that "the cures offered by the elitist theorists are worse than the problem they address; democracy's very goals are ignored in its defense" (Dalton, 2018: 267). An all-out, across-the-board increase of citizen participation may not be the cure to all democracy's ills, but the opposite approach—reducing participation, or letting it fade away—resembles the once popular leech therapy. Drawing blood from an ailing organism may help its recovery in a few circumstances, but in most cases, it ends up weakening it, harming it, and sometimes killing it.

But if less participation is not the answer, is more participation what democracies need today? When we started this project, a vast body of literature (e.g., Dalton & Wattenberg, 2000) argued that a decline of political participation—at least in its institutional forms such as voting, party membership, and volunteering for campaigns—was occurring, that this was problematic for democracy, and that at least part of the responsibility lay in how the mass media, particularly television, had reconfigured the relationship between citizens and political actors (Entman, 1990; Putnam, 2000; Dahlgren, 2009). A more nuanced, "realist" position suggests that citizen participation does not affect public policy as much as the most enthusiastic proponents of democracy suggest, because most people vote on the basis of partisan loyalties and group identities that have little to do with punishing or rewarding governments and parties for their records or proposals (Achen & Bartels, 2017). Still, the proponents of this view highlight that democratic processes and procedures, chief among which are popular participation in elections, entail some important democratic benefits, such as legitimizing who shall rule, facilitating turnover in government, incentivizing power holders to tolerate opposition, and helping citizens develop civic competence and other democratic and human virtues (Achen & Bartels, 2017: 316–319).

However, we should not simplistically assume that reversing the participatory decline that occurred toward the end of the twentieth century, an endeavor to which social media seem to be contributing, is necessarily a positive end in and of itself. The *quality* of participation is as important as its *quantity*, if not more. An important debate is taking place on this issue. Hedrick and colleagues caution us against what they see as "a central assumption shared among the research communities that study political, civic, and fan participation: […] that all participation is earnest and well-meaning" (Hedrick et al., 2018: 1062). Andrew Chadwick (2019) observes that this assumption, which he terms "the engagement gaze," has led scholars to overlook the goals of those who participate, the risk that some forms of engagement may threaten democratic norms, and the longer-term implications for political and civic cultures. Thorsten Quandt has proposed the concept of "dark participation" to identify the ways in which citizens make "negative, selfish or even deeply sinister contributions" to online news (Quandt, 2018: 40). Participation has always come in many shapes and sizes, and treating all of it as equal, let alone as equally desirable, obscures important nuances that are key to evaluating its contribution to democracy.

How, then, to assess the implications of our findings for the quality of participation? An honest first answer is that we did not specifically measure such quality, as intended by the authors we have just cited. What we measured is citizens' recall of engaging in six specific behaviors, as explained in Chapter 2: financing a party, candidate, political leader, or campaign; taking part in public meetings and electoral rallies; distributing leaflets to support a political or social cause; contacting a politician to support a cause; signing petitions and subscribing referenda; and trying to convince someone to vote for a party, leader, or candidate. We did not measure the quality of these behaviors, neither by comparing one action against the others ("Is donating money to a party more democratically desirable than attending rallies?"), nor by discriminating the performance of the same action based on the goals it pursued ("Is financing party X more democratically desirable than financing party Y?") or the means it employed ("Is trying to persuade others based on accurate information more democratically desirable than doing so based on false information?"). These are by no means rhetorical questions but speak to core normative democratic values. We will now address each of these limitations.

Instead of differentiating the democratic desirability of different modes of political action, we used an additive index combining six activities, each of which weighted equally as the others. Consistent with our definition of participation repertoires as multifaceted and hybrid, we developed an inclusive compound measure that captures a variety of relevant behaviors without discriminating between them. However, in Chapter 4 we also shed light on the specific relationships between the political experiences on social media we study and each of the six modes of participation we assessed. This exercise showed that the relationships differ in magnitude when comparing different forms of political action, but the findings mostly point in the same direction, i.e., that political experiences on social media are positively associated with most forms of participation. Readers who attribute different values to particular modes of participation can thus assess social media's contribution to democracy based on those specific analyses.

The issue of which goals an active citizen pursues and how well, or poorly, those goals fulfill democratic ideals is more complex. We did not ask our respondents what type of political outcomes they were hoping to advance when they took the actions we inquired about. Measuring the quality of the objectives people aim to achieve when they participate would have required us to decide whether, for instance, trying to convince someone to vote for Hillary Clinton in the U.S. 2016 presidential election is of higher or lower democratic quality than trying to convince others to vote for Donald Trump—or for any of the other candidates. While we share the widespread public and scholarly concern with the rise of authoritarian populists, we also believe in Max Weber's lesson that social scientists should strive as much as possible for value freedom when conducting research (Weber, 1922). Using normative criteria to empirically differentiate acts of participation on the basis described earlier would have, in our view, jeopardized this principle.

This does not mean that we cannot ask empirical questions about the relationship between social media and participation among voters of different ideological leanings, or among voters who did and did not vote for populist political actors. These questions have clear normative implications amid widespread concern that authoritarian populists aim to weaken democracy, damage rational debate, and sow intolerance in our societies (Norris & Inglehart, 2019) but can be answered without confounding empirical and value-based concerns. When we tackled these issues in Chapter 5, we found very few differences in the relationships between the political experiences on social media we studied and participation among voters who placed themselves at different points in the left–right spectrum. Notably, we found no evidence that respondents who are ideologically more extreme receive a larger participatory boost from these experiences—if anything, the opposite occurred. Moreover, we did not detect any differences between respondents who voted for populist parties or presidential candidates and those who voted for other political actors. From a normative standpoint, these null findings provide some grounds for moderate optimism on social media's contribution to democracy. At the very least, our analyses fail to substantiate the argument that digital platforms are disproportionately aiding populist political actors.

Finally, illuminating the means by which individuals participate is crucial at a time when concerns for disinformation, hate speech, inauthentic behavior, and intolerance online are on the rise (Bennett & Livingston, 2018; Chadwick, 2019; Miller & Vaccari, 2020). That political actors and their supporters sometimes rely on these means as part of their online and offline propaganda is concerning for anyone who believes in democracy. Regardless of how widespread and effective these behaviors are, they poison the well of public debate and could, in David Karpf's words, "undermine the democratic myths and governing norms that stand as a bulwark against elite corruption and abuse of power" (Karpf, 2019). If self-interested elites come to believe that most voters can be duped by disinformation or coerced into submission by trolling and hate speech spread via social media thanks to sophisticated targeting and digital mobs of supporters and botnets, they may be less likely to restrain themselves and abide by implicit and explicit democratic norms. The possibility that voters can "throw the rascals out," i.e., replace a government that does not benefit them, is a powerful constraint on elite behavior (Sartori, 1987), but it rests on the assumption that citizens can identify the rascals and make their voices heard against them before and during elections. If digital media help pollute mass political behavior with unfair means, many cracks risk opening in the delicate edifice of democratic governance.

How democratically clean, or poisoned, is the water springing from different media wells is an important question for contemporary political communication research (Van Aelst et al., 2017). In this book, we could not shed adequate light on these issues because survey self-reports are poorly equipped to precisely measure all these problematic behaviors, especially in combination with one another. Spreading disinformation, engaging in hate speech, trolling, and manifesting intolerance are socially undesirable conduct, and thus people who perform these acts tend to be reluctant to admit to them when answering survey questions. Moreover, for their most egregious perpetrators, these activities would not even qualify as problematic. To a racist, racism is common sense. To a callous partisan, disinformation is clever propaganda. To a troll, trolling is just fooling around. To a hater, hatred is legitimate retaliation against some injustice or conspiracy. We do not aim to push this argument to the extreme position that none of these behaviors can be measured in a survey—after all, we and many other scholars have employed surveys to measure the spread of misinformation and disinformation on social media (Chadwick et al., 2018; Rossini et al., 2020). However, these measurement challenges become much more severe when survey research tries to simultaneously measure multiple political behaviors and to gauge whether people employed problematic means while performing them. For these reasons, most research has focused on one set of antinormative behaviors at a time. As we were interested in studying multiple forms of participation across face-to-face and digital environments, we decided to focus on *what* our respondents did when they participated in politics rather than *how* they did so.

Political Participation and Democratic (E)Quality

Our findings directly address another important normative argument: that democracy is founded, among other things, on political equality and inclusiveness. Large inequalities in who participates weaken this foundation. Two main strands of the literature have addressed this issue: research on political participation, mainly rooted in political science, and studies of deliberation and the public sphere, mainly rooted in communication.

Scholars of political participation often emphasize the value of equality in who participates and the dangers for democracy when participation becomes a weapon of the strong and leaves out relevant sectors of the population. As Verba and colleagues (1995: 509) eloquently put it, "meaningful democratic participation requires that the voices of citizens in politics be clear, loud, and equal," and participatory equality is necessary "so that the democratic ideal of equal responsiveness to the preferences and interests of all is not violated." Participation communicates information to policymakers on the preferences of the population and provides incentives for elites to take those preferences into account in governing. Equality of participation is also an important way in which the broader democratic value of equality among all citizens comes to life (Dahl, 2006)— which, as we will see, is a relevant point for deliberation theorists as well.

In their study of the United States in the 1980s and 1990s, Verba and colleagues (1995) found Americans' political voice to be loud and clear, but deeply unequal. In a follow-up analysis covering the first decade of the twenty-first century, the same authors noted that "the disparities in political voice across various segments of society are so substantial and so persistent as to preclude equal consideration" (Schlozman et al., 2013: 6). Similar studies in the United Kingdom concurred with this somber assessment (Pattie et al., 2004; Whiteley, 2011b). Declines in voter turnout across Western democracies have been linked to reduced levels of mobilization of socially marginal voters, meaning that their interests and preferences are less likely to affect election outcomes (Gray & Caul, 2000). And while participatory inequalities are partly explained by socioeconomic status, the strongest predictor of participation is political interest (Verba et al., 1995). Interest in politics, however, is not just a transient individual preference but tends to be very stable over time (Prior, 2010). This is why our finding that political experiences on social media can narrow, or even close, participatory gaps among voters with different levels of political interest—as well as attentiveness to campaigns, which is a more context-sensitive measure of involvement—is particularly important in terms of democratic equality.

Political scientists mostly focus on equality of participation because of the *outcomes* it is expected to generate—holding elites accountable based on democratic electoral mandates that reflect as broadly as possible the interests and preferences of the population. By contrast, communication scholars are predominantly interested in how equality of participation contributes to the quality of the *processes* by which citizens interact with political elites and with each other. The paradigm of democratic deliberation is arguably the most important theoretical, conceptual, and normative backbone of these approaches.

Deliberation entails a complex set of principles and mechanisms that enable individuals to "arrive at a well-reasoned solution after a period of inclusive, respectful consideration of diverse points of view" (Gastil & Black, 2007: 2). In its pure form, deliberation requires many conditions that are hardly, if ever, fulfilled in public debate, regardless of whether it occurs in face-to-face conversations, town hall meetings, mass media, the Internet, or social media. However, deliberation has been one of the key normative cornerstones of political communication research (Gastil & Black, 2007). How the theoretical requirements for deliberation can be fulfilled in the messy practice of everyday life has been widely debated. For Habermas (1989), deliberation is only possible in an ideal speech situation, where open discussion can facilitate reasoned exchanges and enlightened understanding among participants endowed with equal rights. However, critics have claimed that this view of deliberation is an eminently liberal edifice that accepts, rather than strives to overcome, many entrenched social inequalities that affect who is entitled to speak and to what extent (Calhoun, 1992). A genuinely egalitarian public sphere needs to provide more inclusive spaces that are hospitable to a broader variety of groups, topics, and styles of discussion than those typical of bourgeois liberal democracy as discussed by Habermas (Fraser, 1990). Similar normative tensions have characterized theory and research on how digital media can facilitate various forms of public deliberation. In an overview, Coleman and Moss (2012) argue that most applications of online deliberation have tended to exclude groups that cannot, or do not want to, engage in the formalized practices required by the most orthodox models (see also Hartz-Karp & Sullivan, 2014). Chadwick (2009) observes that, largely as a result of this disconnect between theoretical assumptions and practical constraints, most real-world experiments of online deliberation failed to include more than a few dozen unrepresentative citizens, a far cry from the scale and inclusiveness required by mass democratic governance. This is a classic conundrum in democratic politics. As Dahl (1989), among others, explained, the more effort participation requires, the less inclusive and the more unequal it tends to be.

To overcome these limits, Mansbridge and colleagues (2012) propose the notion of "deliberative systems." This broader perspective on deliberation aims to acknowledge and integrate the role of different actors and communication contexts in making democracy work beyond the more formal and demanding processes highlighted by classic deliberation theories (e.g., Ackerman & Fishkin, 2004). A deliberative system is an assemblage of many different parts, some of which may be very distant from the ideal requirements for deliberation. For instance, partisan media may engage in one-sided propaganda rather than rational argument, but they can still play a useful systemic function if they help voters clarify where the parties stand. This knowledge, albeit acquired in a non-deliberative way, may subsequently enable citizens to engage in deliberative discussions taking place elsewhere. Similarly, conversations where some participants behave in an uncivil way may enable activists to channel their passions and demonstrate their commitment. As highlighted by Diana Mutz (2006), democracy requires both participation and dialogue, but the two do not necessarily occur simultaneously and in the same contexts. Idealized representations of self-contained democratic heavens where all the conflicting and complex values of democratic governance peacefully coexist, always and at the same time, are generally unrealistic models of how democracy actually works.

While it may be impossible to fulfill all the values democracy requires at all places and at all times, a deliberative system as a whole may still achieve those goals. According to Mansbridge and colleagues, a deliberative system should perform three functions: *epistemic* (forming opinions informed by facts and logic), *ethical* (fostering mutual respect), and *democratic* (promoting "an inclusive political process in terms of equality"; Mansbridge et al., 2012: 12). It is worth quoting the authors' discussion of the democratic function at length:

> The inclusion of multiple and plural voices, interests, concerns, and claims on the basis of feasible equality [. . .] is the central element of what makes deliberative democratic processes democratic. Who gets to be at the table affects the scope and content of the deliberation. For those excluded, no deliberative democratic legitimacy is generated. In short, a well functioning democratic deliberative system must not systematically exclude any citizens from the process without strong justification that could be reasonably accepted by all citizens, including the excluded. On the positive side, *it ought also actively to promote and facilitate inclusion and the equal opportunities to participate in the system.* (Mansbridge et al., 2012: 12, emphasis added)

Seen as part of a deliberative ecosystem, then, the political experiences on social media we studied contribute to the democratic function of promoting and facilitating inclusion, as they broaden the pool of citizens who participate. While political communication on social media may not consistently and satisfactorily perform the epistemic and ethical functions, our study shows that it can make an important contribution toward the democratic goal of promoting an inclusive political process.

In sum, our review of the literatures on equality in participation from both political science and communication suggests that one component of participatory *quality* has to be its *equality.* Thus, our finding that political experiences on social media can reduce some participatory gaps in society indicates that they help increase the quality, as well as the quantity, of participation. In a democracy, equality does not just rhyme with quality but it constitutes it. And while social media may be part of many contemporary problems in democratic societies, they can be part of the solution to at least two important democratic ills— citizen disconnection from politics and inequalities between those who choose to exercise their voice and those who prefer to remain silent.

The Dynamic Relationship Between Social Media and Political Context

In this study, we have aimed to overcome the single-country, often U.S.-focused approach of most existing research on digital media and politics to provide systematic evidence on how the relationship between social media and political participation plays out in different institutional settings. In particular, we have shown that engagement with agreeing viewpoints on social media is more strongly associated with participation in countries where electoral competition is majoritarian than in countries where it is proportional. We have also shown that electoral mobilization via social media makes a bigger difference for participation in party-centric political systems than in candidate-centric ones. Instead, we did not find any evidence that the structural characteristics of mass media systems shape the relationship between accidental exposure to political news on social media and participation. That the variables that mattered, albeit in a limited, nine-country comparison, both pertain to the realm of political institutions, is a reminder of Giovanni Sartori's lesson that political phenomena can be understood first and foremost based on other political phenomena—that politics can be explained by politics (Sartori, 1969).

While we have shown that scholars of social media and politics should take into account institutional characteristics, the system-level relationships we uncovered in Chapter 6 were weaker than we expected, when compared with the individual-level factors we included in our explanatory models in Chapters 4 and 5. However, the relationship between political communication and institutions is best described as a dynamic process, not a static state of affairs. Social media are conditioned, in their relationship with participation, by institutional structures, but they may also promote transformations that might consolidate or disrupt those very structures. From this perspective, we speculate, based on our results, that social media may facilitate two potential pathways for institutional change.

Majoritarian electoral rules are designed to promote centripetal party competition, but if citizens in majoritarian democracies who encounter politically congruent opinions on social media become more engaged, as we have shown, and then more radical in their political views, as is conceivable (Lelkes et al., 2017), they may subsequently steer their parties toward more extreme positions. The end result of this process may counterweigh the structural incentives of majoritarian electoral systems, which generally reward parties that act as catch-all bridges between different political and social groups (Norris, 2004; Sartori, 2005). In this sense, social media may play an indirect role in fostering political polarization, not by increasing it among the general population—where they may conceivably reduce it by exposing most users to balanced views, as we showed in Chapter 3 (see also Barberá, 2014; Boxell et al., 2017)—but by boosting the voice and political influence of a minority of activists who engage predominantly with viewpoints they agree with. Thus, social media may weaken one of the conditions that make majoritarian party competition more sustainable— the presence of a shared set of widely agreed-upon values among broad sectors of society—and challenge the functioning of democratic governance to a greater extent than in proportional systems, which can more easily accommodate deep societal divisions through power-sharing among different elite groups (Lijphart, 2012; Powell, 2000).

A similar paradoxical dynamic may be elicited by the differential effects of electoral mobilization via social media between party-centric and candidate-centric systems. In party-centric systems, where we found that online mobilization is comparatively more likely to spur participation, social media may stimulate an influx of political newcomers knocking on the doors of legacy party organizations, eager to take advantage of the structures and opportunities for political action they provide. However, these newcomers may disagree with existing party members and activists about how parties should work and what goals they should pursue, thus becoming powerful change agents within established structures. This new lifeblood of participants recruited via social media may thus disrupt existing equilibria between the organizational "faces" of individual parties—i.e., their membership, their central decision-making bodies, and their elected officials in representative institutions (Katz & Mair, 1995)—as well as between different ideological factions within their constituencies and networks (Bawn et al., 2012). Far from writing parties' obituaries, social media may provide additional chapters and compelling plot twists in their biographies, potentially making them stronger but also more internally competitive and, thus, unstable (see also Chadwick & Stromer-Galley, 2016; Gibson et al., 2017; Dommett, 2020).

Social Media and Politics Between Ideal and Reality

Raffaello Sanzio's masterpiece fresco *The School of Athens* can be admired in the Apostolic Palace in Vatican City. Ancient Greek philosophers Plato and Aristotle occupy the center of the scene, which includes many of the classical thinkers, scientists, and artists who contributed to founding Western civilization. Plato is on the left, his right hand pointing to the sky, his left hand holding his book *Timaeus*, which claims that a benevolent Demiurge created the universe to achieve order and beauty based on scientific laws. Next to Plato is Aristotle, his right hand, wide open, pointing to the ground, his left hand holding his book *Nicomachean Ethics*, which argues that virtue stems not from a set of universal scientific and philosophical principles, but from the practical wisdom, acquired with experience, that enables individuals to make choices supported by good reasons. The contrast between Plato's pointing at the sky and Aristotle's aiming for the ground has long been considered as a symbol of the dialectic between idealism and empiricism in Western culture.

In the span of a decade, social media have moved from the periphery to the center of political communication ecosystems in Western democracies. New questions and concerns over their role in our societies have arisen as a result, reviving the dialectic between idealism and empiricism. For some, 2016 has meant the end of innocence, the shattering of an idealistic quasi-ideology that defined the Internet as an inherently democratic medium—even though this was never an uncontested view among scholars. For others, the post-2016 crisis has finally exposed the Internet's structural role in reproducing hegemonic structures and power imbalances, finally lifting the veil on the naive digital utopias of yesteryear. For others still, and we count ourselves among them, public discourse around digital media is undergoing a healthy empiricist reckoning that requires scholars—us included—to shed some of the myths, useful and otherwise, that have colored our understanding of digital media's contribution to democracy and to ask new, difficult empirical questions in the public interest. We hope our book can be seen as a step in this direction.

And yet, the scene at the center of *The School of Athens* reminds us that there cannot ever be a clear, final winner between Plato and Aristotle, between idealism and realism. They stand together at the core of the painting because they need each other. Democracy is not a once-and-for-all accomplishment, but a perennial struggle aimed at embedding lofty ideals in the everyday praxis of how we live together and govern ourselves in complex societies (Bobbio, 1987). As Peter Dahlgren (2009: 59) notes, "democracy can never be reduced to a mantra, and must be continually discussed and debated." Without an ideal to pursue, that perennial struggle and those continuous debates can seem pointless and exhausting. And without a praxis that is grounded in the best available evidence and informed by an ethical understanding of how we should conduct ourselves, the ideal can become futile or, worse, be used as an excuse to perpetrate violence, oppression, and injustice. When he points his finger to the sky, Plato knows he cannot physically reach it. When he gestures to the ground, Aristotle knows he shares that ground with other human beings toward whom we have moral responsibilities that stem from our shared aspiration to improve our earthly condition beyond self-interest. When we strive for valid knowledge that can help individuals, groups, and institutions achieve a more just order for the way we live together in this world, we move one inch closer to the democratic ideal. The distance between us and the ideal may be ever too long, even incalculable, but that has never stopped humanity from trying to shorten it, one inch at a time. There are definitely enough inches, everywhere around us, to make it worth continuing this pursuit.

Notes

Introduction

1. It should be noted that the Labour membership subsequently experienced a 10% decline between 2017 and 2019 (see Stewart, 2019).

Chapter 1

1. That is, provided that individual members of those networks are using the platform, are paying attention, and have been identified by the algorithms that increasingly curate users' experiences as potentially interested in, and likely to engage with, that content (see Kümpel, 2020).
2. But see Kalogeropoulos et al. (2017), Fletcher and Nielsen (2018), and Heiss and Matthes (2019) for some exceptions.
3. Though often not the same levels of protection against various threats such as disinformation, hate speech, and harassment, as companies' efforts in these areas have not been uniform across the different markets they serve.
4. For instance, one could argue that the *New York Times* (U.S.) and *The Guardian* (U.K.) are both quality newspapers and thus group them under the same category in a comparative analysis of newspapers, or that both the British Broadcasting Corporation (BBC; U.K.) and the Association of Public Service Broadcasting Corporations of the Federal Republic of Germany (ARD; Germany) are public service broadcasters and lump them in the same category when analyzing different types of broadcasters. However, these classifications inevitably obscure some relevant differences between objects in the same class. In these examples, the *New York Times* arguably reports news in a way that is less influenced by its editorial stance than *The Guardian* does, and while the BBC is relatively centralized national organization, ARD is a federation of regional broadcasters.
5. One possible objection to this statement is that Facebook functions differently, at least for politics, in the United States compared with the rest of the world, because its leaders strive to protect their interests and their reputation in the United States more than in other countries. An example of this is the fact that, in response to criticism that breaking news was more difficult to find on Facebook than other platforms, Facebook hired a team of professional journalists who, according to news reports, were tasked with curating the "Trending News" feature on the platform. When news of this initiative broke and controversy ensued that it allegedly was resulting in the silencing of some conservative websites, Facebook dismantled the team and reverted to algorithmic ranking of the news in the Trending section (see Lee, 2016, for a summary). When journalists were in charge of the Facebook Trending

News section in the United States, but not in other countries, this particular Facebook feature in the United States differed from other countries. However, the Trending News box was only a part, arguably a small one, of the user experience on Facebook, and when the experiment with journalists was ended, it can be assumed that the functioning of this feature in the United States went back to resembling that in most other countries. More broadly, Facebook's product development teams routinely test and implement new features and affordances, often during general election campaigns. It is safe to assume that a disproportionate amount of such testing and development occurs in the United States, so in this respect the equivalence between the platform's functioning in the United States and in other Western democracies cannot be assumed to be perfect all of the time and for all its features.

6. By contrast, research on digital media, and social media among them, has to face a massive disadvantage compared with traditional media when it comes to what David Karpf (2012) has identified as the problem of "internet time." This is the fact that, at least in the first twenty years since they became a widespread commodity, digital media have so far changed so quickly and so thoroughly that research cannot safely assume that the theories and findings that were relevant at one point in time will remain relevant even a few years later. We strive to reduce the effects of this important phenomenon by focusing on a relatively narrow time frame, spanning from the spring of 2015 to the spring of 2018. Although we cannot assume that nothing of significance changed in how social media functioned in those three momentous years, this is the smallest temporal window that we must operate in if we are to include general elections in a wide variety of countries, as we do here. Chapter 2 offers some further considerations on these issues.

7. Survey-based voting behavior research usually relies on two measures of general political beliefs: *party identification*, which is based on asking respondents if they identify with, or feel closer to, a party (Holmberg, 2007), and *ideology*, which is measured by asking voters to place themselves on a one-dimensional representation of the political spectrum, either left–right or, in the United States, liberal–conservative (Mair, 2007). While both concepts have been widely used in research on electoral behavior, party identification has been employed much more successfully in party systems, such as the United States and the United Kingdom, with a small number of parties that have remained stable over time, but it has proven less useful in other Western democracies characterized by more complex and fluid party systems. Because our study includes many countries that correspond to the latter profile, we employ ideology rather than party identification in our analyses.

8. We recognize that identifying populist attitudes among respondents solely based on whether they refuse to align themselves with the left or the right is at best an approximation. Unfortunately, we did not measure populist attitudes in our surveys based on the scales that have been developed in the literature on this topic (Akkerman et al., 2014), so our capacity to differentiate respondents on the attitudinal dimension of populism is limited to their refusal of the classic categories of left and right. However, in Chapter 5 we will also present additional analyses that differentiate citizens based on whether they voted for a party that the literature classifies as populist. In this way, we will be able to differentiate respondents more precisely on the behavioral dimension of populism.

9. The same methodological considerations as discussed in the previous note apply to this scenario, and for this reason, in Chapter 5 we will also differentiate respondents based on whether they voted for a right-wing populist party, a left-wing populist party, or a party that the literature does not classify as populist. We will therefore employ more precise behavioral measures of support for authoritarian populists, as well as the less precise attitudinal measure of right-wing ideology.

10. There are also practical reasons why we take this approach. Although the nine countries covered in our book constitute a diverse sample of Western democracies that differ in theoretically fruitful ways, every country is a bundle of properties that are all manifested simultaneously and thus cannot be effectively disentangled—the classic "many variables,

small number of cases" problem that Arend Lijphart (1971) identified a long time ago. Even though nine countries constitute a respectable number of cases—especially given the paucity of comparative research on social media and politics—there are limits to how many hypotheses can be tested simultaneously on that basis.

11. This does not mean that electoral systems are the only factor that influences the breadth and depth of societal cleavages that party systems articulate. As the developments of U.S. politics in the last twenty years show, demographic change, economic disloca- tion, party primaries, campaign finance regulation, and the mass media, among other things, can contribute to increasing levels of political polarization even in what is argu- ably the purest example, among Western democracies, of a majoritarian democracy with an entrenched two-party system. The case of the United Kingdom highlights how the increased salience of an issue—membership in the European Union—can polarize electorates and split parties internally. However, in spite of their recent polarization, the main parties in the United States and the United Kingdom still aim to be relatively more inclusive in their electoral strategies than their counterparts in countries where propor- tional systems incentivize parties to cultivate smaller niches of voters. On the roots of political polarization in the United States, see Nivola and Brady (2008) and Thurber and Yoshinaka (2015).

12. For a discussion of the merits and limitation of this classification of mass media systems, see Chapter 6.

Chapter 2

1. As of this writing, the video counts nearly four billion views (officialpsy, 2012).

2. Unless, that is, these horizontal communications occur in the context of campaigns or other political activities organized by parties, candidates, or interest groups, in which case Verba and colleagues' definition would consider these forms of citizen communication as volunteering for political organizations and, thus, as political participation.

3. It is worth pointing out that none of the definitions proposed by scholars reviewed so far require political actions to achieve their goals for them to constitute legitimate forms of participation. As Downs (1957) and Olson (1965) argued well before the Internet age, no individual political action in a mass society has any realistic chance of achieving any mean- ingful collective goal in isolation. This is another reason why dismissing political action on digital media as ineffective—in the sense of failing to topple a dictator, or to change a policy, or to elect a candidate—does not in and of itself mean it does not constitute political participation.

4. Since 1956, the American National Election Study, the most widely used survey to study American electoral behavior, has asked representative samples of U.S. voters the following question: "Did you wear a campaign button, put a campaign sticker on your car, or place a sign in your window or in front of your house?" Only four other questions measuring cam- paign participation have been asked as consistently throughout the study's existence, which began in 1952 (American National Election Studies, 2020).

5. For more information on questionnaire design, survey fieldwork, and sample composition, see the Online Appendix.

6. We offer a broader discussion of the main advantages and disadvantages of survey data in the study of political participation in the section "Employing Surveys to Study Social Media and Political Participation" of the Online Appendix.

7. In our survey, we asked our respondents two different questions related to signing petitions and referenda: the former focused on performing this action in general, while the latter mentioned exclusively online petitions. As we aim to define political participation in hybrid terms, without discriminating between online and offline activities, we combined answers to these two questions, as described in Table A3 of the Online Appendix, to measure this activity.

8. We asked respondents three different questions related to this activity: the first did not specify which channel had been used, the second referred to email exchanges, and the third to social media conversations. For the same reasons as discussed in the previous note, we have combined answers to the three questions. Further details are available in Table A3 the Online Appendix.

9. Based on publicly available data, the percentages of citizens in the nine countries that used the Internet in the year in which we surveyed them are: 96% for Denmark (2015), 81% for France (2017), 84% for Germany (2017), 67% for Greece (2015), 74% for Italy (2018), 68% for Poland (2015), 79% for Spain (2015), 95% for the United Kingdom (2017), and 86% for the United States (2016). Source: International Telecommunications Union (2020).

10. The boundaries of online and offline domains might be more fluid than we are assuming here. For instance, many Americans attended rallies and important campaign events online during the 2020 presidential election because physical attendance was unsafe or illegal due to the Covid-19 pandemic, so many could be said to have attended public meetings and electoral rallies online. By the same token, leafleting need not only occur offline, for instance, if someone contacts a voter online or over the phone, has a conversation about politics, and then sends a digital leaflet to that person via email or social media. However, these two activities arguably remain more closely bound to physical spaces than the other four activities we measured.

11. This is why in another study we found that individuals who are wary about expressing their political views on social media and who align with more extreme ideological positions are more likely to employ mobile instant messaging services, such as WhatsApp, Snapchat, and Facebook Messenger, which enable them to more carefully control the conservations they entertain; see Valeriani and Vaccari (2018).

12. All the surveys we employ in this book have been fielded between 2015 and 2017, with the sole exception of Italy, where the data were collected in 2018.

13. The twenty-six democracies covered in the study we refer to (We Are Social, 2019) are: Argentina, Australia, Austria, Belgium, Brazil, Canada, Denmark, France, Germany, Ghana, India, Ireland, Italy, Japan, the Netherlands, New Zealand, Poland, Portugal, South Africa, South Korea, Spain, Sweden, Switzerland, Taiwan, the United Kingdom, and the United States. The eighteen non-democracies are: China, Colombia, Egypt, Hong Kong, Kenya, Indonesia, Malaysia, Mexico, Morocco, Nigeria, Philippines, Russia, Saudi Arabia, Singapore, Thailand, Turkey, United Arab Emirates, and Vietnam.

14. The duration of those democratic regimes, however, differs widely. Poland is the youngest, having transitioned to democracy in 1989–1991. The United States, United Kingdom, and Denmark are the oldest, dating back to the eighteenth and nineteenth centuries. France, Germany, and Italy returned to democracy after World War II, and Greece and Spain did so in the mid-1970s.

Chapter 3

1. In particular, we consider as mainly exposed to "one-sided supportive" messages: (a) interviewees who answered that they "always" agree and either "often," "sometimes," or "never" disagree with messages they see on social media; (b) those who "often" agree and "sometimes" or "never" disagree with the social media content they are exposed to; (c) those who "sometimes" agree and "never" disagree with the social media messages they encounter. We apply the same logic, simply inverting the questions, to classify "one-sided oppositional" experiences. It is important to note that here we are using the term "messages" as shorthand for "combinations of messages." When we classify respondents as exposed to "two-sided messages," for instance, we do not mean that they are exposed to individual messages that provide two (or more) sides of a political debate, but that, overall, the balance between the individual messages that people are exposed to entails similar quantities of messages

supporting each side. Studies of political journalism differentiate between "internal pluralism," which entails balance achieved within the same news story, product, or outlet, and "external pluralism," where balance is obtained across (and by comparing and contrasting) different news stories, products, or outlets (Hallin & Mancini, 2004). While it is possible to achieve internal pluralism within the content of a social media post, genre, or account, the large number of sources available online makes it more likely that users will experience external pluralism, and this is the meaning that we attribute to our classifications of agreement and disagreement with political content seen on social media.

2. In all regression analyses presented in the book, these respondents have been grouped together with nonusers of social media. Overall, 7% of our sample reported not to use any social media platforms. These respondents were not asked questions about their experiences on social media. However, to avoid biases resulting from individuals' selecting themselves into using social media, we have included nonusers in our analyses, assigning them a value of 0 in the variables derived from questions on social media uses or experiences—questions they were not asked because they are not social media users.

3. This was at least true during the period in which we conducted our study. Toward the end of the decade, WhatsApp and other platforms seem to be evolving toward a more hybrid model that combines small-group and large-group interactions. There is evidence that these affordances have been used by both news organizations and political actors to broadcast messages to large numbers of users and to organize campaign activities, including to spread disinformation (Kligler-Vilenchik & Tenenboim, 2020; Kligler-Vilenchik et al., 2020; Rossini et al., 2020). Future research should investigate to what extent these messaging apps are becoming less private than was the case when we collected our data and what the implications are for political discussion and communication.

4. An exception is Dubois & Blank (2018), who, however, only measure exposure to disagreement rather than the mix of agreement and disagreement encountered by users. See also note 10 below.

5. We conducted all the regression analyses and effects size estimates presented in this book with the Zelig package in *R* (Choirat et al., 2017).

6. Our models also include respondents who are not social media users as well as social media users who reported to "never" encounter both agreeing and disagreeing views and information, grouped together as "nonpolitical or nonusers." Results for this category are not presented here since they are not relevant to our discussion; however, they are included in Tables A8–A11 in the Online Appendix.

7. The income variable featured 2,605 missing values. In the first place this was because several respondents refused to provide this information (i.e., they chose the "don't remember" or "prefer not to answer" options we offered them). Moreover, due to a clerical error in the Danish questionnaire, we decided to consider as missing values some of the answers from Danish interviewees (see Table A3 in the Online Appendix for a detailed discussion). To avoid excluding a large number of (especially Danish) respondents from our analyses due to listwise deletion, we decided to assign all respondents for whom we did not have a valid income measure the mean value for income in their national subsample. We also added to all our models a dummy variable identifying all respondents whose income had been mean replaced. Given this setting, the coefficient of the income variable should be interpreted as the effect of income on the dependent variable only among respondents whose income measure was originally available and has not been imputed. In all models presented in the book we do not report coefficients for the variable identifying respondents with mean-replaced income since it has no relevance in itself and is exclusively a function of the mean value we have assigned to these respondents (see Vaccari et al., 2015). Coefficients for the variable identifying respondents with mean replaced income are reported in tables provided in the Online Appendix.

8. Most questions related to social media experiences and behaviors have been asked exclusively to social media users in our sample. See note 2 above.

9. Descriptive statistics and question wordings for all variables included in our models are provided in the Online Appendix (Table A3).

10. This finding also confirms the importance of adopting a granular measure of exposure to agreeing and disagreeing information on social media, combining these two potentially coexisting outcomes. In an analysis of U.K. survey data, Dubois and Blank (2018) argue that those who are more interested in politics are more likely to frequently encounter disagreeing political views on social media and thus to avoid echo chambers—contrary to what we find. We suspect that the reason we find the opposite is that, unlike Dubois and Blank, we consider respondents' frequency of exposure to agreeing and disagreeing views in conjunction with each other. Most political junkies are immersed in politics on social media, so they are more likely to report higher frequency of exposure to political content, both agreeable and disagreeable, than the rest of the population.

11. In January 2018, Facebook changed its algorithm so that users would see less content from public pages and more content from private profiles, which resulted in a reduction of referrals to, among others, news organizations. However, this reduction did not mean that exposure to such content had become altogether impossible, especially if a user's contacts shared public affairs via their personal profiles (see Mosseri, 2018).

12. See note 9 above.

13. We chose to transform our dependent variable in this way to make the model results and the predicted probabilities derived from them clearer for readers than they would have been if we had kept the variable as ordinal, and to enable readers to compare our models across our three dependent variables in this chapter. To ensure that this choice did not bias our estimates, we also ran ordered logit regressions where the dependent variable retained the same values as in the original survey question, from never (0) to always (3). The results, which are consistent with those presented here, are available in the Online Appendix (Table A16).

14. The variety of subjects potentially delivering mobilization messages on social media might also make it more difficult for users to remember whether they were targeted directly by political actors or indirectly via their own contacts. For research employing survey data, adopting more specific questions aiming to differentiate between direct and indirect mobilization may not necessarily lead to more valid responses if respondents cannot precisely identify, let alone recall, the sources of the messages they saw.

15. See note 9 above.

16. In all regression analyses presented in the book, respondents who claimed they did not receive mobilization messages on social media have been grouped together with nonusers of social media. See note 2 above.

Chapter 4

1. As highlighted in Chapter 3, these analyses include both respondents who use social media and respondents who, in spite of using the Internet, do not have profiles on any social media platforms. The latter constitute about 7% of our whole sample, and excluding them may skew our analyses, as social media users differ from nonusers in some characteristics (for instance, age and education) that may also be associated with participation.

2. In the section "Causal Inference, Survey Data, and Coarsened Exact Matching" of our Online Appendix, we discuss at greater length CEM's rationale, the specific procedure we employed to preprocess our data with CEM, and why preprocessing our data with CEM increases the internal validity of our findings.

3. Apart from income—on which see note 7 in Chapter 3.

4. We ran separate models testing the relationship between political participation and each one of the three experiences at a time. This was necessary for us to be able to preprocess the data with CEM. Since CEM, as any other type of matching technique, requires that researchers choose one, and only one, variable on which to match units, we ran three

separate CEMs, one for each of the three independent variables we are interested in. Hence, we present three separate models, based on three different sets of preprocessed data, for each of the political experiences on social media we employ as independent variables.

5. The actual value reported in the figure is 87.5%. We rounded up the values of our estimates in the text to make it easier to interpret the figures.

6. In examining absolute and relative probability increases across the left and right panels of Figure 4.2, it is worth noting that the horizontal axes are on different scales because they represent different estimates that are not directly comparable.

7. As we write this chapter, a petition hosted by the U.K. advocacy group 38Degrees and titled "Michael Gove [former Secretary for the Environment]: Protect our Bees" has gathered nearly four hundred thousand signatures (see https://speakout.38degrees.org.uk/campaigns/template-petition-clone-74533280-1b02-4002-a9c0-29e6f8e681db). A petition to the U.K. Parliament titled "Don't kill our bees! Immediately halt the use of Neonicotinoids on crops" gathered nearly one hundred thousand signatures in 2015 (https://petition.parliament.uk/archived/petitions/104796) and as a result was debated in Parliament.

Chapter 5

1. We acknowledge that our discussion of political equality can only address one aspect of it—citizens' different levels of political involvement, which motivates them to participate. Although this is a very strong driver of participation and inequalities in citizens' exercise of their political voice (Verba et al., 1995), other factors, chiefly related to social and economic inequalities, also play a strong role in shaping who participates and who does not. While, as discussed in Chapter 1, there is evidence that social media may be helping bridge some engagement gaps related to age, digital platforms may fail to make a dent in other socioeconomic sources of participatory inequalities, such as income, education, and, to some degree, gender (Bode, 2017). We have decided to focus here on participatory divides rooted in different levels of individuals' political involvement, but this does not mean we should ignore other forms and causes of inequality.

2. Descriptive statistics and question wordings for this variable are provided in the Online Appendix (Table A3).

3. Among the 12 coefficients we estimated (four three-way classifications of populist parties × three categories of the independent variable measuring agreement and disagreement on social media), we found only 2 significant coefficients pertaining to voters of right-wing populist parties. In both cases, results suggest that, all else being equal, when these voters encounter oppositional, but not supportive, messages on social media, their levels of participation increase more than those of respondents who did not vote for populist parties. While this pattern signals that right-wing populist voters may be more resilient to challenges to their opinions on social media than voters of other parties, it does not point to a massive surge in support for right-wing populists derived from echo chambers online. Quite to the contrary, right-wing populists may actually relish being challenged by other social media users who disagree with them. Two other significant coefficients involved voters of left-wing populist parties and indicate that the relationship between exposure to supportive political content and participation is significantly weaker among voters of left-wing populist parties than among voters of non-populist parties. See Tables A42–A45 in the Online Appendix for full results of these models.

Chapter 6

1. Importantly, when we ran CEM we clustered respondents by country of residence, so the algorithm only matched respondents from the same country. This setup enables us to maintain the statistical benefits of CEM when comparing respondents from different countries.

2. Multicollinearity occurs when two or more predictors in a model are so strongly correlated to each other that they bias the estimates, usually underestimating the correlations between the other variables in the model and the dependent variable. In the case of our country groupings, simultaneously modeling direct and differential effects for more than one variable would lead to multicollinearity because we have very few country cases and the systemic variables that we model are correlated to one another. For instance, two out of three countries that we classified as featuring majoritarian patterns of electoral competition (the United Kingdom and the United States) are also both classified as Liberal media systems. Both countries whose media systems we classified as Democratic Corporatist (Denmark and Germany) also feature party-centric political organizations and proportional electoral competition. With only nine countries, the overlaps between the systemic characteristics we measure are too large to guarantee accurate estimates when all three systemic variables are modeled simultaneously.

3. To this end, we used the poisson.gee function, included in the Zelig package in R (Choirat et al., 2017).

4. We use the term "relevant" in the way first suggested by Giovanni Sartori (1976: 121–124); that is, a party is relevant when it can be included in a government coalition (coalition potential) and when it can affect the tactics of party competition, forcing other parties to follow or adapt to its strategy (blackmail potential).

5. U.K. citizens went to the polls again for a General Election in December 2019. The vote resulted in a clear victory for the Conservative Party, which won its largest majority since the end of the 1980s, while Labour lost sixty seats and suffered its worst electoral performance since 1935. Thus, the 2019 election saw the return to one-party government.

6. In the 2019 general elections, 10 parties secured parliamentary seats in a relatively small chamber (179 members), and the government coalition that emerged out of the vote included 4 parties, while the opposition bloc also included 4 parties.

7. In the 2019 elections, the center-right New Democracy party achieved a clear victory, with nearly 40% of the vote resulting in a majority in parliament. The return to single-party government may be the sign that a new process of party system consolidation, facilitated by the electoral law, may have begun. However, the opposition was still fragmented across five different parties that gained seats.

8. In the 2019 general elections, Law and Justice retained its majority in the House but lost it in the Senate.

9. Unfortunately, the Zelig package that we used to estimate these models in R does not calculate the deviance and null deviance when running Poisson regressions with clustered standard, which we use in this chapter. To calculate pseudo-R^2 coefficients that can partially orient readers of this chapter, we have run the same models as presented in Tables 6.1, 6.2 and 6.3, but without clustering standard errors. Thus, the pseudo-R^2 coefficients reported in the tables pertain to slightly different models than those shown in the tables.

10. In July 2019 Luigi Di Maio, then leader of the Five Star Movement, claimed that the digital platform employed by the party for internal consultations and referenda counted one hundred thousand registered users. However, there is no way to verify these numbers (see Pagella Politica, 2019).

Conclusion

1. In Chapter 3, our multivariate models predict the likelihood that individuals of different gender, age, education, employment status, and income undergo the three political experiences on social media that constitute our key independent variables in Chapters 4–6. As the results of these models show, male, younger, and better-educated citizens are more likely to engage with supportive viewpoints on social media (Table 3.1, Model 1); female, younger, unemployed, and poorer citizens are more likely to accidentally encounter political news on social media (Table 3.2, Model 1); and male, younger, better-educated, and

employed citizens are more likely to be targeted by electoral mobilization on social media (Table 3.3, Model 1). Thus, accidental exposure to political news on social media mostly caters to socially peripheral voters, while engagement with supportive viewpoints and electoral mobilization mostly benefit users who are more socially central. All three experiences are more likely to involve younger voters, who are generally less politically engaged. However, our models do not assess whether these experiences differentially enhance participation among voters of different socioeconomic status.

References

Achen, C. H., & Bartels, L. M. (2017). *Democracy for realists: Why elections do not produce responsive government* (Vol. 4). Princeton University Press.

Ackerman, B. A., & Fishkin, J. S. (2004). *Deliberation day.* Yale University Press.

Akkerman, A., Mudde, C., & Zaslove, A. (2014). How populist are the people? Measuring populist attitudes in voters. *Comparative Political Studies, 47*(9), 1324–1353.

Albæk, E., Van Dalen, A., Jebril, N., & de Vreese, C. H. (2014). *Political journalism in comparative perspective.* Cambridge University Press.

Aldrich, J. H., Gibson, R. K., Cantijoch, M., & Konitzer, T. (2016). Getting out the vote in the social media era: Are digital tools changing the extent, nature and impact of party contacting in elections? *Party Politics, 22*(2), 165–178.

Alex-Assensoh, Y. M. (2005). *Democracy at risk: How political choices undermine citizen participation and what we can do about it.* Brookings Institution Press.

Allcott, H., & Gentzkow, M. (2017). Social media and fake news in the 2016 election. *Journal of Economic Perspectives, 31*(2), 211–236.

Alter, C. (November 2, 2020). Inside Joe Biden campaign's plan to get out the vote online. *Time Magazine.* Retrieved December 7, 2020 from https://time.com/5906237/inside-joe-biden-campaigns-plan-to-get-out-the-vote-online/.

American National Election Studies. (2020). Wore a Button or Put a Sticker on the Car 1956–2016. Retrieved November 30, 2020 from https://electionstudies.org/resources/anes-guide/top-tables/?id=74.

Amnå, E., & Ekman, J. (2014). Standby citizens: Diverse faces of political passivity. *European Political Science Review, 6*(2), 261–281.

Andersen, K., Ohme, J., Bjarnøe, C., Bordacconi, M. J., Albæk, E., & De Vreese, C. H. (2020). *Generational gaps in political media use and civic engagement: From baby boomers to Generation Z.* Routledge.

Anspach, N. M. (2017). The new personal influence: How our Facebook friends influence the news we read. *Political Communication, 34*(4), 590–606.

Anstead, N. (2017). Data-driven campaigning in the 2015 UK general election. *The International Journal of Press/Politics, 22*(3), 294–313.

Anstead, N., & Chadwick, A. (2009). Parties, election campaigning, and the Internet. Toward a comparative institutional approach. In A. Chadwick & P. N. Howard (Eds). *Routledge handbook of Internet politics.* Routledge: 57–71.

Arceneaux, K. (2006). Do campaigns help voters learn? A cross-national analysis. *British Journal of Political Science, 36,* 159–173.

Arceneaux, K., & Johnson, M. (2013). *Changing minds or changing channels?: Partisan news in an age of choice.* University of Chicago Press.

Audickas, L., Dempsey, N., & Loft, P. (2019). *Membership of UK Political Parties.* Briefing Paper SN05125, August 9, 2019. House of Common Library. Retrieved August 7, 2019, from https://commonslibrary.parliament.uk/research-briefings/sn05125/.

Babbie, E. (2015). *The practice of social research.* Nelson Education.

Bail, C. (2021). *Breaking the social media prism: How to make our platforms less polarizing.* Princeton University Press.

Bail, C. A., Argyle, L. P., Brown, T. W., Bumpus, J. P., Chen, H., Hunzaker, M. F., . . . & Volfovsky, A. (2018). Exposure to opposing views on social media can increase political polarization. *Proceedings of the National Academy of Sciences, 115*(37), 9216–9221.

Bakshy, E., Messing, S., & Adamic, L. A. (2015). Exposure to ideologically diverse news and opinion on Facebook. *Science, 348*(6239), 1130–1132.

Barberá, P. (2014). How social media reduces mass political polarization. Evidence from Germany, Spain, and the US. *Job Market Paper, New York University, 46.* Retrieved from https://wp.nyu.edu/smapp/wp-content/uploads/sites/1693/2016/04/SocialMediaReduces.pdf.

Barberá, P., Jost, J. T., Nagler, J., Tucker, J. A., & Bonneau, R. (2015). Tweeting from left to right: Is online political communication more than an echo chamber? *Psychological Science, 26*(10), 1531–1542.

Barberá, P., & Rivero, G. (2015). Understanding the political representativeness of Twitter users. *Social Science Computer Review, 33*(6), 712–729.

Bardi, L. (2004). Party responses to electoral dealignment in Italy. In P. Mair, W. C. Müller, & F. Plasser (Eds.). *Political parties and electoral change: Party responses to electoral markets.* Sage Publications: 111–144.

Barnidge, M. (2017). Exposure to political disagreement in social media versus face-to-face and anonymous online settings. *Political Communication, 34*(2), 302–321.

Barnidge, M. (2020). Testing the inadvertency hypothesis: Incidental news exposure and political disagreement across media platforms. *Journalism.* Available at: https://doi.org/10.1177/1464884920915373.

Bastos, M. T., & Mercea, D. (2019). The Brexit botnet and user-generated hyperpartisan news. *Social Science Computer Review, 37*(1), 38–54.

Baum, M. A., & Groeling, T. (2008). New media and the polarization of American political discourse. *Political Communication, 25*(4), 345–365.

Bawn, K., Cohen, M., Karol, D., Masket, S., Noel, H., & Zaller, J. (2012). A theory of political parties: Groups, policy demands and nominations in American politics. *Perspectives on Politics, 10*(3), 571–597.

BBC News Online. (May 25, 2012). Scottish independence: One million Scots urged to sign "yes" declaration. *BBC News.* Retrieved October 16, 2020, from https://www.bbc.com/news/uk-scotland-scotland-politics-18162832.

BBC News Online. (August 12, 2015). Labour leadership: Huge increase in party's electorate. *BBC News.* Retrieved August 7, 2020, from https://www.bbc.com/news/uk-politics-33892407.

Beam, M. A., Hutchens, M. J., & Hmielowski, J. D. (2018). Facebook news and (de) polarization: Reinforcing spirals in the 2016 US election. *Information, Communication & Society, 21*(7), 940–958.

Bechmann, A., & Nielbo, K. L. (2018). Are we exposed to the same "news" in the news feed? An empirical analysis of filter bubbles as information similarity for Danish Facebook users. *Digital Journalism, 6*(8), 990–1002.

Behr, R. (December 23, 2014). Why a year of little change felt like one of sustained crisis. *The Guardian.* Retrieved January 16, 2020, from https://www.theguardian.com/commentisfree/2014/dec/23/year-crisis-digital-revolution-uk-politics-2014.

Beniger, J. (2009). *The control revolution: Technological and economic origins of the information society.* Harvard University Press.

Benkler, Y. (2006). *The wealth of networks: How social production transforms markets and freedom.* Yale University Press.

Benkler, Y., Tilton, C., Etling, B., Roberts, H., Clark, J., Faris, R., Kaiser, J., & Schmitt, C. (2020). Mail-In Voter Fraud: Anatomy of a Disinformation Campaign. *Social Science Research Network (SSRN) E-Library*, Retrieved December 15, 2020 from https://ssrn.com/abstract=3703701.

Bennett, W. L. (1998). The uncivic culture: Communication, identity, and the rise of lifestyle politics. *PS: Political Science & Politics, 31*(4), 741–761.

Bennett, W. L. (2008). Changing citizenship in the digital age. In W. L. Bennett (Ed.). *Civic life online: Learning how digital media can engage youth*. The MIT Press: 1–24.

Bennett, W. L., & Iyengar, S. (2008). A new era of minimal effects? The changing foundations of political communication. *Journal of Communication, 58*(4), 707–731.

Bennett, W. L., & Livingston, S. (2018). The disinformation order: Disruptive communication and the decline of democratic institutions. *European Journal of Communication, 33*(2), 122–139.

Bennett, W. L., & Segerberg, A. (2013). *The logic of connective action: Digital media and the personalization of contentious politics*. Cambridge University Press.

Benoit, K. (2006). Duverger's law and the study of electoral systems. *French Politics, 4*(1), 69–83.

Berger, B. (2009). Political theory, political science and the end of civic engagement. *Perspectives on Politics, 7*(2), 335–350.

Bergman, M. E. (2019). Insights from the quantification of the study of populism. *Representation, 55*(1), 21–30.

Bernstein, R., Chadha, A., & Montjoy, R. (2001). Overreporting voting: Why it happens and why it matters. *Public Opinion Quarterly, 65*(1), 22–44.

Bille, L., & Pedersen, K. (2004). Electoral fortunes and responses of the Social Democratic Party and Liberal Party in Denmark: Ups and downs. In P. Mair, W. C. Müller, & F. Plasser (Eds.). *Political parties and electoral change: Party responses to electoral markets*. Sage Publications: 207–233.

Bimber, B. (2003). *Information and American democracy: Technology in the evolution of political power*. Cambridge University Press.

Bimber, B., Cantijoch, M., Copeland, L., & Gibson, R. (2015). Digital media and political participation: The moderating role of political interest across acts and over time. *Social Science Computer Review, 33*(1), 21–42.

Bimber, B., & Copeland, L. (2013). Digital media and traditional political participation over time in the US. *Journal of Information Technology & Politics, 10*(2), 125–137.

Bimber, B., & Davis, R. (2003). *Campaigning online: The Internet in US elections*. Oxford University Press.

Bimber, B., Flanagin, A., & Stohl, C. (2012). *Collective action in organizations: Interaction and engagement in an era of technological change*. Cambridge University Press.

Blais, A. (2000). *To vote or not to vote? The merits and limits of rational choice theory*. University of Pittsburgh Press.

Blais, A., Gidengil, E., & Nevitte, N. (2004). Where does turnout decline come from? *European Journal of Political Research, 43*(2), 221–236.

Blumler, J. G., & Kavanagh, D. (1999). The third age of political communication: Influences and features. *Political Communication, 16*(3), 209–230.

Bobbio, N. (1987). *The future of democracy: A defence of the rules of the game*. University of Minnesota Press.

Boczkowski, P. J., Mitchelstein, E., & Matassi, M. (2018). "News comes across when I'm in a moment of leisure": Understanding the practices of incidental news consumption on social media. *New Media & Society, 20*(10), 3523–3539.

Bode, L. (2016a). Pruning the news feed: Unfriending and unfollowing political content on social media. *Research & Politics, 3*(3), 1–8.

Bode, L. (2016b). Political news in the news feed: Learning politics from social media. *Mass Communication and Society, 19*(1), 24–48.

Bode, L. (2017). Closing the gap: Gender parity in political engagement on social media. *Information, Communication & Society, 20*(4), 587–603.

Bode, L., & Vraga, E. K. (2018). Studying politics across media. *Political Communication*, 35(1), 1–7.

Bond, R. M., Fariss, C. J., Jones, J. J., Kramer, A. D., Marlow, C., Settle, J. E., & Fowler, J. H. (2012). A 61-million-person experiment in social influence and political mobilization. *Nature*, 489(7415), 295–298.

Bond, R. M., Settle, J. E., Fariss, C. J., Jones, J. J., & Fowler, J. H. (2017). Social endorsement cues and political participation. *Political Communication*, 34(2), 261–281.

Borowiec, P., Sobolewska-Myślik, K., & Kosowska-Gąstoł, B. (2017). Structures of Polish political parties in the second decade of the 21st century. In K. Sobolewska-Myślik, B. Kosowska-Gąstoł, & B. Borowiec (Eds.). *Organizational Structures of Political Parties in Central and Eastern European Countries*. Cambridge University Press: 311–327.

Bosco, A., & Morlino, L. (Eds.). (2007). *Party change in Southern Europe*. Routledge.

Boulianne, S. (2009). Does Internet use affect engagement? A meta-analysis of research. *Political Communication*, 26(2), 193–211.

Boulianne, S. (2015). Social media use and participation: A meta-analysis of current research. *Information, Communication & Society*, 18(5), 524–538.

Boulianne, S. (2019). Revolution in the making? Social media effects across the globe. *Information, Communication & Society*, 22(1), 39–54.

Boulianne, S. (2020). Twenty years of digital media effects on civic and political participation. *Communication Research*, 47(7), 947–966.

Boulianne, S., Koc-Michalska, K., & Bimber, B. (2020). Right-wing populism, social media and echo chambers in Western democracies. *New Media & Society*, 22(4), 683–699.

Boulianne, S., & Theocharis, Y. (2020). Young people, digital media, and engagement: A meta-analysis of research. *Social Science Computer Review*, 38(2), 111–127.

Boutyline, A., & Willer, R. (2017). The social structure of political echo chambers: Variation in ideological homophily in online networks. *Political Psychology*, 38(3), 551–569.

Bowler, S., Donovan, T., & Van Heerde, J. (2005). The United States of America: Perpetual campaigning in the absence of competition. In M. Gallagher & P. Mitchell (Eds.). *The politics of electoral systems*. Oxford University Press: 185–207.

Bowler, S., Lanoue, D. J., & Savoie, P. (1994). Electoral systems, party competition, and strength of partisan attachment: Evidence from three countries. *The Journal of Politics*, 56(04), 991–1007.

Boxell, L., Gentzkow, M., & Shapiro, J. M. (2017). Is the Internet Causing Political Polarization? Evidence from Demographics. *NBER Working Papers*, No. 23258. Retrieved from https://doi.org/10.3386/w23258.

boyd, d. (2014). *It's complicated: The social lives of networked teens*. Yale University Press.

boyd, d., & Crawford, K. (2012). Critical questions for big data: Provocations for a cultural, technological, and scholarly phenomenon. *Information, Communication & Society*, 15(5), 662–679.

boyd, d., & Ellison, N. B. (2007). Social network sites: Definition, history, and scholarship. *Journal of Computer-Mediated Communication*, 13(1), 210–230.

Bright, J., Bermudez, S., Pilet, J.-B., & Soubiran, T. (2020). Power users in online democracy: Their origins and impact. *Information, Communication & Society*, 23, 1838–1853.

Brüggemann, M., Engesser, S., Büchel, F., Humprecht, E., & Castro, L. (2014). Hallin and Mancini revisited: Four empirical types of western media systems. *Journal of Communication*, 64(6), 1037–1065.

Brundidge, J., & Rice, R. E. (2009). Political engagement online: Do the information rich get richer and the like-minded more similar? In A. Chadwick & P. N. Howard (Eds). *Routledge handbook of Internet politics*. Routledge: 144–156.

Bruns, A. (2019). *Are filter bubbles real?* Polity Press.

Bryan, M. L, & Jenkins, S. P. (2016). Multilevel modelling of country effects: A cautionary tale. *European Sociological Review*, 32(1), 3–22.

Bucar, C., & McMenamin, I. (2015). Poland: The presidentialization of parties in a young democracy. In G. Passarelli (Ed.). *The presidentialization of political parties: Organizations, institutions and leaders*. Springer: 107–123.

Bucher, T. (2018). *If ... then: Algorithmic power and politics*. Oxford University Press.

Bucy, E. P., Foley, J. M., Lukito, J., Doroshenko, L., Shah, D. V., Pevehouse, J. C., & Wells, C. (2020). Performing populism: Trump's transgressive debate style and the dynamics of Twitter response. *New Media & Society, 22*(4), 634–658.

Cadwalladr, C. (February 18, 2019). A digital gangster destroying democracy: The damning verdict on Facebook. *The Guardian*. Retrieved October 22, 2020, from https://www.theguardian.com/technology/2019/feb/18/a-digital-gangster-destroying-democracy-the-damning-verdict-on-facebook.

Cadwallar, C., & Graham-Harrison, E. (March 27, 2018). Revealed: 50 million Facebook profiles harvested for Cambridge Analytica in major data breach. *The Guardian*. Retrieved December 10, 2020, from https://www.theguardian.com/news/2018/mar/17/cambridge-analytica-facebook-influence-us-election.

Calhoun, C. J. (1992). *Habermas and the public sphere*. MIT press.

Campus, D., Pasquino, G., & Vaccari, C. (2008). Social networks, political discussion, and voting in Italy: A study of the 2006 election. *Political Communication, 25*(4), 423–444.

Cantijoch, M., Cutts, D., & Gibson, R. (2015). Moving slowly up the ladder of political engagement: A "spill-over" model of Internet articipation. *The British Journal of Politics and International Relations, 18*(1), 26–48.

Casero-Ripollés, A., Feenstra, R. A., & Tormey, S. (2016). Old and new media logics in an electoral campaign: The case of Podemos and the two-way street mediatization of politics. *The International Journal of Press/Politics, 21*(3), 378–397.

Castells, M. (2007). Communication, power and counter-power in the network society. *International Journal of Communication, 1*(1), 29.

Castells, M. (2015). *Networks of outrage and hope: Social movements in the Internet age*. John Wiley & Sons.

Ceron, A., Curini, L., & Iacus, S. M. (2016). *Politics and big data: Nowcasting and forecasting elections with social media*. Taylor & Francis.

Chadwick, A. (2007). Digital network repertoires and organizational hybridity. *Political Communication, 24*(3), 283–301.

Chadwick, A. (2009). Web 2.0: New challenges for the study of e-democracy in an era of informational exuberance. *I/S: A Journal of Law and Policy for the Information Society, 5*(9), 9–42.

Chadwick, A. (2012). Recent shifts in the relationship between the Internet and democratic engagement in Britain and the United States: Granularity, informational exuberance, and political learning. In E. Anduiza, M. Jensen, & L. Jorba (Eds). *Digital media and political engagement worldwide: A comparative study*. Cambridge University Press: 39–55.

Chadwick, A. (2017a). Corbyn, Labour, digital media, and the 2017 UK election. In E. Thorsen, D. Jackson, & D. Lilleker (Eds.). *UK Election Analysis 2017: Media, Voters and the Campaign*, available at http://www.electionanalysis.uk.

Chadwick, A. (2017b). (2nd edition). *The hybrid media system: Politics and power*. Oxford University Press.

Chadwick, A. (2019). *The new crisis of public communication: Challenges and opportunities for future research on digital media and politics*. Loughborough University, Online Civic Culture Centre.

Chadwick, A., & Stromer-Galley, J. (2016). Digital media, power, and democracy in parties and election campaigns: Party decline or party renewal? *The International Journal of Press/Politics, 21*(3), 283–293.

Chadwick, A., Vaccari, C., & O'Loughlin, B. (2018). Do tabloids poison the well of social media? Explaining democratically dysfunctional news sharing. *New Media & Society, 20*(11), 4255–4274.

Chiaramonte, A., Emanuele, V., Maggini, N., & Paparo, A. (2018). Populist success in a hung parliament: The 2018 general election in Italy. *South European Society and Politics, 23*(4), 479–501.

Choirat, C., Honaker, J., Imai, K., King, G., and Lau, O. (2017). *Zelig: Everyone's Statistical Software.* Version 5.1.4.90000. Retrieved May 16, 2019, from http://zeligproject.org/.

Christensen, H. S. (2011). Political activities on the Internet: Slacktivism or political participation by other means? *First Monday, 16*(2). Available at: https://doi.org/10.5210/fm.v16i2.3336.

Clarke, H. D., Goodwin, M., & Whiteley, P. (2017). *Brexit: Why Britain voted to leave the European Union.* Cambridge University Press.

Cogburn, D. L., & Espinoza-Vasquez, F. K. (2011). From networked nominee to networked nation: Examining the impact of Web 2.0 and social media on political participation and civic engagement in the 2008 Obama campaign. *Journal of Political Marketing, 10*(1–2), 189–213.

Cohen, D. (January 23, 2017). Twitter: 12 million inauguration tweets Friday, 11.5 million Women's March tweets Saturday. *Adweek.* Retrieved October 22, 2020, from http://www.adweek.com/digital/twitter-12-million-inauguration-tweets-friday-11-5-million-womens-march-tweets-saturday/.

Coleman, S. (2012). *How voters feel.* Cambridge University Press.

Coleman, S., & Moss, G. S. (2012). Under construction: The field of online deliberation research. *Journal of Information Technology & Politics, 9*(1), 1–15.

Colleoni, E., Rozza, A., & Arvidsson, A. (2014). Echo chamber or public sphere? Predicting political orientation and measuring political homophily in Twitter using big data. *Journal of Communication, 64*(2), 317–332.

Compaine, B. M. (Ed.). (2001). *The digital divide: Facing a crisis or creating a myth?* MIT Press.

Coppock, A., Guess, A., & Ternovski, J. (2016). When treatments are tweets: A network mobilization experiment over Twitter. *Political Behavior, 38*(1), 105–128.

Cramer, K. J. (2016). *The politics of resentment: Rural consciousness in Wisconsin and the rise of Scott Walker.* University of Chicago Press.

Crawford, K. (2009). Following you: Disciplines of listening in social media. *Continuum, 23*(4), 525–535.

Dahl, R. A. (1956). *A preface to democratic theory* (Vol. 115). University of Chicago Press.

Dahl, R. A. (1971). *Polyarchy: Participation and opposition.* Yale University Press.

Dahl, R. A. (1989). *Democracy and its critics.* Yale University Press.

Dahl, R. A. (2006). *On political equality.* Yale University Press.

Dahlgren, P. (2009). *Media and political engagement: Citizens, communication, and democracy.* Cambridge University Press.

Dalton, R. J. (2008a). Citizenship norms and the expansion of political participation. *Political Studies, 56*(1), 76–98.

Dalton, R. J. (2008b). *The good citizen: How a younger generation is reshaping American politics.* CQ Press.

Dalton, R. J. (2018). (7th edition). *Citizen politics: Public opinion and political parties in advanced industrial democracies.* CQ Press.

Dalton, R. J., & Wattenberg, M. P. (Eds.). (2000). *Parties without partisans: Political change in advanced industrial democracies.* Oxford University Press.

Dalton, R. J., & Wattenberg, M. P. (Eds.). (2002). *Parties without partisans: Political change in advanced industrial democracies.* Oxford University Press.

David, E. (1965). *A framework for political analysis.* Prentice Hall.

Davis, R. (2009). Typing politics: The role of blogs in American politics. Oxford University Press.

della Porta, D., Fernandez, J., Kouki, H., & Mosca, L. (2017). *Movement parties against austerity.* Cambridge: John Wiley & Sons.

Delli Carpini, M. X. (2000). Gen.com: Youth, civic engagement, and the new information environment. *Political Communication, 17*(4), 341–349.

Delli Carpini, M. X., Cook, F. L., & Jacobs, L. R. (2004). Public deliberation, discursive participation, and citizen engagement: A review of the empirical literature. *Annual Review of Political Science, 7,* 315–344.

Del Vicario, M., Bessi, A., Zollo, F., Petroni, F., Scala, A., Caldarelli, G., . . . & Quattrociocchi, W. (2016). The spreading of misinformation online. *Proceedings of the National Academy of Sciences, 113*(3), 554–559.

Del Vicario, M., Zollo, F., Caldarelli, G., Scala, A., & Quattrociocchi, W. (2017). Mapping social dynamics on Facebook: The Brexit debate. *Social Networks, 50,* 6–16.

Dennis, J. (2018). *Beyond slacktivism: Political participation on social media.* Springer.

Dennis, J. (2020). A party within a party posing as a movement? Momentum as a movement faction. *Journal of Information Technology & Politics, 17*(2), 97–113.

de Vreese, C. H., & Boomgaarden, H. (2006). News, political knowledge and participation: The differential effects of news media exposure on political knowledge and participation. *Acta Politica, 41*(4), 317–341.

de Vreese, C. H., Esser, F., Aalberg, T., Reinemann, C., & Stanyer, J. (2018). Populism as an expression of political communication content and style: A new perspective. *The International Journal of Press/Politics, 23*(4), 423–438.

de Vreese, C. H., & Neijens, P. (2016). Measuring media exposure in a changing communications environment. *Communication Methods and Measures, 10*(2–3), 69–80.

Diamond, L., & Morlino, L. (Eds.). (2005). *Assessing the quality of democracy.* Johns Hopkins University Press.

Diehl, T., Weeks, B. E., & Gil de Zúñiga, H. (2016). Political persuasion on social media: Tracing direct and indirect effects of news use and social interaction. *New Media & Society, 18*(9), 1875–1895.

DiMaggio, P., Hargittai, E., Neuman, W. R., & Robinson, J. P. (2001). Social implications of the Internet. *Annual Review of Sociology, 27*(1), 307–336.

Dobek-Ostrowska, B. (2012). Italianization (or Mediterraneanization) of the Polish media system. In Daniel Hallin & Paolo Mancini (Eds.). *Comparing media systems beyond the Western world.* Oxford University Press: 26–50.

Dommett, K. (2020). *The reimagined party: Democracy, change and the public.* Manchester University Press.

Downey, J., & Mihelj, S. (Eds.). (2012). *Central and Eastern European media in comparative perspective: Politics, economy and culture.* Ashgate.

Downs, A. (1957). *An economic theory of democracy.* Harper.

Druckman, J. N., & Lupia, A. (2016). Preference change in competitive political environments. *Annual Review of Political Science, 19,* 13–31.

Dubois, E., & Blank, G. (2018). The echo chamber is overstated: The moderating effect of political interest and diverse media. *Information, Communication & Society, 21*(5), 729–745.

Dutton, W. H., Reisdorf, B. C., Blank, G., Dubois, E., & Fernandez, L. (2019). The internet and access to information about politics: Filter bubbles, echo chambers, and disinformation. In Mark Graham & William H. Dutton (Eds.). *Society and the Internet: How networks of information and communication are changing our lives.* Oxford University Press: 228–246.

Duverger, M. (1951). *Les partis politiques.* A. Colin.

Easton, D. (1965). *A framework for political analysis.* Prentice-Hall.

Eatwell, R., & Goodwin, M. (2018). *National populism: The revolt against liberal democracy.* Penguin UK.

Eliasoph, N. (1998). *Avoiding politics: How Americans produce apathy in everyday life.* Cambridge University Press.

Engesser, S., Fawzi, N., & Larsson, A. O. (2017). Populist online communication: Introduction to the special issue. *Information, Communication & Society, 20*(9), 1279–1292.

Enos, R. D., Fowler, A., & Vavreck, L. (2014). Increasing inequality: The effect of GOTV mobilization on the composition of the electorate. *The Journal of Politics, 76*(1), 273–288.

Entman, R. M. (1990). *Democracy without citizens: Media and the decay of American politics*. Oxford University Press.

Eppler, M. J., & Mengis, J. (2004). The concept of information overload: A review of literature from organization science, accounting, marketing, MIS, and related disciplines. *The Information Society, 20*(5), 325–344.

Epstein, L. (1967). *Political parties in Western democracies*. Pall Mall.

Erikson, R. S., MacKuen, M. B., & Stimson, J. A. (2002). *The macro polity*. Cambridge University Press.

Esser, F., & Pfetsch, B. (Eds.). (2004). *Comparing political communication: Theories, cases, and challenges*. Cambridge: Cambridge University Press.

Eveland, W. P., & Hively, M. H. (2009). Political discussion frequency, network size, and "heterogeneity" of discussion as predictors of political knowledge and participation. *Journal of Communication, 59*(2), 205–224.

Feezell, J. T., & Ortiz, B. (2019). "I saw it on Facebook": An experimental analysis of political learning through social media. *Information, Communication & Society*. Available at: https://doi.org/10.1080/1369118X.2019.1697340.

Festinger, L. (1962). *A theory of cognitive dissonance* (Vol. 2). Stanford University Press.

Finkel, E. J., Bail, C. A., Cikara, M., Ditto, P. H., Iyengar, S., Klar, S., . . . & Druckman, J. N. (2020). Political sectarianism in America. *Science, 370*, 533–536.

Fiorina, M. P. (1976). The voting decision: Instrumental and expressive aspects. *The Journal of Politics, 38*(2), 390–413.

Flanagin, A. J. (2017). Online social influence and the convergence of mass and interpersonal communication. *Human Communication Research, 43*, 450–463.

Flaxman, S., Goel, S., & Rao, J. M. (2016). Filter bubbles, echo chambers, and online news consumption. *Public Opinion Quarterly, 80*(S1), 298–320.

Fletcher, R., Cornia, A., & Nielsen, R. K. (2020). How polarized are online and offline news audiences? A comparative analysis of twelve countries. *The International Journal of Press/Politics, 25*(2), 169–195.

Fletcher, R., Newman, N., & Schulz, A. (2020). A Mile Wide, an Inch Deep: Online News and Media Use in the 2019 UK General Election. *SSRN*. Available at: https://doi.org/10.2139/ssrn.3582441.

Fletcher, R., & Nielsen, R. K. (2017). Are news audiences increasingly fragmented? A cross-national comparative analysis of cross-platform news audience fragmentation and duplication. *Journal of Communication, 67*(4), 476–498.

Fletcher, R., & Nielsen, R. K. (2018). Are people incidentally exposed to news on social media? A comparative analysis. *New Media & Society, 20*(7), 2450–2468.

Fomina, J., & Kucharczyk, J. (2016). Populism and protest in Poland. *Journal of Democracy, 27*(4), 58–68.

Fouquet, H. (April 18, 2017). Here's how Bernie Sanders is playing a role in France's Election. *Bloomberg*. Retrieved September 22, 2020, from https://www.bloomberg.com/news/articles/2017-04-18/here-s-how-bernie-sanders-is-playing-a-role-in-france-s-election.

Fraser, N. (1990). Rethinking the public sphere: A contribution to the critique of actually existing democracy. *Social Text* (25/26), 56–80.

Freedom House. (2017). Freedom in the World 2017: Country Scores. Retrieved September 26, 2017, from https://freedomhouse.org/report/fiw-2017-table-country-scores.

Freelon, D., Marwick, A., & Kreiss, D. (2020). False equivalencies: Online activism from left to right. *Science, 369*, 1197–1201.

Freelon, D., McIlwain, C., & Clark, M. (2018). Quantifying the power and consequences of social media protest. *New Media & Society, 20*(3), 990–1011.

Gaines, B. J., & Mondak, J. J. (2009). Typing together? Clustering of ideological types in online social networks. *Journal of Information Technology & Politics, 6*(3–4), 216–231.

Gainous, J., & Wagner, K. M. (2013). *Tweeting to power: The social media revolution in American politics*. New York: Oxford University Press.

Gallagher, M. (2017). Election Indices Dataset. Retrieved September 26, 2017, from http://www.tcd.ie/Political_Science/staff/michael_gallagher/ElSystems/index.php.

Gallagher, M., & Mitchell, P. (2018). Dimensions of variation in electoral systems. In E. S. Herron, R. J. Pekkanen, & M. S. Shugart (Ed.). *The Oxford Handbook of Electoral Systems*. Oxford University Press: 23–40.

Gastil, J., & Black, L. (2007). Public deliberation as the organizing principle of political communication research. *Journal of Public Deliberation*, 4(1). Available at: https://doi.org/10.16997/jdd.59.

Gerber, A. S., & Green, D. P. (2012). *Field experiments: Design, analysis, and interpretation*. WW Norton.

Gest, J. (2016). *The new minority: White working class politics in an age of immigration and inequality*. Oxford University Press.

Gherghina, S. (2014). *Party organization and electoral volatility in Central and Eastern Europe: Enhancing voter loyalty*. Routledge.

Gibson, R. K. (2009). New media and the revitalisation of politics. *Representation*, 45(3), 289–299.

Gibson, R. K. (2015). Party change, social media and the rise of "citizen-initiated" campaigning. *Party Politics*, 21(2), 183–197.

Gibson, R. K., Greffet, F., & Cantijoch, M. (2017). Friend or foe? Digital technologies and the changing nature of party membership. *Political Communication*, 34, 89–111.

Giglietto, F., Iannelli, L., Valeriani, A, & Rossi, L. (2019). "Fake news" is the invention of a liar: How false information circulates within the hybrid news system. *Current Sociology*, 67(4), 625–642.

Gil de Zúñiga, H., Garcia-Perdomo, V., & McGregor, S. C. (2015). What is second screening? Exploring motivations of second screen use and its effect on online political participation. *Journal of Communication*, 65(5), 793–815.

Gil de Zúñiga, H., Jung, N., & Valenzuela, S. (2012). Social media use for news and individuals' social capital, civic engagement and political participation. *Journal of Computer-Mediated Communication*, 17(3), 319–336.

Gil de Zúñiga, H., Koc Michalska, K., & Römmele, A. (2020). Populism in the era of Twitter: How social media contextualized new insights into an old phenomenon. *New Media & Society*, 22, 585–594.

Gil de Zúñiga, H., Molyneux, L., & Zheng, P. (2014). Social media, political expression, and political participation: Panel analysis of lagged and concurrent relationships. *Journal of Communication*, 64(4), 612–634.

Gil de Zúñiga, H., Strauss, N., & Huber, B. (2020). The proliferation of the "news finds me" perception across societies. *International Journal of Communication*, 14, 1605–1633.

Gil de Zúñiga, H., Weeks, B., & Ardèvol-Abreu, A. (2017). Effects of the news-finds-me perception in communication: Social media use implications for news seeking and learning about politics. *Journal of Computer-Mediated Communication*, 22(3), 105–123.

Gillespie, T. (2016). Algorithm. In B. Peters (Ed.). *Digital Keywords: A Vocabulary of Information Society and Culture*. Princeton University Press: 18–30.

Gillespie, T. (2018). *Custodians of the Internet: Platforms, content moderation, and the hidden decisions that shape social media*. Yale University Press.

Graber, D. A. (2001). *Processing politics: Learning from television in the Internet age*. University of Chicago Press.

Graham, T., & Wright, S. (2015). A tale of two stories from "below the line" comment fields at the Guardian. *The International Journal of Press/Politics*, 20(3), 317–338.

Gray, M., & Caul, M. (2000). Declining voter turnout in advanced industrial democracies, 1950 to 1997: The effects of declining group mobilization. *Comparative Political Studies*, 33(9), 1091–1122.

Green, D. P., & Gerber, A. S. (2015). *Get out the vote: How to increase voter turnout*. Brookings Institution Press.

Green, J. (2002). Still functional after all these years: Parties in the United States, 1960–2000. In P. Webb, D. Farrell, & I. Halliday (Eds.). *Political parties in advanced industrial democracies.* Oxford University Press.

Grinberg, N., Joseph, K., Friedland, L., Swire-Thompson, B., & Lazer, D. (2019). Fake news on Twitter during the 2016 US presidential election. *Science, 363*(6425), 374–378.

Groshek, J., & Koc-Michalska, K. (2017). Helping populism win? Social media use, filter bubbles, and support for populist presidential candidates in the 2016 US election campaign. *Information, Communication & Society, 20*(9), 1389–1407.

Grunberg, G., & Haegel, F. (2007). *La France vers le bipartisme?* Presses de Sciences Po.

Guess, A. (2020). (Almost) everything in moderation: New evidence on Americans' online media diets. *American Journal of Political Science.* Available at: https://doi.org/10.1111/ajps.12589.

Guess, A., Nagler, J., & Tucker, J. (2019). Less than you think: Prevalence and predictors of fake news dissemination on Facebook. *Science Advances, 5*(1). Available at: https://doi.org/10.1126/sciadv.aau4586.

Gunther, R. (2005). Parties and electoral behavior in Southern Europe. *Comparative Politics, 37*(3), 253–275.

Habermas, J. (1989). *The structural transformation of the public sphere: An inquiry into a category of bourgeois society.* MIT press.

Haggerty, A. (October 17, 2014). Social media more influential information source than newspapers in Scottish independence referendum, YouGov finds. *The Drum.* Retrieved January 16, 2020, from https://www.thedrum.com/news/2014/10/17/social-media-more-influential-information-source-newspapers-scottish-independence.

Halliday, I. (2002). Spain: Building a parties state in a new democracy. In P. Webb, D. Farrell, & I. Halliday (Eds.). *Political parties in advanced industrial democracies.* Oxford University Press: 248–279.

Hallin, D. C. (2019). Mediatisation, neoliberalism and populisms: The case of Trump. *Contemporary Social Science, 14*(1), 14–25.

Hallin, D. C., & Mancini, P. (2004). *Comparing media systems: Three models of media and politics.* Cambridge University Press.

Hallin, D. C., & Mancini, P. (Eds.). (2011). *Comparing media systems beyond the Western world.* Cambridge University Press.

Hameleers, M., Bos, L., Fawzi, N., Reinemann, C., Andreadis, I., Corbu, N., . . . & Axelsson, S. (2018). Start spreading the news: A comparative experiment on the effects of populist communication on political engagement in sixteen European countries. *The International Journal of Press/Politics, 23*(4), 517–538.

Han, B. (2017). Korean Wave| K-pop in Latin America: Transcultural fandom and digital mediation. *International Journal of Communication, 11,* 2250–2269.

Hanitzsch, T., Hanusch, F., Ramaprasad, J., & De Beer, A. S. (Eds.). (2019). *Worlds of journalism: Journalistic cultures around the globe.* Columbia University Press.

Hargittai, E. (2002). Second-level digital divide: Differences in people's online skills. *First Monday, 7*(4). Available at: https://doi.org/10.5210/fm.v7i4.942.

Hartz-Karp, J., & Sullivan, B. (2014). The unfulfilled promise of online deliberation. *Journal of Public Deliberation, 10*(1), 1–5.

Hassell, H. J., & Monson, J. Q. (2014). Campaign targets and messages in direct mail fundraising. *Political Behavior, 36*(2), 359–376.

Heaney, M. T., & Rojas, F. (2015). *Party in the street: The antiwar movement and the Democratic Party after 9/11.* Cambridge University Press.

Hedrick, A., Karpf, D., & Kreiss, D. (2018). The earnest Internet vs. the ambivalent Internet. *International Journal of Communication, 12*(8), 1057–1064.

Heerwegh, D. (2009). Mode differences between face-to-face and web surveys: An experimental investigation of data quality and social desirability effects. *International Journal of Public Opinion Research, 21*(1), 111–121.

Heidar, K. (2006). Party membership and participation. In R. S. Katz & W. Crotty (Eds.). *Handbook of party politics.* Sage Publications: 301–315.

Heiss, R., & Matthes, J. (2019). Does incidental exposure on social media equalize or reinforce participatory gaps? Evidence from a panel study. *New Media & Society, 21*(11–12), 2463–2482.

Heller, W. B. (2002). Regional parties and national politics in Europe: Spain's estado de las autonomías, 1993 to 2000. *Comparative Political Studies, 35*(6), 657–685.

Henn, P., Jandura, O., & Vowe, G. (2016). The traditional paradigm of political communication research reconstructed. In G. Vove & P. Henn (Eds.). *Political communication in the online world. Theoretical approaches and research designs.* Routledge: 11–25.

Herman, T. (November 2, 2018). BTS' UNICEF "Love Myself" campaign raises over $1.4 million. *Billboard.* Retrieved August 28, 2020, from https://www.billboard.com/articles/news/bts/8483029/bts-unicef-love-myself-campaign-money-raised.

Hermida, A. (2010). Twittering the news: The emergence of ambient journalism. *Journalism Practice, 4*(3), 297–308.

Hersh, E. D. (2015). *Hacking the electorate: How campaigns perceive voters.* Cambridge University Press.

Hibbing, J. R., & Theiss-Morse, E. (2002). *Stealth democracy: Americans' beliefs about how government should work.* Cambridge University Press.

Highfield, T. (2016). *Social media and everyday politics.* Cambridge: Polity Press.

Hindman, M. (2018). *The Internet trap: How the digital economy builds monopolies and undermines democracy.* Princeton University Press.

Hochschild, A. R. (2018). *Strangers in their own land: Anger and mourning on the American right.* The New Press.

Hoerbst, A., Kohl, C. D., Knaup, P., & Ammenwerth, E. (2010). Attitudes and behaviors related to the introduction of electronic health records among Austrian and German citizens. *International Journal of Medical Informatics, 79*(2), 81–89.

Holbert, R. L., Garrett, R. K., & Gleason, L. S. (2010). A new era of minimal effects? A response to Bennett and Iyengar. *Journal of Communication, 60*(1), 15–34.

Hollander, B. A. (2008). Tuning out or tuning elsewhere? Partisanship, polarization, and media migration from 1998 to 2006. *Journalism & Mass Communication Quarterly, 85*(1), 23–40.

Holmberg, S. (2007). Partisanship reconsidered. In R. J. Dalton & H. D. Klingemann (Eds.). *The Oxford handbook of political behavior.* Oxford University Press: 557–570.

Holt, K., Shehata, A., Strömbäck, J., & Ljungberg, E. (2013). Age and the effects of news media attention and social media use on political interest and participation: Do social media function as leveller? *European Journal of Communication, 28*(1), 19–34.

Hopkin, J. (2005). Spain: Proportional representation with majoritarian outcomes. In M. Gallagher & P. Mitchell (Eds.). *The politics of electoral systems.* Oxford University Press: 375–393.

Hosseinmardi, H., Ghasemian, A., Clauset, A., Rothschild, D. M., Mobius, M., & Watts, D. J. (2020). Evaluating the Scale, Growth, and Origins of Right-Wing Echo Chambers on YouTube. *ArXiv:2011.12843 [Cs].* Retrieved from http://arxiv.org/abs/2011.12843.

House of Commons Digital, Culture, Media and Sport Committee. (2019). Disinformation and "FakeNews": Final Report. Retrieved January 31, 2019, from https://publications.parliament.uk/pa/cm201719/cmselect/cmcumeds/1791/1791.pdf.

House of Commons Library. (2018). Membership of UK Political Parties. Retrieved May 21, 2019, from https://researchbriefings.parliament.uk/ResearchBriefing/Summary/SN05125.

Howard, P. N. (2006). *New media campaigns and the managed citizen.* Cambridge University Press.

Howard, P. N. (2010). *The digital origins of dictatorship and democracy: Information technology and political Islam.* Oxford University Press.

Howard, P. N., & Hussain, M. M. (2013). *Democracy's fourth wave?: Digital media and the Arab Spring.* Oxford University Press.

Huberman, B. A., Romero, D. M., & Wu, F. (2008). Social networks that matter: Twitter under the microscope. *arXiv preprint* arXiv:0812.1045. Retrieved April 14, 2021, from https://arxiv.org/abs/0812.1045.

Huckfeldt, R., Johnson, P. E., & Sprague, J. (2004). *Political disagreement: The survival of diverse opinions within communication networks.* Cambridge University Press.

Huckfeldt, R., & Sprague, J. (1992). Political parties and electoral mobilization: Political structure, social structure, and the party canvass. *American Political Science Review, 86*(1), 70–86.

Huckfeldt, R. R., & Sprague, J. (1995). *Citizens, politics and social communication: Information and influence in an election campaign.* Cambridge University Press.

Hughes, D. J., Rowe, M., Batey, M., & Lee, A. (2012). A tale of two sites: Twitter vs. Facebook and the personality predictors of social media usage. *Computers in Human Behavior, 28*(2), 561–569.

Huntington, S. (1975). The United States. In M. Crozier, S. P. Huntington, & J. Watanuki (Eds). *The crisis of democracy: Report on the governability of democracies to the Trilateral Commission.* New York University Press: 59–118.

Iacus, S. M., King, G., & Porro, G. (2012). Causal inference without balance checking: Coarsened exact matching. *Political Analysis, 20*(1), 1–24.

Iacus, S. M., King, G., & Porro, G. (2017). A Theory of Statistical Inference for Matching Methods in Causal Research, unpublished manuscript. Retrieved September 26, 2018 from https://gking.harvard.edu/files/gking/files/multi4.pdf.

Ignazi, P. (1996). The intellectual basis of right-wing anti-partyism. *European Journal of Political Research, 29*(3), 279–296.

Inglehart, R. (1997). *Modernization and postmodernization: Cultural, economic, and political change in 43 societies.* Princeton University Press.

International Telecommunications Union. (2020). Statistics. Retrieved November 30, 2020 from http://www.itu.int/en/ITU-D/Statistics/Pages/stat/default.aspx.

Internet Live Stats. (2017). Internet Users by Country (2016). Retrieved September 26, 2017, from http://www.internetlivestats.com/internet-users-by-country/.

Issenberg, S. (February 15, 2012a). Obama's white whale: How the campaign's top-secret project Narwhal could change this race, and many to come. *Slate.* Retrieved October 23, 2020, from https://slate.com/news-and-politics/2012/02/project-narwhal-how-a-top-secret-obama-campaign-program-could-change-the-2012-race.html.

Issenberg, S. (2012b). *The victory lab: The secret science of winning campaigns.* Broadway Books.

Iyengar, S., & Hahn, K. S. (2009). Red media, blue media: Evidence of ideological selectivity in media use. *Journal of Communication, 59*(1), 19–39.

Jenkins, H. (2015). Cultural acupuncture: Fan activism and the Harry Potter alliance. In L. Geraghtly (Ed.). *Popular media cultures.* Palgrave Macmillan UK: 206–229.

Jenkins, H., Shresthova, S., Gamber-Thompson, L., Kligler-Vilenchik, N., & Zimmerman, A. (2018). *By any media necessary: The new youth activism.* NYU Press.

Jones, J. J., Bond, R. M., Bakshy, E., Eckles, D., & Fowler, J. H. (2017). Social influence and political mobilization: Further evidence from a randomized experiment in the 2012 US presidential election. *PloS One, 12*(4). Available at: https://doi.org/10.1371/journal.pone.0173851.

Jun, U. (2011). Volksparteien under pressure: Challenges and adaptation. *German Politics, 20*(1), 200–222.

Jungherr, A. (2015). *Analyzing political communication with digital trace data: The role of Twitter messages in social science research.* Springer.

Kaiser, J., Keller, T. R., & Kleinen-von Königslöw, K. (2021). Incidental news exposure on Facebook as a social experience: The influence of recommender and media cues on news selection. *Communication Research, 48*(1), 77–99.

Kalogeropoulos, A., Negredo, S., Picone, I., & Nielsen, R. K. (2017). Who shares and comments on news? A cross-national comparative analysis of online and social media participation. *Social Media + Society, 3*(4). Available at: https://doi.org/10.1177/2056305117735754.

Karlsen, R. (2015). Followers are opinion leaders: The role of people in the flow of political communication on and beyond social networking sites. *European Journal of Communication, 30*(3), 301–318.

Karnowski, V., Kümpel, A. S., Leonhard, L., & Leiner, D. J. (2017). From incidental news exposure to news engagement. How perceptions of the news post and news usage patterns influence engagement with news articles encountered on Facebook. *Computers in Human Behavior*, 76, 42–50.

Karpf, D. (2012a). *The MoveOn effect. The unexpected transformation of American political advocacy.* Oxford University Press.

Karpf, D. (2012b). Social science research methods in Internet time. *Information, Communication & Society*, 15(5), 639–661.

Karpf, D. (2016). *Analytic activism: Digital listening and the new political strategy.* Oxford University Press.

Karpf, D. (2019). On Digital Disinformation and Democratic Myths. *MediaWell.* Retrieved January 30, 2020, from https://mediawell.ssrc.org/expert-reflections/on-digital-disinformation-and-democratic-myths/.

Katz, E., & Lazarsfeld, P. F. (1955). *Personal influence: The part played by people in the flow of mass communications.* Transaction Publishers.

Katz, R. S., & Mair, P. (1995). Changing models of party organization and party democracy: The emergence of the cartel party. *Party Politics*, 1(1), 5–28.

Katz, J. E., & Rice, R. E. (2002). *Social consequences of Internet use: Access, involvement, and interaction.* MIT Press.

Kaye, B. K., & Johnson, T. J. (2002). Online and in the know: Uses and gratifications of the web for political information. *Journal of Broadcasting & Electronic Media*, 46(1), 54–71.

Kerbel, M. R., & Bloom, J. D. (2005). Blog for America and civic involvement. *Harvard International Journal of Press/Politics*, 10(4), 3–27.

Kim, Y. M., Hsu, J., Neiman, D., Kou, C., Bankston, L., Kim, S. Y., ... & Raskutti, G. (2018). The stealth media? Groups and targets behind divisive issue campaigns on Facebook. *Political Communication*, 35(4), 515–541.

King, G., Tomz, M., & Wittenberg, J. (2000). Making the most of statistical analyses: Improving interpretation and presentation. *American Journal of Political Science*, 347–361.

Klandermans, B. (2013). Instrumental versus expressive action. In D. A. Snow, D. Della Porta, B. Klandermans, & D. McAdam (Eds.). *The Wiley-Blackwell Encyclopedia of Social and Political Movements.* Blackwell Publishing Ltd: 614–616.

Kligler-Vilenchik, N. (2021). Friendship and politics don't mix? The role of sociability for online political talk. *Information, Communication & Society*, 24(1), 118–133.

Kligler-Vilenchik, N., Baden, C., & Yarchi, M. (2020). Interpretative polarization across platforms: How political disagreement develops over time on Facebook, Twitter, and WhatsApp. *Social Media + Society*, 6(3), 2056305120944393. Available at: https://doi.org/10.1177/2056305120944393.

Kligler-Vilenchik, N., & Tenenboim, O. (2020). Sustained journalist–audience reciprocity in a meso news-space: The case of a journalistic WhatsApp group. *New Media & Society*, 22(2), 264–282.

Knapp, A. (2002). France: Never a golden age. In P. Webb, D. Farrell, & I. Halliday (Eds.). *Political parties in advanced industrial democracies.* Oxford University Press: 107–150.

Kouki, H., & González, J. F. (2018). Syriza, Podemos and mobilizations against austerity: Movements, parties or movement-parties? In J. Roose, M. Sommer, & F. Scholl (Eds.). *Europas Zivilgesellschaft in der Wirtschafts-und Finanzkrise: Protest, Resilienz und Kämpfe um Deutungshoheit.* Springer: 123–140.

Kreiss, D. (2012). *Taking our country back: The crafting of networked politics from Howard Dean to Barack Obama.* Oxford University Press.

Kreiss, D. (2016). *Prototype politics: Technology-intensive campaigning and the data of democracy.* Oxford University Press.

Kreiss, D., & Howard, P. N. (2010). New challenges to political privacy: Lessons from the first US Presidential race in the Web 2.0 era. *International Journal of Communication*, 4, 1032–1050.

Kreiss, D., & McGregor, S. C. (2018). Technology firms shape political communication: The work of Microsoft, Facebook, Twitter, and Google with campaigns during the 2016 US presidential cycle. *Political Communication, 35*(2), 155–177.

Kreiss, D., & McGregor, S. C. (2019). The "arbiters of what our voters see": Facebook and Google's struggle with policy, process, and enforcement around political advertising. *Political Communication, 36*(4), 499–522.

Kreuter, F., Presser, S., & Tourangeau, R. (2008). Social desirability bias in CATI, IVR, and web surveys: The effects of mode and question sensitivity. *Public Opinion Quarterly, 72*(5), 847–865.

Krueger, B. S. (2006). A comparison of conventional and Internet political mobilization. *American Politics Research, 34*(6), 759–776.

Ksiazek T. B., Malthouse E. C., & Webster J. G. (2010). News-seekers and avoiders: Exploring patterns of total news consumption across media and the Relationship to civic participation. *Journal of Broadcasting & Electronic Media, 54*(4), 551–568.

Kümpel, A. S. (2020). The Matthew Effect in social media news use: Assessing inequalities in news exposure and news engagement on social network sites (SNS). *Journalism, 21*(8), 1083–1098.

Laakso, M., & Taagepera, R. (1979). "Effective" number of parties: A measure with application to West Europe. *Comparative Political Studies, 12*(1), 3–27.

Larson, J. M., Nagler, J., Ronen, J., & Tucker, J. A. (2019). Social networks and protest participation: Evidence from 130 million Twitter users. *American Journal of Political Science, 63*(3), 690–705.

Lasswell, H. (1936). *Politics: Who gets what, when, how.* Whittlesey House.

Lawson, K. (Ed.). (1980). *Political parties and linkage: A comparative perspective.* Yale University Press.

Lazer, D., Pentland, A. S., Adamic, L., Aral, S., Barabasi, A. L., Brewer, D., . . . & Jebara, T. (2009). Life in the network: The coming age of computational social science. *Science, 323*(5915), 721.

Lears, R. (Director). (2019). *Knock Down the House* [Motion Picture]. Netflix.

Lee, H. K. (June 8, 2020). K-pop stars take part in Black Lives Matter movement. *ABC News.* Retrieved August 28, 2020, from https://abcnews.go.com/International/pop-stars-part-black-lives-matter-movement/story?id=71131938.

Lee, S., & Xenos, M. (2020). Incidental news exposure via social media and political participation: Evidence of reciprocal effects. *New Media & Society.* Available at: https://doi.org/10.1177/1461444820962121.

Lee, T. B. (November 16, 2016). Facebook's fake news problem, explained. *Vox.* Retrieved September 22, 2020, from https://www.vox.com/new-money/2016/11/16/13637310/facebook-fake-news-explained.

Leigh, D., & Manthey G. (October 29, 2020). President Donald Trump and former Vice President Joe Biden have set new spending records for political ads on social media this election. *ABC7.* Retrieved November 26, 2020, from https://abc7.com/presidential-race-campaign-spending-trump-political-ads-biden/7452228/.

Leighley, J. E., & Nagler, J. (2013). *Who votes now? Demographics, issues, inequality, and turnout in the United States.* Princeton University Press.

Lelkes, Y. (2016). Mass polarization: Manifestations and measurements. *Public Opinion Quarterly, 80*(S1), 392–410.

Lelkes, Y., Sood, G., & Iyengar, S. (2017). The hostile audience: The effect of access to broadband Internet on partisan affect. *American Journal of Political Science, 61*(1), 5–20.

Lijphart, A. (1971). Comparative politics and the comparative method. *American Political Science Review, 65*(3), 682–693.

Lijphart, A. (1997). Unequal participation: Democracy's unresolved dilemma presidential address, American Political Science Association, 1996. *American Political Science Review, 91*(1), 1–14.

Lijphart, A. (2012). *Patterns of democracy: Government forms and performance in thirty-six countries.* Yale University Press.

Lilleker, D., & Jackson, N. (2013). *Political campaigning, elections and the Internet: Comparing the US, UK, France and Germany.* Routledge.

Lipset, S. (1960). *Political man: The social bases of politics.* New York: Doubleday.

Lord Ashcroft. (2019). How Britain Voted and Why: My 2019 General Election Post-Vote Poll. *Lord Ashcroft Polls.* Retrieved January 8, 2020, from https://lordashcroftpolls.com/2019/12/how-britain-voted-and-why-my-2019-general-election-post-vote-poll/.

Lorenz, T., Browning, K., Frenkel, S. (June 21, 2020). TikTok teens and K-pop stans say they sank Trump rally. *The New York Times.* Retrieved August 28, 2020, from https://www.nytimes.com/2020/06/21/style/tiktok-trump-rally-tulsa.html.

Lupia, A. (2015). *Uninformed: Why people know so little about politics and what we can do about it.* Oxford University Press.

Lupia, A., & McCubbins, M. D. (1998). *The democratic dilemma: Can citizens learn what they need to know?* Cambridge University Press.

MacKuen, M. B. (1990). Speaking politics: Conversational choice, public opinion, and the prospects for deliberative democracy. In J. Ferejohn and J. Kuklinski (Eds.). *Information and democratic processes.* University of Illinois Press: 59–99.

Mainwaring, S., & Torcal, M. (2006). Party system institutionalization and party system theory after the third wave of democratization. In R. Katr & W. Crotty (Eds.). *Handbook of Party Politics.* Sage: 204–227.

Mair, P. 2007. Left-right orientations. In R. J. Dalton & H. D. Klingemann (Eds.). *The Oxford handbook of political behavior.* Oxford University Press: 206–222.

Mair, P. (2013). *Ruling the void: The hollowing of Western democracy.* Verso Trade.

Mansbridge, J., Bohman, J., Chambers, S., Christiano, T., Fung, A., Parkinson, J., . . . & Warren, M. E. (2012). A systemic approach to deliberative democracy. In J. Parkinson & J. Mansbridge (Eds.). *Deliberative systems: Deliberative democracy at the large scale.* Cambridge University Press: 1–26.

Margetts, H. (2006). Cyber parties. In Richard S. Katz & William Crotty (Eds.). *Handbook of Party Politics.* Sage: 528–535.

Margetts, H., John, P., Hale, S., & Yasseri, T. (2016). *Political turbulence: How social media shape collective action.* Princeton University Press.

Margolis, M., & Resnick, D. (2000). *Politics as usual: The cyberspace "Revolution."* Sage.

Margulies, B. (2018). Nativists are populists, not liberals. *Journal of Democracy, 29*(1), 141–147.

Martin, J. A. (2015). Mobile news use and participation in elections: A bridge for the democratic divide? *Mobile Media & Communication, 3*(2), 230–249.

Marwick, A. E., & boyd, d. (2011). I tweet honestly, I tweet passionately: Twitter users, context collapse, and the imagined audience. *New Media & Society, 13*(1), 114–133.

Matthes, J., Knoll, J., Valenzuela, S., Hopmann, D. N., & Von Sikorski, C. (2019). A meta-analysis of the effects of cross-cutting exposure on political participation. *Political Communication, 36*(4), 523–542.

Matthes, J., Nanz, A., Stubenvoll, M., & Heiss, R. (2020). Processing news on social media. The political incidental news exposure model (PINE). *Journalism, 21*(8), 1031–1048.

McClurg, S. D. (2004). Indirect mobilization: The social consequences of party contacts in an election campaign. *American Politics Research, 32*(4), 406–443.

McClurg, S. D. (2006). The electoral relevance of political talk: Examining disagreement and expertise effects in social networks on political participation. *American Journal of Political Science, 50*(3), 737–754.

McKelvey, T. (July 20, 2020). Coronavirus: Why are Americans so angry about masks? BBC News. Retrieved August 23, 2020, from https://www.bbc.com/news/world-us-canada-53477121.

Merten, L. (2020). Block, hide or follow—personal news curation practices on social media. *Digital Journalism.* Available at: https://doi.org/10.1080/21670811.2020.1829978.

Messing, S., & Westwood, S. J. (2014). Selective exposure in the age of social media: Endorsements trump partisan source affiliation when selecting news online. *Communication Research, 41*(8), 1042–1063.

Miller, M. L., & Vaccari, C. (2020). Digital threats to democracy: Comparative lessons and possible remedies. *The International Journal of Press/Politics, 25*, 333–356.

Min, S. J. (2010). From the digital divide to the democratic divide: Internet skills, political interest, and the second-level digital divide in political internet use. *Journal of Information Technology & Politics, 7*(1), 22–35.

Min, S. J., & Wohn, D. Y. (2018). All the news that you don't like: Cross-cutting exposure and political participation in the age of social media. *Computers in Human Behavior, 83*, 24–31.

Möller, J., Trilling, D., Helberger, N., & van Es, B. (2018). Do not blame it on the algorithm: An empirical assessment of multiple recommender systems and their impact on content diversity. *Information, Communication & Society, 21*(7), 959–977.

Molloy, A. (August 22, 2014). Scottish independence: #YesBecause hashtag shows "unfiltered reality" of Yes campaign. *The Independent*. Retrieved January 18, 2020, from https://www.independent.co.uk/news/uk/scottish-independence/scottish-independence-yesbecause-hashtag-shows-unfiltered-reality-yes-campaign-9683541.html.

Mondak, J. J. (1993). Public opinion and heuristic processing of source cues. *Political Behavior, 15*(2), 167–192.

Morton, R. B., & Williams, K. C. (2010). *Experimental political science and the study of causality: From nature to the lab*. Cambridge University Press.

Mosca, L., Vaccari, C., & Valeriani, A. (2015). An Internet-fuelled party? The Five Star Movement and the Web. In F. Tronconi (Ed.). *Beppe Grillo's Five Star Movement: Organisation, communication and ideology*. Ashgate: 127–151.

Mossberger, K. (2009). Toward digital citizenship. Addressing inequality in the information age. In A. Chadwick & P. N. Howard (Eds). *Routledge handbook of Internet politics*. Routledge: 173–185.

Mosseri, A. (June 29, 2016). Building a better news feed for you. *Facebook Newsroom*. Retrieved October 12, 2020, from https://about.fb.com/news/2016/06/building-a-better-news-feed-for-you/.

Mosseri, A. (January 11, 2018). Bringing people closer together. *Facebook Newsroom*. Retrieved October 12, 2020, from https://about.fb.com/news/2018/01/news-feed-fyi-bringing-people-closer-together/.

Mudde, C. (2004). The populist zeitgeist. *Government and Opposition, 39*(4), 541–563.

Munger, K. (2019). The limited value of non-replicable field experiments in contexts with low temporal validity. *Social Media + Society, 5*(3), 2056305119859294.

Munger, K., Egan, P., Nagler, J., Ronen, J., Tucker, J. (2016). Learning (and Unlearning) from the Media and Political Parties: Evidence from a YouGov-SMaPP 2015 UK Election Survey. *SMaPP Working Paper*. Retrieved August 8, 2017, from https://18798-presscdn-pagely.netdna-ssl.com/smapp/wp-content/uploads/sites/1693/2016/01/Munger_et_al_Tucker_CP_Yale_2017_01.pdf.

Munger, K., & Phillips, J. (2020). Right-wing YouTube: A supply and demand perspective. *The International Journal of Press/Politics*. Available at: https://doi.org/10.1177/1940161220964767.

Mutz, D. C. (2001). Facilitating communication across lines of political difference: The role of mass media. *American Political Science Review, 95*(1), 97–114.

Mutz, D. C. (2002). The consequences of cross-cutting networks for political participation. *American Journal of Political Science, 46*(4), 838–855.

Mutz, D. C. (2006). *Hearing the other side: Deliberative versus participatory democracy*. Cambridge University Press.

Nagle, A. (2017). *Kill all normies: Online culture wars from 4chan and Tumblr to Trump and the alt-right*. John Hunt Publishing.

Nechushtai, E. (2018). From liberal to polarized liberal? Contemporary US news in Hallin and Mancini's typology of news systems. *The International Journal of Press/Politics, 23*(2), 183–201.

Nechushtai, E., & Lewis, S. C. (2019). What kind of news gatekeepers do we want machines to be? Filter bubbles, fragmentation, and the normative dimensions of algorithmic recommendations. *Computers in Human Behavior, 90*, 298–307.

Negrine, R., & Papathanassopoulos, S. (1996). The "Americanization" of political communication: A critique. *Harvard International Journal of Press/Politics, 1*(2), 45–62.

Neuman, W. R., Just, M. R., & Crigler, A. N. (1992). *Common knowledge: News and the Construction of Political Meaning*. University of Chicago Press.

Newton, K. (1999). Mass media effects: Mobilization or media malaise? *British Journal of Political Science, 29*(4), 577–599.

Nickerson, D. W. (2007). Does email boost turnout? *Quarterly Journal of Political Science, 2*(4), 369–380.

Nickerson, D. W. (2008). Is voting contagious? Evidence from two field experiments. *American Political Science Review, 102*(1), 49–57.

Nickerson, R. S. (1998). Confirmation bias: A ubiquitous phenomenon in many guises. *Review of General Psychology, 2*(2), 175.

Niedermayer, O. (2020). Parteimitglieder in Deutschland: Version 2020. Retrieved December 15, 2020, from https://refubium.fu-berlin.de/bitstream/handle/fub188/27961/P-PMIT20_Nr_31.pdf?sequence=1&isAllowed=y.

Nielsen, R. K. (2012). *Ground wars: Personalized communication in political campaigns*. Princeton University Press.

Nielsen, R. K., & Vaccari, C. (2013). Do people "like" politicians on Facebook? Not really. Large-scale direct candidate-to-voter online communication as an outlier phenomenon. *International Journal of Communication, 7*, 24.

Nir, L. (2011). Disagreement and opposition in social networks: Does disagreement discourage turnout? *Political Studies, 59*(3), 674–692.

Nivola, P. S., & Brady, D. W. (Eds.). (2008). *Red and blue nation?: Consequences and correction of America's polarized politics*. Brookings Institution Press.

Norris, P. (2000). *A virtuous circle: Political communications in postindustrial societies*. Cambridge University Press.

Norris, P. (2001). *Digital divide: Civic engagement, information poverty, and the Internet worldwide*. Cambridge University Press.

Norris, P. (2002). *Democratic phoenix: Reinventing political activism*. Cambridge University Press.

Norris, P. (2003). Preaching to the converted? Pluralism, participation and party websites. *Party Politics, 9*(1), 21–45.

Norris, P. (2004). *Electoral engineering: Voting rules and political behavior*. Cambridge University Press.

Norris, P. (2011). *Democratic deficit: Critical citizens revisited*. Cambridge University Press.

Norris, P., & Inglehart, R. (2019). *Cultural backlash: Trump, Brexit, and authoritarian populism*. Cambridge University Press.

Norris, P., & Van Es, A. A. (Eds.). (2016). *Checkbook elections?: Political finance in comparative perspective*. Oxford University Press.

North, D. C. (1990). *Institutions, institutional change and economic performance*. Cambridge University Press.

officialpsy. (2012). PSY—GANGNAM STYLE. Retrieved November 29, 2020, from https://www.youtube.com/watch?v=9bZkp7q19f0.

O'Hara, K. P., Massimi, M., Harper, R., Rubens, S., & Morris, J. (2014). Everyday dwelling with WhatsApp. In *Proceedings of the 17th ACM conference on computer supported cooperative work & social computing*. ACM: 1131–1143.

Ohme, J., de Vreese, C. H., & Albæk, E. (2018). From theory to practice: How to apply van Deth's conceptual map in empirical political participation research. *Acta Politica, 53*(3), 367–390.

Olson, M. (1965). *The logic of collective action: Public goods and the theory of groups.* Harvard University Press.

Orriols, L., & Cordero, G. (2016). The breakdown of the Spanish two-party system: The upsurge of Podemos and Ciudadanos in the 2015 general election. *South European Society and Politics, 21*(4), 469–492.

Oser, J., Hooghe, M., & Marien, S. (2013). Is online participation distinct from offline participation? A latent class analysis of participation types and their stratification. *Political Research Quarterly, 66*(1), 91–101.

O'Sullivan, D. (June 21, 2020). TikTok users are trying to troll Trump's campaign by reserving tickets for Tulsa rally they'll never use. *CNN.* Retrieved August 28, 2020, from https://edition.cnn.com/2020/06/16/politics/tiktok-trump-tulsa-rally-trnd/index.html.

Pagella Politica. (2019). Uno, nessuno e 100 mila: l'enigma degli iscritti a Rousseau. Retrieved October 22, 2020, from https://pagellapolitica.it/blog/show/389/uno-nessuno-e-100-mila-lenigma-degli-iscritti-a-rousseau.

Papacharissi, Z. (Ed.). (2011). *A networked self: Identity, community, and culture on social network sites.* Routledge.

Papacharissi, Z. (2015). *Affective publics: Sentiment, technology, and politics.* Oxford University Press.

Pappas, T. S. (2009). Patrons against partisans: The politics of patronage in mass ideological parties. *Party Politics, 15*(3), 315–334.

Pariser, E. (2011). *The filter bubble: What the Internet is hiding from you.* Penguin UK.

Parmelee, J. H., & Bichard, S. L. (2012). *Politics and the Twitter revolution: How tweets influence the relationship between political leaders and the public.* Lexington Books.

Partito Democratico. (2019). Congresso 2019. *Partito Democratico website.* Retrieved June 7, 2019, from https://www.partitodemocratico.it/congresso-2019/ecco-i-nomi-dei-tre-candidati-alle-primarie-del-3-marzo/.

Pasek, J. (2015). When will nonprobability surveys mirror probability surveys? Considering types of inference and weighting strategies as criteria for correspondence. *International Journal of Public Opinion Research, 28*(2), 269–291.

Pasquino, G. (2001). The new campaign politics in Southern Europe. In P. N. Diamandouros & R. Gunther (Eds.). *Parties, politics, and democracy in the new Southern Europe.* Johns Hopkins University Press: 183–223.

Pasquino, G. (2005). Italy and America: Politics and culture: Americanization of Italian politics? *Journal of Modern Italian Studies, 10*(1), 3–9.

Passarelli, G. (2018). Electoral systems in context: Italy. In E. S. Herron, R. J. Pekkanen, & M. S. Shugart (Eds.). *The Oxford handbook of electoral systems.* Oxford University Press: 851–870.

Passarelli, G., & Tuorto, D. (2012). *Lega & Padania: storie e luoghi delle camicie verdi.* Il mulino.

Pattie, C., Seyd, P., & Whiteley, P. (2004). *Citizenship in Britain: Values, participation and democracy.* Cambridge University Press.

Penney, J. (2017). *The citizen marketer: Promoting political opinion in the social media age.* Oxford University Press.

Persily, N. (2017). The 2016 US election: Can democracy survive the Internet? *Journal of Democracy, 28*(2), 63–76.

Phillips, W. (2015). *This is why we can't have nice things: Mapping the relationship between online trolling and mainstream culture.* MIT Press.

Pickard, S. (2018). Momentum and the movementist "Corbynistas": Young people regenerating the Labour Party in Britain. In S. Pickard & J. Bessant (Eds.). *Young people re-generating politics in times of crises.* Palgrave Studies in Young People and Politics. Palgrave Macmillan: 115–137.

Pingree, R. J. (2007). How messages affect their senders: A more general model of message effects and implications for deliberation. *Communication Theory, 17*(4), 439–461.

Plasser, F., & Plasser, G. (2002). *Global political campaigning: A worldwide analysis of campaign professionals and their practices.* Greenwood Publishing Group.

Popkin, S. L. (1994). *The reasoning voter: Communication and persuasion in presidential campaigns.* University of Chicago Press.

Postill, J., & Pink, S. (2012). Social media ethnography: The digital researcher in a messy web. *Media International Australia, 145*(1), 123–134.

Powell, G. B. (1986). American voter turnout in comparative perspective. *American Political Science Review, 80*(1), 17–43.

Powell, G. B. (2000). *Elections as instruments of democracy: Majoritarian and proportional visions.* Yale University Press.

Pressmann, J., & Chenoweth, E. (2018). Crowd Size Estimates, 1/21/2017. Retrieved March 12, 2018, from https://docs.google.com/spreadsheets/d/1xa0iLqYKz8x9Yc_rfhtmSOJQ2EG-geUVjvV4A8LsIaxY/htmlview?sle=true.

Prior, M. (2005). News vs. entertainment: How increasing media choice widens gaps in political knowledge and turnout. *American Journal of Political Science, 49*(3), 577–592.

Prior, M. (2007). *Post-broadcast democracy: How media choice increases inequality in political involvement and polarizes elections.* Cambridge University Press.

Prior, M. (2009). The immensely inflated news audience: Assessing bias in self-reported news exposure. *Public Opinion Quarterly, 73*(1), 130–143.

Prior, M. (2010). You've either got it or you don't: The stability of political interest over the life cycle. *The Journal of Politics, 72*(3), 747–766.

Prior, M., & Lupia, A. (2008). Money, time, and political knowledge: Distinguishing quick recall and political learning skills. *American Journal of Political Science, 52*(1), 169–183.

Przeworski, A. (2019). *Crises of democracy.* Cambridge University Press.

Putnam, R. D. (2000). *Bowling alone: The collapse and revival of American community.* Simon and Schuster.

Quandt, T. (2018). Dark participation. *Media and Communication, 6*(4), 36–48.

Rainie, L., & Wellman, B. (2012). *Networked: The new social operating system.* MIT Press.

Reuters Institute for the Study of Journalism. (2019). *Reuters Digital News Report 2019.* Retrieved January 11, 2020, from http://www.digitalnewsreport.org/.

Rieder, B., Matamoros-Fernández, A., & Coromina, Ò. (2018). From ranking algorithms to "ranking cultures." Investigating the modulation of visibility in YouTube search results. *Convergence, 24*(1), 50–68.

Robinson, M. J. (1976). Public affairs television and the growth of political malaise: The case of "The Selling of the Pentagon." *American Political Science Review, 70*(2), 409–432.

Rodon, T., & Hierro, M. J. (2016). Podemos and Ciudadanos shake up the Spanish party system: The 2015 local and regional elections. *South European Society and Politics, 21*(3), 339–357.

Roemmele, A., & Gibson, R. (2020). Scientific and subversive: The two faces of the fourth era of political campaigning. *New Media & Society, 22*, 595–610.

Rojas, H., & Valenzuela, S. (2019). A call to contextualize public opinion-based research in political communication. *Political Communication, 36*(4), 652–659.

Rooduijn, M. (2019). State of the field: How to study populism and adjacent topics? A plea for both more and less focus. *European Journal of Political Research, 58*(1), 362–372.

Rosanvallon, P. (2008). *Counter-democracy: Politics in an age of distrust.* Cambridge University Press.

Rose, R., & Munro, N. (2003). *Elections and parties in new European democracies.* CQ Press.

Rosenstone, S. J., Behr, R. L., & Lazarus, E. H. (2018). *Third parties in America: Citizen response to major party failure.* Princeton University Press.

Rosenstone, S. J. H., & Hansen, J. M. (1993). *Mobilization, participation, and democracy in America.* Macmillan Publishing Company.

Rossini, P. (2020). Beyond incivility: Understanding patterns of uncivil and intolerant discourse in online political talk. *Communication Research.* Available at: https://doi.org/10.1177/0093650220921314.

Rossini, P., Stromer-Galley, J., Baptista, E. A., & Veiga de Oliveira, V. (2020). Dysfunctional information sharing on WhatsApp and Facebook: The role of political talk, cross-cutting exposure and social corrections. *New Media & Society,* Available at: https://doi.org/10.1177/1461444820928059.

Rustow, D. A. (1968). Modernization and comparative politics: Prospects in research and theory. *Comparative Politics, 1*(1), 37–51.

Saeed, S. (April 10, 2017). Jean-Luc Mélenchon: The video game. *Politico*. Retrieved September 22, 2020, from https://www.politico.eu/article/jean-luc-melenchon-the-video-game/.

Sartori, G. (1969). From the sociology of politics to political sociology. *Government and Opposition, 4*(2), 195–214.

Sartori, G. (1970). Concept misformation in comparative politics. *American Political Science Review, 64*(4), 1033–1053.

Sartori, G. (1976). *Parties and party systems: A framework for analysis*. Cambridge University Press.

Sartori, G. (1987). *The theory of democracy revisited*. Chatham House Publishers.

Sartori, G. (1997). *Comparative constitutional engineering: An inquiry into structures, incentives, and outcomes*. NYU Press.

Sartori, G. (2005). Party types, organisation and functions. *West European Politics, 28*(1), 5–32.

Scammell, M. (1998). The wisdom of the war room: US campaigning and Americanization. *Media, Culture & Society, 20*(2), 251–275.

Schlozman, K. L., Verba, S., & Brady, H. E. (2010). Weapon of the strong? Participatory inequality and the Internet. *Perspectives on Politics, 8*(2), 487–509.

Schlozman, K. L., Verba, S., & Brady, H. E. (2013). *The unheavenly chorus: Unequal political voice and the broken promise of American democracy*. Princeton University Press.

Schradie, J. (2019). *The revolution that wasn't: How digital activism favors conservatives*. Harvard University Press.

Schudson, M. (1997). Why conversation is not the soul of democracy. *Critical Studies in Media Communication, 14*(4), 297–309.

Schudson, M. (1998). *The good citizen: A history of American public life*. New York: Free Press.

Schumpeter, J. A. (1942). *Socialism, capitalism and democracy*. Harper and Brothers.

Searle, J. R. (1969). *Speech acts: An essay in the philosophy of language*. Cambridge University Press.

Seawright, J., & Gerring, J. (2008). Case selection techniques in case study research: A menu of qualitative and quantitative options. *Political Research Quarterly, 61*(2), 294–308.

Settle, J. E. (2018). *Frenemies: How social media polarizes America*. Cambridge University Press.

Shah, D. V. (2016). Conversation is the soul of democracy: Expression effects, communication mediation, and digital media. *Communication and the Public, 1*(1), 12–18.

Shah, D. V., Cappella, J. N., & Neuman, W. R. (2015). Big data, digital media, and computational social science: Possibilities and perils. *The ANNALS of the American Academy of Political and Social Science, 659*(1), 6–13.

Shehata, A., & Strömbäck, J. (2021). Learning political news from social media: Network media logic and current affairs news learning in a high-choice media environment. *Communication Research, 41*(1), 125–147.

Sherman, A. (2020). TikTok reveals detailed user numbers for the first time. Retrieved October 12, 2020, from https://www.cnbc.com/2020/08/24/tiktok-reveals-us-global-user-growth-numbers-for-first-time.html.

Shulman, S. W. (2009). The case against mass e-mails: Perverse incentives and low quality public participation in US federal rulemaking. *Policy & Internet, 1*(1), 23–53.

Singh, T., & Hill, M. E. (2003). Consumer privacy and the Internet in Europe: A view from Germany. *Journal of Consumer Marketing, 20*(7), 634–651.

Song, H., Cho, J., & Benefield, G. A. (2020). The dynamics of message selection in online political discussion forums: Self-segregation or diverse exposure? *Communication Research, 47*(1), 125–152.

Soroka, S., Andrew, B., Aalberg, T., Iyengar, S., Curran, J., Coen, S., . . . & Rowe, D. (2013). Auntie knows best? Public broadcasters and current affairs knowledge. *British Journal of Political Science, 43*(4), 719–739.

Statista. (2020a). Number of Facebook Users Worldwide from 2015 to 2020. Retrieved October 12, 2020, from https://www.statista.com/statistics/490424/number-of-worldwide-facebook-users/.

Statista. (2020b). Number of Monthly Active Instagram Users from January 2013 to June 2018. Retrieved October 12, 2020, from https://www.statista.com/statistics/253577/number-of-monthly-active-instagram-users/.

Stavrakakis, Y., & Katsambekis, G. (2014). Left-wing populism in the European periphery: The case of SYRIZA. *Journal of Political Ideologies, 19*(2), 119–142.

Stein, P., & Somashekhar, S. (January 3, 2017). It started with a retiree. Now the Women's March could be the biggest inauguration demonstration. *Washington Post.* Retrieved March 12, 2018, from https://www.washingtonpost.com/national/it-started-with-a-grandmother-in-hawaii-now-the-womens-march-on-washington-is-poised-to-be-the-biggest-inauguration-demonstration/2017/01/03/8af61686-c6e2-11e6-bf4b-2c064d32a4bf_story.html?utm_term=.37af692ef918.

Stewart, H. (February 5, 2019). Labour membership falls 10% amid unrest over Brexit stance. *The Guardian.* Retrieved October 20, 2020, from https://www.theguardian.com/politics/2019/feb/05/labour-membership-falls-10-amid-unrest-over-brexit-stance.

Stolle, D., Hooghe, M., & Micheletti, M. (2005). Politics in the supermarket: Political consumerism as a form of political participation. *International Political Science Review, 26*(3), 245–269.

Stroud, N. J. (2011). *Niche news: The politics of news choice.* Oxford University Press.

Suciu, P. (November 17, 2020). Social media proved crucial for Joe Biden—it allowed him to connect with young voters and avoid his infamous gaffes. *Forbes.* Retrieved December 7, 2020, from https://www.forbes.com/sites/petersuciu/2020/11/17/social-media-proved-crucial-for-joe-biden--it-allowed-him-to-connect-with-young-voters-and-avoid-his-infamous-gaffes/?sh=902099341482.

Sunstein, C. R. (2002). *Republic.com.* Princeton University Press.

Sunstein, C. R. (2009). *Republic.com 2.0.* Princeton University Press.

Sunstein, C. R. (2017). *#Republic: Divided democracy in the age of social media.* Princeton University Press.

Surowiec, P., Kania-Lundholm, M., & Brodowska-Winiarska, M. (2020). Towards illiberal conditioning? New politics of media regulations in Poland (2015–2018). *East European Politics, 36*(1), 27–43.

Swanson, D. L., & Mancini, P. (Eds.). (1996). *Politics, media, and modern democracy: An international study of innovations in electoral campaiging and their consequences.* Greenwood Publishing Group.

Szczerbiak, A. (2001). Party structure and organizational development in post-communist Poland. *Journal of Communist Studies and Transition Politics, 17*(2), 94–130.

Taber, C. S., & Lodge, M. (2006). Motivated skepticism in the evaluation of political beliefs. *American Journal of Political Science, 50*(3), 755–769.

Taylor, S. L., Shugart, M. S., Lijphart, A., & Grofman, B. (2014). *A different democracy: American government in a 31-country perspective.* Yale University Press.

Teixeira, R. A. (1987). *Why Americans don't vote: Turnout decline in the United States, 1960–1984.* Greenwood Publishing Group.

Tenscher, J. (2008). Mass media and political communication in EU countries. In O. W. Gabriel & S. Kropp (Eds.). *A comparison of EU countries: Structures, processes, and political issues.* Springer VS: 412–447.

Tewksbury, D., Weaver, A. J., & Maddex, B. D. (2001). Accidentally informed: Incidental news exposure on the World Wide Web. *Journalism & Mass Communication Quarterly, 78*(3), 533–554.

Theocharis, Y. (2015). The conceptualization of digitally networked participation. *Social Media + Society, 1*(2), Available at: https://doi.org/10.1177/2056305115610140.

Theocharis, Y., Barberá, P., Fazekas, Z., Popa, S. A., & Parnet, O. (2016). A bad workman blames his tweets: The consequences of citizens' uncivil Twitter use when interacting with party candidates. *Journal of Communication, 66*(6), 1007–1031.

Theocharis, Y., & Lowe, W. (2016). Does Facebook increase political participation? Evidence from a field experiment. *Information, Communication & Society, 19*(10), 1465–1486.

Theocharis, Y., & Van Deth, J. W. (2018). The continuous expansion of citizen participation: A new taxonomy. *European Political Science Review*, 10(1), 139–163.

Thorson, K., & Wells, C. (2015). Curated flows: A framework for mapping media exposure in the digital age. *Communication Theory*, 26(3), 309–328.

Thurber, J. A., & Yoshinaka, A. (Eds.). (2015). *American gridlock: The sources, character, and impact of political polarization*. Cambridge University Press.

Tilly, C. (1995). Contentious repertoires in Great Britain, 1758–1834. In M. Traugott (Ed.). *Repertoires and cycles of contention*. Duke University Press: 15–42.

Tilly, C., & Wood, L. J. (2013). *Social Movements 1768–2012*. Routledge.

Toff, B., & Nielsen, R. K. (2018). "I just Google it": Folk theories of distributed discovery. *Journal of Communication*, 68, 636–657.

Tsatsanis, E., & Teperoglou, E. (2016). Realignment under stress: The July 2015 referendum and the September parliamentary election in Greece. *South European Society and Politics*, 21(4), 427–450.

Tucker, J. A., Guess, A., Barberá, P., Vaccari, C., Siegel, A., Sanovich, S., . . . & Nyhan, B. (2018). Social Media, Political Polarization, and Political Disinformation: A Review of the Scientific Literature. *SSRN*. Retrieved October 23, 2020, from https://ssrn.com/abstract=3144139.

Tucker, J. A., Theocharis, Y., Roberts, M. E., & Barberá, P. (2017). From liberation to turmoil: Social media and democracy. *Journal of Democracy*, 28(4), 46–59.

Tufekci, Z. (2014). Engineering the public: Big data, surveillance and computational politics. *First Monday*, 19(7), Available at: https://doi.org/10.5210/fm.v19i7.4901.

Tufekci, Z. (January 27, 2017a). Does a protest's size matter? *The New York Times*. Retrieved October 23, 2020, from https://www.nytimes.com/2017/01/27/opinion/does-a-protests-size-matter.html.

Tufekci, Z. (2017b). *Twitter and tear gas: The power and fragility of networked protest*. Yale University Press.

Tufekci, Z., & Wilson, C. (2012). Social media and the decision to participate in political protest: Observations from Tahrir Square. *Journal of Communication*, 62(2), 363–379.

Turnbull-Dugarte, S. J. (2019). Explaining the end of Spanish exceptionalism and electoral support for Vox. *Research & Politics*, 6(2), Available at: https://doi.org/10.1177/2053168019851680.

Turow, J. (2012). *The daily you: How the new advertising industry is defining your identity and your worth*. Yale University Press.

Twitter. (2019). Political Content. Retrieved October 12, 2020, from https://business.twitter.com/en/help/ads-policies/ads-content-policies/political-content.html.

UK Government. (2019). Online Harms White Paper. Retrieved November 20, 2019, from https://www.gov.uk/government/consultations/online-harms-white-paper/online-harms-white-paper.

UK Electoral Commission. (2014). Scottish Independence Referendum: Report on the referendum held on 18 September 2014. Retrieved November 20, 2019, from http://www.electoralcommission.org.uk/sites/default/files/pdf_file/Scottish-independence-referendum-report.pdf.

Utz, S., Muscanell, N., & Khalid, C. (2015). Snapchat elicits more jealousy than Facebook: A comparison of Snapchat and Facebook use. *Cyberpsychology, Behavior, and Social Networking*, 18(3), 141–146.

Vaccari, C. (2010). "Technology is a commodity": The internet in the 2008 United States presidential election. *Journal of Information Technology & Politics*, 7(4), 318–339.

Vaccari, C. (2013). *Digital politics in Western democracies: A comparative study*. JHU Press.

Vaccari, C. (2017). Online mobilization in comparative perspective: Digital appeals and political engagement in Germany, Italy, and the United Kingdom. *Political Communication*, 34(1), 69–88.

Vaccari, C., & Chadwick, A. (2020). Deepfakes and disinformation: Exploring the impact of synthetic political video on deception, uncertainty, and trust in news. *Social Media + Society*, 6(1), Available at: https://doi.org/10.1177/2056305120903408.

Vaccari, C., Chadwick, A., & O'Loughlin, B. (2015). Dual screening the political: Media events, social media, and citizen engagement. *Journal of Communication, 65*(6), 1041–1061.

Vaccari, C., & Valeriani, A. (2016). Party campaigners or citizen campaigners? How social media deepen and broaden party-related engagement. *The International Journal of Press/Politics, 21*(3), 294–312.

Vaccari, C., Valeriani, A., Barberá, P., Bonneau, R., Jost, J. T., Nagler, J., & Tucker, J. (2013). Social media and political communication: A survey of Twitter users during the 2013 Italian general election. *Rivista italiana di scienza politica, 43*(3), 381–410.

Vaccari, C., Valeriani, A., Barberá, P., Bonneau, R., Jost, J. T., Nagler, J., & Tucker, J. A. (2015). Political expression and action on social media: Exploring the relationship between lower- and higher-threshold political activities among Twitter users in Italy. *Journal of Computer-Mediated Communication, 20*(2), 221–239.

Vaccari, C., Valeriani, A., Barberá, P., Jost, J. T., Nagler, J., & Tucker, J. A. (2016). Of echo chambers and contrarian clubs: Exposure to political disagreement among German and Italian users of twitter. *Social Media + Society, 2*(3), Available at: https://doi.org/10.1177/2056305116664221.

Vaidhyanathan, S. (2012). *The Googlization of everything: (And why we should worry)*. University of California Press.

Vaidhyanathan, S. (2018). *Antisocial media: How Facebook disconnects us and undermines democracy*. Oxford University Press.

Valenzuela, S. (2013). Unpacking the use of social media for protest behavior: The roles of information, opinion expression, and activism. *American Behavioral Scientist, 57*(7), 920–942.

Valeriani, A., & Vaccari, C. (2016). Accidental exposure to politics on social media as online participation equalizer in Germany, Italy, and the United Kingdom. *New Media & Society, 18*(9), 1857–1874.

Valeriani, A., & Vaccari, C. (2018). Political talk on mobile instant messaging services: A comparative analysis of Germany, Italy, and the UK. *Information, Communication & Society, 21*(11), 1715–1731.

Van Aelst, P., Strömbäck, J., Aalberg, T., Esser, F., de Vreese, C., Matthes, J., ... & Stanyer, J. (2017). Political communication in a high-choice media environment: A challenge for democracy? *Annals of the International Communication Association, 41*, 3–27.

Van Biezen, I., Mair, P., & Poguntke, T. (2012). Going, going, ... gone? The decline of party membership in contemporary Europe. *European Journal of Political Research, 51*(1), 24–56.

Van Dijk, J. A. (2005). *The deepening divide: Inequality in the information society*. Sage Publications.

Van Duyn, E. (2018). Hidden democracy: Political dissent in rural America. *Journal of Communication, 68*(5), 965–987.

Van Kempen, H. (2007). Media-party parallelism and its effects: A cross-national comparative study. *Political Communication, 24*(3), 303–320.

Vaterlaus, J. M., Barnett, K., Roche, C., & Young, J. A. (2016). "Snapchat is more personal": An exploratory study on Snapchat behaviors and young adult interpersonal relationships. *Computers in Human Behavior, 62*, 594–601.

Vavreck, L. (2007). The exaggerated effects of advertising on turnout: The dangers of self-reports. *Quarterly Journal of Political Science, 2*(4), 325–343.

Verba, S., & Nie, N. H. (1972). *Participation in America: Political democracy and social equality*. University of Chicago Press.

Verba, S., Schlozman, K. L., & Brady, H. E. (1995). *Voice and equality: Civic voluntarism in American politics*. Harvard University Press.

Vissers, S. (2009). From preaching to the converted to preaching through the converted. Paper presented for the ECPR Joint Sessions of Workshops 2009. Workshop 20: Parliaments, Parties, and Politicians in Cyberspace. April 14–19, 2009, Lisbon.

Vitak, J., Zube, P., Smock, A., Carr, C. T., Ellison, N., & Lampe, C. (2011). It's complicated: Facebook users' political participation in the 2008 election. *CyberPsychology, Behavior, and Social Networking, 14*(3), 107–114.

Vogelstein, F. (March 12, 2018). For news publishers, Facebook is a less reliable friend. *Wired*. Retrieved October 12, 2020, from https://www.wired.com/story/why-facebook-has-been-less-important-to-news-publishers/.

Völker, B., & Flap, H. (2001). Weak ties as a liability: The case of East Germany. *Rationality and Society, 13*(4), 397–428.

Vraga, E. K., Bode, L., Smithson, A. B., & Troller-Renfree, S. (2019). Accidentally attentive: Comparing visual, close-ended, and open-ended measures of attention on social media. *Computers in Human Behavior, 99*, 235–244.

Waisbord, S. (2018). Why populism is troubling for democratic communication. *Communication Culture & Critique, 11*(1), 21–34.

Wallace, T., & Parlapiano, A. (January 22, 2017). Crowd scientists say Women's March in Washington had 3 times as many people as Trump's inauguration. *The New York Times*. Retrieved March 12, 2018, from https://www.nytimes.com/interactive/2017/01/22/us/politics/womens-march-trump-crowd-estimates.html.

We Are Social. (2019). Digital in 2019. Retrieved November 27, 2020, from https://www.slideshare.net/DataReportal/digital-2019-global-digital-overview-january-2019-v01.

We Are Social. (2020). Digital Around the World in 2020. Retrieved November 27, 2020, from https://wearesocial.com/uk/blog/2020/04/digital-around-the-world-in-april-2020.

Webb, P. (2002). Political parties in Britain: Secular decline or adaptive resilience? In P. Webb, D. Farrell, & I. Holliday (Eds.). *Political parties in advanced industrial democracies*. Oxford University Press: 16–45.

Weber, M. (1922). *Gesammelte aufsätze zur religionssoziologie, Vol. I: Die protestantische ethik und der geist des kapitalismus; Die protestantischen sekten und der geist des kapitalismus; Die wirtschaftsethik der weltreligion*. Verlag von JCB Mohr.

Weeks, B. E., Lane, D. S., Hahn, L. B. (2021). Online incidental exposure to news can minimize interest-based political knowledge gaps: Evidence from two U.S. elections. *International Journal of Press/Politics*, Available at: https://doi.org/10.1177/1940161221991550.

Weeks, B. E., Lane, D. S., Kim, D. H., Lee, S. S., & Kwak, N. (2017). Incidental exposure, selective exposure, and political information sharing: Integrating online exposure patterns and expression on social media. *Journal of Computer-Mediated Communication, 22*(6), 363–379.

Weisbaum, H. (April 11, 2018). Trust in Facebook has dropped by 66 percent since the Cambridge Analytica scandal. *NBC News*. Retrieved October 12, 2020, from https://www.nbcnews.com/business/consumer/trust-facebook-has-dropped-51-percent-cambridge-analytica-scandal-n867011.

Wells, C., Cramer, K. J., Wagner, M. W., Alvarez, G., Friedland, L. A., Shah, D. V., Bode, L., Edgerly, S., Gabay, I., & Franklin, C. (2017). When we stop talking politics: The maintenance and closing of conversation in contentious times. *Journal of Communication, 67*(1), 131–157.

Wells, C., Shah, D., Pevehouse, J., Yang, J., Pelled, A., Boehm, F., Lukito, J., Ghosh, S., & Schmidt, J. (2016). How Trump drove coverage to the nomination: Hybrid media campaigning. *Political Communication, 33*(4), 669–676.

Wells, C., & Thorson, K. (2017). Combining big data and survey techniques to model effects of political content flows in Facebook. *Social Science Computer Review, 35*(1), 33–52.

Whiteley, P. F. (2011a). Is the party over? The decline of party activism and membership across the democratic world. *Party Politics, 17*(1), 21–44.

Whiteley, P. F. (2011b). *Political participation in Britain: The decline and revival of civic culture*. Palgrave Macmillan.

Whiteley, P. F., Poletti, M., Webb, P., & Bale, T. (2019). Oh Jeremy Corbyn! Why did Labour Party membership soar after the 2015 general election? *The British Journal of Politics and International Relations, 21*(1), 80–98.

Wojcieszak, M. E., & Mutz, D. C. (2009). Online groups and political discourse: Do online discussion spaces facilitate exposure to political disagreement?" *Journal of Communication, 59*(1), 40–56.

Women's March on Washington. (2016). Women's March on Washington: Origins and Inclusion. Retrieved March 12, 2018, from https://static1.squarespace.com/static/584086c7be6594762f5ec56e/t/5870466186e6c0f36e01cc39/1483753061272/Statement+on+inclusivity.pdf.

Women's March on Washington. (2018a). Partners and Sponsors. Retrieved March 12, 2018, from https://www.womensmarch.com/partners/.

Women's March on Washington. (2018b). Sister Marches. Retrieved March 12, 2018, from https://www.womensmarch.com/sisters.

Wright, S. (2012). Politics as usual? Revolution, normalization and a new agenda for online deliberation. *New Media & Society, 14*(2), 244–261.

Wu, T. (2017). *The attention merchants: The epic scramble to get inside our heads.* Vintage.

Xenos, M., & Moy, P. (2007). Direct and differential effects of the Internet on political and civic engagement. *Journal of Communication, 57*(4), 704–718.

Xenos, M., Vromen, A., & Loader, B. D. (2014). The great equalizer? Patterns of social media use and youth political engagement in three advanced democracies. *Information, Communication & Society, 17*(2), 151–167.

Yang, G. (2016). Narrative agency in hashtag activism: The case of #BlackLivesMatter. *Media and Communication, 4*(4), 13–17.

Yoon, K. (2019). Transnational fandom in the making: K-pop fans in Vancouver. *International Communication Gazette, 81*(2), 176–192.

Zaller, J. (1992). *The nature and origins of mass opinion.* Cambridge University Press.

Zaller, J. (2003). A new standard of news quality: Burglar alarms for the monitorial citizen. *Political Communication, 20*(2), 109–130.

Zhang, Y., Wells, C., Wang, S., & Rohe, K. (2018). Attention and amplification in the hybrid media system: The composition and activity of Donald Trump's Twitter following during the 2016 presidential election. *New Media & Society, 20*(9), 3161–3182.

Zittel, T. (2018). Electoral systems in context: Germany. In E. S. Herron, R. J. Pekkanen, & M. S. Shugart (Eds.). *The Oxford handbook of electoral systems.* Oxford University Press: 781–802.

Zuboff, S. (2015). Big other: Surveillance capitalism and the prospects of an information civilization. *Journal of Information Technology, 30*(1), 75–89.

Zuckerman, A. S. (2005). *The social logic of politics: Personal networks as contexts for political behavior.* Temple University Press.

Zulianello, M., Albertini, A., & Ceccobelli, D. (2018). A populist zeitgeist? The communication strategies of Western and Latin American political leaders on Facebook. *The International Journal of Press/Politics, 23*(4), 439–457.

Index

For the benefit of digital users, indexed terms that span two pages (e.g., 52–53) may, on occasion, appear on only one of those pages.

Note: Tables and figures are indicated by t and f following the page number. Those followed by n refer to notes, with note number.